COMBAT AIRCRAFT
SINCE 1945

Stewart Wilson

Airlife
England

Copyright © 2000 Stewart Wilson and Aerospace Publications Pty Ltd

First published in the UK in 2000
by Airlife Publishing Ltd

First published in Australia by Aerospace Publications Pty Ltd

British Library Cataloguing-in-Publication Data
 A catalogue record for this book
 is available from the British Library

ISBN 1 84037 150 1

Printed in Australia
Back cover artwork by Juanita Franzi

Airlife Publishing Ltd
101 Longden Road, Shrewsbury, SY3 9EB, England
E-mail: airlife@airlifebooks.com
Website: www.airlifebooks.com

INTRODUCTION

Welcome to *Combat Aircraft Since 1945*, a comprehensive directory of the combat aircraft which have served the world's armed forces from 1914 to the present day.

My intention with this book has been to create a single volume which provides information on a large number of aircraft in an easy to access manner, with sufficient data to answer most questions but also to encourage more detailed research into a particular aircraft.

All the major combat aircraft of the post war era are covered along with many of the minor ones plus some of the one-offs and prototypes which didn't achieve production and service. Although comprehensive with 260 entries, I make no claim that the book is definitive as the constraints of time and space have to be considered. Nevertheless, I hope there is much of interest for readers within these pages.

The entries are arranged alphabetically by manufacturer and chronologically within that format. Specification, performance and production data are presented along with a concise history of each type. Many aircraft have multiple entries to allow their evolution to be traced and greater detail to be provided on the particular models.

As has been the case with my previous book in this series (*Airliners Of the World*), one of the problems has been deciding under which manufacturer's name some aircraft should be listed, given the mergers and consolidations that have occurred over the years. The decision has been made, therefore, to present aircraft under the manufacturer by which they are best known, or under which the bulk of production took place.

Taking McDonnell as an example, up to and including the F-101 Voodoo they are listed under the McDonnell heading but from the F-4 Phantom onwards they are included in McDonnell Douglas. Boeing's takeover of McDonnell Douglas adds to the possible confusion and the latest Hornet variant (the F/A-18E) is listed under McDonnell Douglas (Boeing) because the original company developed it but production is now underway as a Boeing product (now BAE Systems).

Many British aircraft have the same problem with the formation of British Aerospace and the traditional manufacturer's name has been used where appropriate. Modernist and revisionist readers will be no doubt be disappointed to discover that aircraft such as the 'Boeing' Sabre and 'British Aerospace' Vampire will not be found in the pages of anything to emerge from the pen of this writer!

Finally, my thanks to Don Stephens for his superb cover artwork and, as always, my sincere appreciation to Jim Thorn and the crew at Aerospace Publications for their ongoing and much valued support. In particular thank you to Gerard Frawley for allowing me access to some of his material and for proofreading, and to production manager Gayla Wilson. Thanks also to Wendy Wilson for doing some of the word processing for me and for cracking the whip!

Stewart Wilson
Buckingham 2000

COMBAT AIRCRAFT
MILESTONES SINCE 1945

The shape of things to come. The Lockheed Martin F-22A Raptor is set to become the USAF's next air superiority fighter. It is scheduled to enter service in 2005, no fewer than 15 years after the YF-22 prototype first flew and eight years after the first production standard F-22A development aircraft took to the air. With their advanced avionics and systems, modern combat aircraft take a long time to develop and get into service.

11 May 1945: Germany surrenders, ending the war in Europe.

6 August 1945: The first atomic bomb to be used operationally is exploded over Hiroshima, Japan. The bomb is dropped from Boeing B-29 Superfortress 44-86292 *Enola Gay* of the USAAF's 509th Composite Group and commanded by Col Paul Tibbets.

9 August 1945: A second atomic bomb is dropped on Nagasaki, Japan from B-29 44-27297 *Bock's Car* commanded by Captain Frederick Bock.

14 August 1945: Hostilities end as Japan agrees to unconditional surrender – World War II is over. The formal surrender is signed on 2 September 1945.

7 November 1945: The first post war world's air speed record is set when Gp Capt H J Wilson RAF takes a Gloster Meteor F.4 to a speed of 606.2mph (975.6km/h).

3 December 1945: The first landings and takeoffs of a jet powered aircraft on an aircraft carrier (HMS *Ocean*) by Captain Eric ('Winkle') Brown RN in the second prototype de Havilland Vampire. The aircraft was modified to incorporate an arrester hook, longer stroke undercarriage and larger flaps.

The Soviet Union's first jet fighter of wholly indigenous design, the MiG-9, first flew in April 1948.

December 1945: The first production Lockheed P-80A Shooting Star handed over to the USAF as the service's first operational jet fighter. The XP-80 prototype had first flown on 8 January 1944.

24 April 1946: First true flight of the MiG-9, regarded as the first Soviet jet fighter of wholly indigenous design. The aircraft had made a brief hop five days earlier.

24 April 1946: On the same day as the MiG-9 (above) the prototype Yakovlev Yak-15, the first Soviet jet combat aircraft to enter regular squadron service, records its maiden flight.

21 July 1946: A McDonnell FH-1 Phantom makes the first landing by an American jet aircraft on an aircraft carrier, the USS *Franklin D Roosevelt*.

24 July 1946: The first manned ejection from an aircraft when – in a planned test – Mr Bernard Lynch departs a Gloster Meteor T.7 while strapped into a Martin-Baker seat.

8 August 1946: First flight of the prototype Convair B-36, the world's first intercontinental strategic bomber.

29 September-1 October 1946: Lockheed P2V-1 Neptune *Truculent Turtle* sets a new distance record of 11,235.6 statute miles (18,081.4km) by flying non stop and unrefuelled between Perth (Western Australia) and Columbus, Ohio.

28 October 1946: First flight of the production McDonnell FH-1 Phantom, the US Navy's first operational jet fighter. The prototype (as the XFD-1) had first flown in January 1945.

July 1947: US Navy squadron VF-17A becomes the world's first carrier based operational jet fighter unit when it receives its first McDonnell FH-1 Phantoms.

18 September 1947: The United Sates Air Force formally established as a separate military service. Until then, it had been the United States Army Air Force.

1 October 1947: First flight of the prototype North American

The Gloster Meteor F.4 (background) set the first post war world's air speed record of 606mph (975km/h), in November 1945. The Meteor NF.11 (foreground) was based on the T.7 trainer, from which the first manned ejection from an aircraft was performed in July 1948.

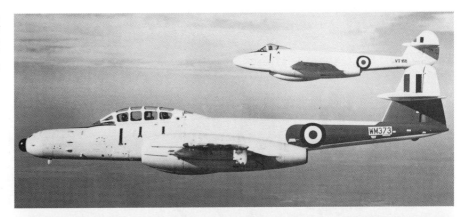

The first production Lockheed F-80A Shooting Star was handed over to the USAAF in December 1945 as America's first operational jet fighter. An F-80C Shooting Star like this one made history in November 1950 when it shot down a MiG-15 over Korea in the first conclusive jet-versus-jet aerial combat. (Lockheed)

The prototype for the MiG-15 first flew in December 1947. The fighter remained pretty much unknown in the West until late 1950 when it appeared in the skies over Korea and caused a major rethink of Soviet capabilities. (Paul Merritt)

The English Electric Canberra, Britain's first jet bomber, flew in May 1949 and went on to be widely used over five decades. This is an Australian built Canberra Mk.20.

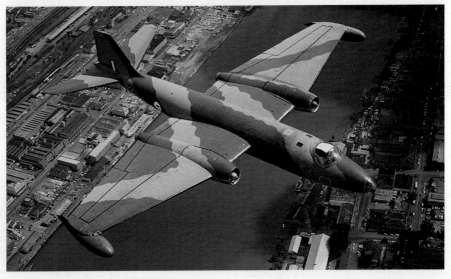

The North American F-86 Sabre was the USAF's first operational swept wing fighter, first flying in October 1947. (Paul Merritt)

XP-86 (later F-86) Sabre, the first swept wing fighter to enter service with the USAF.

14 October 1947: A Bell X-1 flown by Captain Charles ('Chuck') Yeager becomes the first manned aircraft to exceed the speed of sound, achieving Mach 1.015 (670mph/1078km/h) after launch from a Boeing GB-29 Superfortress 'mother' ship.

30 December 1947: First flight of the Mikoyan-Gurevich I-310 jet fighter, prototype for the MiG-15.

17 June 1948: Declaration of a state of emergency in Malaya

to deal with communist terrorists in the country. Operation 'Firedog' – air operations against the terrorists – launched by the RAF and lasts until 1960 until the situation is finally resolved. The campaign involved aircraft from the Royal Air Force, Royal Navy, Royal Malayan Air Force, Royal Australian Air Force and Royal New Zealand Air Force. Even the USAF briefly contributed three Boeing B-29s which were used for bombing operations in July 1953.

3 July 1948: First flight of the North American AJ-1 Savage,

The prototype Avro Vulcan delta winged strategic bomber first flew in August 1952 and entered RAF service in May 1956. This is a Vulcan B.2.

The North American F-100 Super Sabre was the first of the USAF's 'Century Series' of supersonic fighters. It first flew in May 1953 and in August 1955 set the first supersonic and high altitude world's air speed record of Mach 1.25 or 822mph (1,323km/h). This is an F-100D photographed in 1969 while serving in Vietnam. (USAF)

the first naval combat aircraft designed from the outset to carry an atomic bomb.

15 September 1948: A North American F-86A Sabre flown by Major Richard Johnson sets a new world's air speed record of 670.9mph (1079.8km/h).

November 1948: Service entry of the North American B-45A Tornado, the USAF's first four jet bomber and its first combat capable jet bomber of any type. The prototype XB-45 made its first flight on 17 March 1945.

13 May 1949: First flight of the prototype English Electric Canberra, Britain's first jet bomber.

24 August 1949: The North Atlantic Treaty comes into force and with it establishment of the North Atlantic Treaty Organisation (NATO), an alliance of nations to provide military mutual protection against the perceived threat from the Soviet Union and its allies. The possibility of nuclear attack by the Soviets dictated the military philosophies of the member nations for many years

22 December 1949: First flight of the North American F-86D Sabre, the first fighter in regular service to dispense with guns in favour of an all missile armament.

19 January 1950: First flight of the Avro Canada CF-100 twin engined all weather fighter, the first indigenous Canadian jet combat aircraft to enter production.

29 June 1950: Start of the Korean War, the first conflict involving jet-versus-jet aerial combat.

8 November 1950: The first conclusive jet-versus-jet combat when a Lockheed F-80C Shooting Star of the USAF's 51st Fighter Interceptor Wing flown by Lt Russell Brown shoots down a Chinese MiG-15 near the North Korea/China border.

23 February 1951: First flight of the Dassault Mystère, Western Europe's first production swept wing aircraft (in Mystère IIC form from 1954).

6 March 1951: The English Electric Canberra tactical bomber is selected for licence production in the USA for the USAF. The first US built Martin B-57 flies on 20 July 1953.

18 May 1951: First flight of the Vickers Valiant, the first of the RAF's three V-Bombers along with the Avro Vulcan and Handley Page Victor.

20 May 1951: Captain James Jabara of the USAF's 4th Fighter Interceptor Wing becomes the first jet 'ace' when he shoots down his fifth MiG-15 in his North American F-86A Sabre over Korea. Jabara went on to claim 15 kills during the conflict, all MiG-15s.

20 July 1951: First flight of the Hawker P.1067, prototype for the Hunter.

26 November 1951: First flight of the Gloster Javelin, Britain's first purpose built all weather and night jet fighter.

15 April 1952: First flight of the Boeing B-52 Stratofortress.

19 May 1952: First flight of the Grumman XF10F Jaguar, the world's first variable sweep combat aircraft intended for production. The programme was cancelled mainly due to the failure of the aircraft's Westinghouse J40 turbojet but the lessons learned were later put to good use in the General Dynamics F-111 and Grumman F-14 Tomcat.

24 May 1952: First flight of the Mikoyan-Gurevich I-360, prototype for the MiG-19, the first Soviet production fighter capable of supersonic speeds in level flight.

30 August 1952: First flight of the prototype Avro Vulcan delta winged strategic bomber.

20 January 1953: First flight of the Myasishchev M-4, the Soviet Union's first operational four jet strategic bomber.

18 May 1953: Captain James McConnell of the USAF's 16th Fighter Interceptor Squadron becomes the top American ace of the Korean War when he claims his 16th MiG-15 kill of the conflict, flying an F-86 Sabre. McConnell was killed in a Sabre accident the following year.

The Boeing B-52 Stratofortress is set to become the longest serving combat aircraft in history. It first flew in April 1952 and plans are in place to keep it in USAF service until 2040. This is a B-52F unleashing a load of conventional bombs, a common sight in the Vietnam War where the B-52 flew its first missions in June 1965.

Lockheed's 'missile with a man in it' F-104 Starfighter caused a sensation when it first flew in March 1954 and although USAF service was relatively limited, the fighter was exported to some 18 nations and built under licence in Europe, Canada and Japan. This is a Turkish F-104S, built in Italy.

19 May 1953: American Jacqueline Cochrane becomes the first woman to exceed the speed of sound, flying a Canadair Sabre.

25 May 1953: The first of the USAF's 'Century Series' supersonic fighters – the North American F-100 Super Sabre – records its maiden flight.

16 July 1953: The first world's air speed record of over 700mph (1126km/h) is set by Lt Col William Barnes USAF in a North American F-86D Sabre, achieving 715.7mph (1151.8km/h). This beat the previous record of 698.5mph (1124.1km/h) set the year before by Captain J Slade Nash in another F-86D.

7 September 1953: A new world's air speed record of 727.6mph (1170.9km/h) set by a Hawker Hunter F.3 (modified from the first prototype) and flown by Neville Duke.

25 September 1953: Another new world's air speed record set, this time by Mike Lithgow in a Supermarine Swift at 737.7mph (1187.2km/h). In a period where the record was being beaten on a regular basis, this mark was almost immediately passed by a Douglas A4D-1 Skyray which achieved 753.4mph (1212.4km/h).

24 October 1953: First flight of the Convair YF-102A Delta Dagger, the world's first production delta winged fighter and the first designed from the outset to dispense with guns in favour of missiles.

29 October 1953: A North American YF-100A Super Sabre flown by Lt Col F K ('Pete') Everest sets the last low altitude

First flown in November 1956, the highly advanced, delta wing Convair B-58 Hustler was the world's first supersonic bomber to achieve production and service and the first to reach a speed of Mach 2.

and subsonic world's air speed record at a speed of 755.1mph (1215.2km/h).

30 July 1954: First flight of the Grumman F11F Tiger, the first US Navy transonic carrier based fighter.

25 March 1955: First flight of the Vought XF8U-1 Crusader, the US Navy's first supersonic interceptor.

20 August 1955: A North American F-100C Super Sabre flown by Colonel Horace A Haines establishes the first supersonic (and high altitude) world's air speed record, achieving 822.1mph (1323.0km/h) or Mach 1.25.

15 May 1956: First flight of the Dassault Super Mystère B2, the first Western European production aircraft capable of exceeding Mach 1 in level flight.

21 May 1956: A USAF Boeing B-52B Stratofortress drops the first airborne hydrogen bomb over Bikini Atoll in the Pacific Ocean.

11 October 1956: The first British atomic bomb is dropped from an RAF Vickers Valiant over Maralinga, South Australia.

11 November 1956: First flight of the Convair XB-58 Hustler, the world's first production supersonic bomber and the first to achieve Mach 2.

4 April 1957: Release of the infamous British Government Defence White Paper which claims that manned fighters would in the near future be replaced by missiles. This wholly erroneous assertion had a marked negative effect on British military aviation planning and the industry for a considerable time.

15 May 1957: Britain's first hydrogen bomb is dropped from an RAF Vickers Valiant over a Pacific Ocean testing range.

4 April 1957: First flight of the English Electric P.1B, prototype for the Lightning, Britain's first and only wholly indigenous Mach 2 fighter to enter service. Deliveries of the Lightning F.1 to the RAF began in June 1960.

27 May 1958: First flight of the McDonnell YF4H-1 Phantom II fighter for the US Navy, the prototype of what many regard as "the greatest fighter of the post war era".

21 October 1960: First (tethered) flight of the Hawker P.1127, prototype for what would become the Harrier, the world's first operational V/STOL combat aircraft. The first conventional flight was recorded on 13 March 1961.

17 June 1961: First flight of the HAL Marut, India's first indigenous combat aircraft and the first Asian aircraft to exceed Mach 1 in level flight.

The North American A-5 Vigilante carrier based supersonic bomber introduced many 'firsts' including fully variable geometry intakes, multimode radar, a digital computer, 'slab' tailerons, linear weapons bay and numerous other aerodynamic and structural innovations. This is an RA-5C.

18 October 1961: The first USAF deployment to Vietnam, the McDonnell RF-101C Voodoos of the 15th Tactical Reconnaissance Squadron based at Tan Son Nhut.

27 May 1963: First flight of the McDonnell F-4C Phantom II, the USAF version of the US Navy fighter. The F-4C represented the first ever purchase of a USN aircraft by the USAF.

January 1964: The US Navy deploys its first aircraft carrier to the Vietnam theatre of operations, the US *Bonne Homme Richard* with its complement of F-8 Crusaders, A-4 Skyhawks and A-1 Skyraiders.

7 March 1964: First flight of the Helwan HA-300, Egypt's first combat aircraft, designed by Professor Willy Messerschmitt. It was cancelled after two prototypes were flown as performance requirements were not met.

2 March 1965: First of the 'Rolling Thunder' strikes by US forces against targets in North and South Vietnam. Lasting for more than three years, this massive campaign was intended to interrupt the flow of supplies from North to South Vietnam and also force North Vietnam to make concessions at the negotiating table. Neither objective was achieved.

18 June 1965: The first Boeing B-52 Stratofortress combat mission flown in Vietnam, an unsuccessful strike on Viet Cong positions in the South. Thirty bombers flew from Guam, two of them collided and were lost, the bombing was inaccurate and enemy personnel near the target had been forewarned of the raid and had departed the area.

7 September 1965: First flight of the Bell AH-1 HueyCobra, the world's first operational dedicated helicopter gunship.

5 June 1967: Start of the Six Day War when Israeli aircraft launch pre-emptive strikes against Egyptian, Syrian and Jordanian military airfields. More than 450 Arab aircraft are destroyed in the raids for the loss of 46 Israeli aircraft.

17 March 1968: The USAF's controversial General Dynamics F-111A flies its first combat mission in Vietnam. This initial combat deployment was premature and unsuccessful with three of the six (later eight) lost in only 55 missions due to technical problems. A 1972 deployment to Vietnam was considerably more successful.

8 September 1968: First flight of the Sepecat Jaguar, the world's first bi-national combat aircraft to enter production. The Sepecat consortium's main members were France's Breguet and the British Aircraft Corporation.

April 1969: The world's first operational V/STOL combat aircraft, the Hawker Siddeley Harrier GR.1, enters regular squadron service with the Royal Air Force.

September 1969: First flight of IAI Nesher (Eagle), Israel's 're-verse engineered' copy of the Dassault Mirage III. The substantially redesigned and re-engined Kfir first flew in October 1970.

15 January 1973: US President Richard Nixon orders a halt to air attacks against North Vietnam as a prelude to the ceasefire announced 12 days later.

6 October 1973: Start of the Yom Kippur War when Egypt attacks Israel with large scale air strikes. About 120 Israeli aircraft are lost in the first few days but a ceasefire is called on 24 October.

The first USAF deployment to Vietnam was by McDonnell RF-101C Voodoos in October 1961.

20 January 1974: First flight of the prototype General Dynamics F-16, the most numerically important US fighter of the current era with more than 4000 delivered by mid 2000. The F-16 was the first production fighter to feature fly-by-wire controls and relaxed stability for a high level of manoeuvrability.

14 August 1974: First flight of the Panavia MRCA (Multi Role Combat Aircraft – later Tornado), the first major multinational combat aircraft programme and involving the British, German and Italian aerospace industries developing and producing both the airframe and the new RB.199 engine.

The Sepecat Jaguar, the world's first bi-national combat aircraft to enter production. First flight was in September 1968; this is an RAF Jaguar T.2. (Paul Merritt).

First flown in January 1974, the General Dynamics (now Lockheed Martin) F-16 Fighting Falcon has become the most numerically important US fighter of the current era with more than 4000 delivered by late 2000. It was the first production fighter to feature fly-by-wire controls and relaxed stability. (Paul Merritt).

3 June 1975: First flight of the Mitsubishi F-1 prototype, Japan's first indigenous pure combat aircraft since World War II.

September 1976: A Soviet MiG-25 'Foxbat' Mach 3 fighter is flown to Japan by a defecting pilot. After detailed examination, the aircraft is returned to its owner.

1 January 1978: Hawker Siddeley, the British Aircraft Corporation (BAC) and Scottish Aviation merged to form the government owned British Aerospace (BAe). BAe became a public company on 1 January 1981.

18 June 1981: First flight of the pre production Lockheed F-117A Nighthawk 'stealth' fighter-bomber. Although the

F-117A was first delivered to the USAF service in August 1982, the secrecy surrounding the programme meant the aircraft was not publically revealed for the first time until November 1988.

2 April 1982: Start of the Falklands War when Argentinian forces invade the Falkland Islands. A task force including the Royal Navy carriers HMS *Invincible* and *Hermes* is assembled with RAF Harriers and RN Sea Harriers on board. During the course of the war, Sea Harriers were responsible for the downing of 23 Argentinian aircraft for no losses in aerial combat.

1 May 1982: An RAF Vulcan flies a 6830nm (12,650km) round

The Panavia Tornado was the first major multinational combat aircraft, involving the aerospace industries of Britain, Germany and Italy. First flight was in August 1974; this is an RAF Tornado GR.1A. (RAF)

The Lockheed F-117A Nighthawk – the first 'stealth' combat aircraft to enter production – was delivered to the USAF from August 1982. (Paul Merritt)

Like many other aircraft, the world's first operational V/STOL combat aircraft – the Harrier – has undergone several 'brand name' changes over the years as companies have merged or formed joint ventures. What began as the Hawker P.1127 in 1960 has subsequently become the Hawker Siddeley, British Aerospace, McDonnell Douglas and finally Boeing Harrier. This US Marine Corps AV-8B Harrier II represents the final generation of a revolutionary aircraft. (Boeing)

The Eurofighter Typhoon represents Europe's second major multinational combat aircraft programme after the Tornado. It involves the aerospace industries of Britain, Germany, Italy and Spain and first flew in March 1994. (BAE Systems).

trip from Ascension Island (with several flight refuellings) to bomb the Argentine held Port Stanley airfield in the Falklands. Four more of these 'Black Buck' missions were completed between then and 12 June, the only time times the Vulcan was flown in combat. Two other missions were aborted and Argentine forces on the Falklands surrendered two days later.

2 September 1983: A Soviet Sukhoi Su-15 shoots down a Korean Air Lines Boeing 747 north-west of Japan with the loss of all 263 on board. The Soviets claimed they thought the 747 was a USAF RC-135 intelligence gathering aircraft.

14 April 1986: British based USAF General Dynamics F-111s and US Navy aircraft attack targets in Libya in retaliation for terrorist attacks. One F-111 is lost during the mission.

17 July 1989: First flight of the Northrop B-2 flying wing stealth bomber.

2 August 1990: Iraq invades Kuwait, providing the catalyst which resulted in the Gulf War five months later.

17 January 1991: Start of the Gulf War and Operation 'Desert Storm', the air war against Iraq and involving US, British, French, Saudi and other air forces. The campaign was the first combat test for many of the new generation of 'smart' air-to-ground weapons developed in recent years. A ceasefire was called on February 27 with Iraqi forces defeated.

9 December 1992: The first of many US aerospace industry

consolidations and mergers when Lockheed acquires General Dynamics. Lockheed purchased Martin Marietta in August 1994 to form Lockheed Martin.

27 March 1994: First flight of the prototype Eurofighter EF2000 (later Typhoon) jointly developed and manufactured by the aerospace industries of Britain, Germany, Italy and Spain.

28 August 1995: NATO undertakes air attacks on Bosnian-Serb positions in response to continuing unrest in the Balkans. The campaign sees the German *Luftwaffe* in action for the first time since World War II.

15 December 1996: Boeing announces it is taking over McDonnell Douglas, the transaction completed in August 1997. Boeing also took over Rockwell in December 1996.

17 December 1998: Operation 'Desert Fox' begins, a sustained aerial bombardment of Iraq intended to stop production of weapons of mass destruction in the country.

24 March 1999: The start of Operation 'Allied Force', the NATO campaign against targets in Serbia in response to ethnic cleansing activities in Kosova. The attacks continue until 9 June.

18 September 2000: First flight of the Boeing X-32A, the company's technology demonstrator for its Joint Strike Fighter (JSF) entry.

ADA Light Combat Aircraft

Country of origin: India.

Type: Single seat multirole fighter.

Powerplant: Prototypes – one 18,100lb (80.5kN) with afterburner General Electric F404-GE-F2J3 turbofan. Production – one 11,530lb (51.3kN) dry/18,750lb (83.4kN) with afterburner GTRE Kaveri turbofan.

Dimensions: Wing span 8.20m (26ft 11in); length 13.21m (43ft 4in); height 4.39m (14ft 5in); wing area 38.4m² (413sq ft).

Weights: (Estimated) empty 5500kg (12,125lb); takeoff (clean) 8500kg (18,739lb); max takeoff 12,500kg (27,557lb).

Armament: One 23mm twin barrel cannon; one centreline and six underwing pylons for approx 4000kg (8818lb) ordnance including conventional and laser guided bombs, cluster bombs, AAMs and AGMs.

Performance: (Estimated) max speed 918-1033kt (Mach 1.6-1.8/1700-1913km/h); service ceiling 50,000ft.

Production: First of seven prototypes built but not flown by early 2000; Indian requirement for approx 200 production LCAs.

Notes: India's most ambitious indigenous aircraft programme is planned to result in a capable lightweight multirole fighter in the same weight class as the Saab Gripen. It is intended to replace the MiG-21 and MiG-23 in Indian Air Force service. Naval and two seat operational trainer versions are also planned.

The Light Combat Aircraft (LCA) is being developed by India's Aeronautical Development Agency (ADA). Work began in 1983 following go ahead from the Indian Government, initial design work was completed in 1990 and a mockup displayed at the 1993 Avia India Show. Hindustan Aeronautics Ltd (HAL) began construction of the prototype in 1991.

The LCA features a tailless delta configuration and the airframe includes extensive use of composites in its construction, notably in the wings and vertical tail. A fixed aerial refuelling probe is fitted, the cockpit contains the latest technology and the radar is a locally developed multimode unit.

Except for the first two prototypes which have General Electric F404 engines, the LCA will be powered by a new indigenous turbofan called the Kaveri. Developed by India's Gas Turbine Research Establishment (GTRE), the Kaveri was first bench tested in 1994 and flight tested four years later in a Tupolev Tu-16.

The first prototype was rolled out in November 1995, nine months behind schedule. The first flight (originally planned for June 1996) has been continually postponed and by early 2000 had still not occurred. The delay has been largely caused by flight control system reliability concerns with the Lockheed Martin fly-by-wire system, despite the software having previously been tested on a T-33 and F-16.

Despite this major delay, India still claims it can achieve a 2002 initial operational capability (IOC) for the LCA and full operational status in 2005.

By late 2000, the Indian military was expressing substantial concerns that the LCA would never enter service and steps were being taken to rectify an operational aircraft shortage.

Photo: The prototype Light Combat Aircraft.

Aeritalia (Fiat) G.91R

Country of origin: Italy.

Type: Single seat tactical strike/reconnaissance fighter.

Powerplant: One 5000lb (22.2kN) Bristol Siddeley Orpheus 803 turbojet.

Dimensions: Wing span 8.56m (28ft 1in); length 10.29m (33ft 9¹/₄in); height 3.99m (13ft 1¹/₄in); wing area 16.4m² (177sq ft).

Weights: Empty 3269kg (7207lb); max takeoff 5670kg (12,500lb).

Armament: Four 0.50in machine guns (G.91R/1/4) or two 30mm cannon (G.91R/3) in nose; four underwing hardpoints for max 680kg (1500lb) ordnance.

Performance: Max speed 586kt (1086km/h) at 5000ft; economical cruising speed 350kt (648km/h); initial climb 5990ft (1826m)/min; service ceiling 42,980ft; combat radius at sea level (internal fuel) 170nm (315km); ferry range 1000nm (1852km).

Production: 3 G.91 prototypes, 27 pre-production/G.91R/1, 25 G.91R/1A, 345 G.91R/3 (Fiat 50, Dornier 295), 50 G.91R/4 and 142 G.91T (Fiat 120, Dornier 22), total 642.

Notes: In December 1953 NATO announced a competition for a day/clear weather light tactical strike fighter to equip European NATO members' air forces, to be built by a European manufacturer and supplied under the Mutual Weapons Programme. The Bristol Siddeley Orpheus turbojet was the specified powerplant. The idea was for the aircraft to equip all Continental European NATO air forces.

The G.91 – which looked very much like a scaled down F-86 Sabre – was selected but in the event the aircraft was only built for Italy's Aeronautica Militare and Germany's Luftwaffe. It was manufactured in Italy by the parent company and in Germany by a consortium headed by Dornier. Typically, France boycotted the project shortly after its manufacturers' entries in the contest had been rejected in favour of the Italian G.91.

The first of three prototypes flew on 9 August 1956, followed by 27 pre series aircraft from February 1958 of which 23 entered Aeronautica Militare service from February 1959 as the G.91R/1, the 'R' signifying the installation of nose mounted cameras for tactical reconnaissance duties, a standard production feature.

Subsequent Fiat production comprised 25 G.91R/1As (with revised avionics) and 50 G.91R/1Bs (the first batch with Fiat built Orpheus 803 engines) for Italy plus 50 G.91R/3s (with two 30mm cannon in place of the previous four 0.50in machine guns and equipment changes) and 50 G.91R/4s (machine guns reinstated) for Germany. The latter were originally intended for Greece and Turkey but diverted. G.91R/3 deliveries to Germany began in late 1961 and the last was retired in February 1982.

The first of 295 G.91R/3s manufactured by the Dornier consortium flew in July 1965 as the first jet combat aircraft built in Germany since 1945, the whole batch completed within a year. A tandem two seat operational trainer version with lengthened forward fuselage was developed as the G.91T. First flown in May 1960 it was also built in Italy and Germany. The only other G.91 operator was Portugal, which received 74 ex Luftwaffe G.91R/3s and /4s (plus 36 for spares) in several batches between 1965 and 1981.

Photo: Portuguese G.91R/3. (Paul Merritt)

Aeritalia (Fiat) G.91Y

Country of origin: Italy.

Type: Single seat tactical strike/reconnaissance fighter.

Powerplants: Two 2725lb (12.1kN) dry/4080lb (18.1kN) with afterburner General Electric J85-GE-13A turbojets.

Dimensions: Wing span 9.00m (29ft 6½in); length 11.67m (38ft 3½in); height 4.43m (14ft 6½in); wing area 18.1m² (195sq ft).

Weights: Empty 3900kg (8598lb); normal takeoff 7800kg (17,196lb); max overload 8700kg (19,180lb).

Armament: Two 30mm cannon in nose; four underwing hardpoints for max 1814kg (4000lb) ordnance.

Performance: Max speed 600kt (1111km/h) at sea level, 582kt (1078km/h) at 32,800ft; economical cruising speed 432kt (800km/h) at 35,000ft; max initial climb 17,000ft (5182m)/min with afterburner, 7000ft (2133m)/min with dry thrust; time to 40,000ft 4.5min; service ceiling 41,000ft; low altitude combat radius with 1814kg (4000lb) load 200nm (370km) or 305nm (565km) hi-lo-hi; low level combat radius with drop tanks 360nm (669km); ferry range 1890nm (3500km).

Production: 67.

Notes: Although developed as a twin engined and more capable evolution of the G.91R, sharing a common overall designation and similar general configuration with the earlier aircraft, the G.91Y was in reality a completely new design intended to fill an Aeronautica Militare requirement for a day/clear weather ground attack/fighter reconnaissance aircraft.

Development began in 1965, the G.91Y design revealed to be slightly larger and considerably heavier than its predecessor with power provided by a pair of afterburning General Electric J85 turbojets in place of the previous single Bristol Siddeley Orpheus.

Ordnance carrying capacity was more than doubled on the four underwing hardpoints. A greater power-to-weight ratio conferred performance gains and operational enhancements resulted from the incorporation of improved navigation aids and an upgraded nav/attack system. Nose mounted cameras for tactical reconnaissance were standard equipment.

The first of two G.91Y prototypes flew on 27 December 1966 followed by 20 pre series aircraft from July 1968, these entering service in May 1970. Fiat and Finmeccanica merged to form Aeritalia (now Alenia) in 1969, and production G.91Ys were delivered under that name.

The first full production aircraft flew in June 1971 and the initial batch of 35 was delivered to the Aeronautica Militare between September 1971 and mid 1973. An additional batch of 10 was also delivered, the last of these handed over in mid 1976.

Italy's Aeronautica Militare remained the only G.91Y operator, the aircraft serving with two *Stormi* (Wings) before being retired from front line service in 1995.

Several other versions were planned but not built, these including the G.91Y/T tandem two seat trainer and the G.91Y/S single seater designed to meet a Swiss requirement for a ground attack aircraft.

Photo: Aeritalia G.91Y.

Aermacchi MB-326K

Country of origin: Italy.

Type: Single seat light strike.

Powerplant: One 4000lb (17.8kN) Rolls-Royce Viper Mk.632-43 turbojet.

Dimensions: Wing span 10.95m (35ft 7in); length 10.67m (35ft 0¼in); height 3.71m (12ft 2in); wing area 19.3m² (208sq ft).

Weights: Empty equipped 3123kg (6885lb); takeoff (clean) 4645kg (10,240lb); max takeoff 5897kg (13,000lb).

Armament: Two 30mm cannon; six underwing hardpoints for max 1814kg (4000lb) ordnance load including bombs, rocket pods, ASMs, AAMs, gun pods and reconnaissance pods.

Performance: Max speed 480kt (889km/h) at 5000ft, 370kt (685km/h) at 30,000ft; max climb 6500ft (1981m)/min clean or 3750ft (1143m)/min at max weight; service ceiling 47,000ft; low altitude combat radius with 1280kg (2822lb) load 145nm (268km) or 70nm (130km) with 1814kg (4000lb) load; combat radius hi-lo-hi with reconnaissance pod and drop tanks 560nm (1037km); ferry range 1150nm (2130km).

Production: 111 including 73 under licence by Atlas in South Africa as the Impala Mk.2.

Notes: A single seat dedicated light attack version of the highly successful MB-326 two seat jet trainer, the MB-326K was developed well into the aircraft's career, the prototype not flying until 22 August 1970 or nearly 13 years after the first MB-326 flew in December 1957.

Light attack versions of the two seat MB-326 were offered early, culminating in the more powerful and heavily armed MB-326G of 1967 of which 215 were purchased by four countries. Of these, 167 were built under licence in Brazil by Embraer as the AT-26 Xavante. MB-326 production amounted to 761 aircraft of all versions.

Compared to the MB-326G, the K differed in having a more powerful Viper 632-43 engine, the rear cockpit removed, additional fuselage fuel tanks, increased weapons carrying capability and strengthened structure. Two fixed 30mm cannon in the lower fuselage had their ammunition box in the space vacated by the second cockpit, while the previously nose mounted avionics were also located in that area.

The first prototype MB-326K was powered by a 3410lb (15.1kN) Viper 540 turbojet – the same as the MB-326G – but the second prototype which joined the test programme in 1971 had the more powerful Viper 632-43 as offered as standard equipment. Orders were slow to materialise and it wasn't until 1974 that the first MB-326Ks were delivered, six for Dubai.

Subsequent customers were Ghana (9), Tunisia (8), Zaire (6) and South Africa (7), the latter also receiving 73 built under licence by Atlas Aircraft as the Impala 2 and adding to the 191 two seat MB-326/Impalas previously delivered. The first South African Impala 2 was delivered in 1975, these aircraft differing from other MB-326Ks in having the lower powered Viper 540 powerplant.

Aermacchi's successor to the MB-326, the MB-339, first flew in August 1976. A single seat light attack variant (the MB-339K Veltro 2) was launched as a private venture and first flown in May 1980 but failed to attract any buyers.

Photo: Aermacchi MB-326K. (MAP)

Aero L 159 ALCA

Country of origin: Czech Republic.

Type: L 159/A – single seat light multirole fighter. L 159B/T – two seat lead in fighter trainer and light combat aircraft.

Powerplant: One 6300lb (28.0kN) Honeywell/ITEC F124-GA-100 turbofan.

Dimensions: Wing span 9.55m (31ft 4in); length 12.72m (41ft 9in); height 4.77m (15ft 8in); wing area 18.8m² (202sq ft).

Weights: Empty 4160kg (9171lb); max takeoff 8000kg (17,637lb).

Armament: One centreline and six underwing hardpoints for max 2340kg (5158lb) ordnance including AAMs, ASMs, bombs, gun pods, reconnaissance pod, rocket pods, fuel tanks etc.

Performance: L 159/A – max speed 502kt (930km/h) at sea level; max climb 9250ft (2819m)/min; service ceiling 43,300ft; hi-lo-hi combat radius with 454kg (1000lb) bomb load plus two Sidewinder AAMs and two drop tanks 380nm (704km); range (internal fuel) 848nm (1570km); max ferry range 1365nm (2528km).

Production: 2 prototypes and first production aircraft by early 2000; 72 on order for Czech Air Force.

Notes: The L 159 ALCA (Advanced Light Combat Aircraft) is the latest and most advanced development of the L 39/139/59 Albatros family of jet trainers which first flew in November 1968 and has since achieved production of nearly 3000 units.

The L 159 combines a slightly lengthened Albatros airframe with a new generation FADEC equipped Honeywell/ITEC F124 engine, modern avionics and radar.

The Boeing integrated avionics suite is built around a databus linking a headup display, two colour multifunction LCDs, Flight Visions dual mission computers, ring laser gyro INS with GPS navigation system, and the Italian FIAR Grifo L multimode radar with lookdown/shootdown and ground mapping functions.

Other features include HOTAS controls, plus a Sky Guardian radar warning receiver, Vinten chaff and flares countermeasures dispenser and cockpit armour.

Both single and two seat versions are offered, the former featuring an additional fuel tank in place of the aft cockpit but with the two seater's canopy retained.

Four variants have been developed: the basic single seat L 159 for the Czech Republic and L 159A for export; and the two seat L 159B (Czech) and L 159T (export). Most of the 72 ordered by the Czech Air Force will be of the single seat version.

Design work on the L 159 began in 1992, full scale development was approved in April 1995 and the Czech Air Force placed an order for 72 in July 1997. The first prototype (a two seater) flew on 2 August 1997 and the second (a single seater) on 18 August 1998. The first production L 159 was flown on 20 October 1999 with deliveries to begin in 2000. The Czech order is scheduled to be completed in 2002 and the manufacturer has been actively seeking export sales.

Aero, its part owners Boeing and Czech Airlines (CSA) plus engine manufacturer Honeywell (formerly AlliedSignal) have formed a joint marketing team to sell the L 159 on the world market.

Photo: First prototype L 159 ALCA. (Aero Vodochody)

Agusta A 129 Mangusta

Country of origin: Italy.

Type: Two seat attack and scout helicopter.

Powerplants: A 129 – two 881shp (657kW) Rolls-Royce Gem Mk.1004 turboshafts; four bladed main rotor. International – two 1404shp (1047kW) LHTEC (Allison/Honeywell) T800-LHT-800 turboshafts; five bladed main rotor.

Dimensions: Main rotor diameter 11.90m (39ft 0½in); fuselage length 12.45m (40ft 10in); height 3.35m (11ft 0in); main rotor disc area 111.2m² (1197sq ft).

Weights: A 129 – operating empty 2529kg (5575lb); max takeoff 4100kg (9039lb). International – max takeoff 5100kg (11,243lb).

Armament: A 129 – four hardpoints under stub wings for max 1200kg (2645kg) ordnance load including rocket and gun pods, anti tank and other missiles etc. International – ordnance under stub wings plus 20mm cannon in undernose turret.

Performance: A 129 – max speed 149kt (276km/h); max cruise 135kt (250km/h); max climb 2009ft (612m)/min; hovering ceiling 10,300ft IGE or 6200ft OGE; service ceiling 15,500ft; typical mission endurance 2hr 30min. International – max speed 161kt (298km/h); max cruise 150kt (278km/h); max climb 2225ft (678m)/min; vertical climb rate 1062ft (323m)/min; hovering ceiling 13,800ft IGE or 10,800ft OGE; normal range 303nm (561km); ferry range with external tanks 540nm (1000km).

Production: 60 by 2000.

Notes: Agusta instigated full scale development of the A 129 Mangusta (Mongoose) in 1978 to meet an Italian Army requirement for a combat helicopter capable of performing day and night attack and reconnaissance, escort, fire support and area suppression roles.

The prototype first flew on 11 September 1983, features including twin Rolls-Royce Gem turboshafts, the gunner/co pilot (front) and pilot (rear) in separate stepped tandem cockpits, four bladed main rotor, extensive use of composites (45 per cent of structural weight), a computerised and fully redundant integrated flight control/nav/weapons management system, stub wings each with two weapons pylons and low detectability/high survivability characteristics.

Deliveries of 60 to the Italian Army began in October 1990, the Mangusta's only customer by early 2000. The first 45 were built to the basic A 129 standard, the remaining 15 with some of the International model's features including five bladed main rotor and 20mm cannon in the nose plus an uprated transmission and increase in maximum weight to 4600kg (10,141lb). Stinger air-to-air missiles can also be carried.

The A 129 International was developed to attract export orders, a partial standard prototype first flying in 1988 and the fully configured version on 9 January 1995. Compared to the original A 129, the International features more powerful LHTEC T800 engines, increased maximum weight, five bladed main rotors, standard undernose gun, higher rated transmission, some avionics upgrading and a wider choice of weaponry.

Italy requires a further 30 Mangustas in both attack and scout configurations, the latter with mast mounted sights.

Photo: Italian Army Agusta A 129.

AIDC Ching-Kuo

Country of origin: Taiwan.

Type: Single or two seat multirole light fighter/operational trainer.

Powerplants: Two 6300lb (28.0kN) dry/9400lb (41.8kN) with afterburner ITEC TFE1042-70 (F125) turbofans.

Dimensions: Wing span 8.53m (28ft 0in); length (excl nose probe) 13.26m (43ft 6in); height 4.72m (15ft 6in); wing area 24.2m² (261sq ft).

Weights: Empty equipped 6486kg (14,300lb); typical combat 9525kg (21,000lb); max takeoff 12,247kg (27,000lb).

Armament: One 20mm Vulcan rotary cannon; two underwing, two wingtip and two underfuselage hardpoints for max 3900kg (8600lb) ordnance including bombs, AAMs and AGMs.

Performance: (Estimated) max speed 700kt (Mach 1.22/1297km/h) at 36,000ft; max climb 50,000ft (15,240m)/min; service ceiling 54,000ft.

Production: 144 including prototypes/pre-production.

Notes: Named after a former President of Taiwan (Chiang Ching-Kuo) this light air defence and multirole fighter is the country's most ambitious indigenous aircraft design to date.

Development of the Ching-Kuo (originally known as the Indigenous Defensive Fighter – IDF) began in May 1982 as a replacement for Taiwan's F-104 Starfighters and F-5E Tigers following a US ban on licence production of the Northrop F-20 Tigershark and the sale of other advanced fighters to Taiwan.

Despite the ban – and in order to maintain diplomatic sensibilities – US companies were able to work with the Taiwanese industry in the form of technical support.

General Dynamics worked closely with AIDC to develop the airframe while the new International Turbine Engine Corporation (ITEC) TFE1042 afterburning turbofan was developed jointly by AlliedSignal (now Honeywell) and AIDC. The US military designation for the engine is F125.

Other Ching-Kuo elements derived from US technology include the Golden Dragon 53 radar based on the APG-67 originally developed for the F-20 with some influence from the F-16's APG-66 radar; and the infrared Sky Sword I and radar guided Sky Sword II AAMs which are derived from Sidewinder technology.

The first of four Ching-Kuo prototypes flew on 28 May 1989, the others following in September 1989, January 1990 and July 1990 with the latter the first two seater.

These were followed by 10 pre-production aircraft up to late 1993 while the first production model – a single seater – flew on 10 January 1994. The first production two seater was flown the next month and operational capability declared in January 1995.

Taiwan's initial planned buy of 260 Ching-Kuos was halved when the lifting of arms purchase restrictions in the early 1990s allowed Taiwan to purchase F-16s from the USA and Mirage 2000-5s from France to meet most of its needs.

Deliveries were temporarily suspended between October 1995 and June 1996 to sort out problems with the fuel management system. Delivery of the 130 production Ching-Kuos was completed in early 2000.

Photo: AIDC Ching-Kuo.

AMX International AMX/A-1

Countries of origin: Italy and Brazil.

Type: Single seat attack.

Powerplant: One 11,030lb (49.1kN) Rolls-Royce Spey Mk.807 turbofan.

Dimensions: Wing span 8.88m (29ft 1¹/₂in); length 13.23m (43ft 5in); height 4.55m (14ft 11in); wing area 21.0m² (226sq ft).

Weights: Operating empty 6700kg (14,770lb); max takeoff 13,000kg (28,660lb).

Armament: One 20mm Vulcan rotary cannon (Italian aircraft) or two 30mm cannon (Brazilian); one centreline and four underwing hardpoints for max 3629kg (8000lb) ordnance or fuel tanks; plus wingtip stations for two AIM-9L Sidewinder (Italy) or Piranha (Brazil) AAMs.

Performance: Max speed 555kt (1027km/h) at sea level, 506kt (938km/h) at 30,000ft; max climb 10,250ft (3124m)/min; ceiling 42,650ft; combat radius with 2722kg (6000lb) load lo-lo-lo 285nm (528km) or 500nm (926km) hi-lo-hi; ferry range 1800nm (3334km).

Production: Over 210 by early 1999.

Notes: In 1977 the Aeronautica Militare (Italian Air Force) issued a specification for a tactical fighter-bomber to replace the Fiat G.91 and Lockheed F-104 Starfighter, Aermacchi and Aeritalia (now Alenia) jointly developing the concept. Coincidentally and simultaneously, Brazil was defining a similar requirement for the Fôrca Aérea Brasileira (FAB), the two nations signing an agreement to jointly develop an appropriate aircraft in July 1980.

The result was the formation of AMX International owned by Aeritalia (46.7%), Aermacchi (23.6%) and Embraer (29.7%). Assembly lines were established by all three companies but there was no duplication of component manufacture. The non afterburning Rolls-Royce Spey Mk.807 would be built under licence by FiatAvio and Celma-Cio.

The initial agreement covered 266 production aircraft for Italy (187) and Brazil (79) with both single and a lesser number of two seaters planned. In Brazilian service the AMX is known as the A-1 in single seat form or A-1B for the two seat conversion trainer version. The two seater is called the AMX-T by the Italians.

The first of seven prototypes (assembled by Aeritalia) flew on 15 May 1984 followed by the second (Aermacchi) on 19 November 1984. The first from Embraer (and the fifth to fly) took to the air on 16 October 1985. The first production (Italian) AMX flew on 11 May 1988 and the first production Brazilian A-1 on 12 August 1989. Deliveries to Italy began in April 1989 and to Brazil six months later. All AMXs had been single seaters to this point, the first two seater flying on 14 March 1990.

By 1999, AMX production was beginning to wind down with Italy having received the 149 funded aircraft (against a requirement for 238) and deliveries of Brazil's 56 aircraft continuing at a slow rate. Brazil's stated requirement is for 94. However, the AMX's prospects have been boosted by Venezuela, which in 1998 announced it was planning to order 24 examples of an AMX-T development called the AMX-ATA (Advanced Trainer Attack). This will feature a digital cockpit and radar. Anti ship, anti radar and night attack versions have also been studied, along with a variant powered by the Eurojet EJ200 engine.

Photo: A prototype AMX. (AMX International)

Avia S 199

Countries of origin: Germany/Czechoslovakia.

Type: Single seat fighter-bomber.

Powerplant: One 1350hp (1007kW) Junkers Jumo 211F inverted V12 piston engine; three bladed propeller.

Dimensions: Wing span 9.92m (32ft 6½in); length 8.94m (29ft 4in); height 2.59m (8ft 6in); wing area 16.5m² (178sq ft).

Weights: Empty 2860kg (6305lb); max takeoff 3736kg (8236lb).

Armament: Two 13mm machine guns in forward fuselage, two 20mm cannon under wings; one 250kg (551lb) bomb under fuselage.

Performance: Max speed 318kt (589km/h) at 19,700ft, 280kt (518km/h) at sea level; cruise speed 215-249kt (398-461km/h); max climb 2695ft (821m)/min; service ceiling 31,170ft; range with drop tank 459nm (850km).

Production: 493 S 199 and 58 CS 199, total 551.

Notes: Assembly of Germany's Messerschmitt Bf 109 fighter had begun in Czechoslovakia during 1944 at the Avia factory at Prague-akovice, the aircraft built up from sub assemblies from several small factories in the area. The Bf 109G-14 single seater plus the tandem two seat 109G-12 were built, but only a small number had been handed over to the Luftwaffe by the time of the Germans' rapid withdrawal in the face of the advancing Soviets in 1945.

A large quantity of parts (and the factories) remained intact, these collected with a view to completing more aircraft. A second assembly line was established at the Letov facility at Letnany. Twenty-two additional aircraft were initially assembled, comprising 20 Bf 109G-14s (locally named the S 99) and two G-12s (CS 99), these delivered to the Czech National Air Guard during 1945.

Plans to continue production were put in place but the building in which the stock of Daimler-Benz DB 605 engines was stored burnt down in September 1945, leaving the need to find an alternate source of appropriate engines.

The only engine readily available was the Jumo 211 for the Heinkel He 111H bomber, and although far from ideal for a fighter, Avia adapted the 109 design to take the new powerplant. As the S 199, this first flew on 25 March 1947 and the first two seat CS 199 on 24 January 1949. The aircraft was universally disliked by pilots thanks to its vicious swing on takeoff, over sensitive controls, sluggish acceleration, extremely difficult landing characteristics and poor general handling. The derisive nickname *Mezec* (Mule) was quickly applied.

Despite this, 551 were built up to 1951 including 129 at the Letov factory. Deliveries to the Czech Air Force began in 1948 and 25 were exported to Israel in the same year, the newly formed nation desperate for anything with which to equip its air force. Paid for in highly prized US dollars, the S 199s were surreptitiously supplied despite an arms embargo. Israeli pilots disliked the S 199 as much as the Czech flyers had, but the 'Mule' was nevertheless used in combat against Egyptian Air Force aircraft and ground targets. Most of the S 199's losses were due to accidents resulting from its handling difficulties.

Photo: Avia S 199.

Avro Lincoln B.1/B.2

Country of origin: United Kingdom.

Type: Seven crew heavy bomber.

Powerplants: B.1 – four 1750hp (1305kW) Rolls-Royce Merlin 85 V12 piston engines. B.2 – four 1750hp (1305kW) Packard Merlin 68 or 300; four bladed propellers.

Dimensions: Wing span 36.57m (120ft 8in); length 23.86m (78ft 3½in); height 5.27m (17ft 3½in); wing area 132.0m² (1421sq ft).

Weights: B.1/2 – empty 19,686-20,026kg (43,400-44,150lb); max takeoff 37,195kg (82,000lb).

Armament: Two 0.50in machine guns in each of nose, dorsal and tail turrets (some with two 20mm cannon in dorsal turret); max bomb load 6350kg (14,000lb).

Performance: B.1 – max speed 256kt (475km/h) at 15,000ft; cruising speed 187kt (346km/h); initial climb 800ft (244m)/min; service ceiling 22,000ft; range with 6350kg (14,000lb) bomb load 2294nm (4250km); max range with bomb bay tanks 3519nm (6519km).

Production: 550 in UK by Avro (3 prototypes, 52 B.1, 116 B.2), Metropolitan Vickers (28 B.1, 52 B.2) and Armstrong Whitworth (2 B.1, 297 B.2) plus 1 Mk.XV in Canada by Victory Aircraft.

Notes: A direct development of the Lancaster, the Avro Type 694 Lincoln was intended for service in the Pacific War against Japan but was subject to large order cancellations when the conflict suddenly ended in August 1945. What became known as the Lincoln B.1 and B.2 were originally named the Lancaster IV and V with Rolls-Royce and Packard Merlins, respectively.

Compared to the Lancaster, the Lincoln featured a lengthened fuselage, increased span wings, more powerful engines (driving four rather than three bladed propellers), improved defensive armament, increased fuel capacity and increased weights. The prototype first flew on 9 June 1944 and initial deliveries were to the RAF's No 57 Squadron at Scampton in August 1945, initially for service trials. Regular squadron service began in early 1946, the aircraft by then having a relatively low priority. The RAF received its 529th and last Lincoln in April 1951. The B.2 was delivered from 1948 and the projected Lincoln III maritime patrol variant was developed into the Shackleton.

The Lincoln equipped 23 RAF bomber squadrons and was the mainstay of the RAF's heavy bomber force until the jets entered service. It saw action against communist terrorists in Malaya from 1950 and the Mau-Mau in Kenya from 1953. Withdrawn from front line RAF service in 1955, some aircraft were retained for training and use by five Signals Command squadrons, their 60 Lincolns converted from B.2s as the Mk.4 and fitted with electronic jamming equipment. The last RAF Lincoln was retired in May 1963. Many Lincolns were used for experimental work including as engine, de-icing and flight refuelling testbeds.

Canada's Victory Aircraft had built 430 Lancasters during the war and planned to also manufacture Lincolns. The end of hostilities resulted in only one being built (as the Mk.XV) in 1945. Argentina received 30 Lincolns (12 ex RAF and 18 new) from 1947, these seeing action in the 1955 revolution and 1956 counter-revolution and serving until the early 1960s. Others were built under licence in Australia (see next entry).

Photo: Lincoln B.2. (BAe)

Avro/GAF Lincoln Mk.30/31

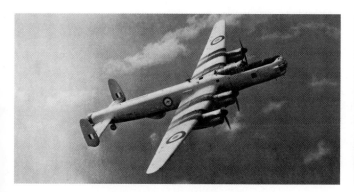

Countries of origin: Australia/United Kingdom.

Type: Mk.30 – seven crew heavy bomber. Mk.31 – 11 crew general/maritime reconnaissance bomber.

Powerplants: Four 1750hp (1305kW) Rolls-Royce Merlin 66 or 85B or 1775hp (1323kW) CAC built Merlin 102 V12 piston engines; four bladed propellers.

Dimensions: Mk.30 – wing span 36.57m (120ft 0in); length 23.86m (78ft 3½in); height 5.27m (17ft 3½in); wing area 132.0m² (1421sq ft). Mk.31 – length 25.84m (84ft 9½in).

Weights: Empty equipped 19,958-20,367kg (44,000-44,900lb); max takeoff 34,020-37,195kg (75,000-82,000lb).

Armament: Two 0.50in machine guns in each of nose and tail turrets, two 20mm cannon in dorsal turret; max bomb load 6350kg (14,000lb).

Performance: Max speed 269kt (499km/h) at 18,300ft; max cruise 226kt (418km/h) at 20,000ft; range cruise 187kt (346km/h); initial climb 800ft (244m)/min; service ceiling 28,000ft; range with max bomb load 2433nm (4507km); max range with bomb bay tanks 3728nm (6905km).

Production: 73 of which 20 converted to Mk.31 configuration.

Notes: Australia began investigating local production of a large bomber in 1941, early thoughts revolving around the Avro Manchester. In early 1943 the Lancaster was selected with an order for 346 recommended. Formal approval for the manufacture of an initial 50 aircraft by the Australian Department of Aircraft Production (later Government Aircraft Factories/GAF) was given in November 1943, this later changed to the Lincoln. Seventy-three Avro aircraft were contracted in July 1945 comprising 61 Lincolns and 12 Tudor airliners. This was subsequently amended to 73 Lincolns and none of the ill-fated Tudors.

The Australian built Lincoln was dubbed the Mk.30 with the first five assembled from British components. The first example flew on 12 March 1946. The initial 25 aircraft were built as basic Mk.30s and the remaining 47 as Mk.30As with structural modifications allowing increased weights. The initial powerplant was the Merlin 85 but some aircraft were fitted with Merlin 66s from RAAF stocks. Others had Merlin 102s built in Australia by the Commonwealth Aircraft Corporation. Production was at a leisurely pace, the final aircraft delivered in September 1953.

The major variant was the unique to Australia Mk.31 'long nose' Lincoln with the nose stretched by 1.98m (6ft 6in) to house a tactical navigator and three sonobuoy operators. As the (GR) Mk.31 for maritime duties, the new variant first flew in 1952 and of the 20 converted, eight were built from existing Mk.30As and the remainder delivered new after conversion on the production line. Ten were subsequently upgraded to (MR) Mk.31 standards with improved operational equipment, the first delivered in March 1955.

The Lincoln served with five RAAF squadrons. No 1 Squadron flew operationally against communist terrorists in Malaya for eight years from July 1950. The last (MR) Mk.31s were retired in June 1961 after the discovery of severe wing spar corrosion and replaced by Neptunes.

Photo: Lincoln Mk.31.

Avro Shackleton MR.1/2

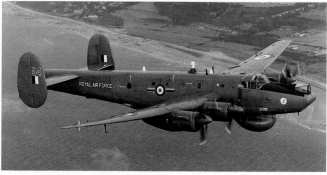

Country of origin: United Kingdom.

Type: 10 crew maritime patrol and anti submarine bomber.

Powerplants: Four 2450hp (1827kW) Rolls-Royce Griffon 57/57A V12 piston engines; six bladed counter-rotating propellers.

Dimensions: MR.1 – wing span 36.57m (120ft 0in); length 23.62m (77ft 6in); height 5.10m (16ft 9in); wing area 132.0m² (1421sq ft). MR.2 – length 26.59m (87ft 3in).

Weights: MR.2 – empty 24,585kg (54,200lb); max takeoff 39,010kg (86,000lb).

Armament: MR.2 – two 20mm cannon in each of nose and dorsal turrets (later deleted); max bomb/depth charge load 6804kg (15,000lb).

Performance: MR.2 – max speed 257kt (476km/h) at 18,300ft; range cruise 174kt (322km/h); service ceiling 25,700ft; max range 3737nm (6920km).

Production: 191 Shackletons of all models including 3 prototypes, 77 MR.1 and 69 MR.2.

Notes: Developed from the Lincoln Mk.III, a planned anti submarine and maritime patrol version of the bomber, the Avro Type 696 Shackleton was the last of the line of aircraft which began with the Manchester in 1939 and progressed through the Lancaster and Lincoln. Optimised for the maritime role, it basically combined the Lincoln's wing and undercarriage with a new more spacious fuselage and Rolls-Royce Griffon engines driving contraprops.

Built to Air Ministry Specification R.5/46, the first of three prototypes flew on 9 March 1949 followed by the first production Shackleton GR.1 (MR.1 from 1951) on 24 October 1950. RAF squadron service began in April 1951 with No 120 Squadron at Kinloss; nine others also flew the initial version. The designation MR.1A was applied from the 30th aircraft onwards, these featuring minor powerplant modifications.

The first Shackleton MR.2 flew on 17 June 1952, this differing from the MR.1 in having a lengthened nose with two 20mm cannon installed, a dorsal turret also with two cannon (later deleted) and the undernose 'chin' radome replaced with a retractable 'dustbin' radome for the ASV radar mounted under the lower rear fuselage. Deliveries of the MR.2 began in January 1953, the aircraft serving with the same ten RAF squadrons which had flown the MR.1/1A.

Apart from their normal maritime duties, some Shackleton MR.2s of No 42 Squadron were used as bombers during the Omani rebellion of 1957. Many MR.2s were converted to MR.2 Phase 3 standards from 1959 with some of the updated equipment fitted to the later MR.3 (see next entry) installed. The last MR.2s were retired from RAF service in April 1972.

Shackleton versions created by conversion were the 16 T.4 and two MR.2(T) crew trainers (from the MR.1 and MR.2, respectively) and most importantly, the AEW.2 early warning aircraft, a successful 'cobble up' fitted with APS-20 radar in a large radome under the forward fuselage.

The first of 12 conversions flew in September 1971 and despite being regarded as a temporary expedient the AEW.2 remained in RAF service until 1991 following the failure of the Nimrod AEW version. The Shackleton was finally replaced by the Boeing E-3 Sentry AWACS.

Photo: Shackleton AEW.2. (MoD)

Avro Shackleton MR.3

Country of origin: United Kingdom.

Type: 10 crew maritime patrol and anti submarine bomber.

Powerplants: Four 2450hp (1827kW) Rolls-Royce Griffon 57A V12 piston engines; six bladed counter-rotating propellers; two auxiliary 2700lb (11.1kN) Bristol Siddeley Viper 203 turbojets added later.

Dimensions: Wing span 36.52m (119ft 10in); length 28.19m (92ft 6in); height 7.11m (23ft 4in); wing area 132.0m² (1421sq ft).

Weights: Empty 29,166kg (64,300lb); max takeoff 45,360kg (100,000lb).

Armament: Two 20mm cannon in nose; max bomb/depth charge load 5443kg (12,000lb).

Performance: Max speed 262kt (486km/h); max cruise 220kt (407km/h); long range cruise 174kt (322km/h); initial climb 850ft (259m)/min; service ceiling 19,200ft; range 3180nm (5891km).

Production: 191 Shackletons of all models including 42 MR.3.

Notes: The final version of the Shackleton, the MR.3 featured several major modifications over the previous versions. The most obvious of these was the installation of a nosewheel rather than tailwheel undercarriage to improve crosswind handling on the ground and to cope with increased operating weights. Smaller twin wheels were fitted to all undercarriage legs in place of the previous single units.

Other changes included providing increased fuel capacity in external wingtip tanks, deletion of the dorsal gun turret (also removed from the MR.2 during its service life), and fitting a revised clear view canopy for improved visibility from the cockpit.

Maximum takeoff weight was increased substantially and the structure strengthened, underwing hardpoints were fitted to carry rocket projectiles and operational equipment was upgraded. The MR.3's interior was also redesigned. With sortie times of up to 18 hours it was often necessary to carry a duplicate crew and improved accommodation was provided for better working and rest conditions including a 'soundproof' wardroom. Of course, when it came to the Shackleton, the word 'improved' was relative!

The first Shackleton MR.3 was flown on 2 September 1955 but operational service of the 34 aircraft delivered to the RAF didn't start until August 1957. The last aircraft was delivered in June 1959.

The MR.3 served with six RAF operational squadrons but never completely replaced the MR.2 in service and was the first to be withdrawn, in September 1971, seven months before the earlier model.

Two major upgrade programmes were carried out, the first involving fitting an Autolycus exhaust trail detector for 'sniffing' submarines on the surface (MR.3 Phase 2); while the MR.3 Phase 3 modification programme undertaken from 1964 saw the aircraft refurbished and fitted with a Viper turbojet in each outer engine nacelle to boost takeoff performance at high weights.

The only export customer for the Shackleton was the South African Air Force, which received the first of eight new production MR.3s in May 1957 and operated them well into the 1980s.

Photo: Shackleton MR.3. (Stewart Wilson)

Avro Vulcan B.1

Country of origin: United Kingdom.

Type: Five crew strategic bomber.

Powerplants: Four 11,000lb (48.9kN) Bristol Siddeley Olympus 101; 12,000lb (53.4kN) Olympus 102; or 13,500lb (60.0kN) Olympus 104 turbojets.

Dimensions: Wing span 30.17m (99ft 0in); length (B.1A) 29.59m (97ft 1in); height 8.08m (26ft 6in); wing area 330.2m² (3554sq ft).

Weights: Normal max takeoff 75,751kg (167,000lb); max overload 86,184kg (190,000lb).

Armament: Up to 9525kg (21,000lb) of conventional bombs; or one 4536kg (10,000lb) Blue Danube or 3175kg (7000lb) Yellow Sun nuclear bomb.

Performance: Max speed 543kt (1006km/h) at 36,000ft; cruising speed 527kt (977km/h) at 50,000ft; service ceiling 55,000ft; max range 3910nm (7242km); range with max bomb load 2607nm (4828km).

Production: 135 Vulcans of all models (plus 1 fatigue test airframe) including 2 prototypes and 45 B.1.

Notes: One of the most distinctive and charismatic combat aircraft of the post war era, Avro's 'tin triangle' delta winged bomber represented one-third of Britain's nuclear deterrent V-Bomber force (along with the Vickers Valiant and Handley Page Victor) and remained in its designed bombing role for longer than either. Originally intended for high altitude missions, it was switched to low altitude penetration duties relatively early in his career. The Vulcan's primary mission was and remained retaliatory attacks on the Soviet Union during the Cold War.

Design studies for a Lincoln replacement began in 1945 but the issue of a demanding Air Ministry specification in early 1947 led to earnest development of a jet bomber designed to carry Britain's first atomic bomb, the Blue Danube. The study of captured German documentation contributed to adoption of the Vulcan's radical and distinctive tailless delta wing configuration.

The first prototype flew on 30 August 1952 powered by four Rolls-Royce Avon engines instead of the planned Bristol Olympus as these were not ready. The second prototype was Olympus powered and first flew in September 1953. Both were fitted with pure delta wings with straight leading edges. The name 'Vulcan' was bestowed in late 1952.

Early testing revealed wing compressibility buffet and stall problems when pulling 'g' at high altitudes, this leading to development of the Phase 2 wing with 'kinked' leading edge incorporating three different sweep angles.

The new wing was applied to production Vulcan B.1s, the first of which flew on 4 February 1955, although aircraft to full production standards did not appear until the second half of 1956. The Vulcan's Operational Training Unit received its first aircraft in May 1956 and the first of five RAF operational squadrons to fly the B.1 a year later. Final delivery was in April 1959.

Conversion of 29 Vulcan B.1s to B.1A standards by Armstrong-Whitworth was conducted in 1960-63, this variant incorporating the electronic countermeasures equipment developed for the B.2 (see next entry) mounted in an 86cm (34in) extension to the tailcone. The Vulcan B.1A was retired from RAF front line service in 1967.

Photo: Vulcan B.1A. (AWM)

Avro Vulcan B.2

Country of origin: United Kingdom.

Type: Five crew strategic bomber.

Powerplants: Four 17,000lb (75.6kN) Bristol Siddeley Olympus 201 or 20,000lb (89.0kN) Olympus 301 turbojets.

Dimensions: Wing span 33.83m (111ft 0in); length (excluding refuelling probe) 30.45m (99ft 11in); height 8.25m (27ft 1in); wing area 368.2m² (3964sq ft).

Weights: Normal max takeoff 92,534kg (204,000lb); max overload 102,060kg (225,000lb).

Armament: Up to 9525kg (21,000lb) of conventional bombs; one Avro Blue steel standoff nuclear missile or one Yellow Sun or WE177 nuclear weapon.

Performance: Max speed 560kt (1038km/h) at 36,000ft; cruising speed 539kt (998km/h) at 55,000ft; service ceiling 60,000ft; max high altitude range 4000nm (7409km); max low altitude range 3000nm (5557km).

Production: 135 Vulcans of all models (plus one fatigue test airframe) including 88 B.2.

Notes: The Vulcan B.2 represented a notable improvement over the original thanks to incorporation of the more powerful Olympus 200/300 series of engines, the addition of electronic countermeasures equipment in an extended tailcone and the ability in some aircraft to carry the Blue Steel rocket powered standoff weapon.

Other significant changes introduced to the B.2 include increased weights, a restressed structure and most significantly the Phase 2C wing with increased span and area, improved aerodynamic properties for the very high subsonic speeds and altitudes at which the Vulcan operated and changes to the flight control system.

The second prototype Vulcan was fitted with the new wing and reflown in 31 August 1957. The first true B.2 flew on 19 August 1958 and deliveries to the RAF began in July 1960. The first 44 aircraft were powered by Olympus 201 engines and the remainder by more powerful Olympus 301s. Twenty-six were equipped to carry Blue Steel and designated B.2A. Final delivery was in January 1965 while eight were converted to SR.2 (sometimes B.2MRR) standards from 1973 for maritime radar reconnaissance missions.

The Vulcan's high altitude strategic bomber role switched to low level penetration from 1963 following Britain's main nuclear deterrent duties being taken over by the Royal Navy's Polaris submarines. This necessitated some minor structural modifications to help cope with the rougher air 'down low' and the fitting of terrain following radar and a radar warning receiver.

RAF Vulcan operations were due to wind down in early 1982 but the outbreak of the Falklands War in April of that year provided a temporary reprieve and the only time the Vulcan was used in anger. Six very long range 'Black Buck' missions (the longest in history to that point) were flown against Port Stanley in April-June, some of them anti radar sorties using four AGM-45 Shrike missiles mounted on makeshift underwing pylons. The conflict also prompted rapid development of six Vulcan K.2 tanker conversions.

All Vulcan bombers had been withdrawn from service by the end of 1982 but the tankers remained until March 1984.

Photo: Vulcan B.2.

Avro Canada CF-100

Country of origin: Canada.

Type: Two seat all weather fighter.

Powerplants: Mks.2/3 – two 6000lb (26.7kN) Orenda 2/8 turbojets. Mk.4A – two 6500lb (28.9kN) Orenda 9. Mks.4B/5 – two 7275lb (32.3kN) Orenda 11/14.

Dimensions: Mk.3 – wing span 15.85m (52ft 0in); length 15.94m (52ft 3³⁄₄in); height 4.73m (15ft 6¹⁄₂in); wing area 50.2m² (540sq ft). Mk.5 – wing span 17.68m (58ft 0in); length 16.48m (54ft 1in); wing area 54.9m² (591sq ft).

Weights: Mk.3 – empty 9798kg (21,600lb); normal loaded 15,422kg (34,000lb); max takeoff 18,030kg (39,750lb). Mk.5 – empty 10,478kg (23,100lb); normal loaded 16,783kg (37,000lb); max takeoff 20,639kg (45,500lb).

Armament: Mk.3 – eight 0.50in machine guns in ventral pack. Mk.4 – guns or 48 2.75in (70mm) unguided missiles in ventral pack plus 58 in two wingtip pods. Mk.5 – wingtip missiles only.

Performance: Mk.3 – max speed 552kt (1022km/h) at 10,000ft, 492kt (911km/h) at 40,000ft; initial climb 9200ft (2804m)/min; service ceiling 47,000ft. Mk.5 – max speed 565kt (1046km/h) at 10,000ft, 510kt (945km/h) at 40,000ft; initial climb 8500ft (2590m)/min; service ceiling 54,000ft; combat radius 565nm (1046km).

Production: 2 Mk.1, 10 Mk.2, 70 Mk.3, 137 Mk.4A, 144 Mk.4B, 329 Mk.5, total 692.

Notes: Designed in late 1946 to meet a Royal Canadian Air Force requirement, the CF-100 was a large, twin engined and radar equipped all weather fighter of conventional all metal construction. Regarded by some as the best of its type during the 1950s, the CF-100 was not only a wholly indigenous Canadian design but was also powered by the locally developed Avro Canada (later Orenda Engines) Orenda axial flow turbojet.

The two prototypes were designated CF-100 Mk.1 and were powered by Rolls-Royce Avon engines, the first of them flying on 19 January 1950. Ten unarmed pre-production Mk.2s with Orendas followed from June 1951 and deliveries of the initial production Mk.3 with a ventral gun pack began in September 1952.

The Mk.4A with more powerful Orenda 9 engine, improved radar and provision for a battery of unguided 2.75in missiles (or guns) in the ventral pod plus others in wingtip pods first flew on 24 October 1953. The Mk.4B was similar except for its more powerful Orenda 121 engines with a two-stage turbine. Tip tanks could be fitted in lieu of the missile pods. The final and major production version was the Mk.5 with Orenda 11s or similarly rated 14s, modified structure and increased span wings and tailplane. The converted prototype flew in September 1954 and the first production model in October 1955. Belgium was the only export customer for the CF-100, receiving 53 Mk.5s. Production ended in 1957 despite several developed versions being proposed including the Mk.6 with afterburning engines and Sparrow air-to-air missiles.

The RCAF operated its CF-100s at home and as part of NATO's forces in Europe. Front line service had ended by 1961 but many were converted to trainers and electronic warfare aircraft. The last was retired as late as 1981.

Photo: CF-100 Mk.5.

Avro Canada CF-105 Arrow

Country of origin: Canada.

Type: Two seat long range all weather interceptor.

Powerplants: Mk.1 – two 12,500lb (55.6kN) dry/23,500lb (104.5kN) with afterburner Pratt & Whitney J75-P-3 turbojets. Mk.2 (proposed) – two 19,250lb (85.6kN) dry/26,000lb (115.6kN) with afterburner Orenda PS-13-3 Iroquois turbojets.

Dimensions: Wing span 15.24m (50ft 0in); length 23.72m (77ft 10in); height 6.48m (21ft 3in); wing area 113.8m² (1225sq ft).

Weights: Empty 22,244kg (49,040lb); max takeoff 31,118kg (68,602lb).

Armament: Six Falcon or eight Sparrow air-to-air missiles in internal weapons bay.

Performance: Mk.1 – max speed 1320kt (Mach 2.3/2445km/h) at 36,000ft; max cruise 527kt (977km/h) at 36,000ft; combat radius 356nm (660km).

Production: 5 Mk.1s flown, 5 Mk.2s complete or virtually complete but unflown.

Notes: A highly advanced Mach 2, two seat missile armed fighter intended to intercept Soviet bombers approaching North America, the Arrow met an ignominious end at the hands of politicians.

Five Arrows were flown before the project was abruptly terminated at a time when some in the corridors of power were convinced that the day of the manned fighter had passed and that missiles would take over. At a stroke, the innovative Canadian aircraft industry's ability to design and produce state-of-the-art combat aircraft was destroyed.

The advanced design of the aircraft was impressive enough; equally impressive was the fact that production versions would be powered by the locally developed Orenda Iroquois afterburning axial flow turbojet, at the time regarded as the most advanced engine of its kind. Bench testing began in December 1954 and flight testing in 1956 in a pod on the rear fuselage of a B-47 Stratojet.

The Arrow was developed to meet a 1952 Royal Canadian Air Force requirement and it was decided that for safety's sake, early aircraft would be powered by the proven Pratt & Whitney J75. Orders were placed covering 13 J75 powered Mk.1 development aircraft and 37 production standard Mk.2s with Iroquois engines. When rolled out in October 1957, the Arrow was revealed to be a large and attractive delta winged fighter with substantial vertical tail surfaces. A large diameter radar dish scanner in the nose, an internal weapons bay for up to eight AAMs was provided and the aircraft's structures and systems design was highly advanced.

The prototype first flew on 25 March 1958 and achieved Mach 1.5 on its third flight. Four other J75 powered Arrow Mk.1s were flown in August, September and October 1958 plus January 1959. These were the only five Arrows to fly, as the programme was cancelled on 20 February 1959 and all flying ceased. A sixth Arrow – the first Mk.2 – was ready to join the test programme when it was cancelled and four others were virtually complete.

When it was realised that manned fighters did have a future after all, the RCAF was forced to by second hand F-101B Voodoos from the USAF to fill its all weather interceptor needs.

Photo: CF-105.

BAe Nimrod

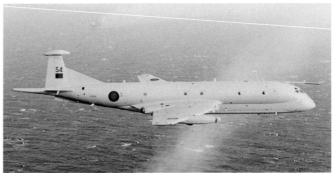

Country of origin: United Kingdom.

Type: 12 crew maritime patrol.

Powerplants: Four 12,140lb (54.0kN) Rolls-Royce Spey RB.168-20 Mk.250 turbofans.

Dimensions: Wing span 35.00m (114ft 10in); length 38.63m (126ft 9in); height 9.06m (29ft 8½in); wing area 197.0m² (2121sq ft).

Weights: MR.2 – empty equipped 39,010kg (86,000lb); normal max takeoff 80,514kg (177,500lb); max overload 87,091kg (192,000lb).

Armament: Max 6124kg (13,500lb) ordnance in weapons bay and two underwing hardpoints including two AGM-84 Harpoon ASMs, Stingray torpedoes, bombs, depth charges and up to four AIM-9 Sidewinder AAMs for self defence.

Performance: Max speed 500kt (926km/h); max cruise 475kt (880km/h); economical cruise 425kt (787km/h); two engined low level patrol speed 200kt (370km/h); operating ceiling 42,000ft; typical endurance 12 hours; max endurance with one refuelling 19 hours; ferry range 4500-5000nm (8335-9261km).

Production: 2 prototypes (converted from Comet 4Cs), 46 MR.1 and 3 R.1.

Notes: Developed as a replacement for the Avro Shackleton in RAF service, design of the Nimrod (as the Hawker Siddeley HS.801) began in 1964. Based on the Comet 4C airliner, the Nimrod differed in having Spey turbofans in place of the Avon turbojets, a shortened fuselage and a new, enlarged and unpressurised lower fuselage containing a weapons bay and equipment accommodation.

The nose was lengthened and deepened (with search radar installed), other external changes including the installation of a magnetic anomaly detector (MAD) boom extending from the rear fuselage and ESM sensors mounted in a fairing above the fin.

The two prototypes were converted from unsold Comet 4C airframes, the first of them (with Spey engines) flying on 23 May 1967. The second prototype retained the original Avons. In service, the Nimrod can patrol with two of its Speys shut down.

The first of 46 production Nimrod MR.1s flew on 28 June 1968 and deliveries to the RAF began in October 1969. Of these, 11 were later allocated to the aborted Nimrod AEW programme and 32 were upgraded to MR.2 standards with a new central tactical system, computer, processors, communications suite and EMI Searchwater radar. The first modified aircraft was redelivered in August 1979.

Subsequent upgrades with inflight refuelling capability and wingtip ESM pods have resulted in the designation MR.2P. Three additional Nimrods were delivered as R.1 electronic intelligence gathering aircraft in 1971-72, these lacking the MAD boom. A fourth was later converted.

The Nimrod MRA.4 is a substantial rebuild of 21 aircraft involving re-engining with 15,500lb (68.9kN) BMW Rolls-Royce BR710 turbofans, fitting new and larger wings, refurbishing the fuselage (some 80 per cent of the total structure is new) and installing the latest technology mission systems, sensors, navigation/communications systems, weapons and EFIS cockpit. Work began in 1997 but delays have pushed the in service date back to 2005.

Photo: Nimrod MR.2. (MoD)

BAe Harrier GR.1/3 and AV-8A

Country of origin: United Kingdom.

Type: Single seat close support and reconnaissance fighter.

Powerplant: GR.1 – one 19,000lb (84.5kN) Rolls-Royce Pegasus Mk.101 vectored thrust turbofan. GR.1A/early AV-8A – 20,500lb (91.2kN) Pegasus Mk.102/F402-RR-400. GR.3/AV-8A – 21,500lb (95.6kN) Pegasus Mk.103/F402-RR-401.

Dimensions: GR.3 – Wing span 7.70m (25ft 3in); length 13.92m (45ft 8in); height 3.52m (11ft 6½in); wing area 18.7m² (201sq ft).

Weights: GR.3 – empty 5734kg (12,640lb); max takeoff 11,794kg (26,000lb).

Armament: Provision for two 30mm cannon in underfuselage pods; four underwing hardpoints for max 2404kg (5300lb) ordnance.

Performance: GR.3 – max speed (clean) 642kt (1189km/h) at low level or 573kt (1062km/h) with typical external load; time to 40,000ft 2.3min; service ceiling 51,200ft; low level combat radius with 1996kg (4400lb) load 200nm (370km); max ferry range 1850nm (3427km).

Production: 6 P.1127, 9 Kestrel GR.1, 84 Harrier GR.1, 40 GR.3, 102 AV-8A, 11 AV-8S (plus 43 T.2/2A/4/4N/TAV-8A/TAV-8S).

Notes: The revolutionary Harrier was the world's first practical V/STOL (vertical/short takeoff and landing) combat aircraft, its origins lying in the Hawker P.1127 developed from 1957 and designed around the equally revolutionary Bristol BS.53 (later Pegasus) vectored thrust turbofan. The engine's four exhaust nozzles could be pivoted through more than 90 degrees, allowing vertical or short takeoffs (and landings) plus the ability to hover and even fly backwards.

The first of six P.1127 prototypes made its initial tethered hovering flight on 21 October 1960 and its first transition to horizontal flight in September 1961. A new anhedral tailplane and redesigned wing with more sweep was introduced to the later prototypes.

Nine further modified pre-production Kestrel FGA.1s followed, the first flying on 7 March 1964. These were operated by a joint British, German and US 'Tripartite' evaluation unit and on 31 August 1966 the first of six development batch Harrier GR.1s was flown. The first full production GR.1 for the RAF with Pegasus 101 engine flew on 28 December 1967 and regular squadron service began in April 1969. Most were converted initially to GR.1As with the more powerful Pegasus 102 and also to GR.3 standards with Pegasus 103 and a Marconi laser target seeker in a lengthened nose. New GR.3s were also built, the first one flying in January 1976.

The US Marine Corps ordered the Harrier as the AV-8A, the first of these flying on 20 November 1970. It was fitted with some US equipment and could carry Sidewinder AAMs, the purchase leading to a co-operation programme between Hawker Siddeley (later BAe) and McDonnell Douglas which resulted in the upgraded AV-8B/Harrier II.

Spain was another customer, receiving 11 as the AV-8S Matador from 1975. The Thai Navy received seven ex Spanish aircraft in 1996 for operation from the carrier *Chakri Naruebet* as the last operator of the first generation Harrier, but by 1999 they were effectively out of service due to a shortage of spares and funds. The first of several two seat operational trainer versions of the Harrier flew in October 1969, these used by all operators of the single seaters.

Photo: Harrier GR.3. (BAe)

BAe Sea Harrier

Country of origin: United Kingdom.

Type: Single seat shipboard multirole V/STOL fighter.

Powerplant: One 21,500lb (95.6kN) Rolls-Royce Pegasus Mk.104 (FRS.1) or Mk.106 (F/A.2) vectored thrust turbofan.

Dimensions: FRS.1 – wing span 7.70m (25ft 3in); overall length (incl nose probe) 14.50m (47ft 7in); height 3.71m (12ft 2in); wing area 18.7m² (201sq ft). F/A.2 – length 14.15m (46ft 5in).

Weights: FRS.1 – operating empty 6298kg (13,884lb); max takeoff 11,884kg (26,200lb). F/A.2 – operating empty 6616kg (14,585lb); max takeoff 11,885kg (26,200lb).

Armament: Two 30mm cannon under fuselage; max 2268kg (5000lb) ordnance on four underwing and two underfuselage hardpoints including air-to-air, air-to-ground and anti shipping missiles, bombs and rockets.

Performance: Max speed 635kt (1176km/h) at sea level, 527kt (977km/h) at 36,000ft (10,970m); max cruise 450kt (833km/h) at low level; combat radius (high altitude intercept) 405nm (750km); combat radius (low level attack) 305nm (565km).

Production: 57 Sea Harrier FRS.1, 23 FRS.51 and 18 F/A.2 (plus 29 converted from FRS.1).

Notes: Operating the Harrier from ships was always regarded as a significant part of its future with the first trials conducted by the original P.1127 prototype from the carrier HMS *Ark Royal* in February 1963. Full development of the Sea Harrier was announced in May 1975, the aircraft to replace conventional fixed wing aircraft in Royal Navy service and operate from the new *Invincible* class of 'Through Deck Cruisers' – 'Harrier Carriers' in popular parlance.

Development of the 'ski jump' ramp for these ships transformed the performance potential of the Sea Harrier as it allowed it to take off with a much heavier warload than would be possible using a flat or vertical takeoff procedure.

The first Sea Harrier FRS.1 flew on 20 August 1978. It differed from land based Harriers mainly in having a redesigned forward fuselage with raised cockpit and the vital addition of Ferranti Blue Fox multimode radar in the nose, allowing air intercept missions to be performed. The Sea Harrier entered RN service in June 1979 and the 'ski jump' system became operational in 1981. The Indian Navy received 23 new Sea Harrier FRS.51s in 1982-92. RN Sea Harriers proved their worth in air-to-air combat during the 1982 Falklands War when they destroyed 23 Argentinian aircraft for no losses in that area of operation.

The Sea Harrier FRS.1 was withdrawn from RN service in 1995, replaced by the F/A.2 (originally FRS.2) which was instigated as a mid life upgrade conversion with enhanced capability due to Ferranti Blue Vixen multimode radar (in a reshaped radome) with lookdown/shootdown, multiple target tracking and improved surface detection capabilities. The cockpit, avionics and systems were upgraded, weapons options increased and a small fuselage stretch incorporated behind the wing to house an equipment bay.

The converted aerodynamic prototype first flew on 19 September 1988 and the first production conversion was delivered in April 1993. Deliveries of 18 new build F/A.2s began in 1995 and the last was handed over in January 1999.

Photo: Sea Harrier FRS.1. (Bill Lines)

BAe Hawk 200

Country of origin: United Kingdom.

Type: Single seat light multirole fighter.

Powerplant: One 5845lb (26.0kN) Rolls-Royce Adour Mk.871 turbofan.

Dimensions: Wing span 9.40m (30ft 10in); length 11.35m (37ft 3in); height 3.99m (13ft 1in); wing area 16.7m² (180sq ft).

Weights: Empty 4450kg (9810lb); max takeoff 9100kg (20,062lb).

Armament: Max 3000kg (6614lb) ordnance on one centreline, four underwing and two wingtip hardpoints; options include up to four AIM-9 Sidewinder AAMs, Maverick AGMs, bombs, rocket launchers, ECM pod, reconnaissance pod or 30mm cannon pod on centreline.

Performance: Max speed 540kt (1000km/h) at sea level; max climb 11,510ft (3508m)/min; service ceiling 45,000ft; combat radius with 1814kg (4000lb) bombs and two Sidewinders (internal fuel) 100nm (185km); with 907kg (2000lb) bombs, two Sidewinders and drop tanks 290nm (537km); with reconnaissance pod, two Sidewinders and drop tanks 490nm (907km); ferry range 1300nm (2408km).

Production: Over 560 BAe Hawks of all models ordered by early 2000 including 62 Hawk 200s; also 234 Boeing/BAe T-45A Goshawks for US Navy.

Notes: The Hawker Siddeley HS.1182 was selected in October 1971 to replace the Folland Gnat advanced trainer in RAF service. As the Hawk T.1, the prototype first flew on 21 August 1974 and deliveries to the RAF began in November 1976. Since then, the two seat Hawk has been offered in several upgraded versions and sold to 16 nations.

All Hawks have weapons carrying capability but in June 1984 British Aerospace decided to launch a dedicated single seat light multirole combat version capable of performing air defence, close air support, battlefield interdiction, maritime support and strike and reconnaissance roles.

Compared to the two seaters, the Hawk 200 features a redesigned forward fuselage and nose to accommodate the single crew member, Lockheed Martin (Westinghouse) APG-66H radar (similar to that used in the F-16), a new 'combat wing' with fixed manoeuvring slats, greater weapons carrying capability, upgraded avionics, cockpit multifunction display, head-up display and hands-on-throttle-and-stick (HOTAS) controls. A more powerful Ardour 871 is fitted and an aerial refuelling probe is optional.

The privately funded prototype Hawk 200 first flew on 19 May 1986 but crashed just over six weeks later due to the pilot suffering a g-induced loss of consciousness. A second aircraft flew in April 1987 and a fully representative production demonstrator (with radar and other operational equipment fitted) in February 1992. Meanwhile, the first order had been placed by Oman (in July 1990) and the first production aircraft flew in September 1993. Other orders were subsequently placed by Indonesia and Brunei, all three having also purchased two seaters.

The two seat Hawk 100 and its LIFT (lead in fighter trainer) variant has the 200's Ardour 871, combat wing, weapons options and upgraded cockpit/equipment but lacks radar. It has 80 per cent commonality with the single seater and has been ordered by eight customers.

Photo: Hawk 200. (BAe)

BAC TSR.2

Country of origin: United Kingdom.

Type: Two seat attack/reconnaissance bomber.

Powerplants: Two 19,610lb (87.2kN) dry/30,610lb (136.1kN) with afterburner Bristol Siddeley Olympus 22R Mk.320 turbojets.

Dimensions: Wing span 11.28m (37ft 0in); length 27.13m (89ft 0in); height 7.31m (24ft 0in); wing area 65.0m² (700sq ft).

Weights: Empty 20,344kg (44,850lb); typical mission takeoff 36,288kg (80,000lb); max takeoff 43,500kg (95,900lb).

Armament: Up to 2722kg (6000lb) conventional or nuclear bombs in weapons bay plus up to 1814kg (4000lb) ordnance on four underwing pylons including air-to-surface missiles and rocket launchers or drop tanks; optional weapons bay reconnaissance pallet.

Performance: Max speed 1177kt (Mach 2.05/2180km/h) at high altitude, 730kt (Mach 1.1/1352km/h) at sea level; operating ceiling 54,000ft; combat radius with 907kg (2000lb) bomb load or nuclear weapon 1000nm (1852km) hi-lo-hi or 695nm (1288km) lo-lo-lo; combat radius with max bomb load 400nm (741km); max ferry range 3700nm (6854km).

Production: 2 prototypes completed and others under construction but only 1 flown.

Notes: One of the great 'what ifs' of the post war combat aircraft era and one of the most controversial, the TSR.2 highly advanced strike, interdiction and reconnaissance aircraft was cancelled by the British Government early in its flight test programme and after the expenditure of large sums of money. General Dynamics F-111s were ordered instead, but these were also cancelled, leaving the RAF with a substantial gap in its strike capability for many years.

The TSR.2 (for 'Tactical Strike Reconnaissance') was conceived to meet a September 1957 requirement for an English Electric Canberra replacement. In January 1959 it was announced that English Electric and Vickers (later combined to form the British Aircraft Corporation) would jointly develop the airframe and that Bristol and Armstrong Siddeley (who would also merge) would develop an afterburning version of the Olympus turbojet. A development contract covering nine aircraft was placed in October 1960.

The design that emerged was optimised for low level strike missions with twin engines, a small wing, two crew members seated in tandem and advanced avionics including a headup display and advanced multimode Ferranti radar with terrain following capability, a world's first.

Throughout the TSR.2's lengthy and expensive development period, the British Labour opposition under Harold Wilson vowed it would cancel the project if it came to power. It won the October 1964 general election, shortly after the first prototype had flown on 27 September. One other was completed but not flown by the time the axe fell in April 1965. The early, underdeveloped engines revealed problems (which were being sorted out) but the TSR.2's handling characteristics were superb, especially in the crucial low altitude area.

Australia was a potential customer but was officially discouraged by the British Government and ordered F-111s instead. In truth, the TSR.2's range was probably insufficient for the RAAF anyway.

Photo: TSR.2 prototype.

BAC Strikemaster

Country of origin: United Kingdom.

Type: Two seat light strike/trainer.

Powerplant: One 3360lb (14.9kN) Rolls-Royce Viper Mk.535 turbojet.

Dimensions: Wing span 11.23m (36ft 10in); length 10.27m (33ft 8^1/$_2$in); height 3.10m (10ft 2in); wing area 19.9m^2 (214sq ft).

Weights: Operating empty 2844kg (6270lb); takeoff (clean) 4218kg (9300lb); max takeoff 5216kg (11,500lb).

Armament: Two 7.62mm machine guns in lower intake lips; four underwing hardpoints for max 1361kg (3000lb) ordnance including rockets, bombs, practice bombs, gun pods, drop tanks, reconnaissance pods.

Performance: Max speed (clean) 418kt (774km/h) at 18,000ft; max climb 5250ft (1600m)/min; service ceiling 40,000ft; combat radius hi-lo-hi with max weapons load 215nm (398km) or 500nm (925km) with 454kg (1000lb) load; combat radius lo-lo-lo with max weapons load 126nm (233km) or 240nm (445km) with 454kg (1000lb) load; max range 1200nm (2223m).

Production: 151.

Notes: The last in the long series of jet trainers which began with the original Hunting Jet Provost of 1954 (the Royal Air Force's first jet trainer and itself derived from the piston engined Provost), the BAC 167 Strikemaster was a private venture light attack/counter insurgency development of the last of the Jet Provost line, the T.5.

Popularly known as the JP5, this differed from earlier models mainly in having a revised forward fuselage with enlarged canopy covering a pressurised cockpit. Production of all Jet Provost variants amounted to 591 aircraft for the RAF and export.

Compared to the JP5, the Strikemaster featured a more powerful Viper Mk.535 engine, strengthened structure and four underwing hardpoints capable of carrying a combined ordnance load of 1361kg (3000lb). The Strikemaster was capable of operating from rough airstrips and its simple design, low cost and low maintenance requirements made it ideal for many smaller air forces as an advanced trainer, weapons trainer and light strike aircraft.

The prototype Strikemaster first flew on 26 October 1967 and deliveries began the following year. The aircraft quickly found a modest but ready market, with several customers placing repeat orders. Series production ended in 1978 but a further batch of 10 was built in 1980-81 in anticipation of further orders. These were delivered to Sudan in 1984.

The air forces of eight nations ordered Strikemasters: Saudi Arabia (25 Mk.80 and 22 Mk.80A), Singapore (four ex Saudi as Mk.81 and 16 new Mk.84), Oman (12 Mk.82 and 12 Mk.82A), Kuwait (12 Mk.83), Kenya (six Mk.87), New Zealand (16 Mk.88), Ecuador (16 Mk.89) and Sudan (10 Mk.90). New Zealand's aircraft were locally nicknamed 'Blunties'. By early 2000 only one country still operated the aircraft – Sudan with three. Oman retired its 12 Strikemasters in January 2000.

A developed version of the Strikemaster with a more powerful Viper 632 engine was briefly mooted during the 1970s but was not proceeded with as it offered no major operational advantage over the standard model and would cost more to operate.

Photo: RNZAF Strikemaster Mk.88. (Richard Kuluz)

Bell UH-1C/E Iroquois

Country of origin: USA.

Type: Attack/assault helicopter.

Powerplant: UH-1C/E – one 1100shp (820kW) Lycoming T53-L-9/11 or (UH-1C only) 1400shp (1044kW) T-53-L-13 turboshaft.

Dimensions: Main rotor diameter 13.41m (44ft 0in); fuselage length 11.71m (38ft 5in); height 4.44m (14ft 7in); main rotor disc area 141.2m^2 (1520sq ft).

Weights: UH-1C – max takeoff 4309kg (9500lb). UH-1E – empty 2147kg (4734lb); max takeoff 3856kg (8500lb).

Armament: Air-to-ground ordnance mounted on external pylons plus guns in cabin including: 48 2.75in FFARs (folding fin aerial rockets), 40mm grenade launchers, four 7.62mm machine guns, two or four 0.50in machine guns, six TOW missiles in two pods, two 20mm cannon side mounted pods, six barrel 7.62mm Miniguns, 19 round rocket pods etc.

Performance: UH-1E – max speed 120kt (222km/h); typical cruise 98kt (182km/h); initial climb 1985ft (605m)/min; service ceiling 19,700ft; range 243nm (450km).

Production: Over 10,400 UH-1s (single engined versions) of all models including 766 UH-1C and 192 UH-1E (plus commercial Model 204s).

Notes: The ubiquitous Bell UH-1 Iroquois utility helicopter has been by far the most widely used rotorcraft of its type since the 1960s, serving with some 70 nations and built in both single and twin engined forms. The Vietnam War generated mass production of Iroquois versions capable of carrying 8-14 troops and as a helicopter gunship. The nickname 'Huey' was universally applied, derived from the original designation HU-1.

The prototype Bell XH-40 first flew on 22 November 1956 and initial deliveries of the HU-1A to the US Army began in June 1959. The UH-1B was the major production version of this original 'short fuselage' family of Iroquois, followed by the stretched UH-1D (first flight August 1961) and mass produced UH-1H from 1967. Civilian versions also sold widely.

The need to arm Hueys in Vietnam resulted in field modifications involving the fitting of weapons pylons outboard of the cabin doors and flexibly mounted guns firing through the door aperture. The concept was taken a step further with the UH-1C 'Huey Dog' which was built from scratch to be armed and had features intended to negate the performance penalties imposed on modified UH-1Bs.

These included the fitting of broader chord rotors which provided increased speed, manoeuvrability and an increase in maximum weight; a modified vertical fin; increased fuel capacity; a new engine cowling design; and dual hydraulic systems for protection against ground fire. UH-1C deliveries began in September 1965.

The US Marine Corps' UH-1E was also based on the UH-1B and intended as an armed assault support helicopter. Delivered from February 1964, it lacked the UH-1C's major modifications but was normally heavily armed, some aircraft fitted with a chin turret for two 7.62mm machine guns. Some of the US Army's UH-1Cs were modified to UH-1M 'Night Fighter' standards for use in Vietnam from 1967, these featuring low light level television (LLTV) and searchlights to help aim the two six barrel Miniguns usually fitted.

Photo: Royal Australian Navy UH-1C Iroquois. (Paul Sadler)

Bell AH-1G/F/P/Q/S HueyCobra

Country of origin: USA.

Type: Two seat attack helicopter.

Powerplant: AH-1G/Q – one 1400shp (1044kW) Avco Lycoming T53-L-13 turboshaft. AH-1F/S/P/E – one 1800shp (1342kW) T53-L-703 turboshaft; two bladed main rotor.

Dimensions: Main rotor diameter 13.41m (44ft 0in); fuselage length 13.59m (44ft 7in); height 4.09m (13ft 5in); main rotor disc area 141.2m² (1520sq ft).

Weights: AH-1G – empty 2755kg (6073lb); max takeoff 4309kg (9500lb). AH-1F – empty 2994kg (6600lb); max takeoff 4536kg (10,000lb).

Armament: Two 7.62mm Miniguns or two 40mm grenade launchers in nose turret (AH-1G) or three barrel 20mm cannon slaved to helmet sights (AH-1F); four hardpoints under stub wings for rockets, machine gun pods, missiles etc.

Performance: AH-1F – max speed 122kt (226km/h); max climb 1620ft (494m)/min; service ceiling and hovering ceiling IGE 12,200ft; range 273nm (506km).

Production: 1127 AH-1G, 100 AH-1P, 98 AH-1E, about 300 AH-1F.

Notes: The world's first operational dedicated helicopter gunship, the HueyCobra was intended as an interim design pending the introduction to service of the larger but ultimately abandoned Lockheed AH-56 Cheyenne. It served in Vietnam, drawing on experience gained from operating UH-1 Iroquois gunship conversions in the conflict.

Development began as a private venture in early 1965 as the Bell 209, combining the Iroquois' powerplant, transmission and rotor system with a new fuselage featuring two seats in tandem (pilot in the rear, co-pilot/gunner in the front), stub wings to carry weapons and a nose gun. The prototype first flew on 7 September 1965, just six months after design work had begun. The US Army subsequently ordered the Model 209 into production as the AH-1G HueyCobra and the helicopter was quickly sent to Vietnam after deliveries began in June 1967.

The AH-1G was followed by the AH-1Q conversion, an interim anti armour version capable of carrying Hughes TOW anti tank missiles. It first flew in 1973 and 92 conversions were performed. Hot and high performance was found to be lacking, resulting in the AH-1S with more powerful T53-L-703 engine; 179 AH-1Gs and Qs were converted to AH-1S standards. New production versions were built in 1977-79 as the AH-1P (100) and AH-1E (98) with progressive equipment and mechanical improvements including a universal nose turret capable of carrying different guns (usually a three barrel 20mm cannon), improved stores management and upgraded electrical power.

The AH-1F (149 delivered to the US Army 1979-86) combines the various upgrade features of the AH-1S/P/E, while 378 AH-1Gs were upgraded to 'F' standard between November 1979 and June 1982 with further modifications incorporated. The HueyCobra was also exported to Bahrain, Israel, Jordan, Pakistan, South Korea, Turkey and Japan, where it is built under licence by Fuji. In US service, it was still flying with the National Guard and Army Reserve in 2000.

Photo: Pakistan Army AH-1S. (Bell)

Bell AH-1J/T/W SeaCobra and SuperCobra

Country of origin: USA.

Type: Two seat attack helicopter.

Powerplants: AH-1J – one 1800shp (1342kW) Pratt & Whitney Canada T400-CP-400 (PT6T Twin-Pac) twin turboshaft. AH-1T – 1970shp (1469kW) T400-WV-402. AH-1W – two 1690shp (1260kW) General Electric T700-GE-401 turboshafts; two bladed main rotor.

Dimensions: AH-1J – main rotor diameter 13.41m (44ft 0in); fuselage length 13.60m (44ft 7½in); height 4.15m (13ft 7½in); main rotor disc area 141.2m² (1520sq ft). AH-1T – main rotor diameter 14.63m (48ft 0in). AH-1W – main rotor diameter 14.63m (48ft 0in); fuselage length 13.87m (45ft 6in); height 4.34m (14ft 3in); main rotor disc area 168.1m² (1810sq ft).

Weights: AH-1J – empty 2950kg (6503lb); max takeoff 4536kg (10,000lb). AH-1T – empty 3642kg (8030lb); max takeoff 6350kg (14,000lb). AH-1W – empty 4672kg (10,300lb); max takeoff 6690kg (14,750lb).

Armament: One three barrel 20mm cannon in nose; four hardpoints under stub wings for variety of weapons including TOW or Hellfire anti tank missiles, rocket pods, gun pods, iron bombs; AGM-122A Sidearm ASMs or two AIM-9L Sidewinder AAMs on AH-1W.

Performance: AH-1J – max speed 140kt (259km/h); initial climb (clean) 2230ft (680m)/min; operational ceiling 10,000ft; hovering ceiling OGE 4200ft; range 288nm (533km). AH-1W – max speed 152kt (281km/h); max climb 2000ft (610m)/min; vertical climb 645ft (196m)/min; service ceiling 18,000ft; hovering ceiling IGE 14,750ft; hovering ceiling OGE 3000ft; range 320nm (593km).

Production: 271 AH-1J, 57 AH-1T, 286 AH-1W ordered.

Notes: The AH-1J/T SeaCobra and AH-1W SuperCobra are twin engined variants of the HueyCobra developed specifically for the US Marine Corps. A 1968 evaluation of the AH-1G led to an order for the AH-1J SeaCobra, this differing from the earlier version in having the Pratt & Whitney Canada T400 turboshaft, the military version of the PT6T Twin-Pac, two PT6 turboshafts coupled together and driving a common transmission. The first AH-1J flew in November 1969 and 69 were delivered to the USMC from mid 1970 plus 202 for Iran.

The improved AH-1T SeaCobra first flew in May 1976 and differed from the J in having the more powerful T400-WV-402 engine, substantially increased maximum weight, uprated transmission, longer fuselage and larger main rotor blades. Deliveries began in October 1977.

The AH-1W SuperCobra was developed to meet an Iranian requirement and features two General Electric T700 turboshafts plus the rotor blades and lengthened fuselage of the AH-1T. Iran's interest lapsed with the fall of the Shah in 1979 but the design was then adapted to meet USMC needs with a T700 powered prototype converted from an AH-1T flown in December 1983. Production standard AH-1Ws began appearing in March 1986 against orders for 213 from the USMC and exports to Taiwan (63) and Turkey (10).

USMC AH-1Ws destroyed 97 tanks, 104 armoured vehicles, 16 bunkers and two anti aircraft gun sites during Operation Desert Storm in 1991. They are being rebuilt to AH-1Z Viper standards with a four bladed rotor, Litton avionics and new sensors.

Photo: AH-1W SuperCobra. (Bell)

Beriev Be-6

Country of origin: Soviet Union.

Type: Eight crew maritime patrol and general reconnaissance flying boat.

Powerplants: Two 2300hp (1715kW) Shvetsov ASh-73TK radials; three bladed propellers.

Dimensions: Wing span 33.00m (108ft 3¹/₄in); length (without MAD boom) 23.57m (77ft 4in); length (with MAD boom) 25.60m (84ft 0in); height 7.65m (25ft 1in); wing area 120.0m² (1292sq ft).

Weights: Empty 18,827kg (41,506lb); max takeoff 23,400kg (51,587lb).

Armament: One 23mm cannon in bow turret, two in remotely controlled dorsal turret and two in tail turret (latter deleted when MAD boom installed); offensive load of mines, depth charges or torpedoes on underwing pylons.

Performance: Max speed 224kt (415km/h) at 7875ft; cruising speed 182-215kt (337-398km/h); service ceiling 20,000ft; max endurance 16 hours; max range 2645nm (4900km).

Production: Estimated at 'several hundred'.

Notes: During World War II it was decided by the Soviet hierarchy that all seaplane and flying boat development effort would be concentrated in the design bureau headed by Georgi M Beriev at Taganrog on the Sea of Azov in Russia. Work on a new maritime patrol and reconnaissance flying boat began in 1945 shortly after the end of hostilities, this resulting in a twin engined aircraft with twin tails and gull wings designated the LL-143. A prototype was flown in 1947, further refinement resulting in acceptance of a revised design for production under the designation Be-6.

Compared to the LL-143, the Be-6 featured a redesigned forward hull, provision for a retractable radar scanner radome aft of the hull step and more powerful engines. Defensive armament comprised five 23mm cannon in three turrets, the dorsal installation remotely controlled. The aircraft was also capable of carrying a substantial offensive load of mines, depth charges and torpedos on pylons outboard of the engines.

The first production Be-6 was flown in 1949, NATO subsequently allocating the codename 'Madge'. The Be-6 went on to become the most widely used flying boat operated by the *Aviatsiya-Voenno Morskikh Flota* (A-VMF – Naval Air Fleet) for patrol, maritime reconnaissance and anti submarine duties. To assist it in the latter, many aircraft were retrofitted with a magnetic anomaly detector (MAD) boom, this necessitating the removal of the rear turret.

The Be-6 had been largely withdrawn from front line duties by the late 1960s but remained in service for a decade after that on search and rescue and general duties including fishery patrol and personnel and freight transport. It was also used for submarine co-operation tasks in the Arctic.

The Be-6's planned successor was the Be-10 advanced twinjet flying boat powered by 14,300lb (63.6kN) Lyulka AL-7PB turbojets mounted in the roots of the highly swept high wing. Codenamed 'Mallow' by NATO, the Be-10 made its first public appearance in 1961 and set 12 class speed/altitude/payload records including a speed of 566.69mph (911.97km/h). Only three or four were built and the Be-6's actual successor was the turboprop Be-12 (see next entry).

Photo: Beriev Be-6.

Beriev Be-12 Tchaika

Country of origin: Soviet Union.

Type: Five crew anti submarine and maritime patrol amphibian.

Powerplants: Two 4190shp (3124kW) Ivchenko AI-200D turboprops; four bladed propellers.

Dimensions: Wing span 29.77m (97ft 8in); length 30.17m (99ft 0in); height 7.01m (23ft 0in); wing area 98.9m² (1065sq ft).

Weights: Empty 21,700kg (47,840lb); max takeoff 36,000kg (79,365lb).

Armament: Internal weapons bay and two underwing hardpoints for max 4536kg (10,000lb) torpedos, depth charges, mines, sonobuoys, unguided rockets and air-to-surface missiles.

Performance: Max speed 329kt (610km/h); economical patrol speed 173kt (320km/h); initial climb 2990ft (911m)/min; service ceiling 37,000ft; range with combat load 2160nm (4000km); max range 4050nm (7500km).

Production: Approximately 120.

Notes: The turboprop powered Be-12 Tchaika (Gull) was developed as a replacement for the piston engined Be-6 after being selected for service ahead of the Be-10 jet, only three or four of which were built in the early 1960s.

Of similar general appearance and configuration to the Be-6, the Be-12 was nevertheless considerably redesigned with a longer and reworked hull, spray dams along the nose to minimise engine water ingestion, nose mounted radar and a pair of Ivchenko AI-20D turboprops. A major change was the fact that the Be-12 was an amphibian with retractable tailwheel landing gear.

The magnetic anomaly detector (MAD) boom on the tail indicated its anti submarine role while the three gun turrets which featured on the Be-6 were deleted. Armament was carried in an internal weapons bay and on two underwing pylons. The NATO codename 'Mail' was applied.

The prototype Be-12 first flew in 1960, the type's first public appearance was at the 1961 Soviet Aviation Display day at Tushino Airport, Moscow, and it entered service with the Soviet Naval Air Fleet in 1964 on 'inshore' anti submarine, search and rescue and surveillance duties out to about 200nm (370km) from shore bases. The Be-12 set an impressive 44 world speed, altitude and payload records for its class between 1964 and 1983, although that class – for turboprop powered amphibians and seaplanes – was a very small one with no real competition!

Apart from its basic roles, the Be-12 has also been used for Arctic and Siberian resource exploration, geophysical mapping and search and rescue. These alternative roles have become a more significant part of the Be-12's activities in recent years as the Ilyushin Il-38 and Tupolev Tu-142 (plus helicopters) took over most ASW tasks.

Several Tchaikas have been upgraded for firefighting duties within the Russian Federation as the Be-12P. The conversion involves the installation of water tanks in the former weapons bay, intake systems for scooping water during aquaplaning and from airfield facilities as well as a water dropping system.

By 2000 the Be-12 still serves with Russia and Ukraine and others have found their way into Vietnamese service. Some were based in Egypt in the early 1970s for operations over the Mediterranean, carrying Egyptian markings but crewed by Soviet Navy personnel.

Photo: Be-12 Tchaika.

Boeing B-50 Superfortress

Country of origin: USA.

Type: 10 crew heavy bomber.

Powerplants: Four 3500hp (2610kW) Pratt & Whitney R-4360-35 Wasp Major 28-cylinder radials; four bladed propellers.

Dimensions: Wing span 43.05m (141ft 3in); length 30.17m (99ft 0in); height 9.96m (32ft 8in); wing area 164.2m² (1768sq ft).

Weights: B-50D – empty 36,742kg (81,000lb); max takeoff 78,473kg (173,000lb).

Armament: 13 0.50in machine guns in five turrets; max bomb load 9072kg (20,000lb).

Performance: B-50D – max speed 330kt (611kt); normal cruise 241kt (446km/h); long range cruise 204kt (378km/h); service ceiling 37,000ft; max range 4260nm (7890km).

Production: 79 B-50A, 45 B-50B, 222 B-50D and 24 TB-50H, total 370.

Notes: A more powerful and capable direct derivative of the famous wartime B-29 Superfortress (of which 3960 were built 1942-46), the B-50 began life in 1944 under the Boeing designation Model 345-2, differing mainly in having Pratt & Whitney R-4360 Wasp Major engines instead of the B-29's Wright R-3350s. The engines were successfully tested on a B-29 (redesignated XB-44) and an order was placed for 200 under the designation B-29D in July 1945.

The designation was changed to B-50 in late 1945, ostensibly to differentiate the new model but in reality to create the impression it was an entirely new aircraft at a time of post war budget cuts and politicians who were reluctant to allocate money to mere variants of existing designs.

The first B-50A (there was no prototype as such) flew on 25 June 1947, three months before the United States Army Air Force became the independent US Air Force. The USAF's bomber fleets were controlled by Strategic Air Command (SAC) which had been established in March 1946.

Apart from its new engines, the B-50 differed from its predecessor in having increased weights, strengthened undercarriage, the use of more durable alloys in the structure and a notably taller fin and rudder. Defensive armament remained as before with 13 0.50in machine guns in computer and remotely controlled turrets.

The B-50A entered service in February 1948. Other new production models were the B-50B with increased maximum weight (first flight December 1948); the major production B-50D with redesigned nose glazing and provision for external fuel tanks and aerial refuelling (first flight May 1949), and the final production TB-50H unarmed bombing and navigation trainer. The last was delivered in March 1953. The B-50C was to be powered by 4500hp (3355kW) Wasp Major engines but remained only a project.

The B-50 had a short career as a bomber and had been replaced by the B-47 Stratojet by the end of 1955. There were several models created by conversion, most notably the RB-50B photo-recce version (on all but one of the 45 B-50Bs) and 112 KB-50J tankers converted from B-50Ds with two auxiliary underwing 5620lb (25.0kN) GE J47 turbojets and three refuelling hose reels. The similar KB-50K (16 converted) was based on the TB-50H.

Photo: B-50D Superfortress.

Boeing B-47A/B Stratojet

Country of origin: USA.

Type: Three crew medium strategic bomber.

Powerplants: B-47A – six 5200lb (23.1kN) General Electric J47-GE-11 turbojets. B-47B – J47-GE-11 or 5800lb (25.8kN) J47-GE-23 turbojets; 18 1000lb (4.4kN) Aerojet RATO units.

Dimensions: Wing span 35.35m (116ft 0in); length 33.48m (109ft 10in); height 8.51m (27ft 11in); wing area 132.7m² (1428sq ft).

Weights: B-47B – max takeoff 90,720kg (200,000lb).

Armament: B-47B – two 0.50in machine guns in tail barbette; max conventional bomb load 9072kg (20,000lb) or up to four 1152kg (2540lb) B28 atomic bombs.

Performance: B-47B – max speed 536kt (993km/h) at 10,600ft; range 3400nm (6300km).

Production: 2042 B-47s of all models including 2 XB-47; 10 B-47A (all by Boeing); and 399 B-47B by Boeing (380), Douglas (10) and Lockheed (9).

Notes: A highly significant bomber of the Cold War era, the B-47 Stratojet seemed to be always overshadowed by its B-52 Stratofortress stablemate but formed the backbone of the Strategic Air Command until the B-52 arrived in quantity. An extremely advanced design for its day, the B-47 was built in large numbers, served with 36 USAF Bomber Wings and in its reconnaissance versions flew dangerous covert intelligence gathering missions over China and the Soviet Union.

After numerous turboprop and jet powered configurations for the new bomber had been examined, the final, futuristic configuration was settled in late 1945 as the Model 450. The USAF ordered two XB-47 prototypes in April 1946. Six engines were needed to provide barely sufficient power and their novel (for the time) underwing podded installation was adopted after no fewer than 50 alternatives had been examined. The tandem main undercarriage with outriggers added to the B-47's futuristic appearance.

The first XB-47 prototype flew on 17 December 1947 and the second in July 1948, both aircraft powered by 3750lb (16.7kN) thrust General Electric J35s. An initial production order for only 10 aircraft was placed in September 1948, the first of these B-47As flying in June 1950. They were powered by the definitive J47 engine plus 18 RATO units in the rear fuselage to help improve takeoff performance. A very long and lumbering takeoff roll remained a feature of the B-47 throughout its life. The B-47As were not considered to be operational aircraft and were used for testing, development, evaluation and training.

The first true production model was the B-47B, first flown in April 1951 and featuring reduced nose glazing, a smaller bomb bay, square fin tip shape, increased weights and – strangely and controversially – deletion of the crew ejection seats. Aerial refuelling capability was installed as were remotely controlled rear defensive guns and optional underwing fuel tanks.

The first 87 B-47Bs had J47-GE-11 turbojets and the remainder more powerful J47-GE-23s. Service entry was October 1951. An upgrade modifying nearly 200 aircraft to near B-47E standards in 1954-56 resulted in the new designation B-47B-II while others were converted to RB-47B photo-recce and TB-47B crew training aircraft.

Photo: B-47A Stratojet.

Boeing B-47E Stratojet

Country of origin: USA.

Type: Three crew medium range strategic bomber.

Powerplants: Six 6000lb (26.7kN) dry/7200lb (32.0kN) with water/alcohol injection General Electric J47-GE-25A turbojets; 33 jettisonable 1000lb (4.4kN) Aerojet RATO bottles for takeoff.

Dimensions: Wing span 35.35m (116ft 0in); length 33.48m (109ft 10in); height 8.52m (27ft 11in); wing area 132.7m² (1428sq ft).

Weights: B-47E-II – empty 36,631kg (80,756lb); normal max takeoff 93,760kg (206,700lb); max overload 99,792kg (220,000lb).

Armament: Two 20mm cannon in tail barbette; max conventional bomb load 9072kg (20,000lb) or up to four 1152kg (2540lb) B28 atomic bombs.

Performance: Max speed 526kt (975km/h) at 16,300ft, 484kt (896km/h) at 38,500ft; cruising speed 430kt (797km/h); initial climb 2300ft (700m)/min; service ceiling 38,000ft; range with max bomb load 2780nm (5150km); range with four atomic bombs 3476nm (6438km).

Production: 2042 B-47s of all models including 1341 B-47E by Boeing (691), Douglas (264) and Lockheed (386); plus 240 RB-47E, 35 RB-47H and 15 RB-47K (all by Boeing).

Notes: The B-47E was by far the most numerous of the Stratojet versions thanks to the influence of the Korean War, accounting for two-thirds of production and mass produced by Boeing, Douglas and Lockheed. The latter pair had also built a small number of B-47Bs.

The B-47E had numerous improvements including the installation of J47-GE-25 engines on early aircraft and then boosted water/alcohol injected -25As later, a strengthened structure, more weight increases, further reduced nose glazing, installation of a drag parachute for landing, upgrading the rear guns to 20mm cannon and – much to the relief of crews – reinstatement of ejection seats. The fixed internal RATO equipment was deleted and replaced with 22 or 33 jettisonable bottles mounted on a rear fuselage 'collar'. Despite these and the more powerful engines, the B-47's takeoff performance remained poor.

The first Boeing built B-47E flew on 30 January 1953 and the last in October 1956. The 1341st and final B-47E from any source emerged from Lockheed in February 1957. The B-47E was subject to a major structural upgrade from 1959, the more than 1000 modified aircraft given the new designation B-47E-II. Other new build Stratojet variants were the RB-47E photo-reconnaissance, RB-47H electronic intelligence gathering and RB-47K weather reconnaissance (with secondary photo-recce capability) models. Further weather reconnaissance, electronic countermeasures and test versions were created by conversion.

The 36 Strategic Air Command Wings which operated the B-47 flew them from bases in the USA and also overseas with deployments to Britain and parts of Europe a permanent feature. Covert spying operations over the Soviet Union, Eastern Europe and China were common with at least one aircraft shot down and others damaged by intercepting fighters. Some RB-47Hs operated in Vietnam in 1966-67, marking the end of the B-47's front line career. The last of the bombers had been withdrawn by 1965.

Photo: B-47E Stratojet.

Boeing B-52A-C Stratofortress

Country of origin: USA.

Type: Six crew strategic bomber.

Powerplants: B-52B – eight 9700lb (43.1kN) dry/11,000lb (48.9kN) wet Pratt & Whitney J57-P-1W or (late B and C) 10,500lb (46.7kN) dry/12,100lb (53.8kN) wet J57-P-19W/29W turbojets.

Dimensions: Wing span 56.39m (185ft 0in); length 47.72m (156ft 7in); height 14.72m (48ft 3¹/₂in); wing area 371.6m² (4000sq ft).

Weights: B-52B – empty 74,427kg (164,081lb); max takeoff 190,512kg (420,000lb).

Armament: Four 0.50in machine guns in tail; max bomb load 19,505kg (43,000lb).

Performance: Max speed 546kt (1011km/h); unrefuelled combat radius 3110nm (5760km).

Production: 744 B-52s of all models including 1 XB-52, 1 YB-52, 3 B-52A, 23 B-52B, 27 RB-52B and 35 B-52C.

Notes: One of the most significant combat aircraft of any era, the eight engined B-52 strategic bomber took the general concept of the B-47 and developed it with a completely new and much larger design, creating an aircraft destined to have the longest career in military aviation history.

Ironically, a service life of only a few years was planned as it was assumed that the rapid march of technological progress in the 1950s would soon come up with a more advanced successor. The 'Buff' – 'Big Ugly Fat Fella' in its polite version – entered service in June 1955 and an operational career of 75 years is probable.

The USAAF issued a broad requirement for a long range turbine engined bomber in April 1945, various concepts covering pure jet and turboprop powered aircraft emerging over the next few years. The final Boeing Model 464 configuration was accepted and two prototypes – the XB-52 and YB-52 Stratofortress – were approved. An extremely large aircraft for its time, the B-52 featured eight podded J57 engines with water injection, a massive steerable double tandem (with outriggers) undercarriage design and aerial refuelling capability.

The XB-52 was scheduled to fly in early 1952 but substantial damage caused by a pneumatic system 'blow up' during ground testing meant the YB-52 was the first to take to the air on 15 April 1952. Both differed externally from production B-52s by having a fighter style canopy with tandem seating for the pilots – subsequent aircraft would have a more conventional cockpit with side by side seating.

The first three production aircraft were designated B-52A and used for trials purposes only. The first one flew on 5 August 1954, this model incorporating several hundred engineering changes including a slightly lengthened fuselage and the installation of operational equipment. The full production B-52B (first flight 25 January 1955) was built in pure bomber and bomber-reconnaissance (RB-52B) versions, the latter with a removable pressurised capsule for cameras, ECM equipment and two crew members in the bomb bay.

The B-52C combined the features of late production B-52Bs with a revised fuel system (including external tanks) and upgraded nav/attack system. First flown in March 1956, it remained in front line service for a decade and after use as a trainer was retired in 1971.

Photo: XB-52 Stratofortress. (Boeing)

Boeing B-52D/E/F Stratofortress

Country of origin: USA.

Type: Six crew strategic bomber.

Powerplants: B-52D/E – eight 10,500lb (46.7kN) dry/12,100lb (53.8kN) wet Pratt & Whitney J57-P-19W turbojets. B-52F – eight 11,200lb (49.8kN) dry/13,750lb (61.1kN) wet J-57-P-43W/WA/WB turbojets.

Dimensions: Wing span 56.39m (185ft 0in); length 47.72m (156ft 7in); height 14.72m (48ft 3^1/$_2$in); wing area 371.6m^2 (4000sq ft).

Weights: B-52D – empty 80,657kg (177,816lb); max takeoff 204,120kg (450,000lb).

Armament: Four 0.50in machine guns in tail; max bomb load 27,216kg (60,000lb).

Performance: B-52D – max speed 551kt (1020km/h) at 20,200ft; service ceiling (at mid weight) 46,200ft; unrefuelled combat radius 3012nm (5579km); max unrefuelled range 6520nm (12,077km).

Production: 744 B-52s of all models including 170 B-52D, 100 B-52E and 89 B-52F.

Notes: The B-52 was a truly 'global' bomber with impressive range which could be multiplied substantially with the use of aerial refuelling. It formed a major part of the USA's nuclear deterrent during the Cold War, equipping 38 Strategic Air Command Wings by 1963.

The prototype and early production B-52s had been built at Boeing's Seattle facility but the next three versions – B-52D, E and F were manufactured in larger numbers at both Seattle and the company's Wichita (Kansas) plant. The B-52D (first flight 4 June 1956) was generally similar to the C apart from lacking photo-recce capability and although intended as an atomic bomber was substantially modified for conventional bombing during its career.

Spurred by the needs of the Vietnam War, the 'Big Belly' modification of the mid 1960s allowed the D to carry a maximum bomb load of 27,216kg (60,000lb) internally and on underwing racks. The first B-52 Vietnam mission was flown in June 1965 and the last in the region (on Cambodia and Laos) in 1973. The B-52D remained in service until 1983 after flying with 30 SAC Wings.

The B-52E first flew on 3 October 1957 and served with eight SAC wings before being withdrawn from use in March 1970. Mechanically similar to the D, the B-52E differed mainly in its more capable nav/attack and associated systems. Like the D, further upgrades were incorporated as lower altitude operations became more prevalent.

The last of the 'tall tail' Stratofortresses, the B-52F featured more powerful J57-P-43W/WA/WB engines and upgraded internal systems. First flown on 6 May 1958, the B-52F equipped eight SAC Wings with most retired by 1973 and a few surviving in service until 1978.

Some B-52Fs underwent modifications which allowed them to carry larger conventional bomb loads, although not to the same extent as the B-52D's 'Big Belly' upgrade. It was B-52Fs from the 7th and 320th Bomb Wings which performed the first 'Buff' mission of the Vietnam War on 18 June 1965. Flying from Guam, 30 aircraft attacked Viet Cong positions in the South but the mission was a disaster with a collision between two aircraft and inaccurate bombing.

Photo: B-52D Stratofortress.

Boeing B-52G Stratofortress

Country of origin: USA.

Type: Six crew strategic bomber.

Powerplants: Eight 11,200lb (49.8kN) dry/13,750lb (61.1kN) wet Pratt & Whitney J57-P-43WB turbojets.

Dimensions: Wing span 56.39m (185ft 0in); length 49.05m (160ft 11in); height 12.40m (40ft 8in); wing area 371.6m^2 (4000sq ft).

Weights: Empty 76,407kg (168,445lb); max takeoff 221,357kg (488,000lb).

Armament: Four 0.50in machine guns in tail; over 22,680kg (50,000lb) conventional or nuclear bombs or two underwing AGM-28 Hound Dog nuclear cruise missiles; 12 AGM-86 air launched cruise missiles and eight AGM-69 short range attack missiles or eight Harpoon anti shipping missiles after upgrades.

Performance: Max speed 551kt (1021km/h) at 20,800ft; cruising speed 442kt (819km/h); low altitude penetration speed 352-365kt (652-676km/h); service ceiling 47,000ft; combat radius 3550nm (6575km); max unrefuelled range 7300nm (13,52km).

Production: 744 B-52s of all models including 193 B-52G.

Notes: The most numerous of the Stratofortress variants, the B-52G was also the most modified version. Externally, the major difference was the fitting of much shorter vertical tail surfaces. The B-52F's engines were retained but there were major changes under the skin. The B-52G was also the first Stratofortress variant to carry a 'standoff' weapon (or cruise missile in modern parlance), the supersonic North American Hound Dog with nuclear warhead.

There were numerous systems modifications, a modified flight control system (including with ailerons deleted and roll control performed by spoilers), the fin's size was reduced following further testing of asymmetric handling characteristics and all six crew members were grouped together in the forward fuselage area for the first time, necessitating a substantial redesign of consoles and hatches.

Rearranging the aircraft's rear end as a result of the gunner moving forward allowed relocation of the braking parachute, installation of tracking radar and a TV camera for the now remotely controlled defensive guns and a rear fuselage extension to carry this equipment plus other items. A significant change was the incorporation of a 'wet' wing which increased the G's internal fuel capacity by a substantial 31 per cent.

The first B-52G flew on 26 October 1958 with deliveries beginning the following February. The last was delivered in February 1961. The G was subject to extensive weapons, structural, systems and equipment upgrades during a career which saw it equip 28 SAC Wings. Weapons upgrades included the introduction of cruise missiles, Harpoon anti shipping missiles, short range attack missile and others, while an ever increasing array of avionics, optical viewing and ECM equipment led to more and more fairings and radomes appearing on the aircraft.

The B-52G played a prominent role in the 1991 Gulf War, after which its numbers in USAF service reduced from 90 in 1991 to 50 the following year. The last was retired in 1994.

Photo: B-52G Stratofortress.

Boeing B-52H Stratofortress

Country of origin: USA.

Type: Six crew strategic bomber.

Powerplants: Eight 17,000lb (75.6kN) Pratt & Whitney TF33-P-3 turbofans.

Dimensions: Wing span 56.39m (185ft 0in); length 49.05m (160ft 11in); height 12.40m (40ft 8in); wing area 371.6m^2 (4000sq ft).

Weights: Empty 78,355kg (172,740lb); max takeoff 229,068kg (505,000lb); war limit after aerial refuelling 256,738kg (566,000lb).

Armament: One 20mm Vulcan rotary cannon in tail; offensive payload of over 22,680kg (50,000lb); typical 1990s armament of 51 227kg (500lb) bombs on underwing pylons and in bomb bay; or up to 20 air launched cruise missiles under wings and in bomb bay; or combination of 12 missiles and eight gravity nuclear bombs.

Performance: Max speed 547kt (1013km/h) at 23,800ft; cruising speed 443kt (820km/h); low level penetration speed 310kt (574km/h); service ceiling 47,700ft; unrefuelled combat radius 4176nm (7735km); practical max range with payload 8684nm (16,085km); max unrefuelled range approx 10,000nm (18,520km).

Production: 744 B-52s of all models including 102 B-52H.

Notes: The final Stratofortress variant and the one that will remain in service until well into the 21st century, the B-52H nearly didn't happen as the B-52G was supposed to the final version to enter production.

The highly advanced, supersonic North American B-70 Valkyrie's failure to progress beyond an experimental project, the continuation of the Cold War, the development of the Douglas Skybolt air launched ballistic missile and Pratt & Whitney coming up with the TF33 turbofan engine (JT3D in civil guise) all resulted in the B-52H being ordered.

The main difference between the B-52H and G was the installation of the TF33, offering more power and a marked improvement in fuel efficiency. Unrefuelled combat radius increased by over 600nm (1110km). Other changes included a new tailcone design incorporating a multi barrel 20mm Vulcan rotary cannon.

The Skybolt was cancelled in 1962 leaving the Hound Dog standoff weapon as the B-52H's primary weapon until the mid 1970s when it was phased out. After that, the H carried basically the same weaponry as the B-52G and has also been subject to numerous structural, systems and avionics upgrades. Subsequent armament installations included SRAMs, ALCMs and the Harpoon air-to-surface missile.

The first B-52H was flown on 6 March 1961 and the last delivered in March 1963. Like its immediate predecessor, the H was built exclusively at Boeing's Wichita (Kansas) facility. Nicknamed 'Cadillac' by its crews, the H quickly established its long range credentials by setting two distance records in 1962. One of them was the absolute unrefuelled non stop distance in a straight line when a flight between Okinawa and Madrid was performed covering a distance of 12,532.3 statute miles (20,168.23km).

Just over 90 B-52Hs remained in USAF service by 2000 with more updates planned and service not expected to end until about 2040. The 'Cadillac' has meanwhile seen action over Iraq and Yugoslavia.

Photo: B-52H Stratofortress.

Boeing X-32 JSF

Country of origin: USA.

Type: Advanced multirole fighter concept demonstrator in conventional takeoff and landing (CTOL), short takeoff/vertical landing (STOVL) and carrier capable versions.

Powerplants: One 35,000lb (155.7kN) class Pratt & Whitney SE614 (F119 derivative) turbofan.

Dimensions: CTOL versions – wing span 10.97m (36ft 0in); length 13.72m (45ft 0in); wing area 54.8m^2 (590sq ft).

Weights: Estimated – empty 10,000kg (22,046lb) for USAF version, 10,900kg (24,030) for USN version; max takeoff 22,680kg (50,000lb).

Armament: Internal 20mm rotary cannon on USAF version, optional on others; internal weapons bay for AAMs or bombs up to 2722kg (6000lb); external stores capability 5443-7711kg (12,000-17,000lb) depending on version.

Performance: Estimated – max speed 918kt (Mach 1.6/1700km/h) at altitude; radius of action USAF version 850nm (1574km), USMC version 600nm (1112km), USN version 750nm (1389km).

Production: Total planned procurement of 3002 (see below).

Notes: The X-32 is a concept demonstrator of Boeing's contender for the US Joint Strike Fighter programme, potentially the world's largest arms project. The project started in 1990 with the Common Affordable Lightweight Fighter study launched by the US Advanced Research Project Agency.

The stealthy, multirole JSF is intended to be built in conventional, carrier capable and STOVL versions, using a common basic airframe for all three to keep costs down. The UK became a 10 per cent development partner in the JSF programme in December 1995 with the aim of replacing RN Sea Harriers and now also RAF Harrier GR.7/9s.

By June 1996 Boeing, Lockheed Martin and McDonnell Douglas had submitted their design proposals to the JSF project office, with Boeing and Lockheed Martin then selected to build two JSF demonstrators each. Boeing's X-32 and Lockheed Martin's X-35 demonstrators will be evaluated with the winning design scheduled to be selected in 2001. Current planning envisages the USAF taking 1763 JSFs (X-32A), the USMC 609 (X-32B), the USN 480 (X-32C), RAF 90 and RN 60. USAF initial operational capability is planned for 2008.

The X-32 will be powered by a P&W SE614 turbofan, while the STOVL variant will use a Harrier style thrust vectored direct lift system designed by Rolls-Royce. Boeing is projecting more than 80 per cent overall commonality between its three JSF variants. The company originally proposed a blended delta wing configuration, but in February 1999 announced production aircraft would feature a revised design with a trapezoid wing, conventional horizontal tail and twin vertical tails, and a revised inlet design.

Boeing announced further revisions to its design in November 1999, with straightened wingtips and small inlets either side of the cockpit. Common features on production Boeing JSFs would include the structure, systems and outer mould line, two-dimensional thrust vectoring nozzle, blended trapezoid wing, variable geometry chin inlet, side fuselage internal weapons bays, leading edge flaps, and twin fin tail. The first X-32A recorded its maiden flight on 18 September 2000.

Photo: The first X-32A on its maiden flight. (Boeing)

Boeing (MDC/Hughes) AH-64 Apache

Boeing-Sikorsky RAH-66 Comanche

Country of origin: USA.

Type: Two seat attack helicopter.

Powerplants: AH-64A – two 1723shp (1285kW) General Electric T700-GE-701 turboshafts. AH-64D – two 1890shp (1409kW) T700-GE-701C turboshafts; four bladed main rotor.

Dimensions: AH-64D Apache Longbow – main rotor diameter 14.63m (48ft 0in); fuselage length 15.06m (49ft 5in); height 4.95m (16ft 3in); main rotor disc area 168.0m^2 (1809sq ft).

Weights: AH-64D Apache Longbow – empty 5352kg (11,800lb); typical combat 7530kg (16,600lb); max takeoff 10,107kg (22,283lb).

Armament: One 30mm cannon in nose turret; four pylons under stub wings for a variety of ordnance including up to 16 AGM-114 Hellfire anti armour missiles, rocket pods, Stinger or Sidewinder AAMs etc.

Performance: AH-64D Apache Longbow – max speed 143kt (265km/h); max climb 2415ft (736m)/min; vertical climb rate 1475ft (450m)/min; hovering ceiling IGE 13,690ft; hovering ceiling OGE 9480ft; range (internal fuel) 220nm (407km); max endurance 3.2 hours.

Production: Over 1000 of all models ordered by 2000.

Notes: The Boeing (formerly McDonnell Douglas and Hughes) Apache was developed to meet the US Army's Advanced Attack Helicopter (AAH) requirement of 1973, the Army sponsoring development of the Hughes Model 77 (YAH-64) and Bell YAH-63 for a competitive fly-off. The first of two YAH-64 prototypes flew on 30 September 1975 and as the AH-64A Apache, it was selected for further development in November 1976. A prototype was modified to production configuration in November 1978.

The procurement programme was slow, however, and the first of 821 production AH-64As for the US Army was not flown until January 1984 with deliveries beginning a year later. Design features include crew armour, a high degree of survivability, aerobatic capability and a nose mounted Lockheed Martin AAQ-11 target acquisition and designation sight/pilot night vision sensor comprising a FLIR, TV camera, laser spot tracker and laser target rangefinder/designator. US Army AH-64As were successful in combat during the Gulf War.

The US Army plans to upgrade 530 AH-64As to AH-64D standards with more powerful engines and improved digital avionics housed in enlarged cheek fairings. Of these, 500 will become AH-64D Apache Longbows with mast mounted Northrop Grumman Longbow radar, which can guide the Hellfire anti armour missile.

The AH-64D is offered in new production or converted forms and the first example flew on 15 April 1992. The first production model was rolled out in March 1997. The Apache Longbow achieved IOC (initial operational capability) with the US Army in June 1998.

British Army WAH-64Ds (mostly assembled by Westland) are powered by 2100shp (1566kW) Rolls-Royce Turboméca RTM322 turboshafts, the first of 67 rolled out in September 1998, a prototype having meanwhile been flown on 29 May 1998. Other AH-64 customers by 2000 were Egypt, Greece, Israel, the Netherlands, Saudi Arabia, Singapore and the United Arab Emirates.

Photo: AH-64A Apache. (MDC)

Country of origin: USA.

Type: Two seat all weather multirole battlefield helicopter.

Powerplants: Two 1432shp (1068kW) LHTEC T800-LHT-801 turboshafts; five bladed main rotor.

Dimensions: Main rotor diameter 11.90m (39ft 0½in); fuselage length 13.20m (43ft 4in); height 3.39m (11ft 0½in); main rotor disc area 111.2m^2 (1197sq ft).

Weights: Empty 3942kg (8690lb); typical mission 4807kg (10,597lb); max takeoff 7896kg (17,408lb).

Armament: One 20mm three barrel cannon in undernose turret; internal weapons bays for six Hellfire anti armour or Stinger air-to-air missiles; removable stub wings for additional eight Hellfire or 16 Stinger missiles.

Performance: Max speed 175kt (324km/h); max cruise 165kt (305km/h); max sideways/backwards speed 45kt (83km/h); max vertical climb rate 1418ft (432m)/min; time to turn 180deg 4.7 seconds; ferry range with external fuel 1260nm (2334km); endurance with standard fuel 2hrs 30min.

Production: 1292 required by US Army, 2 prototypes built by 2000.

Notes: An extremely advanced (and expensive) multirole combat helicopter, the Comanche is designed to provide the US Army with an armed general reconnaissance battlefield helicopter capable of high speed and agility and low observability and one which can be configured for air combat and light attack.

When first mooted in 1982, the US Army's Light Helicopter Experimental (LHX) programme was intended to find a single airframe successor to some 5000 UH-1 Iroquois, AH-1 HueyCobra, OH-6 Cayuse and OH-58 Kiowa helicopters, but by the time the formal requests for proposals had been issued in June 1988, the requirement had been modified to cover 1292 scout/reconnaissance helicopters.

The Boeing-Sikorsky design was selected as the winner over proposals from Bell and McDonnell Douglas in April 1991 and the go ahead given for the building of prototypes as the YRAH-66.

The first prototype flew on 4 January 1996 and the second in March 1999.

The Comanche has numerous advanced features including a relatively compact, all composites airframe of faceted design to reduce the radar cross section; five bladed composite main rotor with swept tips and bearingless hub; and eight bladed shrouded tail rotor.

Other features include an internal weapons bays; detachable stub wings of various sizes for ordnance; new technology LHTEC T800 turboshafts; night vision goggles compatible EFIS cockpits with 3D moving map displays; triple redundant fly-by-wire flight controls; sidestick cyclic control; helmet mounted sights; Longbow radar, FLIR and a laser designator.

The Comanche programme has suffered a number of delays, mainly due to budget cuts and funding uncertainties. Only the two YRAH-66 prototypes had flown by 2000 with a further six pre-production aircraft planned for 2001 and 13 evaluation models from 2004. Service entry is now scheduled for 2006.

Photo: First prototype Comanche.

Breguet Alizé

Country of origin: France.

Type: Three seat carrier borne anti submarine warfare.

Powerplant: One 2100ehp (1566kW) Rolls-Royce Dart RDa 7 Mk.21 turboprop; four bladed propeller.

Dimensions: Wing span 15.60m (51ft 2in); length 13.87m (45ft 6in); height 5.00m (16ft 5in); wing area 36.0m² (388sq ft).

Weights: Empty equipped 5700kg (12,566lb); max takeoff 8200kg (18,078lb).

Armament: Internal weapons bay for one homing torpedo or three 160kg (353lb) depth charges; two underwing hardpoints for 160kg (353lb) or 175kg (386lb) depth charges, six 0.5in rockets or two AS 12 air-to-surface missiles.

Performance: Max speed 248kt (459km/h) at sea level, 280kt (518km/h) at 10,000ft; cruising speed 200kt (370km/h); typical patrol speed 130kt (241km/h); initial climb 1380ft (420m)/min; service ceiling 26,250ft; range 1350nm (2500km); max endurance 7.5hrs.

Production: 92.

Notes: Still in Aéronavale service in 2000 after more than 40 years, the Alizé (Tradewind) began life in 1948 with the start of design work on a carrier borne strike aircraft. The resulting Br.960 Vultur (Vulture) first flew on 3 August 1951, this featuring an Armstrong Siddeley Mamba turboprop in the nose and an auxiliary Rolls-Royce Nene jet in the tail. The Vultur was never ordered, Breguet instead using the design as the basis for the Br.1050 anti submarine warfare aircraft.

As the Alizé, the new design featured a Rolls-Royce Dart turbo-prop instead of the Mamba (with the auxiliary jet deleted), search radar mounted in a retractable radome in the lower rear fuselage, main undercarriage legs which retracted forwards into underwing pods which also carried sonobuoys, and a crew of three – pilot and radar operator side-by-side in the front cockpit and sensor operator behind.

An aerodynamic prototype (converted from a Vultur) flew on 26 March 1955 followed by the first of two Alizé prototypes on 6 October 1956. These were in turn followed by three pre-production models with first deliveries to the Aéronavale occurring in May 1959 for operation from the carriers *Foch* and *Clemenceau*.

Manufacture ended in 1962 after 75 production aircraft had been delivered to France and 12 to India, which also later acquired 12 ex French aircraft.

France's Alizé fleet gradually declined during the 1970s and was down to 39 by the end of the decade. Two major upgrades were then undertaken, the first from 1980 when 28 aircraft received Thomson-CSF Iguane radar plus updated navigation/communications systems and ESM capability; and in 1990 when the 24 survivors were fitted with a datalink and upgraded tactical data processing system.

India's Alizés were retired in 1992 after spending their last five years shore based following the carrier *Vikrant's* refit with a ski ramp for Harrier operations. This meant that conventional carrier based aircraft could no longer use the ship. France still had nine Alizés in service by early 2000.

Photo: A French Navy Alizé. (Paul Merritt)

CAC Mustang

Countries of origin: Australia/USA.

Type: Single seat fighter-bomber.

Powerplant: Mks.20/21/22 – one 1720hp (1283kW) Packard Merlin V-1650-7 V12 piston engine. Mk.23 – one 1655hp (1234kW) Rolls-Royce Merlin 70; four bladed propeller.

Dimensions: Wing span 11.28m (37ft 0in); length 9.83m (32ft 3½in); height 3.71m (12ft 2in); wing area 22.3m² (240sq ft).

Weights: Mk.21 – operational empty 3567kg (7863lb); normal loaded 4309kg (9500lb); max overload 4763kg (10,500lb).

Armament: Six 0.50in machine guns in wings; two 227kg (500lb) bombs or six 5in rockets under wings.

Performance: Max speed 380kt (703km/h) at 25,000ft, 343kt (636km/h) at 5000ft; max climb 3475ft (636m)/min; time to 20,000ft 7.3min; service ceiling 41,900ft; range (internal fuel) 825nm (1529km); range with drop tanks 1434nm (2655km).

Production: 80 Mk.20, 26 Mk.21, 28 Mk.22 and 66 Mk.23, total 200.

Notes: The Royal Australian Air Force was a major user of the North American P-51D/K Mustang, operating a total of 499 from 1945, including 200 built under licence in Australia by the Commonwealth Aircraft Corporation (CAC). These were the only Mustangs manufactured outside the United States.

The decision to manufacture the Mustang in Australia was made in April 1944 after an extensive evaluation of available types including the Supermarine Spitfire, which had been in RAAF service 'at home' since 1942 and with British based squadrons since 1941. Relative ease of manufacture and range were major factors in the decision in favour of the Mustang.

Initial orders covered 690 aircraft but with the end of the war the need for them reduced (especially as nearly 300 North American built aircraft had been delivered), this resulting in just 200 being built at a leisurely pace with production 'stretched out' to keep CAC's workforce employed in the lean post war years.

Local production was preceded by the arrival of a P-51D 'pattern' aircraft in 1944, although this was used for extensive ground testing and didn't fly in Australia until April 1945, just one month before the first CAC CA-17 Mustang Mk.20 took to the air.

All CAC Mustangs were based on the P-51D with minor modifications, the 200 comprising 80 Mk.20s (built up from sets of imported components); 26 CA-18 Mk.21s (the first wholly Australian built version); 28 CA-18 Mk.22 tactical reconnaissance versions with two cameras in the rear fuselage; and 66 CA-18 Mk.23s with a Rolls-Royce rather than Packard Merlin engine.

The production rate was sluggish and stretched out largely to keep the factory occuppied. The first batch of 80 Mk.20s had been handed over by July 1946 but it would be another year before deliveries of the next group started. The last CAC Mustang (a Mk.22) was delivered in August 1951.

A handful of CAC Mustangs flew with the P-51Ds of No 77 Squadron in the Korean War in 1950-51 but most locally manufactured aircraft equipped Australian based squadrons and then the RAAF's five Citizen Air Force squadrons. The last of these was disbanded in June 1960.

Photo: CAC Mustang Mk.22. (RAAF)

CAC Avon-Sabre

Country of origin: Australia.

Type: Single seat fighter-bomber.

Powerplant: One 7500lb (33.4kN) Rolls-Royce/CAC Avon RA.7 Mk.20 or 26 turbojet.

Dimensions: Wing span 11.30m (37ft 1in); length 11.43m (37ft 6in); height 4.39m (14ft 5in); wing area 28.1m² (302sq ft).

Weights: Empty 5443kg (12,000lb); normal loaded 8038kg (17,720lb); max takeoff 9621kg (21,210lb).

Armament: Mk.32 – two 30mm cannon in nose; two AIM-9B Sidewinder AAMs, up to 24 air-to-ground rockets or two 227kg (500lb) or 454kg (1000lb) bombs under wings.

Performance: Mk.32 – max speed 609kt (1126km/h) at sea level, 528kt (977km/h) at 38,000ft; typical cruise 478kt (885km/h); initial climb 12,000ft (3658m)/min; time to 50,000ft 11.1min; service ceiling 52,000ft; range with drop tanks 1000nm (1850km).

Production: 1 CA-26 prototype, 22 CA-27 Mk.30, 20 CA-27 Mk.32 and 69 CA-27 Mk.32, total 112.

Notes: After an extensive evaluation which included the Hawker P.1081 and Hunter (correctly adjudged to be running late), the North American F-86 Sabre was chosen for the Royal Australian Air Force in early 1951, to be produced under licence by the Commonwealth Aircraft Corporation (CAC). The standard General Electric J47 was to be replaced by a Rolls-Royce Avon also built under licence by CAC. Another major change was the substitution of two 30mm Aden cannon in the nose in place of the standard six 0.50in Browning machine guns.

The engine change necessitated a substantial redesign of the Sabre's fuselage as the Avon needed more air (requiring an enlarged intake), was shorter and lighter (it had to be moved aft to maintain centre of gravity) and was of greater diameter. The result was recognised as the best day fighter Sabre variant but at the cost of needing to redesign 60 per cent of the airframe.

CAC ordered 100 sets of F-86F major components to help expedite production and the prototype CA-26 Avon-Sabre first flew on 3 August 1953 powered by an imported Avon 20 engine. The initial production CA-27 Sabre Mk.30 first flew on 13 July 1954 and was handed over to the RAAF two months later. Regular squadron service began in April 1955, but considerable work had to be done to cure engine surge problems when the guns were fired.

All 22 Sabre Mk.30s were fitted with the standard F-86F slatted wing and all but the last six with imported Avons, CAC built engines installed from there. The Mk.31 introduced the '6-3' fixed and extended wing leading edges (20 delivered July 1955-September 1956) and the earlier models were upgraded. The definitive Sabre Mk.32 (69 delivered September 1956-December 1961) had several significant modification including the 'surge free' locally built Avon 26, additional fuel in the wing leading edges and 'dual store' wing with additional hardpoints and the ability (from 1960) to carry a pair of Sidewinder missiles.

The Avon-Sabre flew with five RAAF squadrons and remained in front line service until the Mirage III began to replace it in 1965. It was withdrawn in July 1971 but 16 examples were given to both the Malaysian and Indonesian air forces as part of Australian foreign aid.

Photo: CAC Sabre Mk.32.

Canadair Argus

Country of origin: Canada.

Type: 15 crew maritime patrol and anti submarine.

Powerplants: Four 3400hp (2535kW) dry/3700hp (2759kW) with water injection Wright R-3350-32W Turbo-Compound 18-cylinder radials; three bladed propellers.

Dimensions: Wing span 43.37m (142ft 3½in); length 39.09m (128ft 3in); height 11.20m (36ft 9in); wing area 192.8m² (2075sq ft).

Weights: Empty 36,968kg (81,500lb); max takeoff 71,215kg (157,000lb).

Armament: Two internal weapons bays for max 3629kg (8000lb) bombs, depth charges, homing torpedoes and mines; two underwing pylons for total 3447kg (7600lb) ordnance.

Performance: Max speed 274kt (507km/h) at 20,000ft, 250kt (463km/h) at sea level, economical cruise 194kt (359km/h); typical low level patrol speed 165kt (306km/h); initial climb 1700ft (518m)/min; service ceiling 29,000ft; max range 5127nm (9495km); max endurance 24 hours.

Production: 1 prototype, 12 Mk.1 and 20 Mk.2, total 33.

Notes: Built to a 1952 requirement to replace the Lancaster Mk.10 as the Royal Canadian Air Force's maritime patrol aircraft, the Canadair CL-28 Argus (military designation CP-107) was based on the Bristol Britannia airliner, combining its wings, tail surfaces and landing gear with an entirely new unpressurised fuselage incorporating two weapons bays located fore and aft of the centre section structure.

American APS-20 radar was installed in a chin radome and a magnetic anomaly detection (MAD) 'stinger' was fitted in the tail. Normal crew complement was 15 working in shifts due to the length of patrols – three pilots, two flight engineers, three navigators and seven sensor operators. Sonobuoys were stored in the rear fuselage and fired through dispensers. Various items of electronic countermeasures equipment (ECM) were carried as was a diesel exhaust detector. Two underwing weapons pylons were fitted, intended for the abandoned Petrel air-to-surface missile and were seldom used in operational service.

The Britannia's four Bristol Proteus turboprops were replaced with Wright Turbo-Compound piston engines, these – like the unpressurised fuselage – chosen because most of the Argus' flying would be conducted at low level. Canadair acquired a licence to manufacture the Britannia in 1954, and apart from the Argus, developed the CL-44 series of transports with a lengthened version of the original's fuselage and Rolls-Royce Tyne turboprop engines.

The prototype Argus first flew on 28 March 1957 and deliveries to the RCAF began in May 1958. The first 12 production aircraft were completed to Mk.1 standards with APS-20 radar but production then switched to the Mk.2 with more advanced British ASV-21 radar mounted in a smaller radome and upgraded communications, navigation and ECM equipment. Production ended in July 1960.

The Argus served with four RCAF (later Canadian Armed Forces) Maritime Command squadrons, some remaining in service until 1981 before being replaced by the CP-140 Aurora, a Lockheed P-3 Orion derivative.

Photo: Argus Mk.1.

Canadair Sabre

Country of origin: Canada.

Type: Single seat fighter-bomber.

Powerplant: Mks.2/4 – one 5200lb (23.1kN) General Electric J47-GE-13 turbojet. Mk.5 – one 6355lb (28.3kN) Avro Canada Orenda 10 turbojet. Mk.6 – 7275lb (32.4kN) Orenda 14.

Dimensions: Wing span 11.30m (37ft 1in); length 11.43m (37ft 6in); height 4.44m (14ft 7in); wing area 28.2m² (304sq ft).

Weights: Mk.6 – empty 5054kg (11,143lb); max takeoff 7988kg (17,610lb).

Armament: Six 0.50in machine guns in nose; max 907kg (2000lb) underwing ordnance.

Performance: Mk.6 – max speed 617kt (1143km/h) at sea level, 539kt (998km/h) at 36,000ft; initial climb 11,800ft (3597m)/min; time to 40,000ft 6.0min; service ceiling 54,000ft; tactical radius (clean) 316nm (585km); range with drop tanks 1300nm (2408km).

Production: 1 Mk.1 prototype, 350 Mk.2, 1 Mk.3, 438 Mk.4, 370 Mk.5 and 655 Mk.6, total 1815.

Notes: Needing to fill its post war defensive and NATO commitments, Canada decided to manufacture the North American F-86 Sabre for the RCAF, the programme undertaken by Canadair. Initially, only 100 Canadair Sabres were planned but by the time production ended the total was 1815, of which more than 40 per cent were exported. Early Canadair Sabres contained only 10 per cent local content but this increased to 90 per cent in later aircraft, including the Canadian designed and built Avro Orenda axial flow turbojet.

The single CL-13 Mk.1 prototype was assembled from F-86A components and like the early marks which followed, was powered by the standard General Electric J47 engine. It first flew on 9 October 1950 and was followed in 1951 by the series production Mk.2, based on the F-86E. Of the 350 built, 287 went to the RCAF, three to the Royal Air Force and the remaining 60 to the USAF as the F-86E-6 for service in Korea.

The one-off Mk.3 was the Orenda powered prototype (some fuselage structural modifications were necessary) but the next production version was the J47 powered Mk.4 of which all but 10 of the 438 built were delivered to the RAF in 1952-53 as the Sabre F.1. The aircraft was supplied under the US Mutual Defence Assistance Programme and became necessary due to delays with the Hawker Hunter and Supermarine Swift.

The last two Canadair Sabre variants were the CL-13A Mk.5 (first flight July 1953) and CL-13B Mk.6 (first flight November 1954) powered by the Orenda 10 and more powerful Orenda 14, respectively. Based on the F-86F, the Mk.5 and early Mk.6 had the slatless '6-3' wing but most Mk.6s were fitted with a wider chord wing with leading edge slats.

All of the 370 Mk.5s were delivered to the RCAF and of the 655 Mk.6s, 390 went to Canada, six to Colombia, 34 to South Africa and 225 to West Germany, most of the latter subsequently modified to carry a pair of Sidewinder AAMs. The last Canadair Sabre was built in October 1958.

Second hand aircraft were later sold to Italy, Yugoslavia, Greece and Turkey. Sales to Argentina were frustrated by a lack of funds and to Israel by the 1956 Arab-Israeli war.

Photo: Canadair Sabre Mk.6.

Cessna A-37 Dragonfly

Country of origin: USA.

Type: Two seat light attack.

Powerplants: A-37A – two 2400lb (10.7kN) General Electric J85-GE-5 turbojets. A-37B – two 2850lb (12.7kN) GE J85-GE-17A turbojets.

Dimensions: Wing span 10.93m (35ft 10½in); length 8.93m (29ft 3½in); height 2.70m (8ft 10½in); wing area 17.1m² (184sq ft).

Weights: A-37B – empty equipped 2817kg (6211lb); max takeoff 6350kg (14,000lb).

Armament: One 7.62mm machine gun in forward fuselage; eight underwing hardpoints for max 2576kg (5680lb) ordnance including bombs, rockets and gun pods.

Performance: A-37B – max speed 440kt (815km/h); max cruise 425kt (787km/h); typical cruise with stores 260kt (482km/h); max climb 6990ft (2130m)/min; service ceiling 41,765ft; range with 1860kg (4100lb) ordnance 400nm (740km); ferry range 878nm (1626km).

Production: 39 A-37A conversions and 577 A-37B.

Notes: Investigations into developing an armed version of the Cessna T-37B jet trainer for the counter insurgency (COIN) role began in 1962 when the USAF's Special Air Warfare centre evaluated two aircraft to assess their suitability for the role. This led to both aircraft being modified to YAT-37D standards in which the original pair of 1025lb (4.6kN) Continental J69 turbojets were replaced with General Electric J85-GE-5s with more than twice the power of the originals. The first of these flew on 22 October 1963.

The concept languished for a time but was revived to meet a need resulting from the USAF's experiences in the Vietnam War. In 1966, Cessna was contracted to convert 39 T-37Bs to A-37A Dragonfly standards (Cessna Model 318D) with J85s, an internal gun, eight underwing hardpoints, additional fuel capacity in wingtip tanks, armour protection, revised avionics and a substantial increase in maximum weight. Deliveries began in May 1967 and 25 A-37As were operationally evaluated in Vietnam by the 604th Air Commando Squadron at Bien Hoa. They were passed on to the South Vietnamese Air Force in 1970.

Cessna had meanwhile built the prototype of a further developed version (Model 318E) which first flew in September 1967. This was ordered into production as the A-37B, changes including more powerful J85-GE-17A engines, a restressed structure, increased internal fuel capacity and provision for a flight refuelling probe. Deliveries began in May 1968 and 577 were built between then and the final delivery in 1975.

The A-37B was supplied to the USAF and several other nations including South Vietnam, Chile, El Salvador, Guatemala, Honduras, Peru, South Korea, Uruguay, Colombia, Ecuador, the Dominican Republic and Thailand, while even the North Vietnamese Air Force had a few captured examples on strength towards the end of the conflict. Eight Central and South American nations still flew the Dragonfly in 2000, as did South Korea.

The USAF modified 130 A-37Bs as the OA-37B for forward air control (FAC) duties with appropriate avionics installed. A lightly armed version of the T-37 trainer was also developed as the T-37C with two underwing hardpoints.

Photo: A-37B Dragonfly.

Chengdu J-7 and F-7

Country of origin: China.

Type: Single seat fighter.

Powerplant: J-7 – one 11,243lb (50.0kN) with afterburner WP-7A (Tumansky) turbojet. F-7 II/F-7M – one 9700lb (43.1kN) dry/14,550lb (64.7kN) with afterburner WP-7BM turbojet.

Dimensions: F-7M – wing span 7.16m (23ft 6in); length 13.94m (45ft 9in); height 4.10m (13ft 5$^{1}/_{2}$in); wing area 23.0m^2 (248sq ft).

Weights: F-7M – empty 5275kg (11,630lb); normal loaded 7531kg (16,603lb); max takeoff 8880kg (19,577lb).

Armament: F-7M – two 30mm cannon; four underwing hardpoints for max 1000kg (2205lb) ordnance including PL-2/-2A/-7 or Matra R550 Magic AAMs, rockets and bombs.

Performance: F-7M – max speed 1173kt (Mach 2.04/2173km/h) above 36,000ft; max climb 35,435ft (10,800m)/min; service ceiling 59,710ft; intercept combat radius with three AAMs and drop tanks 350nm (648km); ferry range 945nm (1750km).

Production: Approximately 1000.

Notes: The J-7 (F-7 for export) series of fighters are fundamentally Chinese copies of the MiG-21F but with local variations continually developed for the People's Liberation Army Air Force and export. The aircraft remains an integral component of China's air defence inventory with some 500 in service by 2000.

China acquired a licence to build the MiG-21F-13 ('Fishbed C') and its Tumansky R.11 turbojet in 1961. Assembly of aircraft built up from kits began in 1964 but the programme was delayed when China and the Soviet Union severed ties before the technology transfer activities had been completed, forcing China to 'reverse engineer' the aircraft for local production.

The first Chinese manufactured J-7 flew on 17 January 1966 and production began the following year at Shenyang. It was soon transferred to the Chengdu Aircraft Factory where subsequent development took place. Production was temporarily halted by the 'cultural revolution' but resumed under the designation J-7 I. Some were exported to Albania and Tanzania as the F-7A.

The much improved F-7 II with more powerful engine, aft rather than forward hinged canopy, continuously variable (instead of three position) intakes, optional Matra AAMs and new ejection seat first flew on 30 December 1978 and was exported to Egypt and Iraq.

The F-7M Airguard for export was based on the F-7 II but with Western radar and avionics, improved ejection seat, increased weapons options, additional fuel, an advanced weapons control system and upgraded systems. It was sold to Bangladesh, Egypt, Iran, North Yemen, Myanmar, Somalia, Sudan and Zimbabwe. The F-7P Skybolt for Pakistan differs in having a Martin Baker ejection seat, upgraded radar and Sidewinder AAM capability.

Other variants include the J-7E with more agile cranked double delta wing, more powerful engine and extra hardpoints and the J-7 III (first flight April 1984) all weather fighter. The latest version (F-7MG) flew in 1993 and has the J-7E's wing plus modern, mostly Western avionics, systems and weapons. Two seat operational trainer versions have also been developed.

Photo: F-7MG.

Convair B-36

Country of origin: USA.

Type: 15 crew strategic bomber.

Powerplants: B-36B – six 3500hp (2610kW) Pratt & Whitney R-4360-41 Wasp Major 28-cylinder radials; B-36D – six R-1460-41s and four 5200lb (23.1kN) General Electric J47-GE-19 turbojets in paired underwing pods. B-36F/H/J – six 3800hp (2833kW) P&W R-4360-53s plus four J47-GE-19 turbojets.

Dimensions: Wing span 70.10m (230ft 0in); length 49.40m (162ft 1in); height 14.22m (46ft 8in); wing area 443.3m^2 (4772sq ft).

Weights: B-36B – empty 68,040kg (150,000lb); max takeoff 126,100kg (278,000lb). B-36D – empty 81,194kg (179,000lb); max takeoff 162,162kg (357,500lb). B-36J – max takeoff 185,976kg (410,000lb).

Armament: 16 20mm cannon in six retractable and remotely controlled fuselage turrets plus nose and tail turrets; max bomb load 32,659-38,102kg (72,000-84,000lb).

Performance: B-36D – max speed 381kt (706km/h); cruising speed 195kt (362km/h); initial climb 1740ft (530m)/min; service ceiling 45,200ft; range 6517nm (12,070km). B-36J – max speed 357kt (661km/h) at 36,400ft; cruising speed 340kt (629km/h); initial climb 1920ft (585m)/min; service ceiling 39,900ft; range 5909nm (10,945km).

Production: 1 XB-36, 1 YB-36, 22 B-36A, 73 B-36B, 22 B-36D, 17 RB-36D, 34 B-36F, 24 RB-36F, 83 B-36H, 73 RB-36H, 33 B-36J, total 383. Also numerous conversions including 64 B-36B to B-36D, 7 B-36B to RB-36D, 1 YB-36 and 21 B-36A to RB-36E.

Notes: Developed from 1941 as the first true intercontinental bomber, the B-36 (sometimes called 'Peacemaker') was designed to carry a 4536kg (10,000lb) bomb load from bases in the USA to European targets and return.

Delayed by having a low wartime priority, the B-36 was the largest and heaviest aircraft in the world when it appeared, the fuselage featuring forward and aft pressurised sections joined by a 24.4m (80ft) trolley tunnel over four weapons bays. The six Wasp Major radial engines in the wing trailing edges drove 5.8m (19ft) diameter pusher propellers. The prototype XB-36 first flew on 8 August 1946 followed by the YB-36 with production standard raised cockpit roof and then (as the YB-36A) double bogie main undercarriage units.

The first production B-36A flew in August 1947, this unarmed model used for training and followed by the armed B-36B (first flight July 1948); B-36D (March 1949) the first with four podded underwing J47 jets to boost takeoff performance (but shut down in cruising flight), built new and by conversion; B-36F (November 1950) with and more powerful piston engines; B-36H (April 1952) with cockpit improvements; and B-36J (September 1953) with increased fuel capacity and heavier weights. The last was delivered in August 1954.

The RB-36 reconnaissance versions carried 14 cameras in two of the weapons bays, while other experimental models were created by conversion. The B-36 had a brief (retired in February 1959) and politically controversial USAF career with numerous technical problems.

Photo: B-36D.

Convair F-102A Delta Dagger

Country of origin: USA.

Type: Single seat all weather interceptor.

Powerplant: One 11,700lb (52.0kN) dry/17,200lb (76.5kN) with after-burner Pratt & Whitney J57-P-23 turbojet.

Dimensions: Wing span 11.62m (38ft 1½in); length (incl nose probe) 20.84m (68ft 4½in); height 6.46m (21ft 2½in); wing area 64.6m² (695sq ft).

Weights: Empty 8777kg (19,350lb); max takeoff 12,769kg (28,150lb) clean, 14,187kg (31,276lb) with drop tanks.

Armament: Up to six AIM-4 Falcon or two AIM-26 air-to-air missiles or 24 2.75in (70mm) folding fin unguided rockets.

Performance: Max speed 717kt (Mach 1.25/1328km/h) at 40,000ft; initial climb 13,000ft (3962m)/min; service ceiling 54,000ft; max range with drop tanks 1173nm (2173km).

Production: 4 YF-102A, 875 F-102A, 63 TF-102A, total 942 (plus 10 YF-102).

Notes: The first delta winged fighter and the first to entirely dispense with guns in favour of missiles controlled by advanced avionics, the highly advanced Delta Dagger began life as the XF-92A, itself the world's first powered delta winged aircraft. The single example first flew in September 1948 as part of a research programme for a supersonic fighter. Delta wing pioneer, Germany's Dr Alexander Lippisch, was involved in the design.

The XF-92A led to the Convair Model 8-80, winner of a contest against designs from five other manufacturers. As the YF-102, the first of 10 examples flew on 24 October 1953. Performance was found to be deficient, the YF-102 remaining firmly subsonic. A major redesign followed, the Model 8-90 (or YF-102A) featuring a much lengthened 'coke bottle' fuselage which conformed to Dr Richard Whitcomb's area rule formula. The first of four prototypes flew on 20 December 1954 and went supersonic on its second flight.

Production aircraft were dubbed F-102A (and nicknamed 'Deuce' – '2' in cards), entering USAF Air Defence Command (ADC) service in mid 1956. An early production modification was the incorporation of a taller fin and rudder to cure a roll coupling problem. The last of 875 was delivered in April 1958, by which time 26 ADC squadrons were equipped with the fighter.

The Delta Dagger remained in ADC service until 1969, and with European and Pacific squadrons until 1970. Some of the latter flew the aircraft on combat missions over Vietnam between 1962 and 1969. Nineteen Air National Guard squadrons flew the F-102A until the first half of 1976.

A two seat combat trainer version – the TF-102A – was developed with operational capability. With the two seats side by side in a widened, redesigned forward fuselage, the TF was subsonic in level flight and the first of 63 was flown on 8 November 1955.

The Delta Dagger underwent an upgrade programme from 1957 with a new fire control system, armament revisions, provision for drop tanks and installation of an infrared sighting system. Many became QF-102 armed or PQM-102 unarmed target drones, while ex USAF F-102As were supplied to Greece (20) and Turkey (40).

Photo: F-102A Delta Dagger.

Convair F-106 Delta Dart

Country of origin: USA.

Type: F-106A – single seat all weather interceptor. F-106B – two seat operational trainer.

Powerplant: One 17,200lb (76.5kN) dry/24,500lb (109.0kN) with after-burner Pratt & Whitney J75-P-17 turbojet.

Dimensions: Wing span 11.67m (38ft 3½in); length (incl nose probe) 21.56m (70ft 8¾in); height 6.18m (20ft 3¼in); wing area 64.8m² (698sq ft).

Weights: F-106A – empty 11,029kg (24,315lb); max takeoff 17,779kg (39,195lb).

Armament: Two AIR-2A/B Genie unguided and four AIM-4 Falcon guided air-to-air missiles in weapons bay; some aircraft with one 20mm Vulcan rotary cannon in lieu of one Genie.

Performance: Max speed 1153kt (Mach 2.01/2136km/h) at 35,000ft; max climb 42,800ft (13,045m)/min; service ceiling 57,000ft; combat radius 500nm (926km) clean or 634nm (1175km) with drop tanks; ferry range 1303nm (2414km).

Production: 277 F-106A and 63 F-106B, total 340.

Notes: Originally designated F-102B due it being a development of the F-102A Delta Dagger, Convair's new Model 8-24 fighter was renamed F-106 Delta Dart as the changes became more extensive. The result was a Mach 2 fighter which remained in service for nearly three decades.

The delta wing remained as before but the fuselage was redesigned to accommodate a more powerful J75 turbojet. Variable geometry intakes, upgraded Hughes MA-1 electronic guidance and fire control system (integrated with the USA's Semi-Automatic Ground Environment/SAGE defence system), new undercarriage and upgraded weapons including the AIR-2 Genie unguided nuclear tipped missile were fitted.

No gun was originally installed, although a 1973 upgrade saw a Vulcan M-61 20mm rotary cannon fitted in a semi retractable weapons bay mounting.

The first F-106A flew on 26 December 1956, early testing revealing some performance shortcomings including lower than anticipated maximum speed and acceleration rate plus problems with the MA-1 system. At one stage it appeared the F-106 programme would be scrapped, but it continued albeit in much lower numbers than originally envisaged.

Deliveries to the USAF's Air Defence Command began in July 1959 with the last example handed over two years later. Earlier aircraft underwent modification to the latest production standard in 1960-61, this including fitting supersonic ejection seats, an improved MA-1 and upgraded instrument displays. Other equipment upgrades were also performed over the years.

The F-106A served with 14 ADC squadrons and was the mainstay of the USA's air defence system throughout the 1960s and '70s. Air National Guard units began receiving the aircraft in the early 1970s and service continued until 1988 when conversion of some to QF-106 drones began.

The F-106B operational trainer first flew on 9 April 1958, this accommodating two pilots in tandem cockpits and retaining full operational capability. The improved F-106C/D with P&W JT4D engine and other modifications was not built.

Photo: F-106A Delta Dart.

Convair B-58 Hustler

Country of origin: USA.

Type: Three crew medium bomber.

Powerplants: Four 10,000lb (44.5kN) dry/15,600lb (69.4kN) with afterburner General Electric J79-GE-5B/C turbojets.

Dimensions: Wing span 17.32m (56ft 10in); length 29.49m (96ft 9in); height 9.58m (31ft 5in); wing area 142.3m² (1542sq ft).

Weights: Empty (with weapons pod) 29,083kg (64,115lb); max takeoff 73,937kg (163,000lb); max after aerial refuelling 80,342kg (177,120lb).

Armament: One radar controlled 20mm multi barrel cannon in tail; max 8822kg (19,450lb) nuclear and/or conventional weapons in underfuselage pod.

Performance: Max speed (with weapons pod) 609kt (Mach 0.92/1128km/h) at sea level, 1204kt (Mach 2.1/2230km/h) at 40,000ft; initial climb 17,400ft (5303m)/min; service ceiling 63,000ft; unrefuelled combat radius 1347nm (2495km); max unrefuelled range 4453nm (8247km).

Production: 1 XB-58, 8 YB-58, 21 YB-58A, 86 B-58A, total 116.

Notes: A very high performance technical *tour de force*, the Hustler was the first production supersonic bomber and the first to reach Mach 2. It abounded in advanced and innovative features including a very thin delta wing, four podded afterburning J79 turbojets, area ruled fuselage and extensive use of honeycomb sandwich construction.

Internal weapons storage was discarded in favour of an 18.9m (62ft) long underfuselage pod to carry fuel and a variety of conventional and nuclear weapons. This could be jettisoned after the target had been attacked. A radar controlled 20mm Vulcan rotary cannon in the tail provided defensive capability and the three crew members sat in tandem in individual escape capsules.

The Hustler was the first example of a complete and integrated weapons system purchase contract, the package including not only the airframe, engines, systems, weapons and avionics but also the necessary ground based training and support infrastructure.

The Hustler resulted from a March 1949 USAF requirement for a supersonic bomber, Convair's Model 4 concepts winning a contract to develop the aircraft as the B-58 in December 1952. Thirty prototype/development aircraft were ordered between then and 1958 followed by 86 production models in 1958-60.

The XB-58 prototype first flew on 11 November 1956 followed by 29 development YB-58/As. The first production B-58A flew in September 1959. The first Hustler operational unit, the 43rd BW, was activated in March 1960. Deliveries ended in October 1962. The 305th BW was the only other operational wing to fly the B-58A, both maintaining the aircraft in service until it was withdrawn in January 1970. Cost of operation was the reason given for the Hustler's apparently early retirement, with its high dependence on aerial refuelling also a factor.

Twenty of the development aircraft were brought up to operational standards in 1961 while eight others were converted to TB-58A operational trainers from May 1960 with dual controls fitted and operational equipment deleted.

Photo: B-58A Hustler. (Gerard Frawley)

Dassault Ouragan

Country of origin: France.

Type: Single seat fighter-bomber.

Powerplant: One 5070lb (22.5kN) Hispano-Suiza (Rolls-Royce) Nene 104B turbojet.

Dimensions: Wing span (with tip tanks) 13.16m (43ft 2in); length 10.74m (35ft 3in); height 4.14m (13ft 7in); wing area 23.8m² (256sq ft).

Weights: Empty equipped 4800kg (10,582lb); normal loaded 6950kg (15,322lb); max takeoff 7900kg (17,416lb).

Armament: Four 20mm cannon in lower nose; two 500kg (1100lb) bombs or 16 105mm rockets under wings.

Performance: Max speed 502kt (930km/h) at sea level, 448kt (830km/h) at 39,400ft; initial climb 7874ft (2400m)/min; time to 10,000ft 3.2min; service ceiling 49,200ft; range with tip tanks 540nm (1000km).

Production: 438.

Notes: Famed French aircraft designer and manufacturer Marcel Bloch's brother Paul – a founder of the French Resistance – assumed the codename d'Assault during the war, both men formalising it as Dassault afterwards. Marcel was interned for a time in the notorious Buchenwald prison camp but in 1946 formed a new company under the Dassault name. Its (and France's) first production jet fighter was the MD.450 Ouragan (Hurricane), a useful and reliable combat aircraft which set the scene for Dassault's future by finding an export market.

The basically straight winged (but with a hint of leading edge sweep) Ouragan was a simple and conservative design powered by a Rolls-Royce Nene centrifugal flow turbojet. The first of three prototypes flew on 28 February 1949 powered by a 5000lb (22.2kN) British built Nene 102. The second prototype (first flight July 1949) had a licence built Hispano-Suiza Nene 104B installed, this the powerplant of most production aircraft. Twelve pre-production aircraft followed, these used for an extensive series of tests and trials.

An initial 150 was ordered, this eventually increasing to 350. The first production Ouragan flew in December 1951 and the last in January 1955. The aircraft remained in front line French service until 1961 and as an advanced trainer until the mid 1960s. The first 50 aircraft were built as MD.450As with Rolls-Royce Nenes and the remainder as MD.450Bs with Hispano-Suiza engines and various equipment changes.

The Indian Air Force received 71 new and 33 ex French Ouragans from 1954, these carrying the name 'Toofani' (the Hindi equivalent of Ouragan) and in the case of the new production aircraft, powered by a 5180lb (23.0kN) Nene 105A. They remained in front line Indian service until 1967, in the meantime seeing action against Pakistan and China.

Israel ordered 24 new Ouragans in January 1955 and a further 51 ex French examples subsequently, these seeing a considerable amount of combat culminating in the 1967 Arab-Israeli war where they were employed as ground attack aircraft. The final Ouragan operator was El Salvador, which acquired 18 surviving Israeli aircraft in 1975 and kept them in service well into the 1980s. These were also often used for ground attack operations.

Photo: An Israeli Ouragan.

Dassault Mystère IIC

Country of origin: France.

Type: Single seat fighter-bomber.

Powerplant: One 6173lb (27.4kN) Snecma Atar 101D-2/3 turbojet.

Dimensions: Wing span 11.33m (37ft 2in); length 12.24m (40ft 1³/₄in); height 4.50m (14ft 9in); wing area 30.3m² (326sq ft).

Weights: Empty equipped 5730kg (12,632lb); max takeoff 7450kg (16,424lb).

Armament: Two 30mm cannon in lower nose (provision for underwing ordnance not used).

Performance: Max speed 556kt (1030km/h) at sea level, 516kt (956km/h) at 29,500ft; initial climb 4528ft (1380m)/min; service ceiling 42,650ft; range 648nm (1200km).

Production: 14 prototypes/pre-production, 156 IIC.

Notes: Dassault's fighter design evolution continued with the MD.452 Mystère, fundamentally an Ouragan fitted with 30 degree swept wings and swept horizontal tail surfaces. The name Mystère was subsequently used for other Dassault fighters and later for the corporate jets produced by the company. In its production Mystère IIC form, the aircraft was Western Europe's first swept wing aircraft to enter production, the first all French (airframe and engine) jet fighter and the first Western European fighter capable of exceeding Mach 1 in a dive.

The latter was unintentionally demonstrated for the first time by a USAF pilot in October 1952 during a test flight in one of the prototypes. The flight was part of an evaluation to determine if the Mystère was suitable for the USA's Off-Shore Procurement Scheme, under which foreign military aircraft were purchased for European NATO air forces.

The Mystère IIC served only with the Armée de l'Air although Israel ordered 24 which were never built, the order unfulfilled for political reasons.

The prototype Mystère I first flew on 23 February 1951, this powered by the same Nene engine as the Ouragan. The following 13 prototype and pre-production Mystère IIs were powered by different jet engine types: the 6283lb (27.9kN) Hispano-Suiza (Rolls-Royce) Tay; non afterburning Snecma Atar 101C or 101D as fitted to production IICs; and Atar 101F rated at 8378lb (37.2kN) thrust with afterburning. The axial flow Atar became an extremely important French powerplant, later fitted to the Mystère IV, Etendard and various Mirage fighters.

The transition from testing to production was a slow process for the Mystère, the French military happy to build up jet fighter experience with the Ouragan. The early Mystères were therefore used mainly as test vehicles which had numerous detailed modifications introduced as time went on.

The Armée de l'Air finally ordered its first batch of Mystère IICs in April 1953, eventually receiving 156. The first production aircraft flew in 1954 and the last in January 1957. Front line service was only brief as the Mystère IIC was regarded as an interim type pending introduction of the more advanced Mystère IV and Super Mystère B2. Withdrawal from operational units began only a few months after the last example had been delivered. Only two Armée de l'Air Escadres operated the Mystère IIC.

Photo: Mystère IIC. (Vance Ingham)

Dassault Mystère IV

Country of origin: France.

Type: IVA – single seat fighter-bomber.

Powerplant: IVA – one 6283lb (27.9kN) Rolls-Royce Tay 250A or 7716lb (34.3kN) Hispano-Suiza Verdon 350 (developed Tay) turbojet.

Dimensions: IVA – wing span 11.12m (36ft 5³/₄in); length 12.85m (42ft 2in); height 4.60m (15ft 1in); wing area 32.0m² (345sq ft).

Weights: IVA – empty 5874kg (12,950lb); normal loaded 8210kg (18,100lb); max takeoff 9500kg (20,944lb).

Armament: IVA – two 30mm cannon in lower nose; four underwing hardpoints for up to 907kg (2000lb) of bombs or rocket pods.

Performance: IVA – max speed 600kt (1111km/h) at sea level, 534kt (990km/h) at 40,000ft; initial climb 8860ft (2700m)/min; service ceiling 49,200ft; range (internal fuel) 495nm (917km); range with drop tanks 1231nm (2280km).

Production: 1 prototype, 435 IVA, 10 IVB, 1 IVN, total 447.

Notes: The next step in Dassault's jet fighter evolution, the Mystère IV was ostensibly a more powerful IIC with a thinner and more sharply swept (38deg) wing and new tail surfaces but was in reality an almost completely new design also with a new and larger fuselage, redesigned structure and fully powered controls. Several North American F-86 Sabre design practices were incorporated including the tailplane design and the use of tapered sheet wing skins, a European first.

Originally named the Super Mystère, the Mystère IV was intended to be powered by an afterburning Atar 101G but this was not quite ready. Instead, production Mystère IVAs were powered by a Rolls-Royce Tay centrifugal flow turbojet (the first 50 aircraft) or a more powerful Hispano-Suiza Verdon 350, a locally developed version of the licence built Tay.

The prototype Mystère IVA first flew on 28 September 1952 and after successful evaluation by the USAF, 225 were ordered for the Armée de l'Air by the US Government as part of its Off-Shore Procurement Scheme for European NATO members. France ordered an additional 100 in its own right.

The first production Mystère IVA flew on 29 May 1954, service entry was in May 1955 and the final example delivered in October 1958. Apart from France, deliveries of new aircraft were also made to Israel (60) from April 1956 and India (67) from 1957, the latter also later receiving 33 from French stocks. France's Mystère IVAs saw action during the 1956 Suez crisis while both Israel's and India's aircraft were often used in combat over their long service careers.

Ten prototype and pre-production Rolls-Royce Avon or Snecma Atar powered Mystère IVBs were built (first flight 16 December 1953) along with a single Mystère IVN tandem two seat night and all weather interceptor. Largely redesigned, it was fitted with a lengthened fuselage, afterburning Avon engine, increased fuel capacity and APG-33 intercept radar mounted in a scanner above the redesigned nose intake. First flight was 19 July 1954 but the project was discontinued, the Sud Vautour gaining favour instead.

Photo: Mystère IV.

Dassault Super Mystère

Country of origin: France.

Type: Single seat fighter-bomber.

Powerplant: B2 – one 7400lb (32.9kN) dry/9833lb (43.7kN) with afterburner Snecma Atar 101G-2/3 turbojet.

Dimensions: B2 – wing span 10.51m (34ft 6in); length 13.94m (45ft 9in); height 4.55m (14ft 11¼in); wing area 35.0m² (377sq ft).

Weights: B2 – empty equipped 6392kg (15,282lb); normal loaded 9325kg (20,558lb); max takeoff 10,000kg (22,046lb).

Armament: B2 – two 30mm cannon in lower nose; 35 68mm rockets in retractable fuselage pack; two underwing hardpoints for up to 1000kg (2205lb) bombs or rocket pods.

Performance: B2 – max speed 560kt (Mach 0.85/1037km/h) at sea level, 643kt (Mach 1.12/1191km/h) at 39,400ft; max climb 17,224ft (5250m)/min; service ceiling 55,750ft; range 469nm (869km) clean or 966nm (1790km) with external fuel.

Production: 1 B1, 5 pre-production B2 and 180 production B2 plus 2 B4.

Notes: The last of the line of 'conventional wing' Dassault fighters which began with the Ouragan, the Super Mystère was also by far the most capable with afterburning Atar 101G engine, new wing with 45 degrees of sweep, improved aircraft and weapons systems and the capability to exceed the speed of sound in level flight – a first for a Western Europe production aircraft. North American F-100 Super Sabre design influence was prevalent in the wing and flattened 'lipped' nose intake designs.

Developed via the Mystère IVB development batch, the first Super Mystère B1 powered by a 9546lb (42.4kN) thrust with afterburning Rolls-Royce Avon RA.7R flew on 2 March 1955. Five pre-production Super Mystère B2s (or SMB 2) followed with Atar I01G engines, the first of these flying on 15 May 1956. The Avon was initially the preferred powerplant for production aircraft but the locally developed Atar was ultimately selected.

After delays caused by the Atar development programme, it was finally decided to order 180 SMB 2s for the Armée de l'Air of which 36 were delivered to Israel in 1958. The first production aircraft flew on 26 February 1957 and the final delivery was in October 1959.

Despite being very much only a day fighter, the SMB 2 enjoyed a long career with the Armée de l'Air, not being retired from front line service until 1977. It was in the meantime subject to several upgrades including the fitting of two AIM-9 Sidewinder air-to-air missiles.

Israel's B2s saw considerable action in various wars and in 1972 the survivors were modified to have a non afterburning 9300lb (41.3kN) Pratt & Whitney J52-P-8A turbojet installed instead of the Atar, this engine also powering Israel's A-4 Skyhawks. Eighteen of Israel's B2s were sold to Honduras in 1977 and remained in service until 1989.

The final Super Mystère variant was the B4, two examples of which were flown in February and October 1958 powered by an Atar 9B rated at 13,227lb (58.8kN) thrust with afterburner. These were used to support Atar 9 development for the delta winged Mirage, the aircraft which formed the basis of Dassault's next and highly successful generation of fighters.

Photo: Super Mystère B2.

Dassault Etendard IVM

Country of origin: France.

Type: Single seat naval fighter-bomber.

Powerplant: One 9700lb (43.1kN) Snecma Atar 8B turbojet.

Dimensions: Wing span 9.60m (31ft 6in); length 14.40m (47ft 3in); height 3.92m (12ft 11½in); wing area 28.4m² (306sq ft).

Weights: 5897kg (13,000lb); max catapult launch 9000kg (19,841lb); max takeoff 10,200kg (22,487lb).

Armament: Two fixed 30mm cannon; four underwing pylons for max 1360kg (3000lb) offensive stores and fuel tanks.

Performance: Max speed 585kt (Mach 1.02/1085km/h) at 36,090ft, 593kt (Mach 0.90/1099km/h) at sea level; initial climb 19,685ft (6000m)/min; time to 32,810ft 6.0min; service ceiling 50,850ft; tactical radius 162nm (300km) at sea level or 378nm (700km) at altitude; range (clean) 918nm (1700km); max range with external fuel 1782nm (3300km).

Production: 1 Etendard IV prototype, 6 pre-production IVM, 69 production IVM and 21 IVP, total 97.

Notes: The Etendard ('Standard', as in national flag) was designed in its original form as a private venture to meet a mid 1950s NATO requirement for a lightweight tactical fighter, the competition ultimately won by the Fiat G.91.

Two versions were built as prototypes, the Etendard II with two 2072lb (9.2kN) Turboméca Gabizo turbojet (first flight July 1956) and Etendard VI with a single Bristol Siddeley Orpheus (first flight March 1957).

The larger and more capable Etendard IV with a Snecma Atar engine was also developed as a private venture and first flew in prototype form on 24 July 1956. This transonic design attracted the attention of France's Aéronavale, which was looking for a multirole strike fighter to operate from its carriers *Clemenceau* and *Foch*.

An order for a single Etendard IVM prototype was therefore placed in December 1956 and one for five pre-production models in May 1957. An additional pre-production aircraft was ordered in 1959. Features of the IVM included folding wing tips, long stroke undercarriage with extendable nose leg, catapult spool, arrester hook and AIDA radar in the nose.

The prototype IVM flew on 21 May 1958 followed by the first pre-production example on 21 December 1958, both powered by the production standard Atar 08B engine. One of the pre-production batch was experimentally fitted with an 11,200lb (49.8kN) Rolls-Royce Avon 51 and flap blowing system under the designation Etendard IVB.

The first production Etendard IVM flew in July 1961 and 69 of this model were delivered to the Aéronavale between then and 1965, fulfilling both the intercept and tactical strike roles from the French carriers. The overall tally of 90 production Etendards included 21 completed as IVP unarmed reconnaissance aircraft with cameras replacing the nose radar and two cannon.

After three decades, the Etendard IVM remained in front line Aéronavale service until 1991 and about 10 IVM/Ps remained on strength in early 2000.

Photo: Etendard IVP. (MAP)

Dassault Super Etendard

Country of origin: France.

Type: Single seat naval strike fighter.

Powerplant: One 11,025lb (49.0kN) Snecma Atar 8K-50 turbojet.

Dimensions: Wing span 9.60m (31ft 6in); length 14.31m (46ft 11¹/₂in); height 3.86m (12ft 8in); wing area 28.4m² (306sq ft).

Weights: 6500kg (14,330lb); max takeoff 12,000kg (26,455lb).

Armament: Two 30mm cannon; two 250kg (550lb) bombs under fuselage; four underwing hardpoints for up to 4000kg (8818lb) ordnance including bombs, rocket pods, Exocet anti shipping and Magic air-to-air missiles.

Performance: Max speed 604kt (Mach 1.05/1119km/h) at 39,370ft, 637kt (Mach 0.96/1180km/h) at 985ft; service ceiling 45,000ft; combat radius with one Exocet and two drop tanks 460nm (852km).

Production: 85 (plus three prototypes converted from Etendard IVMs).

Notes: A progressive and much more capable development of the Etendard IV carrier based strike fighter, the Super Etendard was nevertheless very different in detail design incorporating only 10 per cent commonality with the earlier aircraft through its more powerful Atar 8K-50 engine, revised structure, aerodynamic refinements, enhanced weapons carrying capability, upgraded avionics (including Thomson-CSF/Dassault Agave multi mode radar) and upgraded aircraft and weapons systems.

The Aéronavale originally intended replacing its Etendard IVs with a navalised version of the Sepecat Jaguar, but cost and political considerations dictated that Dassault's improved Etendard would be selected instead. The first of three prototypes converted from Etendard IVMs flew on 28 October 1974, the first production aircraft on 24 November 1977 and deliveries began in June 1978. Series production ended in 1983.

Fifty-four of the Aéronavale's Super Etendards have been subject to an upgrade programme intended to extend their service lives to 2008, modifications to the airframe, cockpit and avionics systems being incorporated as well as the ability to carry the ASMP supersonic nuclear standoff weapon.

The first conversion flew in October 1990 and deliveries began in 1992 at a rate of 15 per annum. The naval Rafale M is scheduled to begin replacing the Super Etendard in French service from around 2005.

Argentina ordered 14 Super Etendards for its navy in 1979 of which eight had been delivered by May 1982 when they were used in action during the Falklands War. Operating from shore bases and armed with Exocet anti shipping missiles, the aircraft achieved some notoriety during that conflict when it sank the Royal Navy destroyer HMS *Sheffield* (despite the Exocet failing to explode) and the supporting container ship *Atlantic Conveyer*. Operations from Argentina's aircraft carrier, the *25 de Mayo*, didn't start until after the conflict.

The only other foreign operator of the Super Etendard has been Iraq, which leased five from the French Government in 1982 pending delivery of new Mirage F1Es. By early 2000 France had 52 Super Etendards in service and Argentina 11.

Photo: French Super Etendard. (Dassault)

Dassault Mirage IIIC

Country of origin: France.

Type: Single seat interceptor.

Powerplant: One 9370lb (41.7kN) dry/13,225lb (58.8kN) with afterburner Snecma Atar 9B turbojet; provision for one 3307lb (14.7kN) SEPR 844 rocket booster engine.

Dimensions: Wing span 8.22m (26ft 11¹/₂in); length 15.03m (49ft 4in); height 4.50m (14ft 9in); wing area 34.8m² (375sq ft).

Weights: Empty 5292kg (13,055lb); max takeoff 9727kg (21,444lb).

Armament: Two 30mm cannon; typical intercept armament of one Matra R 511 AAM under fuselage and two AIM-9 Sidewinders under wings.

Performance: Max speed 1204kt (Mach 2.1/2230km/h) at 36,090ft, 750kt (Mach 1.14/1389km/h) at sea level; time to 59,055ft (with rocket) 6.2min; service ceiling (without rocket) 55,755ft; combat radius (internal fuel) 156nm (290km); combat radius with drop tanks 365nm (676km).

Production: 1414 Mirage III/5/50 of all versions including 1 III, 10 IIIA, 77 IIIB and 184 IIIC.

Notes: The combat aircraft which best symbolises France's post war arms export industry, the delta winged Mirage family owes a great debt to the British Government, which in the mid 1950s abandoned further development of the delta concept for fighters despite having captured the world air speed record with the Fairey Delta 2. Dassault already had an exchange of information arrangement with the British company and gained the full benefit of its advanced research.

The original MD.550 Mirage I (at first called the Mystère-Mirage) was a small delta (with 60deg sweep) powered by two Armstrong Siddeley Viper engines and a SEPR 66 rocket booster. It was developed to meet the a 1954 requirement for an all weather interceptor and first flown in June 1955. Adjudged too small, the Mirage I was succeeded (via the unbuilt Mirage II) by the much larger and more ambitious Mirage III powered by a single Snecma Atar turbojet.

The prototype Mirage III with a 9700lb (43.1kN) thrust Atar and rocket booster motor (something which remained an option for much of the Mirage's life) first flew on 17 November 1956 and was capable of a Mach 1.8 maximum speed. From this came the pre-production Mirage IIIA with a larger and thinner wing, redesigned fuselage and more powerful Atar 9B engine. The first of 10 flew on 12 May 1958 and in October 1958 it became the first western European aircraft to achieve Mach 2 in level flight. One of the series was fitted with a 16,000lb (71.1kN) Rolls-Royce Avon 67 in 1961 for evaluation by Australia as the Mirage IIIO but was not produced.

The production interceptor version for the Armée de l'Air was dubbed the Mirage IIIC with Atar 9B, booster rocket (usually) and CSF Cyrano radar. First flight was on 9 October 1960 and deliveries began shortly afterwards. A two seat operational trainer version – the IIIB – had meanwhile flown in October 1959, a full year ahead of the fighter.

Mirage IIIC production amounted to 184 aircraft for France (95), Israel (72 IIICJ), Switzerland (1 IIICS for evaluation) and South Africa (16 IIICZ). Mirage IIIB two seaters were delivered from 1962 to France, Israel, the Lebanon, Switzerland and South Africa.

Photo: Israeli Mirage IIIC.

Dassault Mirage IIIE

Country of origin: France.

Type: Single seat interceptor and close support fighter.

Powerplant: One 9430lb (41.9kN) dry/13,670lb (60.1kN) with after-burner Snecma Atar 9C turbojet; optional 3307lb (14.7kN) SEPR 844 rocket booster engine.

Dimensions: Wing span 8.22m (26ft 11½in); length 15.03m (49ft 3½in); height 4.50m (14ft 9in); wing area 34.8m² (375sq ft).

Weights: Empty 7050kg (15,542lb); takeoff (clean) 9600kg (21,164lb); max takeoff 13,700kg (30,203lb).

Armament: Two 30mm cannon; one centreline and four underwing hardpoints for air-to-air missiles, air-to-surface missiles, bombs, rocket pods or fuel tanks; max external load 3992kg (8800lb).

Performance: Max speed 1263kt (Mach 2.2/2340km/h) at 39,400ft, 750kt (Mach 1.14/1389km/h) at sea level; cruising speed 517kt (957km/h) at 36,000ft; time to 36,000ft 3.0min; time to 49,200ft 6.8min; service ceiling (without rocket) 55,775ft; combat radius (ground attack) 647nm (1198km); max ferry range 2085nm (3862km).

Production: 1414 Mirage III/5/50 of all models including 51 IIID, 440 IIIE and variants, and 111 IIIR.

Notes: The Mirage's potential as a multirole combat aircraft was exploited with the IIIE, with more powerful Atar 9C engine, a slight fuselage stretch to accommodate a larger avionics bay, dual role Cyrano II radar, Marconi Doppler radar for night/bad weather low level navigation, increased fuel, new fire control system and navigation computer, and five external hardpoints for missiles, bombs, rocket pods and fuel tanks.

The result was a versatile fighter-bomber which found a large home and export market and was also built under licence.

The first IIIE was flown on 5 April 1961 and deliveries began in January 1964 to the Armée de l'Air, which eventually received 192. Other customers for Mirage IIIE variants were Argentina (17 IIIEA), Brazil (16 IIIEBR), Spain (24 IIIEE), Lebanon (10 IIIEL), Pakistan (18 IIIEP), Venezuela (10 IIIEV), South Africa (17 IIIEZ), Australia (100 IIIO), and Switzerland (36 IIIS).

Most of the Australian and Swiss aircraft were locally built while the Brazilian, South African and Swiss aircraft have been subject to upgrades including in most cases the fitting of canard foreplanes. The South African upgrades were performed by Atlas Aircraft and renamed the Cheetah.

Other Mirage IIIE variants were the two seat IIID purchased by Australia (16), Argentina (2), Brazil (6), Spain (6), Pakistan (5), Switzerland (2) and South Africa (14), while the camera equipped reconnaissance Mirage IIIR (first flight 31 October 1961) was delivered to France (72), Pakistan (13) Switzerland (18 locally assembled) and South Africa (8).

The one-off Mirage Milan ('Kite') with more powerful Atar 9K-50 and retractable foreplanes was converted from a IIIE and flown in 1969 but none of the proposed production model, the Milan S with upgraded nav/attack system and armament, was sold. Several other upgrades are offered.

Photo: RAAF Mirage IIIO.

Dassault Mirage 5 and 50

Country of origin: France.

Type: 5 – single seat ground attack and day fighter. 50 – multirole fighter.

Powerplant: 5 – one 9430lb (41.9kN) dry/13,670lb (60.1kN) with afterburner Snecma Atar 9C turbojet. 50 – one 11,055lb (49.2kN) dry/15,873lb (70.6kN) with afterburner Atar 9K-50.

Dimensions: Wing span 8.22m (26ft 11½in); length 15.56m (51ft 0½in); height 4.50m (14ft 9in); wing area 34.8m² (375sq ft).

Weights: 5 – empty 6600kg (14,550lb). 5/50 – max takeoff 13,700kg (30,203lb).

Armament: Two 30mm cannon; seven underfuselage and underwing hardpoints for up to 4000kg (8818lb) external ordnance and fuel tanks.

Performance: 5 – max speed 1263kt (Mach 2.2/2340km/h) at 39,400ft, 750kt (Mach 1.14/1389km/h) at sea level; combat radius with 907kg (2000lb) bomb load 700nm (1297km) hi-lo-hi or 350nm (648km) lo-lo-lo. 50 – speeds as M5; max climb 36,600ft (11,155m)/min; service ceiling 59,055ft; intercept combat radius 378nm (700km); combat radius with 800kg (1764lb) bomb load 370nm (685km) lo-lo-lo or 675nm (1250km) hi-lo-hi.

Production: 1414 Mirage III/5/50 of all models including 528 M5 and 12 M50; others converted.

Notes: Originally developed to meet an Israeli requirement, the Mirage 5 was a simplified day/clear weather ground attack fighter-bomber version of the IIIE with the Cyrano II radar and fire control system removed from a lengthened nose, two extra hardpoints fitted and additional fuel capacity.

Many later M5s had some IFR/all weather capability restored and a wide variety of equipment fit was installed in the different customers' aircraft including Cyrano IV, Agave or Aida lightweight radar. Those having a radar/avionics standard close to that of the Mirage IIIE were designated 5E.

Israel ordered 50 Mirage 5Js, the first of them flying on 19 May 1967. Despite being built and paid for, they were never delivered, French President Charles de Gaulle banning their export for political reasons. This action lead to IAI building its own unlicensed versions of the Mirage (see separate entries). The Mirage 5Js eventually found their way into French service as the Mirage 5F.

Other Mirage 5 variants were the two seat 5D and reconnaissance 5R, customers for the series comprising Abu Dhabi (29), Belgium (96, most locally assembled by SABCA), Colombia (18), Egypt (76), Gabon (7), Libya (100), Pakistan (60), Peru (37), Venezuela (4) and Zaire (17).

The Mirage 50 was the final version of the original delta winged Mirage line to achieve production. The converted prototype first flew on 15 April 1979, this variant featuring a more powerful Atar 9K-50 engine (thus the designation), multi function radar/fire control, system, upgraded cockpit/avionics and enhanced performance. Chile received six new build M50s in 1982-83 (plus six converted from ex Armée de l'Air 5Fs in 1980) and also upgraded earlier M5s to the new standard as the ENAER Pantera. Venezuela ordered six new M50s as well as converting 10 IIIEs and 5s. The Venezuelan M50s were the last of the line, delivered in 1991.

Photo: Venezuelan Mirage 50EV. (Dassault)

Dassault Mirage IV

Country of origin: France.

Type: Two seat strategic bomber.

Powerplants: Two 10,770lb (47.9kN) dry/14,770lb (65.7kN) with afterburner Snecma Atar 9K turbojets.

Dimensions: Wing span 11.85m (38ft 10½in); length 23.49m (77ft 1in); height 5.41m (17ft 9in); wing area 78.0m² (840sq ft).

Weights: Empty 14,500kg (31,966lb); max takeoff 33,475kg (73,798lb).

Armament: IVA – One AN-11 60kT nuclear free fall weapon semi recessed under fuselage or up to 16 454kg (1000lb) bombs under wings or four Martel ASMs. IV-P – ASMP nuclear supersonic standoff air-to-surface missile.

Performance: Max dash speed 1263kt (Mach 2.2/2338km/h) at 36,000ft; max sustained speed 1062kt (Mach 1.85/1965km/h) at 60,000ft; time to 39,090ft 4.3min; service ceiling 65,600ft; unrefuelled radius of action 669nm (1239km); ferry range with drop tanks 2160nm (4000km).

Production: 66.

Notes: In 1954, France decided to establish a nuclear deterrent of which a new strategic bomber would be a vital component. It was to be used as a launch platform for atomic weapons with the AN-11 60kT free fall bomb the basic unit.

Dassault was put in charge of the project in association with a number of other companies and examined several alternative proposals before settling on the Mirage IV as it finally emerged. These ranged from a development of the Sud Vautour to a new and much larger design powered by two Pratt & Whitney J75 turbojets and about the size of the Convair B-58 Hustler.

What finally emerged was a smaller Mach 2, twin engined delta winged bomber which looked like a scaled up Mirage III fighter. Powered by two Snecma Atar turbojets, the aircraft carried its nuclear weapon semi recessed under the fuselage.

The design evolved along with the precise requirement, the final version taking into account the development of aerial refuelling techniques. At best a medium range bomber even with external tanks, the Mirage IV relied on aerial refuelling to achieve the ability to attack targets in the Soviet Union and return. The Armée de l'Air took delivery of Boeing KC-135F tankers to support the bombers.

The prototype Mirage IVA first flew on 17 June 1959 and the first of three pre-production aircraft on 12 October 1961. The first production version flew on 23 January 1963 and 62 were delivered to the Armée de l'Air in 1964-68.

The Mirage IV was subject to several upgrades during its career including 12 aircraft modified to carry a strategic reconnaissance pod. A more substantial upgrade to 18 aircraft which enabled them to carry the ASMP standoff nuclear missile was carried out in 1983-87, modified aircraft redesignated the Mirage IV-P. The last Mirage IV strategic bomber unit was disbanded in July 1988 and in 1996 all but five of the IV-Ps were retired, the suitably equipped survivors flying strategic reconnaissance missions into the 21st century.

Photo: Mirage IVP.

Dassault Mirage F1

Country of origin: France.

Type: Single seat multirole fighter.

Powerplant: One 11,023lb (49.0kN) dry/15,873lb (70.6kN) with afterburner Snecma Atar 9K-50 turbojet.

Dimensions: Wing span 8.40m (27ft 7in); length 15.30m (50ft 2½in); height 4.50m (14ft 9in); wing area 25.0m² (269sq ft).

Weights: F1C – empty 7400kg (16,314lb); takeoff (clean) 10,900kg (24,030lb); max takeoff 16,200kg (35,714lb).

Armament: Two 30mm cannon; four underwing, one centreline and two wingtip pylons for max 6100kg (13,448lb) load of AAMs, ASMs, rocket pods, bombs and fuel tanks.

Performance: Max speed 1263kt (Mach 2.2/2338km/h) at 39,400ft, 792kt (Mach 1.2/1468km/h) at sea level; max climb 41,930ft (12,780m)/min; service ceiling 65,600ft; combat radius with 3500kg (7716lb) bomb load 230nm (426km); combat radius with one Exocet ASM and drop tanks 378nm (700km); combat air patrol endurance 2.25hrs; max ferry range 1781nm (3300km).

Production: 731.

Notes: Developed from 1964 in parallel with the larger Mirage F2 tandem two seat all weather fighter (flown in prototype form only in December 1966), the single seat and scaled down F1 was selected as a replacement for the Armée de l'Air's Mirage IIIC interceptors.

The F1 was substantially different from previous Mirages, dispensing with the familiar delta wing and replacing it with a conventional swept wing and tail surfaces. Incorporating numerous high lift devices, the F1 provided lower approach speeds and therefore much better airfield performance than its predecessor.

Increased fuel capacity, more powerful Atar 9K engine, enhanced manoeuvrability, upgraded weapons and improved radar completed the package.

Originally developed as a private venture, the prototype first flew on 23 December 1966. Official backing followed with three pre-series aircraft ordered in September 1967, the first of these flying on 20 March 1969. The first production F1C basic interceptor version flew in February 1973.

Like the Mirage III before it, the F1 was developed into several versions: the F1A simplified ground attack version lacking radar, F1E multirole air superiority/ground attack; F1B two seat operational trainer (first flight 26 May 1976); F1C-200 with aerial refuelling probe (some new build and some converted); F1CT (55 French F1Cs modified for ground attack from 1991); F1D two seater based on the F1E; and F1CR-200 reconnaissance version.

Like its predecessor, the Mirage F1 found a ready export market with sales to Ecuador, Greece, Iraq, Jordan, Kuwait, Libya, Morocco, Qatar, Spain and South Africa. France received 164 F1C/F1C-200s, 64 F1CRs and 20 F1Bs.

One was flown with an 18,740lb (83.3kN) thrust with afterburner Snecma M53 turbofan in December 1974 as the F1.M53, this developed for the contract to replace the F-104G Starfighter in Belgian, Danish, Norwegian and Dutch service but won by the General Dynamics F-16. Mirage F1 production ended in 1990.

Photo: Mirage F1CR. (Thomson-CSF)

Dassault Mirage 2000C/E

Country of origin: France.

Type: Single seat multirole fighter.

Powerplant: One 12,235lb (54.5kN) dry/19,840lb (88.2kN) with afterburner Snecma M53-5; 14,400lb (64.0kN) dry/21,400lb (95.2kN) with afterburner M53-P2; or 22,050lb (98.1kN) with afterburner M53-P20 turbofan.

Dimensions: Wing span 9.13m (29ft 11^1/$_2$in); length 14.36m (47ft 1^1/$_2$in); height 5.21m (17ft 1in); wing area 41.0m^2 (441sq ft).

Weights: Empty 7500kg (16,534lb); typical combat 9525kg (21,000lb); max takeoff 17,000kg (37,478lb).

Armament: Two 30mm cannon in lower fuselage; four underwing and five underfuselage hardpoints for max 6300kg (13,889lb) stores including Matra Magic 2 and Super 530D AAMs, laser guided and conventional bombs, AS 30L, Armat and Exocet ASMs, fuel tanks etc.

Performance: Max speed 1347kt (Mach 2.35/2495km/h) at 39,370ft, 792kt (Mach 1.23/1467km/h) at sea level; max initial climb 56,000ft (17,070m)/min; climb to 49,000ft 4.0min; operational ceiling 58,000-60,000ft; intercept mission combat radius 435nm (805km); range with 1000kg (2205lb) bomb load 837nm (1550km); max ferry range 1900nm (3519km).

Production: Over 500 Mirage 2000s of all models by 2000.

Notes: Dassault returned to the delta wing for the Mirage 2000, although it had nothing in common with the original Mirage III/5/50 series. New technology enabled most of the earlier aircraft's performance and handling disadvantages (high approach speeds, poor airfield performance and manoeuvrability penalties) to be overcome, the Mirage 2000 incorporating a high power-to-weight ratio, advanced aerodynamics, leading edge slats and fly-by-wire controls.

Composites were used in parts of the structure and power was provided by a Snecma M53 turbofan. The latest technology was incorporated in the 2000's radar, weapons systems and cockpit displays.

The Mirage 2000 was selected to become the Armée de l'Air's new single seat interceptor and air superiority fighter in December 1975, the first of four prototypes flying on 10 March 1978. A fifth prototype – the Mirage 2000B company funded two seat operational trainer version – first flew on 11 October 1980 and was later also ordered by the Armée de l'Air.

The first of 136 production Mirage 2000Cs for the Armée de l'Air flew on 20 November 1982 and operational capability was achieved in July 1984. The first 37 2000Cs were powered by an M53-5 engine; subsequent aircraft had the more powerful M53-P2.

Other single seat Mirage 2000 variants are the 2000E multirole export version (first delivery 1984) and its 2000ED two seater equivalent; 2000R with reconnaissance pod; 2000-3 upgrade (first flight March 1988) with Rafale type cockpit; and the multirole 2000-5 (first flight October 1994) with further enhanced radar, cockpit and systems. Thirty-seven French Mirage 2000Cs were upgraded to -5 standards from 1997 while new aircraft have been ordered for export.

Apart from France, single seat Mirage 2000s have been ordered by Abu Dhabi, Egypt, Greece, India, Peru, Taiwan and Qatar.

Photo: Mirage 2000-5. (Dassault)

Dassault Mirage 2000D/N

Country of origin: France.

Type: 2000N – two seat low altitude nuclear strike. 2000D – all weather strike.

Powerplant: One 14,400lb (64.0kN) dry/21,400lb (95.2kN) with afterburner Snecma M53-P2 or 22,050lb (98.1kN) with afterburner M53-P20 turbofan.

Dimensions: Wing span 9.13m (29ft 11^1/$_2$in); length 14.55m (47ft 9in); height 5.16m (16ft 11in); wing area 41.0m^2 (441sq ft).

Weights: 2000D – empty 7600kg (16,755lb); max takeoff 17,000kg (37,478lb).

Armament: 2000D – four underwing and five underfuselage hardpoints for max 6300kg (13,889lb) ordnance including laser guided and conventional bombs, air-to-ground and anti ship missiles, defensive air-to-air missiles, 30mm cannon pods, cluster bombs etc. 2000N – typically one Aerospatiale ASMP 150kT or 300kT standoff guided nuclear missile plus two Magic AAMs.

Performance: 2000D – max speed over 1263kt (Mach 2.2/2338km/h) at 39,370ft, 792kt (Mach 1.23/1467km/h) at sea level; low level penetration speed 600kt (1110km/h) combat radius with two Magic AAMs, 1000kg (2205lb) ordnance and drop tanks 648nm (1200km); max ferry range 1900nm (3519km).

Production: Over 500 Mirage 2000s of all models by 2000.

Notes: Investigations into the development of two seat strike versions of the Mirage 2000 began in the mid 1970s as the Armée de l'Air began thinking about finding a replacement for the Mirage IV nuclear bomber. Dassault received a contract to build a nuclear attack version of the 2000 in 1979 under the designation 2000P (for *Pénétration*), this subsequently changed to 2000N (*Nucléaire*) to better reflect its role.

Based on the two seat Mirage 2000B conversion trainer, the 2000N's airframe differs mainly in being strengthened for low level operations but its avionics suite is substantially changed. Its key element is the Dassault/Thomson-CSF Antilope V radar with terrain following, ground mapping, navigation, air-to-sea and air-to-air modes. Primary weapon is the ASMP standoff guided nuclear missile carried on the centreline with two Magic AAMs on the wingtips for self defence also usually carried. No internal gun is fitted and two subvariants were produced: the nuclear only 2000N-K1 and nuclear and conventional weapons capable K2.

The Armée de l'Air ordered 75 Mirage 2000Ns, the first of which was flown on 3 February 1983 with initial delivery in January 1987.

The Mirage 2000D (*Diversifie*) is similar to the 2000N-K2 expect that it can only carry conventional weapons and is dedicated to all weather day and night air-to-surface attack. The Antilope V terrain following radar is retained, this allowing automatic flight down to a height of 300ft and a speed of up to 600kt (1110km/h). Like the 2000N, no fixed gun is fitted but 30mm cannon pods can be installed along with a wide variety of air-to-air and air-to-ground ordnance on the four underwing and five underfuselage pylons.

The first Mirage 2000D flew on 19 February 1991 against French orders for 86 with deliveries beginning in July 1993. An export version – the Mirage 2000S (for 'strike') – with a flight refuelling probe was offered but by 1999 was no longer being marketed.

Photo: Mirage 2000N. (Armée de l'Air)

Dassault Rafale

Country of origin: France.

Type: Single (Rafale C/M) or two seat (B) multirole fighter.

Powerplant: Two 11,250lb (50.0kN) dry/16,850lb (74.9kN) with afterburner Snecma M88-2 turbofans.

Dimensions: Wing span 10.79m (35ft 5in); length 15.30m (50ft 2¹/₂in); height 5.33m (17ft 6in); wing area 45.7m² (492sq ft).

Weights: C – empty 9060kg (19,974lb); max takeoff 19,500kg (42,989lb). M – empty 9670kg (21,318lb); max takeoff 19,500kg (42,989lb).

Armament: B/C – one internal 30mm cannon; 14 hardpoints (six underwing, two wingtip, six underfuselage) for max 8000kg (17,637lb) ordnance including AAMs, AGMs, ASMs, ASMP nuclear standoff missile, laser guided and conventional bombs, weapons dispensers, recce/ECM pods, fuel tanks etc. M – 13 hardpoints.

Performance: C – Max speed 1148kt (Mach 2.0/2126km/h) above 36,000ft, 750kt (Mach 1.13/1390km/h) at low level; max climb 60,000ft (18,288m)/min; operational ceiling 55,000ft; low altitude combat radius with 3000kg (6614lb) bomb load 800nm (1480km).

Production: French requirement for 95 Rafale C and 139 Rafale B (Armée de l'Air) plus 86 Rafale M (Aéronavale); 61 production aircraft funded by 2000.

Notes: Development of an advanced multirole fighter for the French military in both land based and naval forms began in April 1983 with the decision to build a technology demonstrator called the *Avions de Combat Experimental* (ACX). The aircraft featured a compound sweep delta wing, foreplanes, digital fly-by-wire controls and extensive use of airframe composites.

Subsequently named Rafale A ('Squall'), the ACX first flew on 4 July 1986, initially powered by two General Electric F404-GE-400 turbofans. Production Rafales would be powered by the new Snecma M88 turbofan, the prototype first flying with one of these engines in the port engine bay in February 1990.

Definitive Rafales are slightly smaller than the ACX prototype, have larger foreplanes and some structural composites replaced with superplastic formed diffusion bonded titanium. Design features include a blended fuselage/wing, fully integrated internal early warning system, Thomson-CSF RBE2 electronic scanning multi function radar, LCD cockpit displays, side stick controller, helmet mounted sight, voice controls, HUD and infrared, television and laser rangefinder optronics.

Three basic versions have been developed: Rafale C single seater (first flight 19 May 1991) and Rafale B two seater with full operational capabilities (first flight 30 April 1993) for the Armée de l'Air; and navalised single seat Rafale M (first flight 12 December 1991) for operation from the Aéronavale's new carrier, the *Charles de Gaulle*. The generic designation Rafale D is used to cover both Armée de l'Air versions. The first production Rafale (a B) flew in November 1998.

By early 2000, contracts covering 61 production Rafales had been signed against an overall French requirement for 95 Cs, 139 Bs and 86 Ms. The Rafale M is scheduled to enter regular Aéronavale service in 2001 with Armée de l'Air service starting two years later.

Photo: The first Rafale C. (Dassault)

Dassault-Breguet Atlantic

Country of origin: France.

Type: 10-12 crew maritime patrol and anti submarine warfare.

Powerplants: Two 6100ehp (4549kW) Rolls-Royce Tyne RTy.20 Mk.21 turboprops; four bladed propellers.

Dimensions: Wing span (over tip pods) 37.46m (122ft 11in); length 31.72m (104ft 1in); height 11.33m (37ft 2in); wing area 120.3m² (1295sq ft).

Weights: ATL1/2 – empty equipped 25,300-25,700kg (55,776-56,658lb); typical mission weight 44,200kg (97,443lb); max takeoff 46,200kg (101,852lb).

Armament: Internal weapons bay for up to eight torpedoes, air-sea rescue containers, depth charges and bombs or (ATL2 only) two Exocet or Martel ASMs; four underwing hardpoints for ASMs and AAMs.

Performance: ATL1/2 – max speed 350kt (648km/h); cruising speed 300kt (556km/h); patrol speed 169kt (313km/h); initial climb 2000ft (610m)/min; service ceiling 30,000ft; max range 4200nm (7780km); max endurance 18hrs.

Production: 91 ATL1 (including prototypes) and 28 ATL2.

Notes: Designed to meet a 1958 NATO requirement to find a replacement for the Lockheed P-2 Neptune in the service of various European countries, the Breguet Br.1150 won the ensuing contest against 24 designs submitted by manufacturers from nine countries.

Named the Atlantic, the aircraft was the first completely multi national combat aircraft, the manufacturing consortium led by Dassault and Breguet (who merged in 1971) and comprising Sud-Aviation (later part of Aerospatiale), Belgium's ABAP (Fairey, SABCA and FN), Germany's Dornier, the Netherlands' Fokker and Italy's Aeritalia. The Tyne engines were built by Rolls-Royce, France's Snecma and Germany's MAN.

Design features include a double bubble fuselage with the lower, unpressurised section containing a weapons bay. The first of two prototypes flew on 21 October 1961 and the first of two pre-production aircraft (with lengthened fuselage) on 25 February 1963. Eighty-seven production Atlantics were built, delivered to France (40), Germany (20), the Netherlands (9) and Italy (18) in two batches between December 1965 and July 1974. Four (plus two for spares) ex French Atlantics were delivered to Pakistan in the mid 1970s.

Development of the second generation Atlantique 2 (ATL2 – originally ANG for *Atlantique Nouvelle Generation*) began in September 1978, this featuring modernised avionics and systems including a Thomson-CSF Iguane radar, pod mounted FLIR in the nose, a new magnetic anomaly detector (MAD) system, new ESM suite, processors and other equipment.

The first ATL2 (converted from an earlier aircraft) was flown 8 May 1981 and the first true ATL2 on 19 October 1988. Twenty-eight were ordered by France with deliveries beginning in October 1989 and ending in 1998. The proposed Atlantique 3 features Allison AE2100H engines driving advanced six bladed propellers, a two crew EFIS cockpit and further upgraded systems, avionics and weapons capability.

Photo: Atlantique 2. (Dassault)

de Havilland Vampire 1 and 3

Country of origin: United Kingdom.

Type: Single seat fighter.

Powerplant: One 3100lb (13.8kN) de Havilland Goblin 2 turbojet.

Dimensions: Wing span 12.19m (40ft 0in); length 9.37m (30ft 9in); height 2.69m (8ft 10in); wing area 24.7m² (266sq ft).

Weights: F.1 – empty 2890kg (6372lb); max takeoff 4754kg (10,480lb). F.3 – empty 3236kg (7134lb); max takeoff 5430kg (11,970lb).

Armament: Four 20mm cannon in lower nose.

Performance: F.1 – max speed 469kt (869km/h) at sea level, 443kt (821km/h) at 31,000ft; range 634nm (1174km). F.3 – max speed 461kt (855km/h) at sea level, 439kt (813km/h) at 30,000ft; initial climb 4375ft (1333m)/min; service ceiling 43,500ft; max range 995nm (1843km).

Production: 2957 single seat Vampires of all models including 3 prototypes, 249 F.1, 206 F.3 and 30 Sea Vampire F.20.

Notes: Britain's second operational jet fighter (after the Meteor), the Vampire was built to Specification E.6/41 around the de Havilland H.1 (later Goblin) centrifugal flow turbojet designed by Major Frank Halford.

It went on to form the basis of a long line of fighters sharing a distinctive twin tailboom configuration, the numerous Vampire variants becoming the most produced of all British post war combat aircraft (over 4000) and exported widely. Initially nicknamed 'Spider Crab', the compact Vampire featured a fuselage 'pod' constructed of plywood and balsa like the Mosquito.

The first of three prototypes flew on 20 September 1943, the Vampire quickly becoming the first Allied aircraft to exceed 500mph (805km/h) in level flight. The first production order was placed in May 1944 and manufacture was entrusted to English Electric as de Havilland was fully occupied with Mosquitos. The first production Vampire F.I (later F.1 when Arabic numerals were applied to British military aircraft designations) flew on 20 April 1945, less than three weeks before the war in Europe ended.

The RAF received 174 and regular service began in April 1946 with No 247 Squadron (replacing Hawker Tempests) and exports were made to Sweden (70) and Switzerland (4 for evaluation), this leading to licence production of later models. France acquired 30 ex RAF Vampire 1s from late 1948 and Dominica obtained 25 from Sweden in 1952. Canada received a single example.

The Vampire F.III (later F.3) differed in having rounded rather than square vertical tail surfaces, a lowered tailplane, increased internal fuel capacity and the ability to carry drop tanks. First flown on 4 November 1946, the F.3 was also built by English Electric and supplied to the RAF (117) and Canada (85) while Mexico bought 15 from Canada in 1961.

The suitably modified second prototype Vampire made history on 3 December 1945 when it performed the world's first operations from an aircraft carrier (HMS *Ocean*) by a jet aircraft. Successful trials by other fully navalised Vampires led to an order for 30 Sea Vampire F.20s from the RN Fleet Air Arm with clipped wings, larger dive brakes and longer stroke undercarriage. The F.20's airframe was based on the Vampire FB.5 (see separate entry) and the first example flew in October 1948.

Photo: Vampire F.3. (Paul Merritt)

de Havilland Nene-Vampire

Countries of origin: United Kingdom (F.2), Australia (F.30/FB.31) and France (Mistral).

Type: Single seat fighter-bomber.

Powerplant: FB.30/31 – one 5000lb (22.2kN) CAC (Rolls-Royce) Nene 2-VH turbojet. Mistral – one 5000lb (22.2kN) Hispano-Suiza (Rolls-Royce) Nene 104.

Dimensions: FB.31/Mistral – wing span 11.58m (38ft 0in); length 9.37m (30ft 9in); height 2.69m (8ft 10in); wing area 24.3m² (262sq ft). F.30 – wing span 12.19m (40ft 0in); area 24.7m² (266sq ft).

Weights: FB.31 – empty 3447kg (7600lb); max takeoff 4990kg (11,000lb). Mistral – empty 3480kg (7672lb); max takeoff 4960kg (10,935lb).

Armament: FB.31/Mistral – four 20mm cannon in lower nose; max 907kg (2000lb) ordnance under wings. F.30 – guns only.

Performance: FB.31 – max speed 495kt (917km/h) at sea level, 476kt (882km/h) at 30,000ft; initial climb 4800ft (1463m)/min; service ceiling 43,000ft; normal range 684nm (1267km). Mistral – max speed 500kt (925km/h) at sea level, 484kt (896km/h) at 20,000ft; initial climb 7087ft (2160m)/min; service ceiling 49,210ft.

Production: 2957 single seat Vampires including: UK – 3 F.2; Australia – 57 F.30 and 23 FB.31 by DHA; France – 250 Mistral by SNCASE (Sud-Est).

Notes: Three early production Vampire F.1 airframes were completed as F.2s with the standard de Havilland Goblin turbojet replaced with a larger and more powerful Rolls-Royce Nene 1 producing 4500lb (20.0kN) thrust. The first example flew on 6 March 1946 and was subsequently fitted with a pair of upper fuselage 'elephant ears' intakes to help meet the Nene's greater appetite for air. None were ordered for the RAF, the aircraft were used for trials with one going to each of France and Australia preliminary to local licence production.

Production of the Australian Nene-Vampire was undertaken by de Havilland Aircraft, the company building 80 for the RAAF with Nenes built in Australia by the Commonwealth Aircraft Corporation (CAC). The first of 57 F.30 fighters with gun armament only was flown on 29 June 1949 and a further 23 were built as FB.31 fighter-bombers with strengthened undercarriage and stronger clipped wings capable of carrying ordnance. The first was delivered in July 1952 and the last in August 1953. Twenty-four F.30s were converted to FB.31s in 1955-56.

The Australians expended considerable effort attempting to improve intake air flow to the Nene including experimenting with enlarged and rerouted main (wing root) intakes. The 'elephant ears' intakes were finally moved from above to below the fuselage.

Like Australia, France received Vampires from both British production and its own assembly lines, Sud-Est building 250 Nene-Vampires as the Mistral. Powered by a Hispano built Nene, the first of them flew on 1 April 1951 with series production beginning in December of the same year. The last was delivered in March 1954.

Sud-Est solved the air intake problem by enlarging the wing root intakes and adapting the split trunk intake design of the Hawker P.1040 Sea Hawk to the Vampire. Mistrals also had increased fuel capacity and a pressurised cockpit.

Photo: Vampire F2.

de Havilland Vampire FB.5/6/9

Country of origin: United Kingdom.

Type: Single seat fighter bomber.

Powerplant: FB.5 – one 3100lb (13.8kN) de Havilland Goblin 2 or 3350lb (14.9kN) Goblin 3 turbojet. FB.6/9 – Goblin 3.

Dimensions: Wing span 11.58m (38ft 0in); length 9.37m (30ft 9in); height 2.69m (8ft 10in); wing area 24.3m² (262sq ft).

Weights: FB.5 – empty 3290kg (7253lb); max takeoff 5606kg (12,360lb). FB.9 – empty 3303kg (7283lb); max takeoff 5620kg (12,390lb).

Performance: FB.5 – max speed 461kt (853km/h) at sea level, 419kt (776km/h) at 30,000ft; cruising speed 304kt (563km/h); max climb 4050ft (1234m)/min; service ceiling 40,000ft; max range 1017nm (1883km). FB.9 – max speed 476kt (882km/h) at sea level; max climb 4800ft (1463m)/min; max range 1060nm (1964km).

Armament: Four 20mm cannon in lower nose; max 907kg (2000lb) ordnance under wings.

Production: 2957 single seat Vampires of all models including 1656 FB.5s (by de Havilland, English Electric, Fiat/Macchi, SNCASE and HAL); 100 FB.6 (by FFA); and 381 FB.9 (by de Havilland).

Notes: De Havilland continued development of the single seat Vampire with the FB.5 fighter-bomber, this based on the Goblin 2 powered F.3 but with clipped and strengthened wings capable of carrying up to 907kg (2000lb) ordnance, increased maximum weight and a longer stroke undercarriage.

The first Vampire FB.5 flew on 23 June 1948 against orders for 888 from the RAF, these built mainly by English Electric but with contributions from de Havilland's Chester and Hatfield factories.

RAF service began in December 1948, the FB.5 serving with more than 30 home and overseas based squadrons including with the 2nd Tactical Air Force in Germany and in Malaya, where its bombs and rockets were used with good effect against communist terrorists.

The FB.5 was also widely exported, these aircraft usually fitted with the more powerful Goblin 3 engine and sold to New Zealand, Norway, Egypt, Finland, India, Iraq and Venezuela from British production. Licence production (under the designation FB.50) was also undertaken in Italy by Fiat/Macchi (80), India by Hindustan Aeronautics (281) and France by Sud-Est (67 from British components and 183 from local resources).

The designation Vampire FB.6 was applied to 100 similar aircraft built under licence in Switzerland by FFA.

The final single seat Vampire for the RAF was the FB.9, a developed version of the Goblin 3 powered FB.5 but intended for service in the Far East and therefore fitted with cockpit air conditioning. It entered service in January 1952 and 381 were delivered, these flying with front line units until 1956 when they had been replaced by Venoms. In the meantime, the Vampire FB.9 had been used in action against the Mau Mau terrorists in Kenya.

Other Vampire fighter-bomber operators were Dominica (17 ex Swedish FB.50s in 1956) while ex RAF FB.9s were obtained by Ceylon, Jordan and Rhodesia.

Photo: Vampire FB.9.

de Havilland Vampire NF.10

Country of origin: United Kingdom.

Type: Two seat night fighter.

Powerplant: One 3350lb (14.9kN) de Havilland Goblin 3 turbojet.

Dimensions: Wing span 11.58m (38ft 0in); length 10.54m (34ft 7in); height 2.69m (8ft 10in); wing area 24.3m² (262sq ft).

Weights: Empty 3168kg (6984lb); max takeoff 5942kg (13,100lb).

Armament: Four 20mm cannon in lower nose.

Performance: Max speed 467kt (866km/h) at sea level; initial climb 4500ft (1372m)/min; service ceiling 40,000ft; max range 1060nm (1964km).

Production: 78 by de Havilland.

Notes: Considering de Havilland's history of developing numerous sub variants of many of its designs – notably the Mosquito – it was probably inevitable that the Vampire would be further developed from the basic single seat fighter-bomber into two seat night fighter (and trainer) versions. The first such variant was the DH.113 Vampire Night Fighter, developed as a private venture and sold in modest numbers to the RAF as the Vampire NF.10 and for export as the NF.54.

Powered by the same 3350lb (14.9kN) Goblin 3 which was fitted to the single seat Vampire FB.9 and armed only with the standard four 20mm cannon in the lower nose, the NF.10 incorporated a side-by-side two seat cockpit based on that of the Mosquito NF.36 night fighter grafted onto the fuselage pod. An enlarged nose housed AI (airborne intercept) Mk.10 radar, a pair of drop tanks could be carried under the wings and like all other Vampires produced thus far, no ejection seats were fitted.

The first of two civil registered prototypes flew on 28 August 1949 and although the RAF showed no interest at this stage, Egypt did and ordered 12 examples in October 1949. Unfortunately for de Havilland, the British Government then placed an embargo on military sales to Egypt but rescued the situation by ordering the type as an interim night fighter whilst awaiting delivery of Meteors and Venoms for that role.

The first production Vampire NF.10 flew in February 1951 and entered RAF service five months later, eventually equipping three squadrons. When it entered service, the NF.10 was the first jet night fighter to fly with a Western air force. It was replaced as a front line aircraft in the RAF within three years but refurbished examples were supplied to India (29) and Italy (14). One also went to Switzerland for use as a test bed for the systems and equipment which would be used on the Venoms built under licence by the EFW consortium.

The two seat DH.115 Vampire Trainer was a direct development of the NF.10 with radar removed but gun armament retained plus the ability to carry underwing ordnance so as to perform a wide variety of flying and weapons training duties. The first Vampire Trainer flew on 15 November 1950 (also as a private venture) and it went on to become very successful with 1022 built for the RAF and 20 other nations including licence production in Australia and India.. The last new Vampire of any version was a Trainer delivered to Austria in 1961.

Photo: Italian Vampire NF.54.

de Havilland Hornet

Country of origin: United Kingdom.

Type: Single seat fighter-bomber.

Powerplants: Two 2070hp (1544kW) Rolls-Royce Merlin 130/131 V12 piston engines; four bladed propellers.

Dimensions: Wing span 13.72m (45ft 0in); length 11.18m (36ft 8in); height 4.32m (14ft 2in); wing area 33.5m² (361sq ft).

Weights: F.1 – empty 5671kg (12,502lb); max takeoff 8029kg (17,700lb). F.3 – empty 5842kg (12,880lb); max takeoff 9553kg (21,060lb).

Armament: F.1 – four 20mm cannon in nose. F.3 – guns plus provision for two 454kg (1000lb) bombs or eight 27kg (60lb) rockets under wings.

Performance: F.3 – max speed 410kt (759km/h) at 22,000ft, 341kt (632km/h) at sea level; initial climb 4650ft (1417m)/min; service ceiling 37,500ft; max range 2260nm (4185km).

Production: 391 Hornets and Sea Hornets of all models including 2 Hornet prototypes, 60 F.1, 5 PR.2, 132 F.3 and 12 F.4.

Notes: De Havilland began design of the DH.103 Hornet twin engined and high performance single seat strike fighter in 1942 as a private venture, taking advantage of experience gained on the Mosquito. As before, the fuselage was constructed of wood but the wing was of mixed wood/metal construction which pioneered the use of Redux bonding. Other features included 'handed' Merlin 130/131 engines (to nullify the effects of torque on takeoff) in low drag cowlings and wing leading edge radiators.

Unlike the Mosquito, the company did not have to struggle to gain official acceptance of the Hornet and Specification F.12/43 was written around it in 1943, this covering the construction of two prototypes. The first of these flew on 28 July 1944 and quickly proved itself to be a very fast aircraft with a top speed of 485mph (780km/h), notably faster than the early Gloster Meteor jets. Production versions were only slightly slower.

The Hornet was intended as a long range fighter for use in the Pacific War, but deliveries of 60 production Hornet F.1s for the RAF began in early 1946, too late to see action in that conflict. Four RAF Fighter Command squadrons were eventually equipped with the aircraft.

The major production variant was the Hornet F.3 with a dorsal fin for improved directional stability, increased fuel capacity and wing hardpoints for the carriage of various items of ordnance including two 454kg (1000lb) bombs or eight air-to-ground rocket projectiles. The F.3 entered service later in 1946.

Other variants were the PR.2 unarmed photo-reconnaissance version (which did not enter service) and the armed F.4 with a vertical camera in the fuselage.

The Hornet was removed from Fighter Command service in 1951-52 and joined three Far Eastern Air Force squadrons in Malaya, replacing Spitfires and Beaufighters on ground attack duties in the campaign against communist terrorists. The last piston engined fighter-bomber in RAF service, the Hornet was replaced by Vampires in 1956.

Photo: Hornet F.1.

de Havilland Sea Hornet

Country of origin: United Kingdom.

Type: F.20 – single seat naval fighter-bomber. NF.21 – two seat naval night fighter.

Powerplants: F.20 – two 2070hp (1544kW) Rolls-Royce Merlin 130/131 V12 piston engines. NF.21 – two 2030hp (1514kW) Merlin 133/134; four bladed propellers.

Dimensions: F.20 – wing span 13.72m (45ft 0in); length 11.17m (36ft 8in); height 4.32m (14ft 2in); wing area 33.5m² (361sq ft). NF.21 – length 11.28m (37ft 0in).

Weights: F.20 – empty 5307kg (11,700lb); max takeoff 8066kg (17,782lb). NF.21 – empty 6455kg (14,230lb); max takeoff 8859kg (19,530lb).

Armament: Four 20mm cannon in lower nose; provision for 907kg (2000lb) underwing ordnance including two 454kg (1000lb) bombs and eight 27kg (60lb) rockets.

Performance: NF.21 – max speed 373kt (692km/h) at 22,000ft, 317kt (587km/h) at sea level; initial climb 4400ft (1341m)/min; service ceiling 36,500ft; range 1303nm (2414km).

Production: 391 Hornets and Sea Hornets of all models including 79 Sea Hornet F.20, 78 NF.21 and 23 PR.22.

Notes: The Royal Navy's first twin engined, long range strike fighter, the Sea Hornet was developed to meet Specification N.5/44 for a carrier based version of the RAF's Hornet F.3. Two of these were converted to prototypes for the Sea Hornet by Heston Aircraft, modifications incorporated including V-frame arrester hooks, catapult pickup points, high drag flaps and modified longer stroke undercarriage.

The first prototype flew on 19 April 1945 and a third prototype conversion featured powered folding wings. This aircraft began carrier trials aboard HMS *Ocean* in August 1945.

The first of 79 production Sea Hornet F.20s flew on 13 August 1946 but only one operational unit operated the aircraft, No 801 Squadron from June 1947. Most Sea Hornet F.20s were operated in evaluation, training and other secondary roles. The unarmed PR.22 photographic-reconnaissance variant was equipped with cameras for both day and night photography.

The only other Sea Hornet variant was the NF.21, developed to meet an urgent Fleet Air Arm requirement for a radar equipped, carrier based night fighter. The NF.21 differed from the F.20 in having Merlin 133/134 engines and ASH radar mounted in a 'thimble' nose radome. Unlike its predecessor, the NF.21 was a two seater with an observer/radar operator accommodated in a centre fuselage cockpit under a small perspex canopy. Armament was the same as the F.20, including the provision for external ordnance.

Design of the NF.21 was undertaken largely by Heston Aircraft and the prototype with fixed wings first flew on 9 July 1946. The second NF.21 had folding wings. The first production aircraft was flown on 24 March 1948 and operational service began in January 1949 but only one front line RN Fleet Air Arm squadron (No 809) flew the aircraft until 1954 when it was disbanded. Operations were restricted by difficulties which arose when the aircraft was deployed at sea. Service with second line and training units continued until late 1955.

Photo: Sea Hornet F.20. (DoD)

de Havilland Venom FB.1/4

Country of origin: United Kingdom.

Type: Single seat fighter-bomber.

Powerplant: FB.1/50 – one 4850lb (21.6kN) de Havilland Ghost 103 turbojet. FB.4 – one 5150lb (22.9kN) Ghost 105.

Dimensions: Wing span 12.70m (41ft 8in); length 10.06m (33ft 0in); wing area 26.0m² (280sq ft).

Weights: FB.4 – empty 3674kg (8100lb); max takeoff 6945kg (15,310lb).

Armament: Four 20mm cannon in lower nose; two 454kg (1000lb) bombs or eight 27kg (60lb) rockets under wings.

Performance: FB.4 – max speed 519kt (961km/h) at sea level, 484kt (896km/h) at 30,000ft; initial climb 7230ft (2204m)/min; service ceiling 48,000ft; range 934nm (1730km).

Production: 816 single seat Venoms of all versions comprising 2 DH.112 prototypes; 475 FB.1 by de Havilland (375) and EFW (100); 322 FB.4 by de Havilland (172) and EFW (150); and 17 FB.50 (by de Havilland).

Notes: Originally known as the Vampire Mk.8, the DH.112 Venom was a direct development of the earlier aircraft with the more powerful de Havilland Ghost engine, a new thinner and slightly swept back wing of greater area, and additional fuel housed in removable (but non jettisonable) tip tanks.

Armament remained as before and performance was notably improved. The wing root engine intakes were modified to provide the greater volume of air required by the Ghost and the rear of the fuselage pod was slightly reshaped to accommodate the larger engine tailpipe.

The prototype first flew on 2 September 1949 and the first of 375 Venom FB.1s for the RAF in June 1951. Regular squadron service began in August 1952, the date delayed while some aerodynamic problems were sorted out. Early aircraft lacked an ejection seat but these were fitted to later models. Initial plans called for the Venom to be built by both de Havilland and Bristol but order cancellations resulted in them being manufactured only by the parent company in Britain.

Production switched to the Venom FB.4 in 1954, this version featuring the more powerful Ghost 105, powered ailerons, provision for underwing drop tanks and redesigned vertical tail surfaces with flat rather than pointed tops. The first FB.4 flew on 29 December 1953 and the delivery of 150 to the RAF began in May 1954.

Most RAF Venom squadrons were based overseas including in West Germany and the Middle East, the latter seeing action during the Suez crisis of 1956 and in Yemen the following year. RAF Venom squadrons also took part in operations against communist terrorists in Malaya as did Royal New Zealand Air Force crews using aircraft leased from the RAF.

The Venom was also exported to Venezuela (22 FB.4s in 1955-56), Italy (two FB.50s) and Iraq (15 FB.50s) while the EFW consortium in Switzerland built 100 Venom FB.1s and 150 FB.4s under licence for the Swiss Air Force from 1953. The last of these was not retired until 1983 after three decades' service.

Photo: Swiss Venom FB.50.

de Havilland Venom NF.2/3

Country of origin: United Kingdom.

Type: Two seat night fighter.

Powerplant: NF.2 – one 4950lb (22.0kN) de Havilland Ghost 104 turbojet. NF.3 – one 5150lb (22.9kN) Ghost 105.

Dimensions: NF.3 – wing span 13.05m (42ft 10in); length 11.17m (36ft 8in); height 2.59m (8ft 6in); wing area 26.0m² (280sq ft).

Weights: NF.3 – empty 3992kg (8800lb); max takeoff 6532kg (14,400lb).

Armament: Four 20mm cannon in lower nose; two 454kg (1000lb) bombs or eight 27kg (60lb) rockets under wings.

Performance: NF.3 – max speed 501kt (928km/h) at sea level, 482kt (893km/h) at 30,000ft; initial climb 6280ft (1914m)/min; service ceiling 49,000ft; range 870nm (1611km).

Production: 283 Venom night fighters of all versions comprising 1 prototype, 90 NF.2, 130 NF.3 and 62 NF.51.

Notes: The two seat radar equipped night fighter version of the Venom evolved in a similar manner to the Vampire Night Fighter (see separate entry), the forward fuselage pod modified to incorporate a wider cockpit with the radar operator/navigator who sitting slightly behind and to the right of the pilot. The enlarged nose housed the same AI (Airborne Intercept) Mk.10 radar which was installed in the Vampire Night Fighter.

Construction of the fuselage pod remained as before – plywood balsa sandwich – and the crew sat under a heavily framed upwards hinging canopy, although this was later replaced by a clear view canopy which was jettisonable. Ejection seats were not fitted and taller pointed fins were another external distinguishing feature.

Developed as a private venture, the prototype first flew on 23 August 1950, early flight testing revealing some problems including a slow rate of role and excessive yaw, various modifications to the tail surfaces and more responsive ailerons being fitted as a consequence.

The first of 90 production Venom NF.2s for the RAF flew on 4 March 1952 but due to the problems they did not begin reaching the RAF until the following year. Only one squadron operated the NF.2 largely due to the discovery of various defects including a structural weakness in the wings.

A high accident rate during night approaches resulted in the fitting of the clear vision canopy and other modifications were made to the fin and rudder. Modified aircraft were designated NF.2A, these serving with three RAF squadrons.

The Venom NF.3 was a new build version incorporating the NF.2A's modifications along with improved AI Mk.21 radar, powered ailerons, more powerful Ghost 105 engine and a new tailplane design. Ejection seats were still not fitted. The first NF.3 was flown on 22 February 1953 and a total of 130 was built, serving with five RAF squadrons until replaced by Gloster Javelins from 1957. The last was withdrawn in 1961.

There was only one export sale, 62 NF.51s delivered to Sweden as the J33 between 1952 and 1957. These were powered by locally built Ghost engines and remained in service until 1967.

Photo: Venom NF.2.

de Havilland Sea Venom

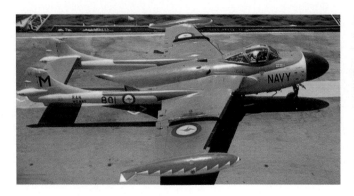

Country of origin: United Kingdom.

Type: Two seat naval all weather fighter.

Powerplant: FAW.20 – one 4850lb (21.6kN) de Havilland Ghost 103. FAW.21/53 one 4950lb (22.0kN) Ghost 104. FAW.22 – one 5150lb (22.9kN) Ghost 105.

Dimensions: Wing span 13.05m (42ft 10in); length 11.17m (36ft 8in); height 2.59m (8ft 6in); wing area 26.0m² (280sq ft).

Weights: FAW.21/53 – empty 4990kg (11,000lb); max takeoff 7212kg (15,900lb).

Armament: Four 20mm cannon in lower nose; provision for max 907kg (2000lb) underwing ordnance.

Performance: FAW.21/53 – max speed 489kt (906km/h) at sea level, 473kt (875km/h) at 30,000ft; initial climb 5750ft (1753m/min); time to 20,000ft 6.1min; service ceiling 40,000ft; max range 870nm (1610km).

Production: 393 Sea Venoms of all versions comprising 3 prototypes, 50 FAW.20, 168 FAW.21, 39 FAW.22, 39 FAW.53 (all by de Havilland) and 94 Aquilon by Sud-Est.

Notes: A navalised version of the Venom night fighter, the Sea Venom resulted from an RN Fleet Air Arm evaluation of the earlier aircraft and ordered it as an interim measure to fill the gap between the piston engined Sea Hornet NF.21 and much more advanced Sea Vixen which was still some years away. As such, it became the RN's first two seat all weather jet fighter.

Changes over the Venom were those associated with 'navalising' the aircraft – folding wings, V-frame arrester hook and stronger, long stroke undercarriage. The Venom NF.2's heavily framed canopy; AI Mk.10 radar and Ghost 103 engine were retained and no ejection seats were fitted. The first of three prototypes flew on 19 April 1951 and the first production FAW.20 in March 1953. Squadron service began a year later, seven FAA operational units eventually flying the type, although the FAW.20 was withdrawn from service after only a year due to problems including the dangerous tendency to break arrester hooks on landing.

The improved FAW.21 first flew in May 1954, this featuring a more powerful Ghost 104, powered ailerons, clear view canopy, AI Mk.21 radar, strengthened arrester hook, anti skid brakes and – finally – ejection seats. The last Sea Venom variant for Britain was the FAW.22 with Ghost 105 engine and the various aerodynamic improvements which had been introduced to the land based Venom night fighter. These were built between 1956 and early 1959. RN Sea Venoms saw action in the Suez crisis of 1956, usually in the ground attack role.

The Sea Venom was also sold to Australia for the RAN (39 FAW.53s in 1955-56, these similar to the FAW.21) and to France where it was built under licence by Sud-Est as the Aquilon. The first Aquilon flew in October 1952 and four versions were built: the Aquilon 201 prototypes; 202 with ejection seats, aft sliding canopy and strengthened undercarriage (first flight March 1954); 203 *single* seater with American APQ 65 radar and clear view canopy (the size of the radar's equipment left space for only one seat); and 204 unarmed trainer.

The Royal Navy's Sea Venoms remained in front line service until 1960, Australia's until 1967 and France's until 1963.

Photo: Royal Australian Navy Sea Venom FAW.53.

de Havilland Sea Vixen

Country of origin: United Kingdom.

Type: Two seat naval all weather strike fighter.

Powerplants: Two 11,230lb (50.0kN) Rolls-Royce Avon 208 turbojets.

Dimensions: Wing span 15.54m (51ft 0in); length 16.94m (55ft 7in); height 3.28m (10ft 9in); wing area 60.2m² (648sq ft).

Weights: FAW.2 – empty 12,679kg (27,952lb); max takeoff 18,858kg (41,575lb).

Armament: FAW.1 – four Firestreak infrared homing AAMs; 28 2in (51mm) rockets in retractable fuselage packs; two 454kg (1000lb) bombs or rocket pods under wings. FAW.2 – provision for Red Top AAMs in place of Firestreaks.

Performance: FAW.2 – max speed 600kt (1110km/h) at sea level; time to 10,000ft 1.5min, to 40,000ft 8.5min; service ceiling 48,000ft; endurance 3.2 hours; max range with drop tanks 1220nm (2260km).

Production: 2 DH.110 prototypes, 1 Sea Vixen prototype, 119 FAW.1 and 29 FAW.2, total 151.

Notes: The last of the de Havilland twin boom jet fighters, the Sea Vixen was in fact far removed from the Vampires and Venoms which preceded it, being a completely new and much larger twin engined and swept wing design which retained only its general configuration in common with the earlier aircraft.

The original DH.110 was developed from 1946 to meet Royal Navy and RAF requirements for an advanced all weather fighter. The RN version was subsequently cancelled but the land based model contested the RAF contract which was eventually won by the Gloster Javelin. The first of two prototypes powered by a pair of 7500lb (33.3kN) Avons flew on 26 September 1951. In September 1952 this aircraft achieved some unwanted fame when it broke up during a demonstration at the Farnborough Air Show, killing pilot John Derry, observer Tony Richards and 29 spectators.

Royal Navy interest in the DH.110 was revived in 1952, resulting in the substantially (80 per cent) redesigned Sea Vixen. A semi navalised prototype was flown on 20 June 1955 following the placing of an order for 78 the previous January and the first fully navalised Sea Vixen FAW.1 in March 1957. This featured folding wings, revised long stroke undercarriage, all flying tailplane, Avon 208 engines, ejection seats, nosewheel steering, GEC AI Mk.18 radar and a main armament of four Firestreak infrared homing AAMs. Deliveries began in November 1958 and operational service in July 1959.

A prototype of the improved Sea Vixen FAW.2 first flew June 1962, this followed by 29 production aircraft between 1963 and 1966. Compared to its predecessor, the FAW.2 differed in having additional fuel capacity stored in forward extensions of the tailbooms and provision to carry the Red Top air-to-air missile. Sixty-seven FAW.1s were converted to the new standard.

With the winding down of RN Fleet Air Arm carrier based fixed wing operations, the last Sea Vixen was withdrawn from front line service in January 1972 but some continued flying with the RN's Air Directors School until 1974. A few were subsequently converted to Sea Vixen D.3 pilotless target drones.

Photo: Sea Vixen F(AW).2. (David McIntosh)

Denel Rooivalk

Country of origin: South Africa.

Type: Two seat attack helicopter.

Powerplants: Two 1845shp (1376kW) Topaz (Turboméca) Makila 1K2 turboshafts; four bladed main rotor.

Dimensions: Main rotor diameter 15.58m (51ft 1½in); fuselage length 16.38m (53ft 9in); height 5.18m (17ft 0in); main rotor disc area 190.6m² (2052sq ft).

Weights: Empty 5730kg (12,632lb); max takeoff 8750kg (19,290lb).

Armament: One 20mm cannon in nose turret; six pylons under stub wings for max 2032kg (4480lb) ordnance including four 19 tube 70mm rocket launchers, up to 16 ZT6 Mokopa anti tank missiles, two or four Mistral AAMs.

Performance: Max cruise 150kt (278km/h); max climb 2620ft (798m)/min; service ceiling 20,000ft; hovering ceiling IGE 19,200ft; hovering ceiling OGE 17,900ft; max range 380nm (704km) on internal fuel or 680nm (1260km) with external fuel; max endurance (internal-external) 3.6-3.9hrs.

Production: 3 prototypes and 7 production aircraft by mid 1999 against orders for 12.

Notes: The AH-2A Rooivalk (Red Kestrel) attack helicopter resulted from a 1981 South African Air Force requirement. It is based on experience Denel (then Atlas) gained from building and flying the XH-1 concept demonstrator, a one-off attack helicopter prototype based on the Alouette III and combining the Alouette's engine, transmission and rotor with a new fuselage with two seats in stepped tandem. The XH-1 first flew in January 1986.

Development of what would become the Rooivalk began in 1984, Denel in the meantime flying the XH-1 plus two Puma medium helicopter testbeds modified as gunships under the designation XTP-1 Beta. The Rooivalk is based on the dynamics of the twin engined Puma but with a completely new fuselage. Some composites are used in both the fuselage and rotor blades.

The XH-2 Rooivalk prototype first flew on 11 February 1990 but the ending of most of the hostilities around South Africa's borders and the resulting defence cuts led to the SAAF's requirement being dropped. The programme continued as a private venture, two more prototypes being flown in 1992 and 1996.

Denel finally got some return on its investment in July 1996 when 12 production AH-2A Rooivalks were ordered to equip one SAAF squadron with a possible requirement for up to 36. The first production AH-2A was handed over to the SAAF in November 1998 and joined 16 Squadron two months later. Deliveries of the 12 on firm order were continuing at the modest rate of four per annum by mid 2000 with completion scheduled for 2001. Initial operational capability was planned for late 2000.

Denel revealed details of a maritime version of the Rooivalk in September 1998, this featuring 360deg chin mounted radar in place of the gun turret, folding main rotor blades and the ability to carry Exocet or Penguin anti-ship missiles. Despite extensive marketing efforts in a crowded field, the Rooivalk had attracted no export orders by mid 2000.

Photo: Pre-production Rooivalk. (BAe)

Douglas AC-47D 'Spooky'

Country of origin: USA.

Type: Six/seven crew gunship.

Powerplants: Two 1200hp (895kW) Pratt & Whitney R-1820-92 Twin Wasp 14-cylinder radials; three bladed propellers.

Dimensions: Wing span 28.95m (95ft 0in); length 19.62m (64ft 5½in); height 5.15m (16ft 11in); wing area 91.7m² (987sq ft).

Weights: Empty approx 8255kg (18,200lb); max takeoff 11,794kg (26,000lb).

Armament: Three General Electric Minigun 7.62mm multi barrel machine guns firing through the main door and two port fuselage windows.

Performance: Max speed 200kt (370km/h); max cruise 161kt (298km/h); initial climb 1200ft (366m)/min; normal gunship operating altitude 3000ft above ground; service ceiling 24,000ft; normal range 1300nm (2408km).

Production: 10,665 US built DC-3/C-47/C-53s of all versions; 32 AC-47D conversions.

History: The versatile C-47 added another role to its long list during the Vietnam War when 32 were converted to AC-47D gunships. Fitted with three General Electric Miniguns mounted in the port side door and two cabin windows, each was capable of firing 6000 rounds per minute. The idea was to fly in a continuous circle from a height of 3000 feet above the ground and thus lay heavily concentrated fire on a target (typically a suspected Viet Cong position) in the centre of the circle.

The result was a spectacular sight and sound which was capable of pouring thousands of rounds into an area about 9.5m (31ft) in diameter in a matter of seconds. Someone suggested that the 'rain of fire' looked like the hot breath of a dragon so the nickname 'Puff The Magic Dragon' (from the popular Peter, Paul and Mary song of the time) was applied. The aircraft initially used the callsign 'Puff' and later 'Spooky'. The designation AC-47D had previously been applied to 26 USAF airways check aircraft – these were redesignated EC-47D.

The idea of flying in a circular pattern to concentrate fire onto the ground was not a new one, having first been tried in the 1920s, but the AC-47D was the first combat application of the concept. Trials were conducted in Vietnam during 1965 using conventional small calibre machine guns firing through aircraft's windows. Installing the Minigun with its massive rate of fire transformed the idea.

The first proper AC-47Ds were operated by the 4th Air Commando Squadron from November 1965. Two other units were also equipped, these operating the aircraft until late 1968 when they were replaced by AC-119 and AC-130 gunships. Some of the 'Puffs' were then transferred to the South Vietnamese and Laotian air forces.

A favourite ploy during night operations was to send two aircraft out, one a standard C-47 equipped with loudspeakers and the other an AC-47D. The C-47 would go in first, broadcasting to the Viet Cong that they should not try to shoot it down or 'great fire, hell and wrath' would descend on them. Naturally, this warning was ignored, so enter the blacked out and hitherto unseen 'Spooky', breathing fire!

Photo: AC-47D guns installation detail.

Douglas A-26 Invader

Country of origin: USA.

Type: Three seat attack bomber.

Powerplants: A-26B/C – two 2000hp (1491kW) Pratt & Whitney R-2800-27/79 Double Wasp 18 cylinder radials. B-26K – two 2500hp (1864kW) R-2800-103W; three bladed propellers.

Dimensions: B-26K – wing span 22.86m (75ft 0in) over tip tanks; length 15.24m (50ft 0m); height 18ft 6in (5.64m); wing area 50.1m² (540sq ft).

Weights: B-26K – empty 10,147kg (22,370lb); max takeoff 19,673kg (43,370lb).

Armament: B-26K – eight 0.50in machine guns in nose; max 4990kg (11,000lb) ordnance in weapons bay and on eight underwing pylons.

Performance: B-26K – max speed (clean) 345kt (639km/h); max cruise 265kt (490km/h); max climb 2990ft (911m)/min; service ceiling 30,000ft; combat radius with 1.5hrs over target (internal fuel) 500nm (926km); max ferry range 3250nm (6020km).

Production: 1 XA-26, 1 XA-26A, 1 XA-26B, 1355 A-26B, 1091 A-26C, 1 XA-26D, total 2450.

Notes: Douglas continued the light attack bomber theme successfully developed by the DB-7/A-20/Havoc/Boston family with the A-26 Invader, a larger, faster, more powerful and more heavily armed aircraft which had its production run cut short by the end of WWII (5254 were cancelled) but continued in service for many years after that, seeing action in Korea and Vietnam.

Three prototypes were ordered in June 1941, the first of them (the XA-26 bomber variant) flying on 10 July 1942. The second prototype (XA-26A) was completed as a night fighter with four 20mm cannon in an underfuselage pack and four machine guns in the dorsal turret, while the third (XA-26B) had a 75mm cannon in its nose.

The solid nose (with machine guns) A-26B close support and ground attack version entered operational service with the USAAF in November 1944 and over the next few months dropped over 18,000 tonnes of bombs on European targets. The A-26C with glazed nose joined it in early 1945 and was often used as a 'lead ship' for bombing formations. Both variants also flew against Japan in the later stages of the Pacific war.

Post war, the Invader was redesignated B-26 (the similarly numbered Martin Marauder having been retired) and enjoyed something of a renaissance, about 450 serving with the USAF in the Korean War while many others were supplied to foreign nations including Brazil, Chile, Colombia, Laos, Indonesia, Nicaragua, Peru and Guatemala.

Several companies performed remanufactured conversions of the aircraft as executive transports, notably California's On Mark Engineering which also developed the YB-26K counter-insurgency (COIN) version. This featured more powerful R-2800-103W engines, permanent wingtip tanks, eight underwing stores pylons and an interchangeable solid (with guns) or glazed nose, the latter for conventional bombing and photo-reconnaissance missions.

The first YB-26K flew in February 1963 and the USAF ordered about 70 as the B-26K (later A-26A). They were used extensively in Vietnam, particularly for night attacks on the Ho Chi Minh trail where their heavy warload and long endurance were assets.

Photo: B-26K/A-26A Invader. (Gerard Frawley)

Douglas Skyraider

Country of origin: USA.

Type: Single or two/four seat naval tactical strike/multirole.

Powerplant: One 3020hp (2252kW) Wright R-3350-26W or 3050hp (2274kW) R-3350-26WB Cyclone 18-cylinder radial; four bladed propeller.

Dimensions: Wing span 15.24m (50ft 0in); length 11.63-12.22m (38ft 2in-40ft 1in); height 4.77m (15ft 8in); wing area 37.2m² (400sq ft).

Weights: AD-2 – empty 4784kg (10,546lb); max takeoff 8284kg (18,263lb). AD-5/A-1E – empty 5585kg (12,313lb); max takeoff 11,340kg (25,000lb). AD-7/A-1J – empty 5486kg (12,094lb); max takeoff 11,340kg (25,000lb).

Armament: Two or four 20mm cannon in wings; max 3629kg (8000lb) external ordnance on 15 hardpoints.

Performance: AD-2 – max speed 279kt (516km/h) at 18,300ft; cruising speed 172kt (319km/h); initial climb 2800ft (853m)/min; service ceiling 32,700ft; range (clean) 795nm (1473km). AD-5/A-1E – max speed 270kt (500km/h) at 18,000ft; initial climb 2300ft (700m)/min; tactical radius 400nm (740km). AD-7/A1-J – max speed 278kt (515km/h) at 18,500ft; initial climb 2300ft (700m)/min; service ceiling 25,400ft; range (clean) 782nm (1448km).

Production: 3180 Skyraiders of all models comprising 25 XBT2D-1, 277 AD-1, 178 AD-2, 194 AD-3, 1051 AD-4, 670 AD-5 (A-1E), 713 AD-6 (A-1H) and 72 AD-7 (A-1J).

Notes: Developed in 1944 for the US Navy as a carrier borne single seat dive/torpedo bomber, the Skyraider went on to become one of the most versatile combat aircraft ever built, produced in a multitude of attack, early warning, anti submarine and electronic warfare variants and surviving in service well into the 1970s.

The first XBT2D-1 flew on 18 March 1945 initially under the name Dauntless II. Deliveries of production AD-1 Skyraiders to the USN and Marine Corps began in late 1946. Some were completed as AD-1Q ECM aircraft with an equipment operator in the spacious rear fuselage; other designation suffixes applied to the various models including W (early warning with large radome under the fuselage), B (nuclear weapon capability), L (with anti and deicing equipment for winter operations in Korea) and N (night operations).

All but the basic AD-1/2/3/4 attack models had additional crew members and each progressively incorporated structural and equipment improvements. The Royal Navy received 40 AD-4W early warning aircraft in 1952 while France's Armée de l'Air flew AD-4s from land.

The AD-5 (A-1E from 1962) had a redesigned and wider fuselage for side-by-side seating (first flight August 1951) and could be used as a 12 seat transport or casevac aircraft. The final single seater attack versions were the AD-6 (A-1H) and AD-7 (A-1J) with strengthened wings for low level tactical strike work. The last Skyraider was an AD-7 delivered in February 1957.

The Skyraider proved its worth in Korea (the conflict extending production) thanks to its load carrying capability, long endurance and survivability. It repeated this in Vietnam where more than 1000 were operated by the USN/MC, USAF and South Vietnamese air force. The 'Spad' (as it was nicknamed) was finally retired from USN service in 1972.

Photo: A-1J Skyraider.

Douglas F3D Skyknight

Country of origin: USA.

Type: Two seat naval all weather fighter.

Powerplants: F3D-1 – two 3250lb (14.4kN) Westinghouse J34-WE-34 turbojets. F3D-2 – two 3400lb (15.1kN) J34-WE-36/36A turbojets.

Dimensions: Wing span 15.24m (50ft 0in); length 13.87m (45ft 6in); height 4.90m (16ft 1in); wing area 37.1m² (400sq ft).

Weights: F3D-1 – empty 6492kg (14,313lb); max takeoff 8468kg (18,668lb). F3D-2 – empty 8237kg (18,160lb); max takeoff 12,180kg (26,850lb).

Armament: Four 20mm cannon in lower nose.

Performance: F3D-1 – max speed 456kt (845km/h) at 20,000ft; initial climb 3710ft (1130m)/min; service ceiling 33,000ft; range (clean) 1127nm (2088km). F3D-2 – max speed 426kt (789km/h) at 15,000ft; cruising speed 304-339kt (563-628km/h); initial climb 2970ft (905m)/min; range (clean) 996nm (1845km).

Production: 3 XF3D-1, 28 F3D-1, 237 F3D-2, total 268.

Notes: Douglas received a contract from the US Navy in April 1946 covering the construction of three prototypes of a new shipboard all weather jet fighter designated the F3D Skyknight. The design Douglas presented was a mid wing side by side two seater powered by two Westinghouse J34 turbojets. The usual naval features were incorporated including folding wings.

Inside, the bulky early generation Westinghouse APQ-35 radar and avionics met the demanding requirement that the aircraft be capable of radar guided interceptions in bad weather or at night 125 statute miles (200km) away from the host aircraft carrier. As was the case with many of the early jet combat aircraft, performance was restricted by the available power, the two J34s leaving the Skyknight considerably underpowered during its career.

The first of three XF3D-1 prototypes flew on 23 March 1948 powered by 3000lb (13.3kN) J34-WE-32 engines. They were followed by the first of 28 production F3D-1s with more powerful J34-WE-34 engines on 13 February 1950.

The major production F3D-2 was supposed to have the Skyknight's lack of power problem remedied by being fitted with 4600lb (20.4kN) Westinghouse J46 engines but this was abandoned and the J34 reverted to in slightly more powerful form. The first F3D-2 flew on 14 February 1951 and initial use was with US Marine Corps units in Korea where it recorded more 'kills' than any other USN/USMC aircraft. The first of these (a MiG-15 on 2 November 1952) was the first time a jet had shot down another during a night interception.

After Korea, the aircraft nicknamed 'Willie the Whale' was largely forgotten but its service continued with new versions and roles created by conversion. These included 16 F3D-2M missile carriers, 35 F3D-2Q ECM and Elint aircraft and 55 F3D-2T and -2T2 trainers for the instruction of radar operators. In 1962 the Skyknight was redesignated as the F-10A (F3D-1) and F-10B (F3D-2). The ECM/Elint EF-10B (F3D-2Q) played a significant but largely anonymous operational role in the Cuban crisis of 1962 (it detected the radar which led to the discovery of Soviet missiles on the island) and in Vietnam from 1965. The last was retired in 1970.

Photo: F3D-1 Skyknight.

Douglas F4D Skyray

Country of origin: USA.

Type: Single seat naval fighter.

Powerplant: One 10,200lb (45.4kN)dry/16,000lb (71.1kN) with afterburner Pratt & Whitney J57-P-8/8B turbojet.

Dimensions: Wing span 10.21m (33ft 6in); length 13.84m (45ft 5in); height 3.96m (13ft 0in); wing area 51.7m² (557sq ft).

Weights: Empty 7268kg (16,024lb); max takeoff 12,300kg (27,116lb).

Armament: Four 20mm cannon in wings; four underwing packs with seven or 19 2.75in (6.98cm) rockets or four Sidewinder air-to-air missiles.

Performance: Max speed 627kt (1162km/h) at sea level, 566kt (1049km/h) at 35,000ft; initial climb 18,300ft (5578m)/min; service ceiling 55,000ft; high altitude combat radius 307nm (568km); max range 1043nm (1931km).

Production: 2 XF4D-1 and 420 F4D-1, total 422.

Notes: The wartime research into tailless delta configurations by Germany's Dr Alexander Lippisch was put to good use by many Allied designers after 1945, including Douglas' Ed Heinemann. One result was the F4D Skyray naval fighter, although this had a wing which was not a pure delta but rather a sweptback design with a very broad chord and low aspect ratio.

Nicknamed 'Ford' (after its designation), the Skyray was capable of high subsonic speeds in level flight (Mach 0.95-0.98) and the only control surfaces apart from the rudder were power operated elevons on the wings. Two XF4D-1 prototypes were ordered in December 1948, the first of these flying on 23 January 1951. The Skyray was designed around the Westinghouse J40 but both prototypes were initially fitted with the 5000lb (22.2kN) Allison J35 pending availability of the more than twice as powerful J40. This was subsequently fitted to both prototypes but it was a failure and cancelled in March 1953.

The decision was therefore made to fit production F4D-1s with the Pratt & Whitney J57, this necessitating some structural and systems redesign. Early F4D-1s were fitted with the 14,500lb (64.5kN) thrust (with afterburner) J57-P-2 but most of the sole production model had the more powerful P-8/8B version installed.

The first production F4D-1 flew on 5 June 1954 but deliveries to the US Navy (and later Marine Corps) didn't start until April 1956 after some developmental problems were sorted out. At its peak, the Skyray equipped 11 USN, six USMC and three Reserve squadrons and remained in service in diminishing numbers until the late 1960s. It was redesignated F-6A in 1962.

The F5D Skylancer was a developed version capable of supersonic flight (max speed 828kt/Mach 1.44 at 35,000ft) thanks to a new wing which retained the span and planform of the original but was much thinner. Originally designated F4D-2, it also had a longer fuselage and taller tail plus increased fuel capacity.

Four F5D-1 prototypes powered by the Skyray's J57-P-8 were flown, the first one on 21 April 1956. Production Skylancers were planned to have the General Electric J79 and a batch of 19 (including the first four) was ordered for evaluation but the programme was cancelled later in 1956, mainly for reasons of political expediency.

Photo: F4D-1 Skyray. (USN)

Douglas A3D (A-3) Skywarrior

Country of Origin: USA.

Type: Three crew carrier based bomber.

Powerplants: A3D-1/A-3A – two 9700lb (43.1kN) Pratt & Whitney J57-P-6 turbojets. A3D-2/A-3B – two 10,500lb (46.7kN) dry/12,400lb (55.1kN) with water injection J57-P-10.

Dimensions: Wing span 22.10m (72ft 6in); length 23.27m (76ft 4in); height 6.95m (22ft 9¹/₂in); wing area 75.4m² (812sq ft).

Weights: A3D-2/A-3B – empty 17,876kg (39,409lb); normal loaded 33,113kg (73,000lb); max takeoff 37,195kg (82,000lb).

Armament: Two 20mm cannon in remotely controlled tail turret; max bomb/depth charge load 5443kg (12,000lb) in weapons bay.

Performance: A3D-2/A-3B – max speed 530kt (982km/h) at 10,000ft, 487kt (900km/h) at 36,000ft; initial climb 3600ft (1097m)/min; service ceiling 41,000ft; tactical radius 912nm (1690km); max range 2520nm (4668km).

Production: 2 XA3D-1, 50 A3D-1 (E-3A), 164 A3D-2 (A-3B), 24 A3D-2Q (EA-3B), 30 A3D-2P (RA-3B) and 12 A3D-2T (TA-3B), total 282.

Notes: The largest aircraft designed to operate from aircraft carriers when it was developed and the world's first carrier based strategic bomber, the Skywarrior resulted from a 1947 US Navy requirement for an aircraft suitable for operations from the super carriers of the USS *Forrestal* type then being planned.

Douglas responded with a swept back high wing design with two podded jet engines underneath, an internal weapons bay, remotely controlled defensive guns in the tail, hydraulically folding wings and fin, and the crew of three grouped forward in a pressurised cockpit.

A contract was awarded to build two XA3D-1 prototypes in March 1949, the first of these flying 28 October 1952 powered by two 7000lb (31.1kN) Westinghouse J40 turbojets. This was the intended power-plant for production models but its failure meant that future Skywarriors would be powered by a pair of Pratt & Whitney J57s.

The first production A3D-1 (redesignated A-3A in 1962) flew on 16 September 1953 and deliveries began to the US Navy's VAH-1 (Heavy Attack) Squadron in March 1956.

The major production bomber variant was the A3D-2 (A-3B) with more powerful engines and provision for flight refuelling from the 124th example. The A3D-2 entered service in 1957 and equipped USN bomber squadrons until the mid 1960s when the Navy relinquished its strategic bomber role.

Subsequent new build versions were the A3D-2Q (EA-3B) electronic countermeasures aircraft with four electronics officers housed in a pressurised compartment in the bomb bay; A3D-2P (RA-3B) with a pressurised compartment for 12 cameras in the forward bomb bay; and A3D-2T (TA-3B) bombardier-navigator trainer with an instructor and five trainees housed in a pressurised bomb bay compartment. Production was completed in 1961.

Other variants were created by conversion including the KA-3B tanker and EKA-3B tanker/ECM aircraft, these remaining in USN service until 1988-89.

The basic Skywarrior concept was developed into a USAF version, the B-66 Destroyer (see next entry).

Photo: A3D-2/A-3B Skywarrior.

Douglas B-66 Destroyer

Country of origin: USA.

Type: Three crew tactical bomber (B-66), photo or electronic reconnaissance (RB-66) and weather reconnaissance (WB-66).

Powerplants: R/B-66B – two 10,200lb (45.4kN) Allison J71-A-11/13 turbojets.

Dimensions: Wing span 22.10m (72ft 6in); length 22.91m (75ft 2in); height 7.19m (23ft 7in); wing area 72.5m² (780sq ft).

Weights: B-66B – empty 19,408kg (42,788lb); max takeoff 37,649kg (83,000lb).

Armament: B-66B – two remotely controlled 20mm cannon in tail turret; max bomb load 6804kg (15,000lb) in weapons bay.

Performance: B-66B – max speed 548kt (1016km/h) at 6000ft, 516kt (956km/h) at 36,000ft; cruising speed 456kt (845km/h); initial climb 3600ft (1097m)/min; service ceiling 38,900ft; range 1303nm (2414km).

Production: 5 RB-66A, 145 RB-66B, 72 B-66B, 36 RB-66C and 36 WB-66D, total 293.

Notes: The needs of the Korean War inspired the USAF to look for a new light tactical bomber and reconnaissance aircraft. In order to expedite things, a 'minimum change' land based version of the US Navy's A3D Skywarrior was selected with naval features such as the folding wings and catapult launching gear deleted.

Unfortunately – as often happens in cases like this – the minimum change concept was largely ignored and although what was called the B-66 Destroyer looked like its USN counterpart it was in reality vastly different with a new wing of revised planform (and with rejigged control surfaces), and a fuselage that structurally bore little relationship with its predecessor's. The B-66's equipment fit was also vastly different and not even the A3D's Pratt & Whitney J57 engines were retained, these replaced by Allison J71s, initially the 9570lb (42.6kN) thrust J71-A-9.

The first of five pre series RB-66A Destroyers with multi camera installation and bombing equipment but intended mainly for night photo-reconnaissance flew on 28 June 1954 followed by production RB-66Bs (first flight March 1955) and B-66B bombers (first flight 4 January 1955). The B-66B was the only Destroyer variant intended purely for the bombing role and like the RB-66 was powered by more powerful J71-A-11 or -13 engine. Deliveries of the B-66B to the USAF began in March 1956 and both it and the RB remained in USAF service until the late 1960s, although by then many had been converted to other roles.

The final new production variants were the RB-66C (first flight October 1955) unarmed electronic countermeasures aircraft with a pressurised compartment for four equipment officers in the bomb bay; and the WB-66D (first flight June 1957) intended to collect weather data in combat areas and having a specialist crew of two operators also housed in the bomb bay. A WB-66D was the last new Destroyer built, in June 1958.

Other specialist variants were created by conversion including the EB-66B/C/E electronic countermeasures versions, these seeing extensive service in Vietnam. Others were based in West Germany between 1969 and 1975 as the final Destroyers in USAF service.

Photo: RB-66B Destroyer.

Douglas A-4A/B/C Skyhawk

Country of origin: USA.

Type: Single seat carrier or land based attack.

Powerplant: A-4A – one 7700lb (34.2kN) Wright J65-W-4 turbojet. A-4B/C – one 7700lb (34.2kN) J65-W-16A or 8500lb (37.8kN) J65-W-20 turbojet.

Dimensions: A-4A – wing span 8.38m (27ft 6in); length 11.91m (39ft 1in); height 4.62m (15ft 2in); wing area 24.1m² (260sq ft). A-4B/C – length (excl nose probe) 12.04m (39ft 6in).

Weights: A-4A – empty 3810kg (8400lb); normal loaded 7711kg (17,000lb); max takeoff (carrier ops) 9072kg (20,000lb). A-4C – empty 4413kg (9728lb); max takeoff (carrier ops) 10,206kg (22,500lb).

Armament: Two 20mm cannon in wing roots; one underfuselage and two underwing hardpoints for typically up to 2710kg (5975lb) ordnance.

Performance: A-4B – max speed 587kt (1088km/h) at sea level; combat radius 400nm (740km); max range with drop tanks 1000nm (1852km).

Production: 2690 Skyhawks of all models including 1 XA4D-1, 165 A4D-1 (A-4A), 542 A4D-2 (A-4B) and 638 A4D-3 (A-4C).

Notes: A successful exercise in compact packaging, the Douglas A4D Skyhawk (A-4 from 1962) attack aircraft was purchased in large numbers by the US Navy and Marine Corps (over 2200) and exported for operation from both the originally intended aircraft carriers and from land. What was nicknamed 'Heinemann's Hot Rod' (after its designer) or 'The Scooter' began life in 1952 as a Skyraider replacement, Ed Heinemann producing a design which seemed impossibly small and light for its claimed capabilities.

Features included a modified delta wing of short span, removing the need for folding wings and their associated weight. Power was provided by a Wright J65 turbojet, a licence built Armstrong Siddeley Sapphire. The US Navy ordered a prototype XA4D-1 and 19 pre-production A4D-1s (later A-4A) in June 1952, the prototype first flew on 22 June 1954, the first of the pre-production models on 14 August 1954 and deliveries to the US Navy began in September 1956.

The A4D-2 (A-4B) first flew in March 1956 and differed from the original version in having a different variant of the J65, provision for aerial refuelling, a dual hydraulic system, powered flying controls and the distinctive 'inside out' rudder with external strengthening ribs, this remaining a feature of the Skyhawk throughout its production life.

The A4D-2N/A-4C (first flight August 1959) had some all weather capacity thanks to the fitting of lightweight Westinghouse APG-53A radar in a slightly lengthened nose plus generally updated weapons systems and avionics and an improved ejection seat. Ninety-nine A-4Bs and Cs later became A-4Ls when fitted with the more powerful J65-W-20 engine and improved avionics housed in the dorsal 'hump' which would be a characteristic of later models.

No new production A-4A/B/Cs were exported but Argentina received more than 75 refurbished ex USN A-4Bs and Cs (as the A-4P and Q) from 1966. Some of these saw action in the Falklands War and the last were retired in early 1988, replaced by later models. The re-engined, A-4B based Singapore Aerospace Super Skyhawk is described separately.

Photo: A-4C Skyhawk.

Douglas A-4E/F/G/H/K Skyhawk

Country of origin: USA.

Type: Single seat carrier or land based attack.

Powerplant: A-4E – one 8500lb (37.8kN) Pratt & Whitney J52-P-6A turbojet. A-4F – one 9300lb (41.3kN) J52-P-8A turbojet.

Dimensions: Wing span 8.38m (27ft 6in); length (excl refuelling probe) 12.23m (40ft 1½in); height 4.62m (15ft 2in); wing area 24.1m² (260sq ft).

Weights: A-4E – empty 4469kg (9853lb); normal loaded 10,160kg (22,398lb); max takeoff (carrier ops) 11,113kg (24,500lb). A-4F – empty 4581kg (10,100lb); max takeoff (land ops) 12,438kg (27,420lb).

Armament: Two 20mm cannon in wing roots; one underfuselage and four underwing hardpoints for typically up to 3719kg (8200lb) ordnance; theoretical maximum 4107kg (9055lb).

Performance: A-4E – max speed 585kt (1083km/h) at sea level; 502kt (930km/h) at 30,000ft; service ceiling 42,650ft; combat radius with 907kg (2000lb) stores 432nm (800km). A-4F – max speed 586kt (1086km/h) at sea level; initial climb 5620ft (1713m)/min; service ceiling 47,900ft; combat radius hi-lo-hi with 1814kg (4000lb) stores 350nm (648km); max ferry range with drop tanks 2120nm (3927km).

Production: 2690 Skyhawks of all models including 499 A-4E, 147 A-4F, 238 TA-4F, 8 A-4G, 2 TA-4G, 90 A-4H, 10 TA-4H, 293 TA-4J, 10 A-4K and 4 TA-4K.

Notes: Ongoing development of the Skyhawk resulted in the 'second generation' A-4E and A-4F models, these featuring major modifications including a more powerful and economical Pratt & Whitney J52 in place of the original Wright J65 (Sapphire) and a largely re-engineered structure for increased weights. This and an additional two underwing hardpoints (giving a total of four plus a single centreline hardpoint) allowed a substantial increase in warload.

The first of two evaluation YA-4Es flew on 12 July 1961 and deliveries of production models was carried out between November 1962 and April 1966. The A-4F (first flight 31 August 1966) was the last version built for the US Navy and offered further improvements including another increase in power, steerable nosewheel, zero-zero ejection seat, wing spoilers and a more comprehensive avionics fit housed in a distinctive dorsal 'hump' behind the cockpit as the Skyhawk's compact airframe allowed no space for it elsewhere. USN and USMC Skyhawks saw extensive service in Vietnam, operating from both carriers and land bases.

Tandem two seater operational trainer versions with a lengthened forward fuselage were built for the USN as the TA-4E, TA-4F and TA-4J, the latter a simplified version of the F with its nav-attack system deleted. The first TA-4E prototype conversion flew in June 1965 and about 550 new production two seaters (mainly Fs and Js) followed.

New build A-4F variants were exported to Australia for carrier operations (A-4G/TA-4G with Sidewinder AAM capability and no dorsal avionics hump), Israel (A-4H/TA-4H with braking parachute and 30mm cannon) and New Zealand (A-4K/TA-4Ks). The A-4H/K introduced a reshaped fin of greater area. Israel, Malaysia and Indonesia also acquired ex USN Skyhawks.

Photo: A-4G Skyhawk. (RAN)

(McDonnell) Douglas A-4M/N Skyhawk

Country of origin: USA.

Type: Single seat carrier or land based attack.

Powerplant: One 11,200lb (49.8kN) Pratt & Whitney J52-P-408 turbojet.

Dimensions: Wing span 8.38m (27ft 6in); length (excl refuelling probe) 12.29m (40ft 4in); height 4.57m (15ft 0in); wing area 24.1m² (260sq ft).

Weights: Empty 4900kg (10,800lb); max takeoff (carrier ops) 11,113kg (24,500lb); max takeoff (land ops) 12,438kg (27,420lb).

Armament: Two 20mm cannon in wing roots; one underfuselage and four underwing hardpoints for max 4153kg (9155lb) ordnance.

Performance: Max speed 582kt (1078km/h) clean or 561kt (1039km/h) with ordnance at sea level; initial climb 8440ft (2572m)/min; tactical radius with 1814kg (4000lb) stores 295nm (547km); max ferry range with drop tanks 1781nm (3300km).

Production: 2690 Skyhawks of all models including 158 A-4M, 117 A-4N, 30 A-4KU and 6 TA-4KU.

Notes: In early 1964, the Vought Corporation won a competition for a new carrier based attack aircraft for the US Navy and Marine Corps which would ultimately replace the A-4 Skyhawk. The resulting A-7 Corsair II was a larger aircraft capable of carrying heavier warloads than its predecessor but was also considerably more expensive and maintenance intensive.

The USN ordered Corsairs but the Marines opted to stay with the Skyhawk, purchasing the final generation A-4M or Skyhawk II as it was dubbed by McDonnell Douglas (formed in 1967 following the merger of the two manufacturers). Externally, the A-4M differed from earlier Skyhawks in having an enlarged canopy and the larger, squarer fin which had first appeared on the A-4H and K.

The A-4M was fitted with the more powerful J52-P-408 engine, a braking parachute, twice the ammunition for the internal guns and uprated electrical system.

McDonnell Douglas calculated the A-4M had an overall combat efficiency improvement of 30 per cent compared to the A-4F. The first A-4M flew on 10 April 1970 and deliveries to the USMC began 12 months later.

The final Skyhawk to leave the line was an A-4M delivered in February 1979. The designation A-4Y was later applied to USMC A-4Ms fitted with an upgraded cockpit and the Hughes Angle Rate Bombing System.

New build A-4M variants were exported to Israel and Kuwait. The Israeli version was the A-4N, first flown in July 1972 and featuring an improved nav-attack system and modified cockpit layout. Some were subsequently fitted with an extended jet pipe to reduce the infrared signature and thus vulnerability to heat seeking missiles.

Kuwait received 30 A-4KU single seaters and six TA-4KU two seaters in 1977 and operated them in the 1991 Gulf War from bases in Saudi Arabia.

Second hand sales of A-4M variants have been made to Argentina (32 A-4Ms refurbished by Lockheed Martin as the A-4AR Fightinghawk with upgraded avionics and radar from 1997); and the Brazilian Navy, which received the first of 26 carrier capable ex Kuwaiti aircraft in September 1998 and designated them AF-1.

Photo: A-4N Skyhawk. (MDC)

English Electric Canberra B.2

Country of origin: United Kingdom.

Type: Two-three seat multirole tactical bomber.

Powerplants: B.2 – two 6500lb (28.9kN) Rolls-Royce Avon Mk.101 turbojets. Mk.20 – two CAC Avon Mk.101 or two 7500lb (33.3kN) CAC Avon Mk.109 turbojets.

Dimensions: Wing span 19.49m (63ft 11½in); length 19.96m (65ft 6in); height 4.75m (15ft 7in); wing area 89.2m² (960sq ft).

Weights: B.2 – empty 10,100kg (22,265lb); max takeoff 20,865kg (46,000lb). Mk.20 – empty 11,521kg (25,400lb); max takeoff 22,680kg (50,000lb).

Armament: Normal max bomb load 2722kg (6000lb) in weapons bay.

Performance: B.2 – max speed 495kt (917km/h) at 40,000ft, 450kt (834km/h) at sea level; initial climb 3800ft (1158m)/min; service ceiling 48,000ft; max range 2310nm (4279km). Mk.20 (Avon 109s) – max speed 504kt (936km/h) at 35,000ft; initial climb 4200ft (1280m)/min; low level combat radius with 2722kg (6000lb) bombs and tip tanks 440nm (814km); max ferry range 3150nm (5835km).

Production: 901 Canberras of all models in UK including 4 prototypes (by EE); 412 B.2 by EE (202), Avro (75), Handley Page (75) and Shorts (60); 35 PR.3 and 72 T.4. Also 48 Mk.20 in Australia by the Government Aircraft Factories.

Notes: Britain's first jet bomber, the versatile Canberra was also one of the most successful early generation combat aircraft, remaining in production until the early 1960s, serving with 17 nations and built under licence in the USA as the Martin B-57 (see separate entry) and Australia. Other foreign operators included Argentina (which used then in the Falklands War, Ecuador, Ethiopia, West Germany, India, New Zealand, Peru, Rhodesia, South Africa and Venezuela.

It was designed by former Westland technical director W E ('Teddy') Petter, who joined English Electric in 1944 to head its newly established design department. English Electric had not previously designed its own aircraft but had built other manufacturers' aircraft during WWII including large numbers of Halifaxes.

The first of four prototypes flew on 13 May 1949 and the first production Canberra B.2 on 8 October 1950. No 101 Squadron at Binbrook received its first aircraft in January 1951 and regular squadron service began the following May. Due to the outbreak of the Korean War and the uncertainties which accompanied that, large orders were placed and production undertaken by Short, Avro and Handley Page as well as the parent company.

The Canberra was also built in reconnaissance and dual control trainer variants, early models being the PR.3 with cameras, increased fuel and slightly longer fuselage (first flight March 1950) and T.4 (June 1952). RAF Canberras flew combat missions against Egyptian military targets during the Suez crisis of 1956, operating from Malta and Cyprus.

The Canberra was built under licence in Australia by GAF as the Mk.20 for the RAAF. Based on the British B.2, the first one flew on 29 May 1953 and the final example was delivered in September 1958. RAAF Canberras saw extensive active service in Vietnam between 1967 and 1971, flying nearly 12,000 sorties with considerable success.

Photo: GAF Canberra Mk.20 (with RNZAF Skyhawk).

English Electric Canberra B.6 and B(I).8

Country of origin: United Kingdom.

Type: Two seat bomber-intruder.

Powerplants: Two 7500lb (33.3kN) Rolls-Royce Avon Mk.109 turbojets.

Dimensions: Wing span 19.49m (63ft 11½in); length 19.96m (65ft 6in); height 4.75m (15ft 7in); wing area 89.2m² (960sq ft).

Weights: B(I).8 – operating empty 12,678kg (27,950lb); max takeoff 24,925kg (54,950lb).

Armament: B.6 – normal max bomb load 2722kg (6000lb) in weapons bay. B(I).6/8 – four 20mm or 30mm cannon in ventral pack plus 1361kg (3000lb) bombs in weapons bay and 907kg (2000lb) under wings.

Performance: B(I).8 – max speed 470kt (871km/h) at 40,000ft, 443kt (820km/h) at sea level; initial climb 3600ft (1097m)/min; service ceiling 48,000ft; range with max bomb load (low altitude) 700nm (1296km); max ferry range (no reserves) 3153nm (5840km).

Production: 901 Canberras of all models in UK including 105 B.6 (EE 56, Short 49), 22 B(I).6, 74 PR.7, 86 B(I).8 (EE 61, Short 25), 23 PR.9 (by Short), 16 B.12, 2 T.54, 8 PR.57 and 59 B.12.

Notes: Development of the Canberra continued with the B.5, this featuring more powerful Avon 109 engines, anti skid brakes, blind bombing radar and additional fuel in wing leading edge integral tanks. Intended to carry a 2268kg (5000lb) nuclear weapon in the tactical role, it was abandoned after a single prototype had been converted from a PR.3.

The B.5's mechanical features (but not the weapons system) were incorporated in the next major production version, the B.6. First flown on 26 January 1954, it entered RAF service the following June. The last 21 Australian built Canberras (see previous entry) were to a similar standard. RAF Canberra operations reached their peak in 1955 when 27 squadrons operated the aircraft. B.6s modified for use in the Near and Far East were redesignated B.15 and B.16.

A variant was the B(I).6 (for bomber/interdictor) with four 20mm cannon mounted in a pack beneath the rear bomb bay and two underwing pylons each capable of carrying a 454kg (1000lb) bomb load. The interdictor/intruder theme was fully exploited in the final bomber Canberra main variant, the B(I).8. The prototype (converted from the B.5) first flew on 23 July 1954 and the first production model on 8 June 1955. This featured the Avon 109s and gun pack of the B(I).6 but had a completely redesigned nose section with an offset and moved aft fighter style canopy under which the two crew members sat in tandem.

Like the earlier model Canberras, the later versions were widely exported and the final new build aircraft was a B(I).12 (similar to the RAF's B(I).8) delivered to South Africa in 1963. Other later models included the PR.7 and PR.9 photo-reconnaissance versions, the latter also with offset canopy and a substantially modified and more powerful derivative with increased span wings developed and built by Shorts.

About 140 Canberras were updated and refurbished between 1960 and 1983 for resale to ten existing or new export customers, generating new mark numbers. Others were converted for specialist training in the RAF and by 2000 the service still operated PR.9s and a handful of others for tests and trials. India and Argentina still flew bomber Canberras in 2000.

Photo: Canberra PR.9. (Bruce Malcolm)

English Electric Lightning F.1/2

Country of origin: United Kingdom.

Type: Single seat fighter.

Powerplants: F.1/1A – two 11,250lb (50.0kN) dry/14,430lb (64.2kN) with afterburner Rolls-Royce Avon 201 turbojets. F.2 – two similarly rated Avon 210s.

Dimensions: F.1/2 – wing span 10.62m (34ft 10in); length (incl probe) 16.84m (55ft 3in); height 5.97m (19ft 7in); wing area 42.6m² (459sq ft). F.2A – wing area 44.0m² (474sq ft).

Weights: F.2 – empty 12,542kg (27,650lb); normal loaded 17,554kg (38,700lb).

Armament: Two 30mm cannon in nose; two Firestreak AAMs under forward fuselage.

Performance: F.2 – max speed 1177kt (Mach 2.05/2180km/h) above 36,000ft, 673kt (Mach 1.02/1248km/h) at sea level; max climb 47,000ft (14,325m)/min; endurance 1.1 hours.

Production: 337 P.1/A/B and Lightnings of all versions including 2 P/1/A, 3 P.1B, 20 pre-production, 19 F.1, 28 F.1A and 44 F.2.

Notes: Britain's first and only wholly indigenous Mach 2 combat aircraft to enter production resulted from a 1947 requirement to develop a supersonic research aircraft. This materialised as the English Electric P.1 in August 1954, designed by W E ('Teddy') Petter. The aircraft featured a very thin and highly swept (60deg) wing with the ailerons mounted on the aft facing 'tips', two unreheated Armstrong Siddeley Sapphire turbojets installed superimposed within the fuselage and a plain intake in the nose.

A further specification for a supersonic fighter resulted in the P.1B, this taking the basic P.1 configuration but extensively redesigning it to incorporate two afterburning Rolls-Royce Avon 200-series turbojets in a considerably deeper fuselage and a shock cone in the intake designed to house advanced Ferranti Airpass radar. The first of three P.1B prototypes flew on 4 April 1957, the same month as the release of the infamous Defence White Paper which decreed that manned aircraft were obsolete and would be replaced by missiles. Despite this, development continued and the P.1B achieved Mach 2 in level flight in November 1958.

The first of 20 pre-production aircraft flew on 3 April 1958 and the first full production Lightning F.1 on 29 October 1959. Deliveries to the RAF began in June 1960. The Lightning F.1 was followed by the F.1A with retractable refuelling probe (first flight 16 August 1960) and then the F.2 with Avon 210s, these similarly rated to the earlier version but featuring infinitely variable afterburners. An autopilot and steerable nosewheel were also installed.

The first F.2 was flown on 11 July 1961 and 31 were modified to F.2A standards with some of the features of the later F.6 (see next entry) including an enlarged ventral fuel tank, larger square tipped fin and a modified wing with kinked and cambered leading edge. Five other F.2s were modified to F.52 standards and delivered to Saudi Arabia in 1966 ahead of a larger order for new production Lightnings.

Once it was established in production and service, the Lightning formed the basis of Britain's air defence system for a quarter of a century, equipping nine squadrons. Operational trainer versions with a widened forward fuselage for side-by-side seating were also developed, the first of them (the T.4 based on the F.1) flying on 6 May 1959.

Photo: A Lightning displays its distinctive wing plan form.

English Electric Lightning F.3 and F.6

Country of origin: United Kingdom.

Type: Single seat fighter.

Powerplants: Two 13,220lb (58.8kN) dry/16,300lb (72.5kN) with afterburner Rolls-Royce Avon 301/302 turbojets.

Dimensions: Wing span 10.62m (34ft 10in); length (incl probe) 16.84m (55ft 3in); height 5.97m (19ft 7in); wing area 44.0m² (474sq ft).

Weights: F.6 – empty 14,062kg (31,000lb); normal loaded 18,117kg (39,940lb); max takeoff 18,915kg (41,700lb).

Armament: F.3 – two Firestreak or Red Top AAMs under forward fuselage. F.6 – missiles plus two 30mm cannon in forward ventral pack. F.53/55 – guns and missiles plus two underwing pylons each for max 454kg (1000lb) load of bombs or rocket launchers.

Performance: F.6 – max speed 1228kt (Mach 2.14/2275km/h) above 36,000ft; 702kt (Mach 1.06/1300km/h) at sea level; max climb 50,000ft (15,240m)/min; max sustained ceiling 57,000ft; range (clean) 695nm (1287km); max ferry range 1350nm (2500km).

Production: 337 P.1/A/Bs and Lightnings of all versions including 62 F.3, 21 T.4, 22 T.5, 62 F.6, 46 F.53 and 8 T.55.

Notes: The fallacy of the 1957 British Defence White Paper's contention that the days of the manned combat aircraft were over had been exposed by the early 1960s, this realisation allowing the development of a 'second generation' of enhanced capability Lightnings. The resulting Lightning F.3 featured more powerful 300-series Avons, upgraded Ferranti AI Mk.23B Airpass fire control radar with collision course intercept capability and 'Advanced Firestreak' missiles, later called the Red Top. A larger, square fin was fitted to compensate for the missiles' destabilising effect.

The nose cannon were deleted and the F.3 continued the great British fighter tradition of having wholly inadequate fuel capacity, remaining as it was in the F.1 and F.2. Provision was made for overwing ferry tanks to help compensate. The first F.3 flew on 16 June 1962 and the fighter was operated by five RAF squadrons, in most cases replacing earlier models. The operational trainer variant was designated T.5, this first flying in March 1962.

The final Lightning for the RAF was the F.6 with a slightly larger wing incorporating extended leading edge camber and 'kink', the square tail, provision for overwing ferry tanks and – finally – increased internal fuel capacity via an enlarged ventral tank. The radar was further upgraded. Later, the gun armament was restored with two 30mm cannon mounted in the forward part of the ventral tank. The first F.6 flew on 17 April 1964 and regular squadron service began in October 1965. The Lightning was retired from RAF front line use in late 1988.

The Lightning F.6 formed the basis of the multirole F.53 which was delivered to Saudi Arabia (34) and Kuwait (12). This featured ground attack capability through its ability to carry bombs or rocket launchers as well as the usual air-to-air missiles and first flew in December 1966. Saudi aircraft were used in action against ground targets in Yemen, the only time the Lightning was flown in anger.

Photo: Lightning F.6. (BAe)

Eurocopter Tiger

Countries of origin: France and Germany.

Type: Two seat battlefield helicopter.

Powerplants: Two 1285shp (958kW) MTU/Turboméca/Rolls-Royce MTR 390 turboshafts; four bladed main rotor.

Dimensions: Main rotor diameter 13.00m (42ft 8in); fuselage length 14.07m (46ft 2in); height 3.81m (12ft 6in); main rotor disc area 132.7m² (1428sq ft).

Weights: Basic empty 3300kg (7275lb); design mission weight 5400-5925kg (11,905-13,062lb); max takeoff 6000kg (13,227lb).

Armament: HAP – one 30mm cannon in chin turret, four Mistral AAMs and four HOT anti tank missiles, or eight Trigat and four Stinger/Mistral AAMs, or combinations of rockets and missiles. HAC and UHT – up to eight HOT or Trigat anti tank missiles and four Mistrals or Stingers on two wing pylons, plus rocket and gun pods.

Performance: Max speed (armed) 145-155kt (269-287km/h); normal cruise 124kt (230km/h); max climb 2264ft (690m)/min; max vertical climb 1260ft (384m)/min; hovering ceiling OGE 11,480ft; range (internal fuel) 432nm (800km); ferry range (external fuel) 702nm (1300km).

Production: Five prototypes flown 1991-96; 427 required for France (215) and Germany (212).

Notes: The Tiger advanced combat helicopter programme resulted from similar requirements being issued by France and Germany, the two nations jointly funding development of the aircraft. The French and German armies separately began studying replacing their MBB Bo 105 and Aerospatiale Gazelle anti tank helicopters in the early 1980s. As a result of the common ground covered by the two requirements, a Memorandum of Understanding was signed in 1984.

An amended MoU was signed in 1987, development approved in December of that year and the main development contracts awarded in late 1989. At the same time, the helicopter was named Tiger, or *Tigre* in French. The helicopter divisions of Aerospatiale and MBB (Deutsche Aerospace) merged in January 1992 to form Eurocopter.

The Tiger is being developed in three versions: the French Army's HAP escort/fire support version with nose gun and roof mounted sight and intended for protection of anti armour helicopters against enemy helicopters and light armour; the HAC French anti tank model armed with 'fire and forget' anti tank missiles; and UHT multirole anti tank/combat support version for Germany which is basically similar to the HAC.

Features of all models include redundant electrical, fuel and hydraulic systems, advanced cockpit displays and the extensive use of composites in a highly crashworthy structure.

The first Tiger development aircraft flew on 27 April 1991 and four other development aircraft followed in April 1993, November 1993, December 1994 and February 1996. The fourth Tiger crashed during a night demonstration to the Australian Army in February 1998. Production contracts covering an initial 80 Tigers each for France and Germany were signed in June 1999 against a total requirement for 215 and 212, respectively. Deliveries are scheduled to begin in 2002.

Photo: The third Tiger prototype in UHT configuration. (Dasa)

Eurofighter Typhoon

Fairchild AC-119 'Shadow' and 'Stinger'

Countries of origin: Germany, UK, Spain and Italy.

Type: Multirole fighter.

Powerplants: Two 13,490lb (60.0kN) dry/20,250lb (90.0kN) with afterburner Eurojet EJ200 turbofans; first two development aircraft initially fitted with two Turbo Union RB199s.

Dimensions: Wing span 10.95m (35ft 11in); length 15.96m (52ft 4½in); height 5.28m (17ft 4in); wing area 51.2m² (551sq ft).

Weights: Basic empty 10,000kg (22,046lb); max takeoff approx 23,000kg (50,705lb).

Armament: One 27mm cannon in starboard wing root (not in RAF version); eight underwing and five underfuselage hardpoints for air-to-ground and air-to-air weapons; max weapons load 6500kg (14,330lb).

Performance: (estimated) max speed 1148kt (Mach 2.0/2126km/h) at altitude; combat air patrol radius of action over 750nm (1389km); radius of action with drop tanks, three laser guided bombs and seven AAMs 750nm (1389km) hi-lo-hi or 350nm (648km) lo-lo-lo.

Production: 7 development aircraft built 1994-1997; project partner requirements for 620 aircraft.

Notes: Initial feasibility studies into a jointly developed European advanced fighter were initiated in 1983 by the UK, Germany, Italy, Spain and France under the designation European Fighter Aircraft (EFA). France dropped out the following year having decided to instead go its own way with the Dassault Rafale.

The Eurofighter consortium was formally established in June 1986 with development and production workshare split between Germany (33%), the UK (33%), Italy (21%) and Spain (13%). The specific concept of the twin engined EFA was formalised in December 1987, British Aerospace in the meantime having flown – in August 1986 – its EAP (Experimental Aircraft Programme) technology demonstrator with the main physical features of the Eurofighter including canard delta configuration and fly-by-wire controls.

The EFA was renamed Eurofighter 2000 in 1992 and then Typhoon in 1998. The new Eurojet EJ200 turbofan for the aircraft is developed and manufactured by a consortium comprising Britain's Rolls-Royce, Germany's MTU, Italy's FiatAvio and Spain's ITP.

The programme was extensively reviewed in 1992 because of German budgetary constraints with various 'cheaper' variants examined. After threatening to withdraw from the project, Germany eventually decided on reduced numbers of a version with some equipment deleted. After considerable delays, the first of seven development aircraft flew in Germany on 27 March 1994 with RB199 engines as used on the Panavia Tornado, followed by the first British aircraft on 6 April. The first Italian example (with EJ200 engines) flew in June 1995 and the first from Spain (also the first two seat operational trainer version) in August 1996.

The Typhoon's advanced features include extensive use of carbon fibre in the structure, multimode Pulse Doppler radar, an infrared search and tracking system, state-of-the-art cockpit and some direct voice input controls. Britain requires 232 aircraft, Germany 180, Italy 121 and Spain 87. A production contract for an initial 148 aircraft was signed in September 1998 with first deliveries planned for 2002, five years later than originally intended. Greece selected the Typhoon in 1999.

Photo: A development batch Typhoon. (Paul Merritt)

Country of origin: USA.

Type: 10 crew gunship.

Powerplants: AC-119G – two 3400hp (2535kW) Wright R-3350-89 Turbo Compound 18-cylinder radials; four bladed propellers. AC-119K – R-3350s plus two 2850lb (12.7kN) General Electric J85-GE-17 turbojets in pods under wings.

Dimensions: Wing span 33.30m (109ft 3in); length 26.36m (86ft 6in); height 8.08m (26ft 6in); wing area 134.4m² (1447sq ft).

Weights: AC-119G – max takeoff 32,977kg (72,700lb). AC-119K – empty 26,437kg (58,282lb); max takeoff 36,469kg (80,400lb).

Armament: AC-119G – four side firing 7.62mm six barrel General Electric Miniguns in port fuselage. AC-119K – Miniguns plus two side firing 20mm cannon.

Performance: AC-119K – max speed 217kt (402km/h) at 10,000ft; max cruise at 10,000ft 190kt (352km/h) with jets operating or 150kt (278km/h) on piston engines only; initial climb 1300ft (396m)/min; range 1720nm (3185km).

Production: 1051 C-119s of all versions; 26 AC-119G and 26 AC-119K conversions.

Notes: Developed in 1967 to replace the AC-47 'Spooky' gunship (which see) for operations in Vietnam, the AC-119 more effectively exploited the concept pioneered by the earlier aircraft by offering heavier armament and more efficient targeting and lighting equipment. Its mode of operation was similar, circling around a target, usually at night, and bringing intensive firepower to bear.

The C-119 Flying Boxcar medium tactical transport had first flown in November 1947 and deliveries began in December 1949. More than 1000 were built up to 1955 in several versions, mainly for the USAF but also for export to Italy, Belgium and India. Others were subsequently sold to Taiwan, Brazil and Ethiopia.

The first gunship version was the AC-119G 'Shadow' intended for 'in country' (ie South Vietnam) service, modifications including the installation of four fixed multi barrel 7.62mm General Electric Miniguns firing from the port side of the fuselage, a night observation sight, a pallet mounted night illumination system, protective armour for the crew, flare launcher and analogue gunfire control system. The first of 26 AC-119G conversions was delivered to the USAF in May 1968 and operational service in Vietnam began in early 1969.

The AC-119K 'Stinger' conversion was intended mainly for night operations in North Vietnam, especially over the Ho Chi Minh Trail. It differed from the 'Shadow' in having two 20mm rotary cannon in addition to the four Miniguns, a forward looking infrared (FLIR) sensor, beacon tracking radar, searchlight and ungraded avionics.

A significant mechanical change was the installation of two podded J85 turbojets under the wings to allow improved takeoff performance and payloads plus greater safety on operations. The AC-119K entered operational service in late 1969 and 26 conversions were performed.

The AC-119 was phased out of USAF service in 1971-72 and the survivors handed over to the South Vietnamese Air Force.

Photo: AC-119G 'Shadow'.

Fairchild A-10 Thunderbolt II

Country of origin: USA.

Type: Single seat anti armour/close support.

Powerplants: Two 9065lb (40.3kN) General Electric TF34-GE-100 turbofans.

Dimensions: Wing span 17.53m (57ft 6in); length 16.25m (53ft 4in); height 4.47m (14ft 8in); wing area 47.0m² (506sq ft).

Weights: Empty equipped 10,600kg (23,370lb); max takeoff 22,680kg (50,000lb).

Armament: One seven barrel 30mm rotary cannon in nose; 11 external stations for max 7258kg (16,000lb) ordnance including Maverick anti armour missiles, cluster bombs, laser guided bombs, conventional bombs, gun pods, jammer pods and drop tanks.

Performance: Max speed (clean) 390kt (722km/h) at sea level; cruising speed 300-342kt (555-633km/h); max climb 6000ft (1829m)/min; combat radius close air support (with 2hrs loiter) 250nm (463km); reconnaissance combat radius 400nm (740km); deep strike combat radius 540nm (1000km); max ferry range 2000nm (3705km).

Production: 2 YA-10A and 713 A-10A, total 715.

Notes: The unsuitability of supersonic fighter-bombers for close support operations during the Vietnam War resulted in the USAF formulating a requirement in 1967 for a dedicated heavily armed, manoeuvrable and long loiter time subsonic ground attack aircraft with a high level of survivability. High speed was considered unimportant for the role.

Designs from Fairchild (YA-10) and Northrop (YA-9) were selected to contest a 60 day, 125 flying hours fly-off competition, the first of two YA-10As flying on 10 May 1972. Fairchild's submission was declared the winner in January 1973 and the first production contracts placed two months later.

A total acquisition of 739 production A-10As for the USAF was originally planned but this was reduced to 713. The first of six development batch A-10As was flown on 15 February 1975 and the first true production version in October 1975. Deliveries to the USAF's Tactical Air Command began in March 1976 and the final example handed over in March 1984. The A-10A quickly acquired the nickname 'Warthog', the official 'Thunderbolt II' not applied until April 1978.

A-10 design features include a large straight wing which provides agility and some shielding for the two TF34 turbofans mounted high on the rear fuselage and separated so that a hit on one will not damage the other. The aircraft is capable of flying with one of its vertical tails severely damaged and the pilot is protected by a titanium bath. Apart from its external ordnance, the A-10's massive General Electric 30mm rotary cannon provides substantial hitting power.

There has been debate about the A-10's survivability on the modern battlefield but it was very successful in the Gulf War against minimal opposition and also extensively used over Kosova in 1999. Some were redesignated OA-10 for the Forward Air Control role from 1989 (with Sidewinder AAMs for self defence) while one of the prototypes was converted to a tandem two seater (with weapons operator) as a night operations demonstrator in 1979 as the YA-10B. None were ordered. About 350 A-10s remained in USAF/ANG/Reserve service by 2000.

Photo: A-10A Thunderbolt II.

Fairey Firefly Mks.4-7

Country of origin: United Kingdom.

Type: Two seat naval fighter-bomber and anti submarine reconnaissance.

Powerplant: One 2245hp (1674kW) Rolls-Royce Griffon 74 V12 piston engine; four bladed propeller.

Dimensions: Wing span 12.55m (41ft 2in); length 11.56m (37ft 11in); height 4.37m (14ft 4in); wing area 30.6m² (330sq ft).

Weights: FR.IV – empty 4472kg (9859lb); max takeoff 7083kg (15,615lb). AS.5 – empty 4388kg (9674lb); max takeoff 7301kg (16,096lb).

Armament: Four 20mm cannon in wings; underwing hardpoints for max 907kg (2000lb) ordnance including bombs, rockets, mines, depth charges, air-sea rescue containers.

Performance: FR.IV – max speed 300kt (555km/h) at 12,500ft, 274kt (508km/h) at sea level; time to 10,000ft 7.2min; service ceiling 29,200ft; range (internal fuel) 506nm (937km); range with drop tanks 930nm (1722km).

Production: 1623 of all models including 160 FR/NF.4, 352 FR/NF/AS.5, 133 AS.6 and 151 AS.7.

Notes: Fairey developed a 'second generation' of Firefly versions following production of over 800 wartime Mks.I and II. The prototype Firefly had flown 22 December 1941 and deliveries to the Royal Navy Fleet Air Arm began in March 1943, the type seeing action against both Germany and Japan before WWII ended.

Already proven to be a versatile and successful carrier borne combat aircraft, the Firefly's usefulness increased further with the post war models, these differing fundamentally from the earlier versions by having the original Rolls-Royce Griffon engine with single-stage supercharger replaced with a more powerful two-stage version. Externally, the new models differed in having the original and ungainly undernose 'beard' radiator replaced with radiators located in the leading edges of the wing roots and leaving the nose clean.

The first Firefly with a two-stage Griffon retained the original radiator layout. Designated Mk.III (and converted from a Mk.I) it first flew in 1943 but subsequent production aircraft had the new radiator arrangement. The first Firefly FR.IV (later FR.4) fighter-reconnaissance version flew on 25 May 1945 and of the 160 built, 40 went to the Royal Netherlands Naval Air Service. A few were built as NF.4 night fighters with radar in a wing leading edge pod.

The Firefly Mk.5 was built in FR, NF and AS (anti submarine) versions between January 1948 and May 1950, these introducing powered rather than manually folding wings during the production run. The Firefly Mks.4 and 5 were flown from four RN and Royal Australian Navy carriers during the Korean War on close support, minelaying and shipping strike duties.

The specialist anti submarine Firefly AS.6 first flew in March 1949 and entered service two months later, this remaining the RN's main anti submarine warfare aircraft until the Fairey Gannet entered service. The final Firefly variant to achieve production was the AS.7 with larger fin and rudder, bulged mid fuselage canopy for two radar operators and reversion to the chin radiator. The last was delivered in May 1955, numerous other subvariants having meanwhile been created by conversion for target towing and training and as pilotless target drones.

Photo: Firefly AS.6.

Fairey Gannet

Country of origin: United Kingdom.

Type: Three seat carrier based anti submarine.

Powerplants: AS.1 – one 2950ehp (2200kW) Armstrong Siddeley Double Mamba 100 turboprop. AS.4 – one 3035ehp (2263kW) Double Mamba 101; counter rotating four bladed propellers.

Dimensions: Wing span 16.56m (54ft 4in); length 13.10m (43ft 0in); height 4.18m (13ft 8½in); wing area 44.9m² (483sq ft).

Weights: AS.1 – empty 6835kg (15,069lb); max takeoff 9798kg (21,600lb). AS.4 – max takeoff 10,209kg (22,506lb).

Armament: Two homing torpedoes, three depth charges or bombs in weapons bay up to max 907kg (2000lb); 16 27kg (60lb) rockets under wings.

Performance: AS.4 – max speed 260kt (482km/h); typical patrol speed 130kt (241km/h); initial climb 2200ft (670m)/min; service ceiling 25,000ft; normal range 575nm (1065km).

Production: 3 prototypes, 182 AS.1, 37 T.2, 44 AEW.3, 75 AS.4 and 8 T.5, total 349.

Notes: Designed to meet a demanding late 1945 specification for an anti submarine aircraft capable of operating from the Royal Navy's smaller fleet carriers while combining the traditionally separated anti submarine hunter/killer roles, what became the Gannet was the RN's standard ASW aircraft during the 1950s and '60s.

Its most significant feature was the use of the Armstrong Siddeley Double Mamba turboprop, this comprising two coupled Mamba turbines driving a pair of co-axial counter-rotating propellers through a common gearbox with a clutch gear that enabled one engine to be shut down to save fuel on patrols. Weapons were housed in a large internal bay.

Fairey won the production contract against competition from the Blackburn YB.1, the prototype flying for the first time on 19 September 1949. Development was protracted due to the customer frequently changing its mind as to the final specification and problems with the Double Mamba, but the first production Gannet AS.1 finally flew in July 1953 and full service began in January 1955.

The improved Gannet AS.4 first flew in April 1956, this featuring a more powerful version of the Double Mamba and upgraded equipment. Many AS.1s were converted to the later standard while some of these were subsequently upgraded to AS.6 specifications with enhanced avionics and ECM equipment. The Gannet T.2 and T.5 with dual controls were operational trainer versions of the AS.1 and AS.4, respectively.

New Gannets were also sold to the Royal Australian Navy (31 AS.1s, 1 AS.4 and 4 T.2s) for operations from HMAS *Melbourne* and the German Navy (15 AS.4s and 1 T.5), while the Indonesian Air Force received 18 ex RN aircraft.

The final Gannet variant was the early warning AEW.3 with a 3875ehp (2890kW) Double Mamba 112, substantially redesigned fuselage, modified tail unit, strengthened undercarriage and a large underside radome housing APS-20 search radar. First flight was in August 1958 and the AEW.3 became the RN Fleet Air Arm's last 'conventional' carrier borne fixed wing aircraft (defining the Sea Harrier as 'unconventional'), retired in 1978.

Photo: Gannet AS.4.

FFA P-16

Country of origin: Switzerland.

Type: Single seat attack fighter.

Powerplant: Mk.II/III – one 11,000lb (48.9kN) Armstrong Siddeley Sapphire ASSa 7 turbojet.

Dimensions: Wing span 11.15m (36ft 7in); length 14.30m (46ft 11in); height 4.24m (13ft 11in); wing area 30.0m² (323sq ft).

Weights: Mk.III – empty 7040kg (15,520lb); max takeoff 11,720kg (25,838lb).

Armament: Mk.III – two 30mm cannon in nose; fuselage launcher for 44 68mm rockets; underwing hardpoints for max 2240kg (4938lb) bombs and rockets.

Performance: Mk.III – max speed 539kt (998km/h) at 26,250ft; initial climb 12,795ft (3900m)/min; service ceiling 46,000ft; range (internal fuel) 800nm (1480km).

Production: 5.

Notes: The FFA (Flug und Fahrzeugwerke AG) P-16 was designed to a 1948 Swiss requirement for an indigenous interceptor and ground support aircraft to meet demanding local requirements. These included high subsonic performance (with supersonic capability in a dive), good manoeuvrability, a high rate of climb with combat load and the ability to operate from short grass airfields. FFA and EFW submitted designs, and both were contracted to build prototypes. The EFW project was abandoned in 1953.

The P-16 featured a low aspect ratio straight wing with high lift devices (including leading edge flaps), permanent wingtip fuel tanks and twin nose and main wheels to assist in operations from grass strips. The first aircraft was powered by a 7900lb (35.1kN) Armstrong Siddeley Sapphire ASSa 6 turbojet and flew for the first time on 28 April 1955. The second flew on 16 June 1956 and recorded the type's first supersonic flight (in a dive) in August 1956.

The first of three pre series aircraft flew in April 1957 as the P-16 Mk.II with more powerful Sapphire ASSa 7 engine. An order for 100 production Mk.IIIs was placed in March 1958 but unfortunately, the first Mk.II was lost only a few days later. The Swiss investigators blamed the aircraft's hydraulic system and their findings (which were disputed by both the manufacturer and experts from the Royal Aircraft Establishment at Farnborough) resulted in the P-16 order being cancelled as it was considered that a modification programme would take too much time to complete.

Despite this, FFA completed two more P-16s to Mk.III production standards on its own initiative, these flying for the first time in July 1959 and March 1960 but failing to generate further interest from the Swiss or export customers.

Despite its failure to enter production, part of the P-16 lives on through its wing. In 1960, William Lear set up the Swiss American Aviation Corporation to manufacture a five/seven passenger light twin engined business jet as the SAAC-23. The original plan was build the aircraft in Switzerland but after the design had been finalised in August 1962 the project was transferred to the USA and the Lear Jet Corporation established at Wichita, Kansas. Renamed the Learjet 23, the first aircraft – complete with the P-16's wing – first flew in October 1963. Subsequent Learjet 24s, 25s, 35s and 36s all flew on the same wing.

Photo: The fifth and final P-16.

FMA IA 58A Pucará

Country of origin: Argentina.

Type: Two seat close support and counter insurgency aircraft.

Powerplants: Two 978shp (729kW) Turboméca Astazou XVIG turbo-props; three bladed propellers.

Dimensions: Wing span 14.50m (47ft 7in); length 14.25m (46ft 9in); height 5.36m (17ft 7in); wing area 30.3m² (326sq ft).

Weights: Empty equipped 4020kg (8862lb); max takeoff 6800kg (14,991lb).

Armament: Two 20mm cannon and four 7.62mm machine guns in forward fuselage; one underfuselage and two underwing hardpoints for max 1500kg (3307lb) ordnance including bombs, rocket pods, torpedos, mines, camera pods and drop tanks.

Performance: Max speed 270kt (500km/h); cruising speed 232-260kt (430-481km/h); max climb 3543ft (1080m)/min; service ceiling 32,800ft; low level combat radius with 1500kg (3307lb) ordnance 121nm (224km) or 310nm (574km) with 800kg (1764lb) ordnance; max ferry range (with external fuel) 2000nm (3705km).

Production: 116.

Notes: The IA 58 Pucará was designed by the Argentine state owned Fabrica Militar de Avions at Cordoba to meet a mid 1960s requirement for a light ground attack and counter-insurgency aircraft. Development began in August 1966, this leading to test flying of an unpowered aerodynamic test vehicle from December 1967.

The first powered prototype – then known as the Delfin – was fitted with two 904shp (674kW) Garrett AiResearch TPE331-U-303 turboprops and first flew on 20 August 1969. The second prototype (flown 6 September 1970) had the definitive Turboméca Astazous installed.

The first and only production version was designated IA 58A Pucará, manufacture getting underway against an initial order for 60 for the Fuerza Aérea Argentina. After a lengthy development period, the first of these flew in November 1974 but deliveries did not begin until early 1976.

It was also in 1976 that the Pucará had its baptism of fire against rebel guerillas in Argentina's north-west, but it was during the Falklands War of 1982 that the aircraft became well known. In this campaign it was unsuccessful, all 24 of the aircraft deployed either destroyed by ground fire, sabotaged by the British SAS troops or captured when Argentine forces were ejected from the Islands. One captured Pucará was evaluated by the RAF.

The Pucará's poor showing in the Falklands resulted in it eventually falling from grace in Argentina, although not before an additional 48 IA 58As were ordered, partly as attrition replacements. The last was built in 1986 and six new aircraft were delivered to Uruguay. Argentina made 40 of its aircraft surplus in 1986 for resale, some of these going to Colombia (3) and Sri Lanka (4). Some early production Pucarás were operated as single seaters with additional fuel capacity where the rear (observer's) seat had been.

Prototypes were flown of the proposed IA 58B with upgraded armament, and the IA 58C single seater with further armament and equipment upgrades, but neither was ordered.

Photo: Argentinian IA 58A Pucará.

Folland Gnat and HAL Ajeet

Countries of origin: United Kingdom/India.

Type: Single seat lightweight fighter.

Powerplant: Gnat – one 4250lb (18.9kN) Rolls-Royce (Bristol) Orpheus Mk.701 turbojet. Ajeet – one 4500lb (20.0kN) HAL built Orpheus Mk.701-01.

Dimensions: Wing span 6.76m (22ft 2in); length 9.07m (29ft 9in); height 2.69m (8ft 10in); wing area 14.7m² (158sq ft).

Weights: Gnat – empty 2177kg (4800lb); max takeoff 3976kg (8765lb). Ajeet – empty 2307kg (5086lb); max takeoff 4170kg (9195lb).

Armament: Two 30mm cannon below wing roots; four underwing hardpoints for two 227kg (500lb) bombs and 68mm rocket pods or drop tanks.

Performance: Gnat – max speed 604kt (1118km/h) at 20,000ft; time to 45,000ft 5.0min; service ceiling 50,000ft; range with drop tanks 852nm (1577km). Ajeet – max speed 595kt (1103km/h) at sea level; 551kt (1020km/h) at 39,000ft, time to 39,000ft 6.0min; low level tactical radius with two 227kg (500lb) bombs 110nm (204km).

Production: Gnat – 61 single seaters in UK (incl 15 for assembly by HAL), 213 single seaters by HAL and 105 T.1 in UK, total 379. Ajeet – 79 by HAL (plus 10 converted from Gnat).

Notes: Although best known in its two seat form as the RAF's advanced trainer through the 1960s and '70s (especially its use by the Red Arrows), the Gnat began life as a single seat lightweight fighter of diminutive proportions. Although not adopted by the RAF it was exported in small numbers to Finland (13 in 1958-59) and Yugoslavia (2) and built under licence in much larger quantities by Hindustan Aeronautics Ltd for the Indian Air Force. HAL also manufactured a locally developed improved version called the Ajeet (Unconquerable).

Folland (later part of Hawker Siddeley) began development of a very small jet fighter in 1951 in an attempt to arrest the ever increasing size and cost of combat aircraft. The initial result was the Fo 139 Midge, powered by a 1640lb (7.3kN) Armstrong Siddeley Viper turbojet, the single prototype flying for the first time on 11 August 1954.

Availability of the more powerful Bristol Orpheus led to the larger (but still relatively tiny) Fo 144 Gnat, the private venture prototype flying on 18 July 1955 and followed by six development aircraft. Despite an intensive marketing campaign, the RAF didn't order the Gnat in its single seat form, but greater success was found with India, which began receiving British and then HAL built aircraft from 1958, the last from HAL delivered in January 1974.

The 214th HAL Gnat was modified as the prototype Ajeet, this featuring a redesigned wing with integral fuel tanks, more powerful Orpheus Mk.701-01 engine, a zero-zero ejection seat, upgraded avionics and new gunsight. The prototype first flew on 6 March 1975 and the last was delivered in February 1982. The prototype of a two seat trainer version was flown in September 1982 but not ordered.

The British built Gnat T.1 trainer for the RAF first flew in August 1959 and the last was delivered in May 1965. It was retired from RAF service in 1979, replaced by the BAe Hawk. Finland's Gnats remained in service until 1972 while India retired its last Ajeets in March 1991.

Photo: HAL Ajeet.

General Dynamics F-111A/E

Country of origin: USA.

Type: Two seat tactical strike.

Powerplants: Two 18,500lb (82.3kN) with afterburner Pratt & Whitney TF30-P-3 turbofans.

Dimensions: Wing span 19.20m (63ft 0in) fully extended, 9.94m (31ft 11½in) fully swept; length 22.40m (73ft 6in); height 5.22m (17ft 1½in); wing area 48.8m² (525sq ft).

Weights: F-111A – empty 20,944kg (46,172lb); max takeoff 41,958kg (92,500lb).

Armament: Internal weapons bay for one 20mm Vulcan multi barrel rotary cannon or two 907kg (2000lb) bombs; six underwing hardpoints for max 13,608kg (30,000lb) ordnance.

Performance: Max speed (clean) 1434kt (Mach 2.5/2656km/h) at 40,000ft, 792kt (Mach 1.2/1468km/h) at sea level; service ceiling over 60,000ft; max range (internal fuel) 2750nm (5094km).

Production: 564 F-111s of all versions including 18 development F-111A, 141 production F-111A and 94 F-111E.

Notes: One of the most controversial and effective (after numerous problems were solved) combat aircraft of the modern era, the F-111 was conceived to meet the 1960 TFX requirement for a 'jack of all trades' aircraft replacing numerous other types and capable of performing tactical strike, strategic bombing, reconnaissance and even naval fleet defence duties. The concept was championed by US Defence Secretary Robert McNamara (a former vice president of Ford) who had the economist's view that defence procurement should be conducted with business like efficiency.

Boeing and General Dynamics were finalists in the TFX programme, the latter's design announced as the winner in November 1962. The design was highly advanced: the first production application of variable sweep wings (ranging from 16 to 72.5 degrees) and afterburning turbofans, advanced (for the time) analogue avionics including terrain following radar (TFR) to allow low altitude and high speed flight in all weathers, and a crew escape capsule rather than individual ejection seats. The planned USAF procurement was 1469 but this was eventually cut by two-thirds mainly due to constantly escalating costs.

The first of 18 development F-111As flew on 21 December 1964 and deliveries began in November 1967. In March 1968 six (later eight) aircraft were prematurely deployed to Thailand for combat trials over Vietnam. Three were lost in only 55 missions due to technical problems, fuelling the controversy the ever more expensive aircraft had already generated. The problems (especially with the wing carry-through box) were gradually and expensively overcome and a second deployment to Vietnam in 1972 was considerably more successful with 4000 missions completed for the loss of seven aircraft, some to enemy action.

The next USAF F-111 variant to appear was the F-111E, first flown in August 1969 and regarded as an interim model pending introduction of the more advanced F-111D. It differed from the F-111A in its more efficient 'Triple Plow 2' engine intakes and improved stores management and TFR systems. Forty-two F-111As were converted to unarmed EF-111A 'Raven' electronic warfare aircraft by Grumman from 1981, these proving effective in the Gulf War.

Photo: The first prototype F-111A. (General Dynamics)

General Dynamics F-111B

Country of origin: USA.

Type: Two seat naval air superiority fighter.

Powerplants: Two 18,500lb (82.3kN) with afterburner Pratt & Whitney TF30-P-3 or (planned) 20,250lb (90.0kN) TF30-P-12 turbofans.

Dimensions: Wing span 21.33m (70ft 0in) fully extended, 10.35m (33ft 11½in) fully swept; length 20.32m (66ft 8in); height 5.08m (16ft 8in); wing area 51.1m² (550sq ft).

Weights: Empty 20,866kg (46,000lb); max takeoff 34,020kg (75,000lb).

Armament: Six AIM-54A Phoenix air-to-air missiles, two internally and four on underwing pylons.

Performance: (Estimated) max speed (clean) 1434kt (Mach 2.5/2656km/h) at 40,000ft, 792kt (Mach 1.2/1468km/h) at sea level; patrol speed 486kt (900km/h) at 36,000ft; max range (internal fuel) 2520nm (4668km).

Production: 564 F-111s of all versions including 7 F-111B.

Notes: Probably the most controversial of all the F-111 variants at a time when the overall programme was attracting enormous criticism, the US Navy's F-111B carrier borne fleet defence fighter was the aircraft which was intended to prove Robert McNamara's 'commonality' concept.... had it worked.

It didn't, and the F-111B was abandoned, the result proving that Boeing – the loser of the TFX/F-111 competition – was correct in its original assertion that it was impossible to fill the various and often disparate requirements with a single airframe. Grumman was the prime contractor on the F-111B programme and the USN planned a procurement of 231.

Externally, the F-111B differed from its land based brethren by virtue of a shorter, upwards folding nose radome (in order to save space) and the longer span wings which would later be fitted to the FB-111A and F-111C. Wing folding was not necessary due to their ability to be swept fully back when embarked. The other major features of the B's airframe and powerplants were similar to the F-111A, apart from those components directly associated with carrier operations. The avionics were also substantially revised.

For its primary role as a fleet air superiority fighter, the F-111B featured Hughes AWG-9 fire control radar housed in the shortened nose in combination with six advanced AIM-54 Phoenix radar guided air-to-air missiles.

The first of what would be only seven F-111Bs flew from Grumman's Long Island, New York plant on 18 May 1965. In July 1968 the programme was cancelled after an unsuccessful battle to bring the aircraft's weight down to practical levels, an impossible task as it turned out. Even the proposed installation of more powerful TF30-P-12 engines couldn't save the F-111B and a near trebling of the unit cost was the final straw.

Apart from anything else, the US Navy was never overly keen in having what was really a modified USAF bomber in its service as a fighter. Grumman went on to build the F-14 Tomcat for the US Navy instead, an aircraft which retained two of the F-111B's features: variable sweep wings and the AWG-9 radar/Phoenix missile combination.

Photo: One of only seven F-111Bs.

General Dynamics F-111D/F

Country of origin: USA.

Type: Two seat tactical strike.

Powerplants: F-111D – two 20,840lb (92.7kN) with afterburner Pratt & Whitney TF30-P-9 turbofans. F-111F – two 25,100lb (111.6kN) TF30-P-100 turbofans.

Dimensions: Wing span 19.20m (63ft 0in) fully extended, 9.94m (31ft 11½in) fully swept; length 22.40m (73ft 6in); height 5.22m (17ft 1½in); wing area 48.8m² (525sq ft).

Weights: F-111D – empty 21,152kg (46,631lb); max takeoff 45,360kg (100,000lb). F-111F – empty 21,537kg (47,481lb); max takeoff 45,360kg (100,000lb).

Armament: Internal weapons bay for one 20mm Vulcan multi barrel rotary cannon or two 907kg (2000lb) bombs; six underwing hardpoints for max 13,608kg (30,000lb) ordnance.

Performance: F-111F – max speed (clean) 1434kt (Mach 2.5/2656km/h) at 40,000ft, 792kt (Mach 1.2/1468km/h) at sea level; max climb (at combat weight) 43,050ft (13,121m)/min; combat ceiling 57,900ft; combat radius hi-lo-hi 1079nm (2000km); max range (internal fuel) 2933nm (5432km).

Production: 564 F-111s of all versions including 94 F-111D and 106 F-111F.

Notes: Development of the F-111 as a highly effective strike aircraft continued with the F-111D, this and the following F-111F continuing to make a mockery of the 'F' prefix to the aircraft's designation. Despite what those planning the TFX might have thought back in 1960, the resulting aircraft was never going to be a fighter in the accepted sense.

In terms of avionics fit, the F-111D represented the most advanced version of the aircraft now universally known as the 'Aardvark' as it incorporated the so-called Mark II system with a digital instead of analogue computer (another first for a tactical combat aircraft), advanced APG-130 radar, Doppler navigation radar and other upgrades. Physically, the F-111D incorporated the Triple Plow 2 intakes matched with more powerful and refined TF30-P-9 engines and the stronger undercarriage of the FB-111A, this allowing increased weights.

The first F-111D was flown in December 1968. Deliveries to the USAF began in June 1970 and the last was handed over in February 1973. The initial requirement for 315 was cut to only 94 mainly due to the chronic unreliability of the much vaunted new avionics. Even in the 1980s the F-111D fleet could only manage an operational availability rate of around 30 per cent.

The final and best Aardvark variant was the F-111F, which combined the Triple Plow 2 intakes with the 25 per cent more powerful and substantially redesigned TF30-P-100 engine, the undercarriage and increased maximum weight of the F-111D, modified wing structure and a revised, simplified (and more reliable) Mark IIB avionics package based around the best from the F-111D and E plus the FB-111A's APG-144 radar.

The F-111F entered service in September 1971 and the final example – the last new production F-111 of any model – was handed over in 1976. Successful in the Gulf War of 1991, the F-111F underwent several weapons and avionics upgrades over the years and was retired from USAF service in July 1996. The USAF kept some EF-111A Raven EW conversions until 1998, leaving Australia as the sole F-111 operator.

Photo: General Dynamics F-111F.

General Dynamics FB-111A and F-111C

Country of origin: USA.

Type: FB-111A – two seat strategic bomber. F-111C – two seat tactical strike.

Powerplants: FB-111A – two 20,350lb (90.5kN) with afterburner Pratt & Whitney TF30-P-7 turbofans. F-111C – two 18,500lb (82.3kN) with afterburner TF30-P-3.

Dimensions: Wing span 21.33m (70ft 0in) fully extended, 10.35m (33ft 11½in) fully swept; length 22.40m (73ft 6in); wing area 51.1m² (550sq ft).

Weights: FB-111A – empty 21,764kg (47,980lb); max takeoff 54,092kg (119,250lb). F-111C – empty 21,457kg (47,303lb); max takeoff 49,896kg (110,000lb).

Armament: FB-111A – two 340kg (750lb) bombs or two AGM-69A ASMs in weapons bay; eight underwing hardpoints for max 17,010kg (37,500lb) ordnance; nuclear capable.

Performance: FB-111A – max speed 1260kt (Mach 2.2/2334km/h) at 40,000ft, 792kt (Mach 1.2/1468km/h) at sea level; rate of climb at combat weight 23,418ft (7138m)/min; service ceiling 50,000ft; combat radius with two AGM-69As and drop tanks 1560nm (2890km); mission range hi-lo-hi 5340nm (9890km).

Production: 564 F-111s of all versions including 76 FB-111A, 24 F-111C and 2 YF-111A.

Notes: The FB-111A was developed for the USAF's Strategic Air Command as an interim replacement for the Convair B-58 Hustler and early model Boeing B-52s pending arrival of the Rockwell B-1. Those responsible for allocating designation prefixes at last made some concession to the F-111's real role!

Compared to the F-111A, the FB-111A featured more powerful TF30-P-7 engines, increased internal fuel capacity with extra tanks in the weapons bay, increased span wings, two additional underwing pylons, strengthened undercarriage, increased maximum weight and avionics appropriate to the strategic bomber role. Terrain following radar was retained.

The first FB-111A (converted from a development F-111A) flew on 30 July 1967 and the first production version in July 1968. Deliveries began in October 1969 and the 76th and last was delivered in 1971, the number reduced from the originally planned 210. With removal of the FB-111A's nuclear role from 1988, the aircraft was redesignated F-111G.

The only nation apart from the USA to purchase F-111s was Australia, the RAAF's F-111Cs combining the F-111A's powerplants and avionics with the FB-111A's long span wings and stronger undercarriage for increased maximum weight. The aircraft were built in 1968 but Australia refused delivery until 1973 when the many technical problems were satisfactorily solved. Four were subsequently modified as RF-111C reconnaissance platforms. Four additional ex USAF F-111As were purchased in 1982 and upgraded to 'C' standards, while a further 15 ex USAF F-111Gs were delivered in 1993-94 to help extend the F-111's RAAF service life to 2020 by allowing fleet rotation. A comprehensive digital avionics upgrade was completed in 1999.

Britain ordered 50 F-111Ks in 1966 to replace the cancelled TSR.2 but these were in turn cancelled two years later. Two partially built F-111Ks were completed as YF-111As and used in research and development programmes by the USAF.

Photo: An RAAF F-111G.

Gloster Meteor F.4

Country of origin: United Kingdom.

Type: Single seat fighter.

Powerplants: Two 3500lb (15.6kN) Rolls-Royce Derwent 5 turbojets.

Dimensions: Wing span 11.33m (37ft 2in); length 12.50m (41ft 0in); height 3.96m (13ft 0in); wing area 32.5m² (350sq ft).

Weights: Empty 5088kg (11,217lb); max takeoff 6598kg (14,545lb).

Armament: Four 20mm cannon in nose.

Performance: Max speed 504kt (933km/h) at 10,000ft; initial climb 7500ft (2286m)/min; time to 30,000ft 6.0min; service ceiling 44,500ft; range (internal fuel) 530nm (982km).

Production: 3886 Meteors of all versions including 680 F.4 in UK by Gloster (635) and Armstrong Whitworth (45); also 1 F.5 and 682 T.7 (by Gloster).

Notes: The only Allied jet fighter to see operational service during WWII, the Meteor went on to be developed into a large family of combat aircraft filling day and night fighter, ground attack and advanced training duties. Most were post war variants for the RAF and for export to a dozen nations.

The first of eight Meteor prototypes flew on 5 March 1943 followed by 20 Meteor Is with Rolls-Royce Welland engines from January 1944 and 210 Meteor IIIs with 2000lb (8.9kN) thrust Derwent I centrifugal flow turbojets from September 1944. F.I squadron service began in July 1944. The first post war variant was the F.IV (later F.4), this extensively modified over its predecessor with a strengthened airframe, pressurised cockpit, reduced span wings (for a greater rate of roll), ventral fuel tank and more powerful Derwent 5 engines. No ejection seat was fitted.

The new Derwent produced 75 per cent more thrust than the earlier version and was a substantially new design – in effect a scaled down version of the more powerful Nene. Of greater diameter than before, the Derwent 5 required larger engine nacelles but also made the Meteor F.4 80kt (148km/h) faster than the F.III and nearly doubled the rate of climb. For a short time in the immediate post war period the Meteor F.4 was the fastest aircraft in the world and set two outright air speed records: 606.379mph (975.845km/h) in November 1945 and 615.778mph (990.971km/h) in September 1946.

The prototype F.4 first flew on 17 May 1945 and squadron service with the RAF began in January 1947. Production was undertaken by Gloster and Armstrong Whitworth and the final example was delivered in April 1950. The RAF received 535 and exports were made to Argentina (100), Belgium (48), Denmark (20), Egypt (12), France (2) and the Netherlands (38 plus 27 ex RAF). The sole Meteor FR.5 was a tactical fighter-reconnaissance variant with cameras and guns but it crashed during its first flight in June 1949 and was not ordered.

Gloster developed a tandem two seater based on the F.4 as the world's first dual control jet trainer. With its forward fuselage lengthened by 76cm (2ft 6in) to accommodate the second cockpit and a heavily framed side hinging canopy, the prototype first flew in March 1948. As the Meteor T.7 it was delivered to the RAF, Royal Navy and nine export nations. Some later versions had the Meteor F.8's 'square' vertical tail surfaces.

Photo: Meteor F.4.

Gloster Meteor F.8 and FR.9

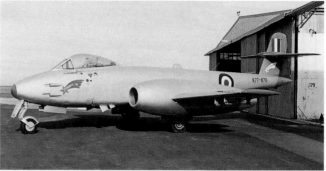

Country of origin: United Kingdom.

Type: F.8 – single seat fighter-bomber. FR.9 – single seat tactical reconnaissance.

Powerplants: Two 3600lb (16.0kN) Rolls-Royce Derwent 8 turbojets.

Dimensions: Wing span 11.33m (37ft 2in); length 13.59m (44ft 7in); height 3.96m (13ft 0in); wing area 32.5m² (350sq ft).

Weights: F.8 – empty 4846kg (10,684lb); normal loaded 7121kg (15,700lb); max takeoff 8664kg (19,100lb).

Armament: F.8 – four 20mm cannon in nose; two 454kg (1000lb) or eight 27kg (60lb) rockets under wings.

Performance: F.8 – max speed 508kt (941km/h) at sea level, 469kt (869km/h) at 30,000ft; initial climb 7000ft (2133m)/min; time to 30,000ft 6.5min; service ceiling 43,000ft; range with ventral tank 666nm (1235km); max range with external fuel 1043nm (1931km).

Production: 3886 Meteors of all models including 1187 F.8 in UK by Gloster (758) and Armstrong Whitworth (429) plus 305 by Fokker and 30 assembled by Fairey in Belgium; also 126 FR.9 and 59 PR.10 (by Gloster).

Notes: Development of what became the Meteor F.8 began in 1947 and the first prototype (a modified F.4) first flew on 12 October 1948. The first production F.8 was flown in September 1949 and deliveries to the RAF began in December 1949.

The Meteor F.8 ultimately equipped 21 regular RAF and 10 RAuxAF squadrons and was exported to Australia (93), Belgium (23 ex RAF plus 150 supplied from licencee Fokker and 30 assembled by Fairey), Brazil (60), Denmark (20), Egypt (12), Israel (11), the Netherlands (5 from the UK plus 155 built by Fokker) and Syria (19).

Compared to the F.4, the F.8 featured Derwent 8 engines initially rated at 3500lb (15.6kN) thrust (and 3600lb/16.0kN later when larger diameter intakes were introduced), a lengthened fuselage aft of the cockpit, increased fuel capacity, an ejection seat, redesigned tail surfaces with 'square' fin and rudder, a one piece 'blown' cockpit canopy (with a metal rear half on early aircraft and then fully transparent), provision for underwing ordnance and some structural strengthening. The longer rear fuselage helped longitudinal stability and also alleviated a centre of gravity problem.

The final single seat Meteors were the FR.9 fighter-reconnaissance version (first flight 23 March 1950) with guns and cameras in a slightly lengthened nose; and the unarmed PR.10 (first flight 19 March 1950) photo-reconnaissance model with the original longer span wing for high altitude operations and cameras in both the nose and rear fuselage. Ex RAF FR.9s also served with Ecuador (12), Israel (7) and Syria (2).

Australia's Meteor F.8s were delivered direct to the RAAF's No 77 Squadron on combat operations in Korea where they replaced P-51D Mustangs from February 1951 and served until the conflict ended in July 1953.

Although outclassed as fighters and used mainly in the ground attack role, RAAF Meteors were nevertheless responsible for three MiG-15 kills in air-to-air combat over Korea. No fewer than 53 were lost to enemy action or operational accidents.

Photo: RAAF Meteor F.8.

Gloster (Armstrong Whitworth) Meteor NF.11-14

Country of origin: United Kingdom.

Type: Two seat night fighter.

Powerplants: NF.11/13 – two 3600lb (16.0kN) Rolls-Royce Derwent 8 turbojets. NF.12/14 – two 3800lb (16.9kN) Derwent 9 turbojets.

Dimensions: NF.11/12/13/14 – wing span 13.11m (43ft 0in); height 4.24m (13ft 11in); wing area 34.7m² (374sq ft). NF.11/13 – length 14.78m (48ft 6in). NF.12 – length 15.21m (49ft 11in). NF.14 – length 15.65m (51ft 4in).

Weights: NF.11 – empty 5452kg (12,019lb); max takeoff 9088kg (20,035lb). NF.14 – empty 5724kg (12,620lb); max takeoff 9616kg (21,200lb).

Armament: Four 20mm cannon in wings.

Performance: NF.11 – max speed 481kt (892km/h) at 10,000ft; initial climb 5800ft (1768m)/min; service ceiling 40,000ft; max range 825nm (1529km). NF.14 – max speed 502kt (930km/h) at 10,000ft; time to 30,000ft 11.2min; service ceiling 40,000ft.

Production: 3886 Meteors of all models including 358 NF.11, 100 NF.12, 40 NF.13 and 100 NF.14 (all by Armstrong Whitworth).

Notes: Developed as an interim all weather/night fighter pending availability of the specialist Gloster Javelin from 1956, the Meteor NF family was based on the fuselage of the tandem two seat Meteor T.7 trainer but with a lengthened nose to accommodate AI Mk.10 air intercept radar. The original longer span wings were fitted and the four 20mm cannon armament moved from the nose to the wings outboard of the engines.

The Meteor F.8's Derwent 8 engines and tail surfaces were retained and the rear cockpit was modified to include radar displays for the operator. No ejection seats were fitted. Due to Gloster's workload with the Meteor F.8 and Javelin at the time, development and production of the Meteor night fighter was entrusted to Armstrong Whitworth Aircraft at Coventry.

The first Meteor NF.11 (converted from a T.7 airframe) first flew on 31 May 1950 and the first production model the following November. Service entry was in August 1951 and 11 RAF squadrons were equipped with the type. The NF.13, a tropicalised version with air conditioning and other equipment changes for service in the Middle East was flown in December 1952 and entered service with two squadrons in March 1952. NF.11 exports were made to Denmark (20) and Belgium (5) while ex RAF NF.13s were sold to Syria, Egypt, France and Israel.

The Meteor NF.12 first flew on 21 April 1953 and entered service in March 1954, equipping nine RAF squadrons. This featured more powerful Derwent 9 engines in an attempt to improve performance plus more capable Westinghouse APS-21 radar (AI Mk.21 in British service) housed in a further lengthened nose which also improved access to the avionics.

The final Meteor version was the NF.14 with Derwent 9s, APS-21 radar, a fully blown clear view canopy and numerous detail changes. First flight was on 23 October 1953 and the last was delivered in May 1955. Twelve RAF squadrons flew the NF.14, the last of them re-equipping with Javelins in June 1959.

Photo: Meteor NF.11. (Paul Merritt)

Gloster Javelin

Country of origin: United Kingdom.

Type: Two seat all weather fighter.

Powerplants: F(AW).1-6 – two 8000lb (35.6kN) Armstrong Siddeley Sapphire ASSa.6 turbojets. F(AW).7 – two 11,000lb (48.9kN) Sapphire ASSa.7. F(AW).8/9 – two 12,300lb (54.7kN) with afterburner Sapphire ASSa.7R.

Dimensions: Wing span 15.85m (52ft 0in); length 17.14m (56ft 3in); height 4.88m (16ft 0in); wing area 86.1m² (927sq ft).

Weights: F(AW).1 – empty 10,886kg (24,000lb); max overload 16,643kg (36,690lb). F(AW).8 – empty 12,610kg (27,800lb); max overload 19,282kg (42,510lb).

Armament: F(AW).1-6 – four 30mm cannon in wings. F(AW).7-9 – two 30mm cannon wings and four Firestreak air-to-air missiles on pylons under wings.

Performance: F(AW).1 – max speed 616kt (1141km/h) at sea level, 532kt (985kmh) at 40,000ft; time to 45,000ft 9.8min; service ceiling 52,500ft. F(AW).8 – max speed 609kt (1128km/h) at sea level, 539kt (998km/h) at 37,000ft; time to 50,000ft 9.3min.

Production: 7 prototypes, 40 F(AW).1, 30 F(AW).2, 22 T.3, 50 F(AW).4, 64 F(AW).5, 33 F(AW).6, 142 F(AW).7 and 47 F(AW).8, total 435.

Notes: Britain's first purpose built jet all weather and night fighter, the Javelin originated as the Gloster GA.5 in response to a 1946 requirement which also produced the de Havilland DH.110. Gloster was awarded a contract for an initial two (later seven) prototypes in April 1949, the twin engined design featuring a large area delta wing but with conventional trailing edge wing flaps and horizontal tail surfaces, these intended to reduce the high angle of attack attained by tailless deltas on approach and landing.

The first prototype flew on 26 November 1951 and the first production Javelin F(AW).1 on 22 July 1954 after a lengthy development period which saw many aerodynamic modifications incorporated to cure various problems. The Javelin finally entered RAF squadron service in the first half of 1956. Although equipped with airborne intercept radar (British AI.17 in the case of the Mk.1), the first six Javelin marks lacked missiles and were armed only with four 30mm cannon in the wings.

Variants were introduced in rapid succession: F(AW).2 (first flight October 1955) with American APQ-43 radar; T.3 (August 1956) operational trainer; F(AW).4 (September 1955) with a powered all-flying tailplane; F(AW).5 (1957) with increased internal fuel capacity and reversion to AI.17 radar; and F(AW).6 with the Mk.5's fuel capacity and APQ-43 radar.

Subsequent Javelins had more powerful engines, Firestreak missiles with two of the guns deleted, a modified flight control system, provision for underwing drop tanks and redesigned rear fuselage. The F(AW).7 with AI.17 radar first flew in November 1957 and the final new production version, the F(AW).8 with APQ-43 radar and a version of the Sapphire engine with limited afterburning capability entered service in November 1959. Seventy-six F(AW).7s were modified to Mk.8 standards in 1960-61 as the F(AW).9. The Javelin was withdrawn from RAF service in 1967-68.

Photo: Javelin F(AW).9.

Grumman F7F Tigercat

Country of origin: USA.

Type: Single seat naval fighter-bomber or two seat night fighter.

Powerplants: Two 2100hp (1566kW) dry/2400hp (1790kW) with water injection Pratt & Whitney R-2800-22W or -34W Double Wasp 18-cylinder radials; three bladed propellers.

Dimensions: F7F-1/3 – wing span 15.70m (51ft 6in); length 13.84m (45ft 5in); height 5.05m (16ft 7in); wing area 42.3m² (455sq ft). F7F-3N/4N – length 14.27m (46ft 10in).

Weights: F7F-3 – empty 7380kg (16,270lb); max takeoff 11,462kg (25,270lb).

Armament: F7F-1/3 – Four 20mm cannon in nose and four 0.50in machine guns in wings; up to 907kg (2000lb) bombs under wings; provision for underfuselage torpedo. F7F-3N/4N – wing guns only.

Performance: F7F-3 – max speed 378kt (700km/h) at 22,200ft, 319kt (590km/h) at sea level; cruising speed 193kt (357km/h); initial climb 4530ft (1380m)/min; service ceiling 40,700ft; normal range 1043nm (1931km).

Production: 2 XF7F-1, 34 F7F-1, 1 XF7F-2N, 65 F7F-2N, 189 F7F-3, 60 F7F-3N and 13 F7F-4N, total 364.

Notes: The first US Navy twin engined fighter to achieve production and the first carrier based combat aircraft with tricycle undercarriage, the F7F Tigercat was conceived in 1941 as a high performance and heavily armed multirole aircraft. Carrying a fixed armament of four cannon in the nose and four machine guns in the wings, it was also capable of carrying a 907kg (2000lb) bomb load under the wings and a torpedo under the fuselage. In the event, all were delivered to the US Marine Corps and the vast majority used for land based operations.

Developed under the company designation G-51, the prototype XF7F-1 first flew on 3 November 1943, by which time 500 had been ordered for the USMC to support 'island hopping' operations in the Pacific. Deliveries of the initial F7F-1 single seater with R-2800-22W engines began in April 1944 but after delays caused largely by changing requirements, deployment was too late to see combat in WWII and about 200 orders were cancelled in late 1945.

New build variants manufactured between then and the end of production in November 1946 were the F7F-2N two seater (with radar operator behind the pilot and nose armament replaced by radar); the major production F7F-3 (similar to the F7F-1 but with R-2800-34W engines); F7F-3N two seat night fighter with longer radar carrying nose and redesigned fin; and the F7F-4N which was similar but had a strengthened structure for carrier operations. Fitted with an arrester hook and other naval equipment, the F7F-4N was the only Tigercat variant cleared for shipborne operations.

Some F7F-3s were modified to F7F-3E electronic warfare and F7F-3P reconnaissance aircraft (about 60) equipped with cameras. The Tigercat equipped a few USMC squadrons in the post war years and some were flown on operations during the Korean War. The last examples were withdrawn from service in 1952. Despite its high performance and versatile operational capabilities, the Tigercat suffered from its timing and was soon out of favour as the new generation of jet fighters and fighter-bombers began to take over.

Photo: F7F-3P Tigercat. (Paul Merritt)

Grumman F8F Bearcat

Country of origin: USA.

Type: Single seat naval fighter-bomber.

Powerplant: One 2100hp (1566kW) dry/2400hp (1790kW) with water injection/2750hp (2050kW) max combat rating Pratt & Whitney R-2800-34W Double Wasp 18-cylinder radial; four bladed propeller.

Dimensions: F8F-1 – wing span 10.92m (35ft 10in); length 8.61m (28ft 3in); height 3.96m (13ft 0in); wing area 22.7m² (244sq ft).

Weights: F8F-1 – empty 3207kg (7070lb); max takeoff 5873kg (12,947lb).

Armament: F8F-1 – four 0.50in machine guns in wings; max 907kg (2000lb) ordnance under wings. F8F-1B/2 – four 20mm cannon in wings plus external ordnance.

Performance: F8F-1 – max speed 372kt (689km/h) at 18,800ft; cruising speed 142-217kt (262-402km/h); max climb 4570ft (1393m)/min; service ceiling 38,700ft; range (internal fuel) 960nm (1778km).

Production: 2 XF8F-1, 770 F8F-1, 111 F8F-1B, 15 F8F-1N, 2 XF8F-2, 293 F8F-2, 12 F8F-2N, 60 F8F-2P, total 1265.

Notes: The last of the Grumman line of single piston engined naval fighters, development of the F8F Bearcat (company designation G-58) began in 1943. It was intended as an air superiority fighter with optimum speed and manoeuvrability, the concept based around fitting the smallest and lightest possible airframe behind the Pratt & Whitney R-2800 engine. Although too late to see combat in WWII, the Bearcat saw action in Indo-China with the Armée de l'Air and the Royal Thai Air Force.

Two XF8F-1 prototypes were ordered in November 1943 and the first of them flew on 21 August 1944. Orders totalling 3899 aircraft were placed with both Grumman (2023) and General Motors (1876 as the F3M) in 1944-45 but the contracts were cut at the end of the war including all of those for General Motors. Grumman's order was reduced to just 770, but subsequent revisions to this saw the total production run exceed 1200 aircraft.

The first of 23 trials aircraft was flown in January 1945 and the first US Navy operational squadron (VF-19) began receiving the Bearcat the following May, just three months before the Pacific War ended. Some 24 USN units were equipped with Bearcats by early 1948.

The initial F8F-1 was followed by the F8F-1B with cannon instead of machine gun armament (some of which were completed as F8F-1N night fighters with a wing mounted radar pod); F8F-2 with cannon, revised cowling shape, taller fin and rudder and structural changes (introduced 1948); F8F-2N night fighter; and F8F-2P armed reconnaissance fighter. Production ended in May 1949.

The USN began withdrawing its Bearcats from front line service in mid 1949 and the last aircraft (F8F-2Ps) were retired in late 1952. Many were refurbished and exported to France (140 F8F-1/1Bs) and Thailand (100 -1s and 29 -1Bs), some of the latter received via France. South Vietnam took over 28 ex French F8F-1s while even communist North Vietnam had some in service, obtained from the same source.

Photo: F8F-1 Bearcat. (USN)

Grumman AF Guardian

Country of origin: USA.

Type: Two seat carrier based anti submarine (AF-2S/3S) or four seat search (AF-2W) aircraft.

Powerplant: One 2400hp (1790kW) Pratt & Whitney R-2800-48W Double Wasp 18-cylinder radial; four bladed propeller.

Dimensions: Wing span 18.49m (60ft 8in); length 13.21m (43ft 4in); height 4.93m (16ft 2in); wing area 52.0m^2 (560sq ft).

Weights: AF-2S – empty 6613kg (14,580lb); max takeoff 11,567kg (25,500lb).

Armament: AF-2S – one 907kg (2000lb) torpedo, two 907kg (2000lb) bombs or two 725kg (1600lb) depth charges in weapons bay.

Performance: AF-2S – max speed 275kt (510km/h); initial climb 1850ft (564m)/min; service ceiling 32,500ft; range 1303nm (2414km).

Production: 3 XTB3F, 193 AF-2S, 153 AF-2W and 40 AF-3S, total 389.

Notes: Grumman began work on a successor to the TBF Avenger three seat naval torpedo bomber in 1943, with two lines of development emerging the following year. The first (designated TB2F) was a large twin engine design powered by two Pratt & Whitney R-2800 radials and capable of carrying a 3630kg (8000lb) war load. Its maximum weight of 20,412kg (45,000lb) was considered too great for carrier operations and it was cancelled in favour of the TSF, a derivative of the F7F Tigercat fighter.

The TSF was itself cancelled in January 1945, the US Navy instead placing an order for three Grumman G-70 prototypes as the XTB3F, a large mid winged monoplane with seating for two crew side-by-side, a weapons bays, and composite powerplants comprising an R-2800 radial piston engine in the nose and a 1600lb (7.1kN) Westinghouse 19XB turbojet in the tail, the latter to give a speed boost when escaping attack.

The first XTB3F-1 prototype flew on 19 December 1945 (with the jet inoperative) but the project was dropped as a torpedo bomber just five days later. It was reinstated but as an anti submarine aircraft with the jet removed and other modifications for the new role incorporated. As the AF Guardian, the basic design was built in two major versions as a 'hunter-killer' combination for shipborne anti submarine duties.

The unarmed 'hunter' AF-2W had a large radome under the fuselage housing APS-20 radar plus an additional two crew members accommodated in the fuselage to operate the detection gear. The armed AF-2S two seater was the 'killer' component of the duo. This carried smaller APS-30 radar in an underwing pod, used to pinpoint a target after the AP-3W had done the main detection work. Prototypes were flown in 1948-49 and the first production AF-2S on 17 November 1949. Deliveries of both models to the US Navy began in late 1950. By then, development of the Guardian's successor, the AF-2 (later S-2) Tracker had already begun.

Guardian production ended in 1953, the last of the line the AF-3S with additional anti submarine warfare equipment including a magnetic anomaly detector (MAD) boom mounted on the starboard fuselage. The Guardian was replaced in USN service by the Tracker in 1955, some units having meanwhile seen combat service in the Korean War.

Photo: AF-2W 'hunter' (foreground) and AF-2S 'killer' Guardians.

Grumman F9F-2/5 Panther

Country of origin: USA.

Type: Single seat carrier based fighter.

Powerplant: F9F-2 – one 5000lb (22.2kN) Pratt & Whitney J42-P-6 (Rolls-Royce Nene) turbojet. F9F-4 – one 6950lb (30.9kN) with water injection Allison J33-A-16. F9F-5 – one 6250lb (27.8kN) dry/7000lb (31.1kN) wet Pratt & Whitney J48-P-6A (Rolls-Royce Tay).

Dimensions: F9F-5 – wing span 11.58m (38ft 0in); length 11.63m (38ft 10in); height 3.73m (12ft 3in); wing area 23.2m^2 (250sq ft).

Weights: F9F-5 – empty 4603kg (10,147lb); max takeoff 8492kg (18,721lb).

Armament: Four 20mm cannon in nose; two 454kg (1000lb) bombs or six 5in (127mm) rockets under wings.

Performance: F9F-5 – max speed 503kt (932km/h) at 5000ft; max cruise 418kt (774km/h); initial climb 5090ft (1551m)/min; service ceiling 42,800ft; range 1130nm (2092km).

Production: 2 XF9F-2, 567 F9F-2, 1 XF9F-3, 54 F9F-3 (all converted to -2), 1 XF9F-4, 109 F9F-4, 1 XF9F-5, 616 F9F-5, 36 F9F-5P, total 1387.

Notes: The chain of events which led to Grumman's first production jet fighter began with the G-75 (military designation XF9F-1) naval night fighter project of 1946 powered by four 1500lb (6.7kN) Westinghouse J30 turbojets mounted in the wings, four engines necessary to achieve the desired power. The concept changed when US Navy evaluation of the 5000lb (22.2kN) thrust Rolls-Royce Nene led to it being built under licence in the USA as the Pratt & Whitney J42.

Availability of the Nene resulted in the single engined Grumman G-79 straight winged naval day fighter, prototypes of which were ordered in September 1946 as the XF9F-2. The first one (with a Nene installed) flew on 24 November 1947. The second prototype was powered by the Pratt & Whitney J42 equivalent and the third by a 4600lb (20.4kN) Westinghouse J33. The permanent wing tip tanks which were a feature of what would be christened the Panther were installed during the flight test programme.

Initial orders were placed for the J42 powered F9F-2 and J33 powered F9F-3, the first production examples of both versions first flying in November 1948. Only small numbers of the F9F-3 were built and these were all converted to -2 standards due to problems with the Westinghouse engine. Deliveries to the US Navy began in May 1949.

Subsequent versions were the F9F-4 with uprated J33 and F9F-5 with the more powerful Pratt & Whitney J48, a version of the Rolls-Royce Tay built under licence. Both featured a 61cm (2ft 0in) longer fuselage and taller fin. The J33 again proved troublesome and many F9F-4s were modified to -5 standards with the J48. The F9F-5 first flew on 21 December 1949 and deliveries began in November 1950. The F9F-5P was a new build photo-reconnaissance version with cameras in a lengthened nose, the F9F-2P a similar conversion of the earlier model.

The Panther was widely used by the USN and Marine Corps including by 24 squadrons in the Korean War, mainly on ground attack duties. On 3 July 1950, F9F-2s of VF-51 and VF-52 flying from USS *Valley Forge* became the first naval jet fighters used in combat, a VF-51 aircraft shooting down two Yak-9s.

Photo: F9F-5 Panther.

Grumman F9F-6/8 Cougar

Country of origin: USA.

Type: Single seat carrier based fighter.

Powerplant: F9F-6/8 – one 7250lb (32.2kN) Pratt & Whitney J48-P8/8A (Rolls-Royce Tay) turbojet. F9F-7 – one 6950lb (30.9kN) Allison J33-A-16A turbojet.

Dimensions: F9F-8 – wing span 10.51m (34ft 6in); length 12.72m (41ft 9in); height 3.73m (12ft 3in); wing area 31.3m² (337sq ft).

Weights: F9F-8 – empty 5382kg (11,866lb); normal loaded 8953kg (19,738lb); max takeoff 11,232kg (24,763lb).

Armament: Four 20mm cannon in nose; four underwing hardpoints for max 907kg (2000lb) ordnance.

Performance: F9F-8 – max speed 562kt (1041km/h) at sea level; initial climb 5750ft (1752m)/min; service ceiling 42,000ft; range 912nm (1690km).

Production: 3 XF9F-6, 646 F9F-6, 60 F9F-6P, 168 F9F-7, 601 F9F-8, 110 F9F-8P, 400 F9F-8T, total 1988.

Notes: Simply a swept wing version of the Panther, the G-93 Cougar retained not only the overall military designation (F9F) of its straight winged predecessor but also its fuselage, tail surfaces, powerplant and undercarriage. The new wing was of thinner section and swept back at 35 degrees. In order to retain desirable handling characteristics (especially at low speeds) it was fitted with leading edge slots, fences, spoilers for roll control instead of conventional ailerons and enlarged trailing edge flaps. The Panther's tip tanks were deleted.

The prototype XF9F-6 Cougar first flew on 20 September 1951 and the first operational unit to receive the production F9F-6 was US Navy squadron VF-32 in November 1952. Powered by a Pratt & Whitney J48-P-8 turbojet, the F9F-6 was joined in production by the F9F-7 (first flight March 1953) which was identical apart from having an Allison J33 powerplant. Sixty were completed as F9F-6Ps with cameras in the nose.

The final single seat Cougar variant was the F9F-8 (Grumman Model G-99), first flown in December 1953. This featured the J48 engine, a slightly lengthened (by 20cm/8in) fuselage to fit additional internal fuel tanks and a modified wing with increased chord. The F9F-8's designation was changed to F-9J in 1962. Subvariants included the new build F9F-8P with cameras and F9F-8B (later AF-9J) attack conversion with LABS (Low Altitude Bombing System) equipment and provision to carry air-to-surface missiles.

The final Cougar production variant was F9F-8T (TF-9J) tandem two seat operational trainer with an 86cm (34in) longer forward fuselage to accommodate the second cockpit. The first F9F-8T flew in April 1956 and the final delivery was in October 1959.

Some F-9Js remained in second line service with USN Reserve units until the early 1970s while the TF-9J trainer was retired in February 1974. Some Cougars were converted to DF-9 drones and QF-9 drone director aircraft. The Cougar was just too late to used in Korea, but a handful of TF-9s saw active service in the Vietnam War in the late 1960s, flown by the US Marine Corps on forward air control duties.

Photo: F9F-7 Cougar.

Grumman F10F Jaguar

Country of origin: USA.

Type: Single seat naval fighter.

Powerplant: Proposed – one 7400lb (32.9kN) dry/10,900lb (48.5kN) with afterburner Westinghouse XJ40-WE-8 turbojet. As flown – one 6800lb (30.2kN) non afterburning J40-WE-6.

Dimensions: Wing span 15.42m (50ft 7in) fully extended, 11.17m (36ft 8in) fully swept; length 16.59m (54ft 5in); height 4.95m (16ft 3in); wing area 43.4m² (467sq ft).

Weights: Proposed production version – empty 9265kg (20,426lb); combat 12,451kg (27,451lb); max takeoff 16,080kg (35,450lb).

Armament: Proposed – four 20mm cannon in nose; two 907kg (2000lb) bombs, 48 2.75in (70mm) or 12 5in (127mm) rockets under wings.

Performance: Estimated for production model – max speed 617kt (1143km/h) at sea level, 550kt (1019km/h) at 35,000ft; initial climb 13,350ft (4069m)/min; service ceiling 45,800ft; combat range 1450nm (2685km). Prototype – max speed 560kt (1038km/h) at sea level.

Production: 1 prototype flown plus 1 other not completed.

Notes: The world's first variable sweep combat aircraft intended for production, the F10F Jaguar came about as a result of US Navy concerns about the increasing stalling speeds (and therefore approach speeds) of jet combat aircraft and the implications for carrier operations. Discussions between Grumman and the USN on the subject of a variable wing geometry design began in early 1948, the manufacturer having some data from the USAF's Bell X-5 variable sweep research aircraft at its disposal.

The philosophy behind variable sweep was to achieve the best of both worlds – lower stalling speeds with the wing swept fully forward and high maximum speeds with it swept back. In the case of the Jaguar, the sweep could be varied between 13.5 and 42.5 degrees, the mechanism driven by a hydraulic actuating system. The shoulder mounted wings also featured high lift devices including full span leading edge slates and trailing edge Fowler flaps covering 80 per cent span.

A contract for two XF10F-1 prototypes was placed in 1950 (spurred on by the USA's involvement in the Korean War) and the first and only example to fly did so for the first time on 19 May 1952. Control and systems problems came to the fore during the 16 minute maiden sortie, setting the scene for the remaining 31 flights conducted by the Jaguar before the project was terminated 11 months later.

The single factor which really ended the Jaguar programme was the failure of the Westinghouse XJ40-WE-8 afterburning turbojet. The Jaguar never flew with the definitive fully rated engine installed, instead having to use the lower powered and non afterburning J40-WE-6. When the J40 was grounded in April 1953, the Jaguar programme went down with it despite orders for 141 having been placed. The second prototype was 90 per cent complete at the time.

Despite the Jaguar's cancellation, it represented a substantial advance in the state-of-the-art. It proved that variable sweep was aerodynamically and structurally feasible and the lessons learned were later put to good use in the General Dynamics F-111 and Grumman F-14 Tomcat.

Photo: XF10-1 Jaguar.

Grumman F11F-1 Tiger

Country of origin: USA.

Type: Single seat carrier based fighter.

Powerplant: One 7450lb (33.1kN) dry/10,500lb (46.7kN) with after-burner Wright J65-W-18 (Armstrong Siddeley Sapphire) turbojet.

Dimensions: Wing span 9.64m (31ft 7½in); length 14.30m (46ft 11in); height 4.03m (13ft 3in); wing area 23.2m² (250sq ft).

Weights: Empty 6091kg (13,428lb); max takeoff 10,641kg (23,459lb).

Armament: Four 20mm cannon; four underwing hardpoints for Sidewinder AAMs or drop tanks.

Performance: Max speed 654kt (Mach 0.99/1211km/h) at sea level, 643kt (Mach 1.12/1190km/h) at 36,000ft; initial climb 16,300ft (4968m)/min; service ceiling 41,900ft; range 963nm (1783km).

Production: 199 F11F-1 and 2 F11F-1F, total 201.

Notes: The US Navy's (and Grumman's) first transonic carrier based combat aircraft, the G-98 Tiger began life as a design study to extract as much performance as possible from the F9F Panther/Cougar family. What resulted was an entirely new and in many ways innovative design which despite this was originally designated the F9F-9 when first ordered in April 1953. The designation was changed to F11F in April 1955 after the first three aircraft had already flown.

Features of the Tiger included an area ruled 'Coke bottle' fuselage design and a new structural technique in the thin and efficient wing in which the main box skins were milled from solid light alloy slabs. Fuel was crammed into every available space in the wings and fuselage with provision for flight refuelling. The planned powerplant was the Wright J65-W-6 afterburning axial flow turbojet, a licence built version of the Armstrong Siddeley Sapphire.

The first Tiger flew on 30 July 1954 originally with a non afterburning J65-W-7 engine. Ongoing problems with the J65-W-6 forced a change in production aircraft to the derated but reliable W-8 version. The result was that the Tiger failed to meet its contract performance guarantees and production was restricted to just 201 aircraft. Several of the early production aircraft were delivered with the non afterburning W-7.

The F11F-1 was the only production version, delivered between November 1954 and January 1959 with regular USN squadron service starting on March 1957.

Tigers from the 43rd example onwards had longer noses for the installation of radar, but this was never fitted in service. The Tiger had only a brief operational career with the USN, phasing out of front line service between 1959 and 1961, most aircraft then used for training duties. It was redesignated F-11A in 1962. The Tiger was a popular mount for the Navy's *Blue Angels* display team, the unit flying it for 11 years from 1957.

The powerplant problems led Grumman to complete two early aircraft as F11F-1F 'Super Tigers' powered by a 15,000lb (66.7kN) with afterburning General Electric J79 turbojet. First flown in May 1956, the F11F-1F was a genuine Mach 2 aircraft with superb manoeuvrability. It also set new world absolute speed and altitude records but was not ordered.

Photo: F11F-1 Tiger. (Keith Myers)

Grumman S-2 Tracker

Country of origin: USA.

Type: Four crew carrier based anti submarine and maritime patrol.

Powerplants: Two 1525hp (1137kW) Wright R-1820-82WA Cyclone nine cylinder radials; three bladed propellers.

Dimensions: S-2E/G – wing span 22.12m (72ft 7in); length 13.26m (43ft 6in); height 5.05m (16ft 7in); wing area 46.1m² (496sq ft).

Weights: S-2E – empty 8633kg (19,033lb); max takeoff 13,222kg (29,150lb).

Armament: Internal weapons bay for max 2182kg (4810lb) ordnance including two homing torpedoes or one depth bomb or mines; six underwing hardpoints for 5in (127mm) rockets, Zuni rockets, torpedoes or 113kg (250lb) bombs.

Performance: Max speed 220kt (407km/h) at 5000ft; patrol speed 130kt (240km/h) at 1500ft; initial climb 1800ft (549m)/min; service ceiling 21,000ft; ferry range 1130nm (2092km); endurance 9 hours.

Production: 2 XS2F-1, 755 S-2A, 77 S-2C, 100 S-2D, 252 S-2E, total 1186 by Grumman plus 100 CS2F-1 by de Havilland Canada.

Notes: The development of new weapons and anti submarine detection systems in the late 1940s rendered the 'hunter/killer' concept of using two aircraft for these roles obsolete and allowed the two functions to be performed by a single airframe. The US Navy initiated a programme for such an aircraft in June 1950, the Grumman G-89 design selected to fill the role as the S2F Tracker.

The twin piston engined Tracker featured tricycle undercarriage, folding wings for shipborne operations, APS-38 search radar in a retractable ventral radome, retractable magnetic anomaly detection (MAD) boom in the tail, sonobuoys carried in the rear of the engine nacelles, a 70 million candlepower searchlight on the starboard wing and an internal weapons bay plus underwing hardpoints. Normal crew complement was four – two pilots, radar operator and MAD operator.

The prototype XS2F-1 first flew on 4 December 1952, the first production S2F-1 (redesignated S-2A from 1962) in July 1953 and service entry with the USN was in February 1954.

Progressive improvements were introduced between then and the end of production in early 1968 via the S-2C/S2F-2 (first flight July 1954) with enlarged weapons bay and modified tail surfaces; S-2D/S2F-3 (May 1959) with increased wing span, extra fuel, modified forward fuselage and equipment upgrades; and S-2E/S2F-3S (first delivery 1962) with further upgrades.

The last new build Trackers were 14 S-2Es for the Royal Australian Navy. Earlier models were also exported to several nations and de Havilland Canada built 100 under licence as the CS2F-1.

Converted versions include the S-2B (S-2As with upgraded operational equipment) and 50 S-2Gs, upgraded and rebuilt S-2Es. Turboprop conversions with systems upgrades (notably by Marsh Aviation and IAI) have also been developed with AiResearch TPE331s.

By 2000, Brazil, South Korea, Uruguay, Argentina and Taiwan still operated Trackers, the latter pair with turboprops. Front line service with the USN ended in December 1975 but a few converted to TS-2A trainers remained operational until March 1979.

Photo: S-2G Tracker.

Grumman A-6 Intruder

Country of origin: USA.

Type: Two seat carrier based all weather attack.

Powerplants: Two 9300lb (41.3kN) Pratt & Whitney J52-P-8A/B turbojets.

Dimensions: Wing span 16.15m (53ft 0in); length 16.69m (54ft 9in); height 4.93m (16ft 2in); wing area 49.1m² (529sq ft).

Weights: A-6E – empty 12,525kg (27,613lb); max takeoff (carrier ops) 26,581kg (58,600lb), 27,397kg (60,400lb) from land.

Armament: A-6E – one centreline and four underwing hardpoints for max 8165kg (18,000lb) ordnance including conventional and laser guided bombs, Harpoon, HARM and SLAM missiles and Skipper laser guided missiles.

Performance: A-6E – max speed 560kt (1037km/h) at sea level; cruising speed 412kt (763km/h) at 30,000ft; initial climb 7620ft (2322m)/min; service ceiling 42,400ft; range with max warload 878nm (1626km); max ferry range 2818nm (5220km).

Production: 482 A-6A (including prototypes), 21 EA-6A and 205 A-6E, total 708.

Notes: Developed to meet a 1956 US Navy requirement for a carrier based strike aircraft capable of first pass blind attacks at low level in any weather or at night, the Grumman G-128 was selected over 10 competing designs in December 1957. The first of eight YA2F-1 Intruder prototypes flew on 19 April 1960, the designation A-6A being applied from 1962.

An interesting design feature was downwards vectoring (to 23deg) jetpipes for the J52 engines to help shorten the takeoff run. Production Intruders lacked this feature, their jetpipes permanently canted downwards at an angle of 7 degrees.

Deliveries of the A-6A to the USN began in February 1963 and to the USMC in October 1964. The Intruder began operating in Vietnam in July 1965, initially with VA-75 flying from USS *Independence*. Of the 482 A-6As built, 19 were converted to A-6Bs with anti radar missiles and 12 to A-6Cs with forward look infra-red (FLIR) and low light level television (LLTV) equipment. A further 78 A-6As were converted to KA-6D tankers while 21 EA-6A electronic countermeasures aircraft were built from 1963. This concept was developed into the EA-6B Prowler (see next entry).

The second major production variant was the A-6E, the prototype of which first flew on 27 February 1970. This featured a substantially upgraded avionics, radar and nav/attack computer fit. Apart from the 205 new build A-6Es, a further 240 were converted from A-6As. The last 21 A-6Es featured a wing of graphite/epoxy construction to alleviate fatigue problems. First test flown in 1987, it was introduced to production the following year and over 170 existing Intruders were subsequently rewinged. The last A-6E was delivered in 1990.

Various weapons, avionics and equipment upgrades were implemented and in November 1987 the first of five converted A-6F prototypes was flown. This featured 10,800lb (48.0kN) General Electric F404 turbofans, the composite wing, additional weapons stations and digital avionics but was abandoned. The A-6G was a proposed similar conversion of the A-6E (but with the J52s retained), this also cancelled. The Intruder was retired in 1997-98.

Photo: A-6E Intruder. (Bill Lines)

Grumman EA-6B Prowler

Country of origin: USA.

Type: Four crew electronic warfare aircraft.

Powerplants: Two 11,200lb (49.8kN) Pratt & Whitney J52-P-408 turbojets.

Dimensions: Wing span 16.15m (53ft 0in); length 18.24m (59ft 10in); height 4.95m (16ft 3in); wing area 49.1m² (529sq ft).

Weights: Empty 14,321kg (31,572lb); typical mission 24,703kg (54,460lb); max takeoff 29,484kg (65,000lb).

Armament: Originally unarmed, later provision for up to four AGM-88 HARM anti radiation missiles on inboard of six underwing hardpoints.

Performance: (with five ECM pods) max speed 530kt (982km/h); cruising speed 418kt (774km/h); initial climb 10,030ft (3057m)/min; service ceiling 38,000ft; range with max external load 955nm (1769km); max ferry range 2085nm (3862km).

Production: 170.

Notes: The US Navy's tactical electronic warfare (EW) aircraft, the EA-6B Prowler is based on the A-6 Intruder attack aircraft. A converted EW version of the Intruder (the EA-6A) was first flown in April 1963, equipment including jammers carried in underwing pods and various antennae housed in a fairing on top of the fin. Twenty-one EA-6As were subsequently built, these seeing service in Vietnam before the last was retired in 1986.

Grumman began development of a specialised ECM version in 1966 to replace the Douglas EA-3. Based on the Intruder, what became the EA-6B Prowler differed from the EA-6A in having a redesigned and lengthened fuselage accommodating four crew members (pilot and three electronic warfare officers) in side-by-side pairs. A large fin tip antennae fairing was fitted and the jammers carried in underwing pods. The first EA-6B aerodynamic test bed (converted from an Intruder) flew on 28 May 1968. Service entry was in 1971 and low rate production continued until 1991.

The first 21 Prowlers were powered by the same J52-P-8 turbojets as fitted to the Intruder but subsequent aircraft had the more powerful J52-P-408. The Prowler's EW systems are collectively called the TJS (Tactical Jamming System), this incorporating antennae, a processing computer and the jammers. All have been progressively updated over the years through both software and hardware changes.

The upgrade programmes were: EXCAP (Expanded Capability); ICAP-1 (Improved Capability-1); ICAP-2; ICAP-2/Block 86 which provided the Prowler with the ability to carry HARM anti radar missiles (these put to good use in the Gulf War); ADVCAP (Advanced Capability); ADVCAP/Block 91 with improvements to the jamming system plus GPS; and ICAP-3 with reactive jamming, new avionics and displays.

With the retirement of the USAF's EF-111s in 1998, the Prowler became the US military's sole dedicated tactical EW jammer aircraft. They are operated by joint USN/USAF squadrons and played an important role in the NATO air campaign over Yugoslavia in 1999. By 2000, more than 120 remained in service.

Photo: EA-6B Prowler. (USN)

Grumman F-14 Tomcat

Country of origin: USA.

Type: Two seat carrier based air superiority fighter.

Powerplants: F-14A – two 20,900lb (93.0kN) with afterburner Pratt & Whitney TF30-P-412 or -414A turbofans. F-14B/D – two 14,000lb (62.2kN) dry/23,100lb (102.7kN) with afterburner General Electric F110-GE-400 turbofans.

Dimensions: Wing span 19.54m (64ft 1½in) fully extended or 11.65m (38ft 2½in) fully swept; length 19.10m (62ft 8in); height 4.88m (16ft 0in); wing area 52.5m² (565sq ft).

Weights: F-14A – empty 18,191kg (40,104lb); max takeoff 33,725kg (74,349lb).

Armament: One 20mm rotary cannon in forward fuselage; typical intercept configuration two AIM-54 Phoenix, two AIM-7 Sparrow and two AIM-9 Sidewinder air-to-air missiles on underfuselage recesses and underwing pylons; max 6577kg (14,500lb) ordnance.

Performance: F-14A – max speed (clean) 1343kt (Mach 2.34/2487km/h) at 40,000ft, 792kt (Mach 1.2/1468km/h) at sea level; initial climb 30,000ft (9144m)/min; service ceiling 64,000ft; tactical radius (at Mach 1.3) 443nm (820km); subsonic patrol radius 665nm (1232km); max ferry range 1735nm (3213km).

Production: 2 prototypes, 636 F-14A, 38 F-14B and 37 F-14D, total 713.

Notes: The failure of the overweight General Dynamics F-111B naval fighter (for which Grumman was prime contractor) led to the development of a new, purpose built fleet defence/air superiority fighter for the US Navy. In 1969, Grumman's advanced Model G-303 twin engined two seater was selected for production as the F-14 Tomcat. The design retained some of the F-111B's features, notably its powerful AWG-9 fire control radar, AIM-9 Phoenix missiles, Pratt & Whitney TF30 engines and variable sweep wings.

The prototype first flew on 21 December 1970 but was lost on its second flight following total hydraulic failure. Another prototype and 12 pre series aircraft were flown during 1971-72 and delivery of production F-14As to the US Navy began in June 1972. The USN received 557 F-14As between then and April 1987, the final 102 of them fitted with an improved version of the TF30 in an attempt to overcome a series of fan blade failures. The pre revolution Imperial Iranian Air Force was the only export customer for the Tomcat, receiving 79 F-14As in 1976-78.

The problems with the TF30 led to the F-14A (Plus), re-engined with General Electric F110 engines and later redesignated F-14B. The first converted prototype flew in September 1986 and the first of 38 new build examples in November 1987. A further 32 F-14As were converted to the new standard.

The final Tomcat variant was the F-14D, this featuring the F110 engine and significant equipment upgrades including digital avionics in place of the previous analogue equipment. First flight was in March 1990 and the last of 37 was delivered in July 1992. A further 18 were converted from F-14As and designated F-14D(R) but additional orders were cancelled in 1991 due to budget cuts. The USN had 350 Tomcats in service by early 2000, by which time the aircraft was widely used for air-to-ground attack and tactical reconnaissance duties with the fitting of laser designator and camera pods.

Photo: F-14B. (USN)

HAL HF-24 Marut

Country of origin: India.

Type: Single seat fighter and light strike.

Powerplants: Mk.1 – two 4850lb (21.6kN) HAL built Rolls-Royce (Bristol) Orpheus Mk.703 turbojets.

Dimensions: Mk.1 – wing span 9.00m (29ft 6½in); length 15.87m (52ft 1in); height 3.60m (11ft 10in); wing area 28.5m² (307sq ft).

Weights: Mk.1 – empty equipped 6195kg (13,658lb); takeoff (clean) 8951kg (19,734lb); max takeoff 10,908kg (24,048lb).

Armament: Four 30mm cannon in forward fuselage and retractable pack for 50 68mm unguided rockets on lower fuselage; four underwing hardpoints for max 1814kg (4000lb) ordnance including bombs, rockets and drop tanks.

Performance: Mk.1 – max speed 613kt (Mach 0.93/1134km/h) at sea level, 585kt (Mach 1.02/1083km/h) at 40,000ft; initial climb 8500ft (2590m)/min; combat radius 214nm (396km) at 40,000ft.

Production: 2 prototypes, 18 pre-production Mk.1, 112 production Mk.1, 12 Mk.1T, total 144.

Notes: Developed under the direction of famed German designer Dr Kurt Tank (responsible also for the wartime Focke-Wulf Fw 190), the Marut ('Wind Spirit') achieved two significant firsts: it was the first indigenous Indian combat aircraft and also the first Asian aircraft to achieve supersonic speeds – just – Mach 1.02 in level flight.

Although a useful ground attack fighter, the Marut failed to reach its full potential due to a lack of power from the two Orpheus turbojets, these built under licence in India by Hindustan Aeronautics Limited's engine division. The HAL Orpheus was also used in the locally built Folland Gnat lightweight fighter and its upgraded derivative, the Ajeet.

HAL began development of the Marut in June 1957, a two seat glider representing the aerodynamic shape of the fighter preceding the real article and used for refining the design. Towed behind a C-47 Dakota, the glider recorded 78 flights between April 1959 and March 1960.

The first of two prototype Maruts flew on 17 June 1961, the first of 18 pre-production Mk.1s in April 1963 and full production Mk.1s from November 1967.

Twelve examples of a tandem two seat trainer version were also produced (first flight 30 April 1970) as the Mk.1T and the last Marut was delivered to the Indian Air Force in 1977.

Investigations into a version fitted with the Turbo Union RB.199 were carried out in 1975 (as the Mk.3) but this was impractical because of the major fuselage redesign required. The Marut was operated by three IAF squadrons and was phased out of service in 1985, replaced by the Sepecat Jaguar.

Several of the pre-production batch were used as test beds under new designations. One became the Mk.1BX with an Egyptian Brandner El-300 turbojet replacing one of the Orpheus engines, this powerplant intended for the Helwan HA-300 supersonic fighter (which see); and the Mks. IE and 1R with afterburning versions of the Orpheus installed.

Photo: Marut Mk.1 (foreground) and two Mk.1Ts.

Handley Page Victor

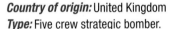

Country of origin: United Kingdom

Type: Five crew strategic bomber.

Powerplants: B.1 – four 11,050lb (49.1kN) Armstrong Siddeley Sapphire 202 or 207 turbojets. B.2 – four 17,250lb (76.7kN) Rolls-Royce Conway Mk.200 turbofans. B.2R – four 20,600lb (91.6kN) Conway Mk.201.

Dimensions: B.1 – wing span (33.53m) 110ft 0in; length 35.02m (114ft 11in); height 8.57m (28ft 1½in); wing area 223.5m² (2406sq ft). B.2 – wing span 35.03m (114ft 11in); height 9.18m (30ft 1½in); wing area 241.2m² (2597sq ft).

Weights: B.1 – max takeoff 92,988kg (205,000lb); B.2 – max takeoff 97,978kg (216,000lb).

Armament: B.1 – Yellow Sun or Blue Danube atomic bombs or up to 15,876kg (35,000lb) conventional bombs. B.2 – normally one Blue Steel standoff weapon.

Performance: B.1 – max speed 545kt (1009km/h) at 40,000ft; service ceiling 56,000ft; range 3040nm (5630km). B.2 – max speed 562kt (1041km/h) at 40,000ft; service ceiling 60,000ft; unrefuelled high altitude combat radius 2000nm (3705km).

Production: 2 prototypes, 50 B.1 and 34 B.2, total 86.

Notes: The third and last of the RAF's 'V-bomber' deterrent force of the 1950s and '60s (along with the Victor and Vulcan), the HP.80 Victor was arguably the best of the trio, being faster, higher flying and capable of carrying a larger warload in a massive bomb bay than even the Avro Vulcan. Features included crescent shaped wings and horizontal tail surfaces, the latter mounted in a T-tail arrangement.

The first of two prototypes powered by 7500lb (33.3kN) thrust Sapphires by flew on 24 December 1952 and the first production Victor B.1 on 1 February 1956. Powered by more powerful Sapphires and featuring a longer forward fuselage and provision for in flight refuelling, the B.1 entered RAF squadron service in January 1958 and equipped five front line units between then and early 1967. From 1960, 24 were upgraded to B.1A standards with additional ECM capability.

The Victor B.2 first flew on 20 February 1959 and entered service in February 1962, equipping only two squadrons after the initial order for 62 was reduced to 34. The B.2 featured much more powerful Rolls-Royce Conway 200 turbofans, a larger wing with Küchemann fairings above the wing trailing edges (to delay the formation of shock waves at high subsonic speeds) and upgraded ECM equipment. Most B.2s were subsequently fitted with still more powerful Conway 201s and redesignated B.2R. Nine were converted to B(SR).2 strategic reconnaissance aircraft from 1965, equipped with cameras and sideways looking radar. The B.2R was phased out of RAF service in late 1968 and the B(SR).2 in early 1975.

The Victor's second career was as a tanker. Thirty-one B.1/1As were converted to K.1/1A tankers from 1965, joined by 24 K.2s (converted from B.2s and SRs) from 1972. Victor tankers served with three squadrons, the K.2 seeing extensive active service in the 1982 Falklands War (where it was also used for maritime reconnaissance) and the 1991 Gulf War. The last was retired in October 1993.

Photo: Victor B.1.

Hawker Sea Fury

Country of origin: United Kingdom.

Type: Single seat carrier based fighter.

Powerplant: One 2550hp (1900kW) Bristol Centaurus XVIII 18-cylinder radial; five bladed propeller.

Dimensions: Wing span 11.70m (38ft 5in); length 10.57m (34ft 8in); height 4.84m (15ft 10½in); wing area 26.0m² (280sq ft).

Weights: FB.11 – empty 4191kg (9240lb); normal loaded 5602kg (12,350lb); max takeoff 6645kg (14,650lb).

Armament: F.10 – four 20mm cannon in wings. FB.11 – guns plus max 907kg (2000lb) ordnance (bombs or rockets) under wings.

Performance: Max speed 400kt (740km/h) at 18,000ft, 360kt (667km/h) at 30,000ft; initial climb 4320ft (1317m)/min; time to 30,000ft 10.8min; service ceiling 35,800ft; range (internal fuel) 608nm (1126km) or 904nm (1674km) with drop tanks.

Production: 4 Fury prototypes, 3 Sea Fury prototypes, 50 F.10, 615 FB.11, 189 F/FB.50/60, 71 T.20/61, total 932.

Notes: Hawker chief designer Sydney Camm's investigations into a lighter version of the Tempest and the accidental (and highly fortuitous) arrival in Britain of a Focke-Wulf Fw 190 were the major catalysts in the development of what would become the Fury and Sea Fury. Firm ideas began to emerge in the second half of 1942 based around a shorter span wing (by eliminating the Tempest's centre section) and the use of a fully monocoque instead of steel tube/monocoque fuselage structure.

Orders were placed for Fury prototypes in late 1943, to be powered by both the Centaurus and Rolls-Royce Griffon vee-12. The first (with a Centaurus) flew on 1 September 1944 and although orders for 200 for the RAF were placed, these were cancelled at the end of WWII.

The navalised Sea Fury was developed in parallel and ordered into production for the Royal Navy, the first prototype flying on 21 February 1945. The first production Sea Fury F.X (later F.10) flew in September 1946 and the aircraft entered service in February 1947. Early Sea Furies were fitted with four bladed propellers instead of the definitive five bladers. The F.10 was armed only with guns and was quickly followed from 1948 by the major production FB.11 with provision for external ordnance. Sea Fury production ended in 1951.

The FB.11 formed the basis for export variants sold to the Royal Australian (101) and Royal Canadian (35) Navies plus F/FB.50/60s for the Netherlands (47 including 25 built by Fokker) and shore based versions for Iraq and Pakistan. Reconditioned aircraft were later sold to Burma and Cuba. A tandem two seat trainer version was developed as the T.20. The first one flew in January 1948 and deliveries were made to Britain, Cuba, Iraq, Burma and Germany.

British and Australian Sea Furies flew operationally from aircraft carriers during the Korean War mainly on ground attack duties although FB.11 pilots from the RN's No 802 Squadron (aboard HMS *Ocean*) downed a MiG-15 and damaged two others in an August 1952 action. The Sea Fury equipped 15 operational and 17 second line Royal Navy squadrons.

Photo: Sea Fury FB.10. (BAe)

Hawker Sea Hawk

Country of origin: United Kingdom.

Type: Single seat carrier based fighter-bomber.

Powerplants: Mks.1-4 – one 5000lb (22.2kN) Rolls-Royce Nene Mk.101 turbojet. FGA.5/6 – one 5200lb (23.1kN) Nene Mk.103.

Dimensions: Wing span 11.89m (39ft 0in); length 12.09m (39ft 8in); height 2.64m (8ft 8in); wing area 25.8m² (278sq ft).

Weights: FGA.6 – empty 4208kg (9278lb); max takeoff 7327kg (16,153lb).

Armament: F.1/2 – four 20mm cannon in nose. FB.3 – guns plus two 227kg (500lb) bombs under wings. FGA.4-6 – guns plus four underwing hardpoints for max 907kg (2000lb) bombs and rockets.

Performance: FGA.6 – max speed 520kt (964km/h) at sea level, 481kt (892km/h) at 36,000ft; initial climb 5700ft (1737m)/min; service ceiling 44,500ft; range (internal fuel) 417nm (772km).

Production: 1 P.1040, 2 P.1045, 95 F.1, 40 F.2, 116 FB.3, 97 FGA.4, 86 FGA.6, 22 FGA.50 and 66 Mks.100/101, total 525.

Notes: Hawker began design work on a land based jet fighter in 1944, design features including a straight tapered wing and a single Rolls-Royce RB.41 (later Nene) engine with bifurcated intakes and exhausts. Development continued as a private venture despite a lack of official interest as the P.1040, a prototype of which was first flown on 2 September 1947.

A navalised version of the basic design was ordered in May 1946 with folding wings, catapult launching gear and arrester hook. As the P.1045, the first of two prototypes flew on 3 September 1948 and the first production Sea Hawk F.1 on 14 November 1951. Service entry with the Royal Navy Fleet Air Arm was in March 1953 and due to Hawker's other commitments (notably the Hunter) all Sea Hawk development and production was transferred to Armstrong Whitworth Aircraft after the 31st F.1.

The Sea Hawk F.2 with powered ailerons followed, this retaining the original's armament of four cannon in the nose. Role versatility was introduced with the FB.3 fighter-bomber (first flight March 1953) with the ability to carry ordnance on two of the underwing hardpoints originally intended for drop tanks. The FGA.4 had two additional hardpoints for bombs and rockets, the 'fighter/ground attack' (FGA) designation reflecting its expanding roles.

Fitting the more powerful Nene 103 to FB.3s and FGA.4s resulted in the designations FGA.5 and FGA.6, respectively, new examples of the latter also being manufactured. The Sea Hawk equipped 11 RN FAA front line squadrons with the last retired in 1960. Three of these (operating from the carriers *Albion*, *Bulwark* and *Eagle*) saw action against Egyptian military targets during the Suez Crisis of 1956.

New and refurbished Sea Hawks were also exported to the Netherlands (FGA.50), Germany (Mks.100/101) and India, and although series production had ended in 1958, an additional batch of FGA.6s was built for the Indian Navy in 1960-1961. India also acquired used Sea Hawks from Britain and later Germany, keeping them in service until as late as 1983 when they were replaced by Sea Harriers.

Photo: Sea Hawk Mk.100.

Hawker Hunter F.1-5

Country of origin: United Kingdom.

Type: Single seat fighter.

Powerplant: F.1/4 – one 7500lb (33.3kN) Rolls-Royce Avon 113/115 turbojet. F.2/5 – one 8000lb (35.6kN) Armstrong Siddeley Sapphire 101 turbojet.

Dimensions: Wing span 10.26m (33ft 8in); length 13.98m (45ft 10½in); height 4.01m (13ft 2in); wing area 31.6m² (340sq ft).

Weights: F.4 – empty 5690kg (12,543lb); normal loaded (clean) 7756kg (17,100lb).

Armament: F.1/2 – four 30mm cannon in lower forward fuselage. F.4/5 – guns plus two underwing pylons for two 454kg (1000lb) bombs, 24 3in (7.62cm) rockets or drop tanks.

Performance: F.4 – max speed 606kt (1122km/h) at sea level, 535kt (991km/h) at 36,000ft; time to 45,000ft 12.5min; service ceiling 48,500ft; max ferry range with drop tanks 1435nm (2658km).

Production: 1972 Hunters of all versions including 3 P.1067 prototypes, 139 F.1, 45 F.2, 725 F.4 and export equivalents (incl 96 by Fokker and 112 by Fairey/SABCA), 105 F.5, 69 T.7 and 10 T.8.

Notes: The RAF's main front line day fighter throughout the 1950s, the Hunter survived early problems with its aerodynamics and engines (early Avons suffered severe surges when the guns were fired, the blast causing air flow disruptions) plus a typically British chronic lack of fuel capacity and endurance to serve with 23 nations and enjoy a long career.

The first of three prototypes flew on 20 July 1951, this and the second prototype powered by a Rolls-Royce Avon and the third by an Armstrong Siddeley Sapphire. Despite the Sapphire proving to be surge free, the vast majority of Hunters were fitted with the Avon.

The first production Hunter F.1 (with Avon) flew in May 1953 and the first Sapphire powered F.2 in October 1953. The F.1 began brief service with three RAF squadrons in August 1954 but was not fully cleared for operational service for some time after that as it was initially unable to fire its guns thanks to the surge problem. The F.2 equipped two squadrons.

The improved Hunter F.4 (Avon) and F.5 (Sapphire) both first flew in October 1954, the F.4 equipping 21 RAF squadrons and the F.5 seven, although service was again relatively brief. Compared to the F.1, the F.4 featured an improved Avon, an 'all flying' tail, a small increase in internal fuel capacity and importantly, the ability to carry drop tanks or a modest ordnance load under the wings. Any increase in fuel capacity was welcome as the Hunter F.1's sortie endurance was a mere 36 minutes with several aircraft lost due to fuel exhaustion.

Externally, undernose blisters to collect spent ammunition belt links were fitted. The F.5 was physically similar. New F.4s were exported to Sweden and Denmark while licence production was undertaken in the Netherlands by Fokker and Belgium by Fairey/Aviolanda.

The original prototype was fitted with an afterburning Avon (and redesignated F.3) to set a new world air speed record of 727.6mph (1170.9km/h) in September 1953 in the hands of Neville Duke. The P.1101 Hunter T.7 side-by-side two seat operational trainer was first flown in June 1955 and the Royal Navy's T.8 had an arrester hook for dry land carrier training.

Photo: Hunter prototype. (BAe)

Hawker Hunter F.6 and FGA.9

Country of origin: United Kingdom.

Type: Single seat fighter-bomber.

Powerplant: One 10,000lb (44.5kN) Rolls-Royce Avon 203 or 10,150lb (45.1kN) Avon 207 turbojet.

Dimensions: Wing span 10.26m (33ft 8in); length 13.98m (45ft 10 1/2in); height 4.01m (13ft 2in); wing area 32.4m² (349sq ft).

Weights: FGA.9 – empty 6610kg (14,572lb); loaded (clean) 8328kg (18,360lb); max takeoff 11,078kg (24,422lb).

Armament: F.6 – four 30mm cannon in lower forward fuselage; four underwing hardpoints for max 1361kg (3000lb) ordnance. FGA.9 – guns plus max 3356kg (7400lb) ordnance.

Performance: FGA.9 – max speed (clean) 622kt (1150km/h) at sea level, 545kt (1009km/h) at 36,000ft; max climb 16,500ft (5029m)/min clean or 8000ft (2438m)/min with typical load; service ceiling 50,000ft; radius of action with two 454kg (1000lb) bombs and two small drop tanks 190nm (352km); max ferry range with four large drop tanks 1595nm (2954km).

Production: 1972 Hunters of all models including 1 P.1099 prototype, 852 F.6 and export equivalents (incl 93 by Fokker and 144 by Fairey/SABCA) and 23 T.66.

Notes: Developed under the company designation P.1099, the Hunter F.6 introduced the more powerful 'large bore' Avon 200 series engine in combination with a modified wing incorporating a drooped and extended outer wing leading edge 'sawtooth' which increased wing area slightly. This was necessary to counter the Hunter's tendency to pitch up at high altitude and high Mach numbers, a problem exacerbated by the new engine.

The P.1099 prototype first flew on 23 January 1954 and the first production F.6 in May 1955. Deliveries to the RAF did not begin until October 1956 while various engine and aerodynamic problems were sorted out. The F.6 equipped 19 RAF operational squadrons and the last was delivered in October 1957. F.6s (and their equivalents) were exported to India, Switzerland, Belgium and the Netherlands, the latter pair building theirs locally under licence. A two seat operational trainer version with the generic designation T.66 was also sold, one of these the last new production Hunter of all and delivered to Jordan in July 1960.

With the Hunter's days as a pure fighter becoming numbered it began a second career as an effective ground attack aircraft with the conversion of large numbers to FGA.9 standards. Based on the F.6 but with structural and systems modifications, the FGA.9 was able to carry a substantially increased ordnance load. The first conversion was flown in July 1959 and the RAF received 128 between early 1960 and 1965 (plus 32 FR.10s with cameras) and the Royal Navy 40 similar GA.11s based on the F.4.

A substantial Hunter refurbishment industry grew out of this project, Hawker selling nearly 400 rebuilt FGA.9 equivalents (and T.70 trainers) to 14 nations up to 1975. It was quickly found that any Hunter version could be converted to any other (including single to two seaters and vice-versa) and a brisk trade was based around airframes repurchased by Hawker from former operators. By 2000 only Zimbabwe and Lebanon still had Hunters in front line service.

Photo: Hunter FGA.9. (BAe)

Hawker Siddeley (Blackburn) Buccaneer

Country of origin: United Kingdom.

Type: Two seat carrier and land based low level strike.

Powerplants: S.1 – two 7100lb (31.6kN) de Havilland (later Bristol Siddeley) Gyron Junior turbojets. S.2 – two 11,100lb (49.4kN) Rolls-Royce Spey Mk.101 turbofans. S.50 – Speys plus 8000lb (35.6kN) Bristol BS.605 rocket booster in rear fuselage.

Dimensions: S.2 – wing span 13.41m (44ft 0in); length 19.33m (63ft 5in); height 4.95m (16ft 3in); wing area 47.8m² (515sq ft).

Weights: S.2 – empty 13,608kg (30,000lb); max takeoff 28,123kg (62,000lb).

Armament: Up to 1814kg (4000lb) ordnance in rotary weapons bay plus up to 5443kg (12,000lb) ordnance on four underwing hardpoints including conventional and laser guided bombs, ASMs, jamming and designator pods, reconnaissance pack, AAMs etc.

Performance: S.2 – max speed 561kt (1040km/h) at sea level, 540kt (1000km/h) at 30,000ft; low level cruise 495kt (917km/h); tactical radius (internal fuel) hi-lo-lo-hi 435-520nm (805-963km); high altitude range with typical weapons load 2000nm (3705km).

Production: 20 prototypes/development, 40 S.1, 84 S.2, 49 S.2B and 16 S.50, total 209.

Notes: Designed to meet a demanding Royal Navy requirement for a two seat, low level/high subsonic speed naval strike aircraft, the Blackburn (later Hawker Siddeley) B.103 design – also known as the N.A.39 and named Buccaneer – was largely unsung but highly effective.

Advanced design features included an area ruled 'coke bottle' fuselage shape, the use of a boundary layer control system (engine bleed air blown over the control surfaces) to reduce minimum speeds and new manufacturing techniques including milling the wing structure from solid billets and machining structural members from steel forgings.

Twenty prototypes and pre-production aircraft powered by de Havilland Gyron Junior turbojets were ordered in May 1955, the first of them flying on 30 April 1958. The first production Buccaneer S.1 flew in January 1962 and front line Fleet Air Arm squadron service began six months later. Although effective in its intended role, the Buccaneer S.1 was underpowered (it was incapable of being launched from a carrier at maximum weight), this resulting in development of the Spey powered S.2 with greatly increased power. The first S.2 flew on 17 May 1963 with regular service entry in April 1965, equipping six FAA squadrons.

Faced with a lack of strike aircraft due to the cancellation of the TSR.2 and F-111K, the RAF began taking over the RN's Buccaneer S.2s from 1969 as FAA fixed wing operations began to wind down. In addition, new S.2Bs with the ability to carry Martel TV guided air-to-surface missiles were built in 1970-77 and others were converted to that standard. Other marks were converted from RN aircraft – S.2A, C and D, the C with Martel capability.

Five RAF squadrons flew Buccaneers until the last was retired in March 1994, three of them in the maritime strike role. Some saw action in the 1991 Gulf War where they were highly effective as laser designator aircraft for their own weapons and for Tornado units. The only export was to South Africa which received 16 S.50s in 1965, these fitted with auxiliary rocket boost engines for hot and high operations.

Photo: Buccaneer S.2B. (BAe)

Helwan HA-300

Countries of origin: Spain/Egypt.

Type: Single seat interceptor.

Powerplant: Prototypes – one 4850lb (21.6kN) Bristol Orpheus Mk.703-S-10 turbojet. Proposed production – one 7500lb (33.3kN) dry/10,582lb (47.1kN) with afterburner Brandner-Helwan HE-300 turbojet.

Dimensions: Wing span 5.84m (19ft 2in); length 12.39m (40ft 8in); height 3.15m (10ft 4in); wing area 16.7m² (180sq ft).

Weights: Proposed production (estimated) – normal loaded 4490kg (9899lb); max takeoff 5443kg (12,000lb).

Armament: Proposed – two 20mm or one 30mm cannon, two infrared homing air-to-air missiles.

Performance: Proposed production (estimated) – max speed at 40,000ft 1148kt (Mach 2.0/2126km/h) clean or 973kt (Mach 1.70/1802km/h) with missiles; maximum climb 35,000-40,000ft (1069-1219m)/min; time to 39,400ft 2.5min; combat radius (clean) 300-390nm (555-722km). Prototype – max achieved speed 648kt (Mach 1.13/1200km/h) at altitude.

Production: 3 prototypes of which 2 flown.

Notes: The first jet combat aircraft to be built in Egypt, the HA-300 began life in the late 1950s as a small and lightweight pure delta interceptor to be built in Spain by Hispano for the Spanish Air Force.

It was designed under the direction of Professor Willy Messerschmitt but the project was transferred to Egypt in 1962 for development and manufacture by the Helwan Air Works in an attempt to introduce a modern aircraft industry to the country. German and Spanish designers, engineers and production line workers were taken to Egypt to establish the enterprise. The facility was formally inaugurated by President Nasser with much fanfare on 25 July 1962. Unfortunately, the great Egyptian aerospace dream did not materialise.

The HA-300 was originally intended to be powered by an afterburning version of the Bristol Orpheus turbojet but with the transfer to Egypt it was decided to install the locally built HE-300 engine designed by Professor Brandner, an Austrian who was put in charge of the aero engine facility at Helwan. The aircraft meanwhile underwent some substantial redesign including the introduction of horizontal tail surfaces.

The first prototype HA-300 was powered by a non afterburning Orpheus 703-S-10 and recorded its maiden flight on 7 March 1964. It was incapable of supersonic flight but the similarly powered second prototype (first flight 22 July 1965) featured redesigned 'supersonic' intakes and other changes. It did achieve supersonic speeds (Mach 1.13) in level flight but at that stage there was little sign the aircraft would be capable of the promised Mach 2.0, even with a more powerful engine.

The third prototype was powered by the HE-300 powerplant and began taxying trials in November 1969, the more than four years' gap between this event and the first flight of the second prototype indicating some of the problems the programme was facing. The project was abandoned shortly afterwards with the third prototype never having flown.

Photo: Helwan HA-300.

Hispano HA-1112

Country of origin: Spain.

Type: Single seat fighter/ground attack.

Powerplant: HA-1109-J/K and HA-1112-K – one 1300hp (969kW) Hispano-Suiza 12Z 89 or 12Z 17 V12 piston engine; three bladed propeller. HA-1112-M – one 1635hp (1219kW) Rolls-Royce Merlin 500-45 V12; four bladed propeller.

Dimensions: HA-1112-M – wing span 9.92m (32ft 6½in); length 9.09m (29ft 10in); height 2.60m (8ft 6½in); wing area 16.1m² (173sq ft). HA-1112-K – length 8.99m (29ft 6in).

Weights: HA-1112-K – empty 2520kg (5555lb); max takeoff 3100kg (6834lb). HA-1112-M – empty 2656kg (5855lb); max takeoff 3180kg (7010lb).

Armament: Two 20mm cannon in wings and eight 80mm rockets under wings.

Performance: HA-1112-K – max speed 332kt (615km/h) at 13,400ft, 301kt (557km/h) at sea level; service ceiling 32,800ft; endurance 1.3 hours. HA-1112-M – max speed 364kt (674km/h) at 13,100ft; initial climb 5580ft (1700m)/min; service ceiling 33,450ft; max range 413nm (765km).

Production: 25 HA-1109-J, 44 HA-1112-K and 170 HA-1112-M.

Notes: Spain's Hispano Aviation acquired a licence to manufacture the Messerschmitt Bf 109G in 1942 but although drawings and 25 incomplete and engineless airframes were supplied in order to start the programme, no production was undertaken until after WWII. The 25 airframes were completed with Spanish built Hispano-Suiza 12Z engines installed in place of the usual Daimler-Benz DB 605, the prototype conversion flying on 2 March 1945 as the HA-1109-J and the remainder in 1947-48.

It was decided to switch to a French version of the 12Z engine for following production, the aircraft thus equipped designated HA-1109-K. A converted prototype was flown in May 1951 and production aircraft delivered from 1952, mostly without armament. Those built with two 20mm cannon in the wings and provision for underwing rockets were designated HA-1112-K. A pair of tandem two seater trainers were also produced as the HA-1110-K, these later converted to Rolls-Royce Merlin engines as the HA-1110-M.

With the Hispano-Suiza engine having gone out of production, it was decided in 1953 to mate the HA-1109/1112 airframe with the Rolls-Royce Merlin. The prototype conversion (the 11th HA-1109-J redesignated HA-1109-M) first flew in its new guise on 1954 and a further three prototypes were also converted.

There was some historical significance associated with the installation of the British powerplant as the original Messerschmitt Bf 109 prototype of 1935 had been powered by a Rolls-Royce Kestrel.

Nicknamed *Buchón* (after a Spanish pigeon), new production aircraft were designated HA-1112-M and entered service with the Spanish Air Force in 1956. Production ended in 1958 and the aircraft remained in service until 1967. Twenty-eight were then purchased for use in the film *The Battle of Britain*, these – and other aircraft made airworthy for the film – making a substantial contribution to the birth of the modern British warbird industry.

Photo: HA-1112-M.

IAI Nesher and Dagger

Country of origin: Israel.

Type: Single seat ground attack and day fighter.

Powerplant: One 9430lb (41.9kN) dry/13,670lb (60.1kN) with afterburner Snecma Atar 9C turbojet.

Dimensions: Wing span 8.22m (26ft 11½in); length 15.56m (51ft 0½in); height 4.50m (14ft 9in); wing area 34.8m² (375sq ft).

Weights: Empty 6600kg (14,550lb); max takeoff 13,700kg (30,203lb).

Armament: Two 30mm cannon; seven underfuselage and underwing hardpoints for up to 4000kg (8818lb) external ordnance and fuel tanks.

Performance: Max speed 1263kt (Mach 2.2/2340km/h) at 39,400ft, 750kt (Mach 1.14/1389km/h) at sea level; combat radius with 907kg (2000lb) bomb load 700nm (1297km) hi-lo-hi or 350nm (648km) lo-lo-lo.

Production: 51 plus 10 two seat trainers.

Notes: Israel – an existing operator of the Dassault Mirage IIIC – was the launch customer for the Mirage 5 day fighter-bomber version (see earlier entry) with an order for 50 examples.

These were built between September 1967 and June 1969 but following the placement of a total arms embargo on Israel by Charles de Gaulle's French Government, they languished at the factory despite having already been paid for. France eventually put the aircraft into Armée de l'Air service and repaid the money.

What resulted was an extraordinary saga of international intrigue which saw the Mirage 5 copied and built by Israel Aircraft Industries (IAI) without the benefit of a licence. Somehow, and after an extraordinary series of espionage events the Israelis obtained the necessary plans and data to build their own Mirages. This in combination with some 'reverse engineering' from Israel's existing Mirage IIICs resulted in the Nesher (Eagle). The aircraft's Atar engines were also duplicated, built by IAI's Bedek Aviation division.

The Nesher differed from the Mirage 5 only in detail, having some local avionics, Martin-Baker ejection seats and the ability to carry Rafael Shafrir or Sidewinder AAMs or ASMs already in Israeli use.

The prototype Nesher was based on a French airframe but with some IAI built components incorporated. It first flew in September 1969 and deliveries began in 1971. The Nesher saw its first action during the 1973 Yom Kippur War. Some two seat operational trainers were also built.

Surplus and refurbished Neshers were offered for export as the Dagger, Argentina taking 35 single seaters and four two seaters in two batches between 1978 and 1982, the total most likely reflecting Israel's entire stock of the surviving aircraft. Argentina flew both Daggers and Mirage IIIEs during the 1982 Falklands War.

Operating at the extreme of their combat radius they were substantially hampered and a combined total of 27 was lost, most to Royal Navy Sea Harriers although some fell to ground fire or ran out of fuel on the way home. By 2000, Argentina still had about 20 Daggers in service.

IAI's experience with the Nesher led to development of the re-engined and largely redesigned Kfir (Lion Cub) as described in the next entry.

Photo: IAI Nesher.

IAI Kfir

Country of origin: Israel.

Type: Single seat multirole fighter.

Powerplant: One 11,890lb (52.9kN) dry/17,860lb (79.4kN) with afterburner IAI built General Electric J79-IAI-J1E turbojet.

Dimensions: Wing span 8.22m (26ft 11½in); length (incl nose probe) 15.65m (51ft 4in); height 4.55m (14ft 11in); wing area 34.8m² (375sq ft).

Weights: C7 – empty 7290kg (16,071lb); max takeoff 16,500kg (36,375lb).

Armament: C7 – two 30mm cannon; five underfuselage and four underwing hardpoints for max 4295kg (9469lb) ordnance including AAMs, ASMs, rockets and conventional or laser guided bombs.

Performance: C7 – max speed 1320kt (Mach 2.3/2445km/h) above 36,000ft, 750kt (Mach 1.13/1389km/h) at sea level; max initial climb 45,930ft (14,000m)/min; operational ceiling 58,000ft; combat radius (high altitude intercept) 419nm (776km); ground attack combat radius (hi-lo-hi) with 1180kg (2600lb) bomb load and two AAMs 640nm (1082km); max ferry range 1744nm (3230km).

Production: 27 C1 and 185 C2/TC2, total 212.

Notes: While IAI was producing its Nesher Mirage 5 copies, the company was also developing an improved version called the Kfir (Lion Cub). Developed under the code name 'Black Curtain', it combined the Mirage airframe with a General Electric J79 turbojet in place of the standard Atar, the installation requiring a shorter rear fuselage of greater diameter to accommodate the new engine. Other features included the incorporation of a dorsal air scoop ahead of the fin for afterburner cooling and Israeli developed avionics in a lengthened nose.

A J79 powered prototype converted from a Mirage IIIC was first flown on 19 October 1970 and a more representative prototype (based on a Nesher airframe) in September 1971. The first true Kfir C1 was flown in June 1973 and deliveries to the IDF/AF began in April 1975.

The Kfir C1 was quickly followed by the C2, this differing from the original in having detachable canard foreplanes mounted on the upper intake trunks, nose strakes and dogtooth wing leading edges, all these intended to enhance manoeuvrability (especially at lower speeds) and to improve airfield performance. The C2 first appeared in 1976 and the production total included some TC2 two seaters from 1981.

Ground attack and interceptor versions were produced (the latter with appropriate radar), all but two of the C1s were upgraded to C2 standards, exports were made to Ecuador (10), Colombia (13) and Sri Lanka (5). The USN and USMC leased the 25 upgraded C1s for 'aggressor' training between 1985 and 1989 as the F-21A.

Most Israeli Kfirs were upgraded to C7 (or TC7) standards from 1983 with two additional hardpoints, a 'combat plus' rating for the engine increasing maximum power to 18,750lb (83.4kN) thrust, and an upgraded cockpit with HOTAS controls. A further upgrade is also offered as the Kfir 2000 (or C10) with new avionics including the multimode radar developed for the IAI Lavi. A further developed version was test flown in 1991 as the Nammer (Tiger).

Photo: Kfir C7. (IAI)

IAI Lavi

Country of origin: Israel.

Type: Single seat multirole fighter.

Powerplant: One 12,500lb (55.6kN) dry/18,600lb (82.7kN) with after-burner Pratt & Whitney PW1120 turbojet.

Dimensions: Wing span 8.79m (29ft 10in); length 14.58m (47ft 10in); height 4.77m (15ft 8in); wing area 33.1m² (356sq ft).

Weights: Empty 6942kg (15,305lb); max takeoff 19,278kg (42,500lb).

Armament: One internal 30mm cannon; seven underfuselage and four underwing hardpoints for max 7257kg (16,000lb) air-to-air and air-to-ground ordnance.

Performance: Max speed 1032kt (Mach 1.8/1912km/h) at 36,000ft; low level penetration speed with two AAMs and eight 340kg (750lb) bombs 538kt (996km/h); combat radius with 680kg (1500lb) ordnance 600nm (1110km) lo-lo-lo or 1150nm (2130km) hi-lo-hi; combat air patrol radius 1000nm (1850km).

Production: 3.

Notes: The Lavi (Young Lion) was developed as a multirole fighter for the Israeli Air Force, primarily as a close air support aircraft and with air defence as its secondary mission. A requirement for about 300 was issued including 60 two seaters with full operational capability.

The programme was given the go ahead in 1980 and full scale development began in October 1982.

The design was basically a tailless delta with close coupled canard foreplanes. An underfuselage intake fed air to the single Pratt & Whitney PW1120 turbojet, this in itself interesting as it reversed normal trends in being a turbojet development of the F100 turbofan as fitted to the McDonnell Douglas F-15 Eagle and some General Dynamics F-16 models.

About 22 per cent of the structure (by weight) was of composite materials, while state-of-the-art Elta multimode radar, headup display (HUD), hands on throttle and stick (HOTAS) controls and cockpit multifunction displays were fitted.

Five prototypes were planned, the first of these (a two seater) flying on 31 December 1996 followed by the second (another two seater) on 30 March 1987. The two aircraft had between them logged about 80 flights by August 1987, at which point the programme was cancelled as a result of severe budget cuts. Both Lavi prototypes were then scrapped.

It was then decided that the Lavi would have some use as a technology demonstrator and a third aircraft was completed at IAI's expense. Another two seater and designated Lavi TD, it first flew on 25 September 1989 and was subsequently used to validate much of the advanced technology that had been developed for the aircraft.

In the late 1990s it was suggested by some military analysts that the Lavi was being used as the basis for China's Chengdu J-10 fighter, with which it has certain similarities including the basic external configuration. Power would be provided by a Russian engine, either a 27,560lb (122.6kN) thrust with afterburner Saturn AL-31F turbofan or a 18,300lb (81.4kN) with afterburner Klimov RD-33. It is thought that a J-10 prototype was flown in March 1998.

Photo: The third Lavi. (IAI)

Ilyushin Il-28

Country of origin: Soviet Union.

Type: Three seat tactical bomber.

Powerplants: Two 5952lb (26.5kN) Klimov VK-1A turbojets.

Dimensions: Wing span 21.45m (70ft 4½in); length 17.65m (57ft 11in); height 6.70m (22ft 0in); wing area 60.8m² (654sq ft).

Weights: Empty equipped 12,890kg (28,417lb); normal loaded 18,400kg (40,564lb); max takeoff 21,000kg (46,296lb).

Armament: Two 23mm cannon in lower forward fuselage and two in tail turret; internal weapons bay for max 3000kg (6614lb) bombs or torpedoes.

Performance: Max speed 486kt (900km/h) at 14,800ft, 424kt (785km/h) at sea level; typical cruise 410kt (759km/h); initial climb 2953ft (900m)/min; service ceiling 40,350ft; low altitude range 613nm (1135km); high altitude range 1177nm (2180km).

Production: Over 2000 Il-28s plus up to 2000 Harbin H-5s.

Notes: Ilyushin gained some experience in the field of jet tactical bombers through the Il-22, a single prototype of which was flown in July 1947.

Inadequately powered with its four 2866lb (12.7kN) Lyulka TR-1 turbojets, the Il-22 served as a stepping stone towards development of the successful and widely used twin engined Il-28. The NATO reporting name 'Beagle' was applied to the aircraft.

The Il-28 began as a private venture in December 1947, the design powered by two Rolls-Royce Nene engines, at that stage the most powerful turbojet in the world. The Nene had been generously supplied by the Attlee socialist government in Britain to its Soviet 'comrades' and was immediately copied. The Nene formed the basis of the Klimov VK-1 engines fitted to the Il-28 and the MiG-15 fighter.

The first Il-28 flew on 8 July 1948 powered by Nenes and was ordered into production for the Soviet Air Force after winning a competition against a Tupolev design. First deliveries were in late 1950, early aircraft powered by two 5000lb (22.2kN) RD-45 turbojets (the direct Nene copy) but the further developed VK-1A was quickly fitted.

Production was at a high rate with more than 2000 Il-28s delivered in four years. Variants included the Il-28T torpedo bomber, Il-28U operational trainer with a second cockpit, IL-28R tactical reconnaissance version and the Il-20, a civil version used by Aeroflot from 1956 on jet route proving trials.

Over 1100 Il-28s were exported to Soviet aligned nations including Egypt, Indonesia, North Korea, North Vietnam, Syria, Yemen and Czechoslovakia, which also built some under licence as the B-228. More than 500 went to China and after it and the USSR severed ties in the 1960s, the Il-28 was copied and built without a licence in China by the Harbin Aircraft factory as the H-5 or B-5 for export. Subvariants included the HJ-5 trainer and HZ-5 reconnaissance aircraft.

The first Chinese built example flew in September 1966 and production continued into the 1980s at a low rate, by which time nearly 2000 had been manufactured. In 2000, China, North Korea and Romania still operated the H-5.

Photo: Ilyushin Il-28. (Sebastian Zacharias)

Ilyushin Il-38

Country of origin: Soviet Union.

Type: 8-10 crew maritime patrol and anti submarine warfare.

Powerplants: Four 4250eshp (3169kW) ZMKB Progress (Ivchenko) AI-20M turboprops; four bladed propellers.

Dimensions: Wing span 37.41m (122ft 9in); length overall 40.08m (131ft 6in); height 10.17m (33ft 4^1/$_2$in); wing area 140.0m^2 (1507sq ft).

Weights: Empty 34,030kg (75,022lb); normal loaded 63,500kg (139,990lb); max takeoff 66,000kg (145,502lb).

Armament: Forward and aft weapons bays for max 5000kg (11,023lb) ordnance including homing torpedoes, sonobuoys, nuclear and conventional depth bombs and mines.

Performance: Max speed 354kt (655km/h); cruising speed 313kt (580km/h); patrol speed 173-216kt (320-400km/h); typical patrol height below 3300ft; service ceiling 36,090ft; range with max weapons load 3615nm (6695km); max endurance 11 hours.

Production: 57.

Notes: The Ilyushin Il-38 is a maritime patrol and anti submarine warfare derivative of the Il-18 80-120 seat turboprop airliner (NATO reporting name 'Coot'), one of the new generation of airliners developed for Aeroflot in the 1950s and first flown in July 1957. The Il-18 went on to achieve a production run of 700-800 and by 2000 some 400 were still in service with mainly CIS and Eastern European airlines.

Some former airliner Il-18s have been converted to fill military roles and given new designations, these including the Il-20 'Coot-A' electronic intelligence/reconnaissance platform first observed in 1978 and the Il-22 'Coot-B' airborne command post. Both feature a variety of external antennae for their role equipment.

The new build Il-38 'May' has a similar relationship to the Il-18 as the Lockheed P-3 Orion does to the Electra airliner. Compared to the Il-18, it features a lengthened fuselage with magnetic anomaly detector (MAD) boom in the tail, the wings are moved forwards and search radar is located in a radome under the lower forward fuselage. Two internal weapons bays are fitted, one forward and one aft of the wing and the cabin houses a tactical commander, sensor operator, communications officer and observers/relief crew in addition to the flight crew of two pilots, navigator and flight engineer.

The Il-38 was first ordered in June 1960 and flight testing of the first fully equipped aircraft began in 1965.

The first production aircraft left Moscow's Znamya Truda (now MAPO) factory in December 1967 and the aircraft was commissioned into service in January 1967. The last of 57 examples was delivered in February 1972.

About 35 Il-38s were in service with the Russian and Ukrainian Navies by 2000, the Russian aircraft divided between the Northern, Pacific and Baltic Fleets based at Severomorsk, Petropavlovsk and Ostrov, respectively.

The Indian Navy received five aircraft in 1975, these still in service in 2000. The standard Il-38 is dubbed 'May-A', the 'May-B' conversion differing in having a retractable drop type radome in place of the forward weapons bay.

Photo: Ilyushin Il-38.

Kamov Ka-50 and Ka-52

Country of origin: Soviet Union/Russia.

Type: Single (Ka-50) or two (Ka-52) seat attack helicopter.

Powerplants: Two 2200shp (1640kW) Klimov TV3-117VMA turboshafts; three bladed counter rotating coaxial rotors.

Dimensions: Ka-50 – main rotors diameter 14.42m (47ft 4in); fuselage length 15.01m (49ft 3in); stub wing span 7.34m (24ft 1in); height 4.93m (16ft 2in); main rotor disc area (each) 165.1m^2 (1777sq ft). Ka-52 – fuselage length 13.54m (44ft 5in)

Weights: Ka-50 – empty 7692kg (16,958lb); normal takeoff 9800kg (21,605lb); max takeoff 10,800kg (23,810lb). Ka-52 – normal takeoff 10,400kg (22,928lb).

Armament: One fixed 30mm cannon; four hardpoints on stub wings for max 1811kg (3992lb) ordnance including rockets, tube launched or laser guided ASMs, gun pods and AAMs.

Performance: Ka-50 – max speed 167kt (309km/h); cruise speed 146kt (270km/h); max climb 2835ft (864m)/min; hovering ceiling OGE 13,125ft; service ceiling 18,045ft; normal range 245nm (454km); ferry range 626nm (1160km).

Production: Ka-50 – five prototypes and about 30 production aircraft by 2000. Ka-52 – prototype only.

Notes: The Ka-50 (NATO codename 'Hokum') was developed simultaneously with the Mil Mi-28 to meet a December 1976 Russian Army requirement for a new generation attack helicopter. The prototype (designated V.80-01) recorded its first hovering flight on 17 June 1982 and its first conventional flight ten days later.

Like other Kamovs, the Ka-50 features counter rotating coaxial main rotors but it is unique among dedicated attack helicopters in having a single seat configuration. To compensate for the higher pilot workload, an advanced autohover system is incorporated. Other features include extensive use of composites in the airframe and an ejection seat for the pilot (a first for an operational helicopter), this operating in conjunction with explosive charges which jettison the rotor blades when the seat is activated.

Production and service entry of the basic Ka-50 ('Hokum-A') has been a protracted affair due to funding problems. Comparative trials with the Mi-28 were held in 1985-86, the first production model was flown in May 1991 and acceptance into Russian Army service was achieved in August 1995. Production was suspended after only 12 had been built but restarted at a very low rate in 1996. A night attack version, the Ka-50N with FLIR/low light TV/laser equipment in a redesigned nose first flew in March 1997.

The Ka-52 Alligator ('Hokum-B') is a side-by-side two seat variant which was developed to address Russian Army concerns over pilot workload in the Ka-50 single seater. The second seat is for a mission officer and dual controls are fitted as well as ejection seats for both crew members. The Ka-52 has about 85 per cent commonality with its predecessor, the main airframe differences being in the redesigned cockpit area. The prototype Ka-52 first flew on 25 June 1997, converted from the 11th production Ka-50.

Israel's IAI and Kamov proposed a joint venture tandem two seat version (the Ka-50-2) with IAI developed glass cockpits and other systems to meet a Turkish requirement (won by the Bell AH-1Z).

Photo: Ka-50 'Werewolf'.

Kawasaki P-2J

Country of origin: Japan.

Type: 10-12 crew maritime patrol and anti submarine warfare.

Powerplants: Two 2850ehp (2125kW) Ishikawajima-Harima built General Electric T64-IHI-10 turboprops and two 3085lb (13.7kN) Ishikawajima-Harima J3-IHI-7C auxiliary turbojets; three bladed propellers.

Dimensions: Wing span over tip tanks 30.87m (101ft 3¹/₂in); length 29.23m (95ft 11in); height 8.93m (29ft 3¹/₂in); wing area 92.9m² (1000sq ft).

Weights: Empty 19,278kg (42,500lb); max takeoff 34,020kg (75,000lb).

Armament: Internal weapons bay for max 3629kg (8000lb) ordnance including homing torpedoes, mines and bombs; underwing attachments for 16 5in (12.7cm) rockets.

Performance: Max cruise 217kt (402km/h); economical cruise 200kt (370km/h); initial climb 1800ft (548m)/min; service ceiling 30,000ft; max range 2400nm (4445km).

Production: 1 prototype (converted from P-2H) and 82 production P-2J.

Notes: Kawasaki Heavy Industries manufactured 48 Lockheed P2V-7/P-2H Neptunes for the Japanese Maritime Self Defence Force between 1959 and 1965 and in 1961 began development work on a more capable version, initially under the designation GK-210. The definitive version which eventually appeared was designated P-2J or P2V-kai (an abbreviation of *kaizo* – 'modified').

Compared to the P-2H, the J differed in having licence built General Electric T64 turboprops in place of the original Wright R-3350 Turbo Compound 18-cylinder radials (driving three rather than four bladed propellers) and Ishikawajima auxiliary turbojets under the wings instead of the previous Westinghouse J34s.

The forward fuselage was lengthened by 1.29m (4ft 3in) to counter the centre of gravity changes introduced by the much lighter turboprops (and to accommodate additional and upgraded search and control system equipment), more compact AN/APS-80 search radar was installed in the smaller ventral radome, the normal crew complement was increased from seven to ten, small diameter dual main wheels replaced the previous large single units, the fin and rudder was slightly enlarged and fuel capacity increased.

The turboprop engines reduced empty weight by more than 3200kg (7000lb) and although the total available power was considerably less than before, the lower maximum takeoff weight this allowed resulted in no significant loss of performance.

The prototype P-2J (converted from a P-2H) first flew on 21 July 1966 and the first of 82 production examples on 8 August 1969. Deliveries to the JMSDF began in October 1969 and the final example was delivered in March 1979, ending 34 years of continuous Neptune production. Subvariants created by conversion were the EP-2J electronic intelligence gathering (Elint) aircraft and the UP-2J for target towing, ECM training and drone launch duties.

The P-2J was replaced in JMSDF service by the Kawasaki assembled P-3C Orion, deliveries of which began in 1982. P-2J numbers gradually declined from then but the last examples remained on strength until 1996.

Photo: Kawasaki P-2J.

Lavochkin La-15

Country of origin: Soviet Union.

Type: Single seat fighter.

Powerplant: One 3505lb (15.6kN) RD-500 (Rolls-Royce Derwent) turbojet.

Dimensions: Wing span 8.83m (28ft 11¹/₂in); length 9.56m (31ft 4¹/₂in); wing area 16.1m² (174sq ft).

Weights: Empty 2575kg (5677lb); max takeoff 3850kg (8488lb).

Armament: Two 23mm cannon in nose.

Performance: Max speed 554kt (1027km/h) at 9800ft; time to 16,400ft 3.1min; service ceiling 42,650ft; range 630nm (1167km).

Production: Approximately 500.

Notes: A rival to the MiG-15, the La-15 (NATO codename 'Fantail') was the only one of several Lavochkin jet fighter designs to achieve production, albeit in relatively limited numbers. Like the early MiGs, Lavochkin's designs benefited from the transfer of jet engine technology from Britain, when examples of the Rolls-Royce Nene and Derwent were sent to the Soviet Union. They were quickly copied and used in several aircraft (the Nene appeared in the MiG-15) and then developed into local versions.

Soviet jet fighter and powerplant development also benefited from captured German hardware and data. Lavochkin's first jet fighter was the La-152 of 1946, a straight wing design powered by a Soviet version of the German Junkers Jumo. It was followed by other designs of similar configuration, the La-152 and La-168.

Development of what led to the La-15 began in 1946 when the Lavochkin bureau was assigned the task of designing advanced swept wing single seat fighters around the Nene (called RD-45) and Derwent (RD-500). The designs had shoulder mounted wings with 37deg sweep, T-tails and undercarriage mounted on the fuselage. The Nene powered La-168 first flew in April 1948 and the 'lightweight' La-172 version with less powerful Derwent engine shortly earlier.

Despite the MiG-15 being selected for large scale production, development continued with the RD-500/Derwent powered La-174, the first of two prototypes flying in August 1948. In the same month, it was ordered into limited production as the La-15 and deliveries to the *Voenno-Vozdushnye Sily* (VVS – Military Aviation Forces) began in mid 1949.

Production was restricted because of the superiority of the MiG-15 and the fact that the La-15's structural design (which used numerous milled parts) was difficult to manufacture. The La-15 had been withdrawn from service by 1955. Two prototypes of a tandem two seat conversion trainer derivative were also built as the La-180 and although ordered into production under the designation La-15UTI, it was cancelled.

Lavochkin followed the La-172D/La-15 with the La-176 which combined the earlier aircraft's fuselage with a new more highly swept wing and the more powerful RD-45F, an afterburning version of the local Nene. First flown in September 1948, the sole prototype exceeded Mach 1 in a dive during flight tests, the first time a Soviet aircraft had achieved supersonic flight. The prototype was lost in early 1949 and the La-176 project abandoned.

Photo: Lavochkin La-15.

Lockheed P-80 Shooting Star

Country of origin: USA.

Type: Single seat fighter.

Powerplant: P-80A – one 3850lb (17.1kN) General Electric J33-GE-11 or 4000lb (17.8kN) J33-A-17 turbojet. P-80B – 4000lb (17.8kN) J33-A-17. P-80C – 4600lb (20.4kN) J33-A-23 or 5400lb (24.0kN) J33-A-35.

Dimensions: Wing span 11.85m (38ft 10½in); length 10.51m (34ft 6in); height 3.45m (11ft 4in); wing area 22.1m² (238sq ft).

Weights: P-80A – empty 3593kg (7920lb); max takeoff 6577kg (14,500lb). P-80C – empty 3819kg (8420lb); max takeoff 7646kg (16,856lb).

Armament: P-80A – six 0.50in machine guns in nose. P-80B/C – guns plus two 454kg (1000lb) bombs or ten 5in rocket projectiles under wings.

Performance: P-80A – max speed 485kt (898km/h) at sea level; initial climb 4580ft (1396m)/min; service ceiling 45,000ft; range (internal fuel) 678nm (1255km). P-80C – max speed 516kt (956km/h) at sea level; initial climb 6870ft (2094m)/min; service ceiling 46,800ft; range 717nm (1328km).

Production: 1 XP-80, 2 XP-80A, 13 YP-80A, 563 P-80A, 114 FP-80A, 240 P-80B, 798 P-80C, total 1731. Also 4992 T-33A and 699 T2V in USA plus 210 by Kawasaki and 656 by Canadair.

Notes: The USA's first operational jet fighter, development of the Shooting Star began in mid 1943 and the prototype XP-80 first flew only 143 days later on 8 January 1944 after a massive effort by Lockheed's design team led by Clarence ('Kelly') Johnson.

The prototype was powered by the Halford (de Havilland) H.1 turbojet which was the intended production powerplant but its non availability meant the aircraft had to be substantially redesigned to accept the General Electric J33. The first J33 powered XP-80A flew in June 1944 followed by 13 YP-80A evaluation aircraft from October 1944. The first production P-80A was handed over to the USAAF in December 1945.

More powerful versions of the J33 engine were developed and applied to new P-80 variants. The P-80B of 1946 had equipment upgrades and the ability to carry some underwing ordnance, while the P-80C (built in 1948-49) was similar but with more power. A modified P-80B set a new world air speed record of 623.8mph (1103.9km/h) in June 1947. USAF Shooting Stars (now designated F-80) saw action in Korea mainly on ground attack duties but one shot down a MiG-15 in November 1950 in what was probably the first conclusive combat between jet fighters.

The RP-80 reconnaissance model with cameras instead of guns was also produced and front line USAF service of the Shooting Star ended shortly after the Korean War. The Air National Guard retained some until 1961. Ex USAF F-80s were supplied to several South and Latin American countries.

The T-33 (originally TF-80C) tandem two seat trainer version first flew on 22 March 1948 and was built in large numbers for the USAF, US Navy (as the T2V SeaStar) and numerous foreign nations under the Military Assistance Programme. It was also built under licence in Japan by Kawasaki and by Canadair as the Silver Star. US production ended in 1959. In 2000 seven nations still flew T-33s.

Photo: F-80B Shooting Star.

Lockheed F-94 Starfire

Country of origin: USA.

Type: Two seat all weather fighter.

Powerplant: F-94A/B – one 6000lb (26.7kN) with afterburner General Electric J33-A-33 turbojet. F-94C – one 6350lb (28.2kN) dry/8750lb (38.9kN) with afterburner Pratt & Whitney J48-P-5/5A turbojet.

Dimensions: F-94B – wing span 11.43m (37ft 6in); length 12.22m (40ft 1in); height 3.86m (12ft 8in); wing area 21.8m² (235sq ft). F-94C – wing span 11.38m (37ft 4in); length 13.56m (44ft 6in); height 4.54m (14ft 11in); wing area 21.6m² (233sq ft).

Weights: F-94B – empty 4565kg (10,064lb); max takeoff 7640kg (16,843lb). F-94C – empty 5764kg (12,708lb); max takeoff 10,970kg (24,184lb).

Armament: F-94A/B – four 0.50in machine guns in nose. F-94C – 24 2.75in (70mm) Mighty Mouse unguided rockets in nose and 12 in each of two wing leading edge pods.

Performance: F-94B – max speed 526kt (975km/h) at sea level; initial climb 6850ft (2088m)/min; normal range 578nm (1070km). F-94C – max speed 556kt (1030km/h) at sea level, 508kt (941km/h) at 30,000ft; initial climb 7980ft (2432m)/min; service ceiling 51,400ft; normal range 700nm (1295km).

Production: 110 F-94A, 357 F-94B, 387 F-94C, total 854 (also 2 YF-94 conversions).

Notes: Development of a radar equipped interim all weather fighter derivative of the T-33 two seat trainer version of the P-80 Shooting Star for the USAF began in January 1949. Two YF-94 prototypes (converted from T-33s) were built, the first one flying on 16 April 1949.

Compared to the T-33, the F-94 Starfire had APG-32 radar fitted to a lengthened nose which also housed four 0.50in machine guns, a rear seat radar operator, an afterburning version of the J33 turbojet to counter substantially increased operating weights and P-80 style tip tanks hung under the wing extremities. Deliveries of production F-94As began in December 1949.

The upgraded F-94B featured revised hydraulics, equipment modifications and larger tip tanks conventionally mounted on the ends of the wings. The prototype YF-94B (converted from the 19th F-94A) first flew on 28 September 1950 and the model entered service in April 1951. Both the F-94A and B had been phased out of front line service by mid 1954 and the proposed F-94D single seat ground attack version was not built.

The F-94A and B had performance shortcomings, especially in rate of climb. The largely redesigned F-94C was developed to address these problems, initially under the designation F-97A. It featured a much more powerful afterburning Pratt & Whitney J48 turbojet (licence built Rolls-Royce Nene), a new and thinner wing, swept back tailplanes and a modified nose carrying 24 Mighty Mouse unguided rockets. Another 24 could be carried in a pair of wing leading edge pods and no guns were fitted.

The first of two YF-94Cs (converted from F-94Bs) flew on 19 January 1950. Production F-94Cs were built between July 1951 and May 1954 although service entry wasn't until June 1953. The F-94C began to be phased out of front line USAF service in 1959 and from the Air National Guard in 1960.

Photo: YF-94 Starfire.

Lockheed P2V-1/4 Neptune

Lockheed P2V-5/6/7 (P-2E/G/H) Neptune

Country of origin: USA.

Type: 9-10 crew maritime patrol and anti submarine.

Powerplants: P2V-2 – two 2800hp (2088kW) wet Wright R-3350-24W Cyclone 18-cylinder radials; three bladed propellers. P2V-3 – two 3200hp (2386kW) wet R-3350-26W; three bladed propellers. P2V-4 – two 3750hp (2796kW) wet Wright R-3350-30W Turbo Compounds; four bladed propellers.

Dimensions: P2V-2/3 – wing span 30.48m (100ft 0in); length 23.72m (77ft 10in); height 8.56m (28ft 1in); wing area 92.9m² (1000sq ft).

Weights: P2V-3 – empty 15,819kg (34,875lb); max takeoff 29,076kg (64,100lb). P2V-4 – max takeoff 33,625kg (74,129lb).

Armament: Weapons bay for up to 3629kg (8000lb) torpedoes, depth charges, bombs and mines; various 20mm cannon and 0.50in machine gun combinations in fixed nose and dorsal and tail turret installations; provision for 16 5in rockets under wings on P2V-3/4.

Performance: P2V-2 – max speed 278kt (515km/h) at 13,500ft; cruising speed 155kt (286km/h); max range 3458nm (6406km). P2V-4 – max speed 306kt (566km/h); max range 3650nm (6760km).

Production: 1181 Neptunes of all models including 1 XP2V-1, 15 P2V-1, 81 P2V-2, 83 P2V-3 and 52 P2V-4.

Notes: Lockheed began work on its Model 26 specialist land based maritime patrol aircraft in September 1941 as a follow on to its successful Ventura and Harpoon designs.

The much larger Model 26's development was delayed by more urgent wartime priorities which saw the project shelved for more than two years before a US Navy contract was placed for what would emerge as the P2V Neptune.

A mid wing design powered by two Wright R-3350 Cyclone radials and fitted with tricycle undercarriage and radar, the Neptune went on to become the mainstay of the USN's maritime patrol force in the 1950s and 1960s and was exported to Britain, Australia, Japan, Portugal, France, the Netherlands, Canada, Brazil and Argentina.

Apart from its primary role, the Neptune appeared in numerous mainly converted subvariants for other roles such as early warning, anti shipping, interdiction, airborne relay, drone launching and electronic reconnaissance. Many of these resulted from the needs of the Vietnam War.

The prototype XP2V-1 first flew on 17 May 1945 and the initial production P2V-1 entered USN service in May 1947. One of these – named *The Turtle* – set an unrefuelled distance record of 11,235 statute miles (18,081km) in September 1946 when it flew non stop from Perth, Western Australia to Columbus, Ohio.

Other early main versions were the P2V-2 (first flight May 1947) with more power, a solid nose containing six 20mm cannon (early Neptunes also had dorsal and tail gun turrets) and provision for JATO bottles on the rear fuselage; the P2V-3 (1948) with a further power upgrade and provision for underwing rockets (some were used in the Korean War as ground attack aircraft and night bombers); and P2V-4 (first flight November 1949) with Turbo Compound engines, wingtip fuel tanks, the ability to carry passive sonobuoys and improved APS-20 radar housed in a larger underfuselage radome.

Photo: P2V-2 Neptune. (Lockheed)

Country of origin: USA.

Type: 7-9 crew maritime patrol and anti submarine warfare.

Powerplants: P2V-5/P-2E – two 3750hp (2796kW) wet Wright R-3350-30W Turbo Compound 18-cylinder radials plus two 3250lb (14.4kN) Westinghouse J34-WE-34 turbojets on P2V-5F. P2V-7/P-2H – two 3700hp (2759kW) wet R-3350-32W and two 3400lb (15.1kN) J34-WE-34; four bladed propellers.

Dimensions: P-2H – wing span over tip tanks 31.65m (103ft 10in); overall length 27.94m (91 ft 8in); height 8.94m (29ft 4in); wing area 92.9m² (1000sq ft).

Weights: P-2E – empty 18,940kg (41,754lb); max takeoff 34,542kg (76,152lb). P-2H – empty 22,650kg (49,935lb); max takeoff 36,240kg (79,895lb).

Armament: Internal weapons bay for typically 3629kg (8000lb) ordnance including torpedoes, depth charges, bombs and mines; provision for eight 5in rockets under wings (if jets fitted) or 16 on early P2V-5. P2V-5 originally fitted with two 20mm canon in nose and tail turrets plus two 0.50in machine guns in dorsal turret.

Performance: P-2H – max speed (all engines) 316kt (586km/h) at 10,000ft or 265kt (491km/h) with pistons only; patrol speed 150-180kt (278-333km/h) at low level; service ceiling 22,400ft; max range 1912nm (3540km) with standard fuel or 3200nm (5927km) with bomb bay tanks.

Production: 1181 Neptunes of all models including 424 P2V-5/P-2E, 83 P2V-6/P-2F and 311 P2V-7/P-2H.

Notes: The P2V-5 (P-2E from 1962) Neptune represented the start of the aircraft's final evolution and was also the first model to be produced in large numbers. First flown in December 1950, the P2V-5 differed from its predecessor in having additional fuel capacity (including in enlarged tip and optional weapons bay tanks), and additional ASW and ECM electronic equipment. Early P2V-5s had nose, dorsal and tail turrets but these gradually disappeared.

The nose position gained a clear glass transparency and further updates saw the fitting of a magnetic anomaly detector (MAD) boom on the tail and the ability to carry the Julie/Jezebel active and passive sonobuoys. These remained in use for many years on both the Neptune and its successor, the P-3 Orion. A major modification to be incorporated was the fitting of two underwing J34 auxiliary turbojets to improve airfield performance and speed over the target. Most were modified and redesignated P2V-5F.

The P2V-6 (first flight October 1952) was designed as a minelayer, torpedo attack, bombing and reconnaissance aircraft. Most were retrofitted with the underwing jets and redesignated P2V-6F (later P-2G).

The final US built Neptune was the P2V-7 (P-2H), first flown on 26 April 1954 and differing externally from the P2V-5F in having a new bulged cockpit canopy design and smaller, more streamlined tip tanks. All but the first few were fitted with the MAD boom and the auxiliary jets were standard. The designation SP-2H was applied to aircraft fitted with Julie/Jezebel and improved ASW/ECM equipment. Front line USN service ended in 1970 but the last Reserve Patrol squadron to fly the Neptune didn't relinquish its aircraft until 1978.

Photo: SP-2H Neptune. (Lockheed)

Lockheed AC-130 Hercules

Country of origin: USA.

Type: 11 crew gunship.

Powerplants: AC-130A – four 3750eshp (2796kW) Allison T56-A-1A turboprops; three bladed propellers. AC-130E – four 4050eshp (3020kW) T56-A-7; four bladed propellers. AC-130H – four 4508eshp (3362kW) T56-A-15; four bladed propellers.

Dimensions: Wing span 40.41m (132ft 7in); length 29.79m (97ft 9in); height 11.66m (38ft 3in); wing area 162.1m² (1745sq ft).

Weights: AC-130E – empty 33,064kg (72,892lb); max takeoff 70,308kg (155,000lb).

Armament: See notes.

Performance: AC-130E – cruising speed 295kt (546km/h); endurance 5 hours. AC-130H – cruising speed 320kt (593km/h); initial climb 1830ft (558m)/min; endurance 5 hours.

Production: Over 2200 Hercules of all models by 2000; 16 AC-130A, 11 AC-130E (of which 10 further converted to AC-130Hs), 13 AC-130U and 9 AC-130H conversions.

Notes: The USAF further developed the concept of the gunship pioneered by the Douglas AC-47 and continued by the Fairchild AC-119 (see separate entries) with the AC-130 Hercules. The bigger aircraft allowed high technology targeting, tracking and lighting equipment to be installed along with even more devastating firepower and substantially increased quantities of ammunition to be carried. As with the AC-47 and AC-119, the aircraft were deployed in Vietnam.

The basic principle remained the same – the aircraft circling around a ground target at a constant rate and pouring thousands of rounds of ammunition into a small area. With the arrival of the AC-130 and its more accurate sensing and tracking equipment, the concept could be extended to more specific targets.

One Hercules was converted to AC-130A standard in 1967 and tested in Vietnam. Its operational equipment included four 20mm Vulcan multi barrel cannon, four 7.62mm multi barrel Minigun machine guns, night observation sight, low light TV, laser rangefinder and beacon tracking radar. The trials were successful with the result that 15 more AC-130As were converted to this 'Plain Jane' standard or to 'Pave Pronto' specifications with two Vulcans, two Miniguns and two 40mm Bofors cannon. The sensor equipment was also upgraded to include an ignition detector and forward looking infrared radar (FLIR).

The next step was the conversion of an initial seven AC-130E gunships by Ling-Temco-Vought, these entering service in 1970. A further four were subsequently converted, called 'Pave Spectre' and featuring one of the 40mm guns replaced by a massive (for an aircraft installation) 105mm recoilless howitzer. Developed from the US Army's M102 weapon and loaded by hand in the aircraft, this gave the AC-130E enhanced tank killing ability.

One AC-130E was lost in action and in 1973 the ten survivors were upgraded to AC-130H standards with more powerful engines. Subsequent Hercules gunship variants are the GAU-12 25mm cannon equipped AC-130U Spectre based on the C-130H, 13 of which were converted by Rockwell (first flight December 1990), and nine more AC-130H Spectres (converted by Lockheed Air Services) from mid 1990.

Photo: AC-130A Hercules.

Lockheed F-104A/C Starfighter

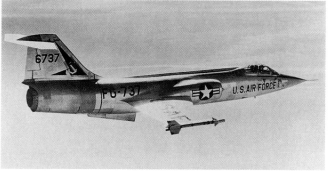

Country of origin: USA.

Type: F-104A – single seat interceptor. F-104C – single seat fighter-bomber.

Powerplant: F-104A – one 9600lb (42.7kN) dry/14,800lb (65.8kN) with afterburner General Electric J79-GE-3B turbojet. F-104C – one 10,000lb (44.5kN) dry/15,800lb (70.3kN) with afterburner J79-GE-7.

Dimensions: Wing span (without tip tanks) 6.68m (21ft 11in); length 16.69m (54ft 9in); height 4.11m (13ft 6in); wing area 18.2m² (196sq ft).

Weights: F-104C – empty 5788kg (12,760lb); max takeoff 12,634kg (27,853lb).

Armament: F-104A – one 20mm six barrel rotary cannon in lower forward fuselage; two Sidewinder AAMs on wingtips. F-104C – gun plus two or four Sidewinders or two 454kg (1000lb) bombs under wings.

Performance: F-104C – max speed 1000kt (Mach 1.74/1852km/h) at 40,000ft; max climb 54,000ft (16,459m)/min; service ceiling 55,000ft; normal range 738nm (1368km).

Production: 2422 Starfighters of all models including 2 XF-104, 15 YF-104A, 153 F-104A, 26 F-104B, 77 F-104C and 21 F-104D.

Notes: Lockheed's Model 83 Starfighter 'missile with a man in it' caused a sensation when it first appeared not only for its appearance – slender fuselage, T-tail and impossibly small wings – but also for its performance. The first operational fighter capable of sustaining speeds above Mach 2, it was also the first aircraft to simultaneously hold the world speed and altitude records. Although not built in large numbers for the US Air Force, the Starfighter later found widespread use with foreign air forces, especially in Europe.

Clarence ('Kelly') Johnson and the Lockheed 'Skunk Works' began design work in late 1952 and the USAF ordered two XF-104 prototypes in March 1953. Both were powered by the 10,000lb (44.5kN) thrust with afterburner Wright XJ65 turbojet (licence built Armstrong Siddeley Sapphire) and the first one flew on 4 March 1954. These were followed from February 1956 by the first of the YF-104A evaluation and trials batch powered by the definitive General Electric J79. Deliveries of production F-104As to the USAF's Air Defence Command began in December 1958. The tandem two seat operational trainer F-104B first flew in February 1957.

A pure interceptor, the F-104A had an armament comprising a Vulcan rotary cannon housed in the lower forward fuselage and a Sidewinder AAM on each wing tip. It was succeeded in production by the F-104C fighter-bomber with more powerful engine, provision for flight refuelling and underwing hardpoints for the carriage of additional missiles or bombs. Detachable wing tip fuel tanks were also fitted. The first F-104C was delivered to Tactical Air Command in October 1958 and the last in June 1959. The two seat equivalent was the F-104D.

The F-104A was relegated to Air National Guard duties in 1960 (some were converted to QF-104 target drones) but were later returned to regular USAF service. They had been retired by the end of 1969 but the F-104C remained in ANG service until 1975. Ex USAF F-104As were supplied to Pakistan (10) and Taiwan (24) during the 1960s, 22 of the latter transferred to Jordan from 1969.

Photo: F-104A Starfighter.

Lockheed F-104G/S Starfighter

Country of origin: USA.

Type: Single seat multirole fighter.

Powerplants: F-104G – one 10,000lb (44.5kN) dry/15,600lb (69.4kN) with afterburner General Electric J79-GE-11A turbojet. F-104S – one 11,870lb (52.8kN) dry/17,900lb (79.6kN) with afterburner J79-GE-19.

Dimensions: Wing span (without tip tanks) 6.68m (21ft 11in); length 16.69m (54ft 9in); height 4.11m (13ft 6in); wing area 18.2m² (196sq ft).

Weights: F-104G – empty 6335kg (13,966lb); max takeoff 13,170kg (29,034lb). F-104S – empty 6700kg (14,770lb); max takeoff 14,062kg (31,000lb).

Armament: F-104G – one 20mm six barrel rotary cannon in lower forward fuselage; two wingtip, one underfuselage and four underwing hardpoints for max 1814kg (4000lb) air-to-air or air-to-ground ordnance. F-104S – gun plus nine external hardpoints for max 3402kg (7500lb) ordnance.

Performance: F-104S – max speed 1250kt (Mach 2.2/2334km/h) at 36,000ft, 792kt (Mach 1.2/1467km/h) at sea level; max climb 55,000ft (16,764m)/min; service ceiling 58,000ft; combat radius with max fuel 673nm (1246km); ferry range 1576nm (2920km).

Production: 2422 Starfighters of all models including 30 F-104F, 1122 F-104G, 126 TF-104G, 194 RF-104G, 200 CF-104, 210 F-104J and 246 F-104S.

Notes: Evolution of the Starfighter continued with the multirole all weather fighter F-104G originally developed for Germany. It featured a strengthened structure, larger tail surfaces (with fully powered rudder), combat manoeuvring flaps, increased fuel capacity, upgraded avionics and provision to carry a useful range of air-to-air and air-to-ground ordnance on external hardpoints.

The F-104G (first flight 7 June 1960) was built by Lockheed for West Germany, Greece, Norway and Turkey but the majority were manufactured in Europe through a co-production agreement for Belgium, Germany, Italy and the Netherlands. Germany alone took 750. Canadair built a similar version as the CF-104 for its own air force plus 140 F-104Gs against a USAF order for supply to Denmark, Greece, Norway, Spain, Taiwan and Turkey. Other related versions were the TF-104G two seater (built by Lockheed), the RF-104G with reconnaissance pack (by Lockheed and in Europe) and the F-104J for Japan, of which most were built by Mitsubishi.

The final new build Starfighter variant was the F-104S developed specifically for Italy. This featured a more powerful J79-GE-17 engine, additional external weapons pylons and the ability to carry both Sidewinder and Sparrow AAMs. The Lockheed built prototype first flew in December 1966 and 245 were manufactured by Fiat (later Aeritalia and Alenia) including 40 for Turkey. The last F-104S was delivered in 1979.

Italy modified 147 of its aircraft to F-104ASA standards in 1985-93 with upgraded radar, avionics, weapons delivery system and weapons carrying capability. Italy was the sole Starfighter operator by 2000 with about 150 in service pending deliveries of the Eurofighter Typhoon.

Photo: F-104S Starfighter. (Paul Merritt)

Lockheed P-3 Orion

Country of origin: USA.

Type: 10 crew maritime patrol and anti submarine.

Powerplants: P-3A – four 4500shp (3355kW) Allison T56-A-10W turboprops. P-3B/C – four 4910ehp (3661kW) T56-A-14 turboprops; four bladed propellers.

Dimensions: Wing span 30.37m (99ft 8in); length 35.61m (116ft 10in); height 10.27m (33ft 10½in); wing area 120.8m² (1300sq ft).

Weights: P-3A – max takeoff 57,698kg (127,200lb). P-3B – max takeoff 61,236kg (135,000lb). P-3C – empty 27,896kg (61,500lb); max overload 64,411kg (142,000lb).

Armament: 10 underwing hardpoints for max 5443kg (12,000lb) rockets, mines or Harpoon anti shipping missiles; internal weapons bay for eight torpedoes or depth bombs or other stores to max 3290kg (7252lb).

Performance: P-3C – max speed 411kt (761km/h); economical cruise 329kt (609km/h); low level patrol speed 206kt (381km/h); initial climb 1950ft (594m)/min; service ceiling 28,300ft; low level mission radius (3hrs on station) 1347nm (2495km); max radius 2071nm (3836km).

Production: 649 by Lockheed comprising 157 P-3A, 144 P-3B and 348 P-3C; also 105 in Japan by Kawasaki.

Notes: Developed to meet a 1957 US Navy requirement for a P2V Neptune replacement, the appropriately named P-3 Orion (the son of Neptune and the God of the Hunt in Greek mythology) was based on the Electra turboprop airliner but with a shortened version of its fuselage incorporating a weapons bay. An aerodynamic prototype converted from an Electra and fitted with a dummy magnetic anomaly detector (MAD) boom flew on 19 August 1958. It was then modified to a full Orion prototype with shorter fuselage and reflown on 25 November 1959 as the YP3V. The Orion's designation was changed to P-3 in 1962.

The initial production P3V-1 (P-3A) flew on 15 April 1961 and deliveries to the US Navy began in August 1962. The improved P-3B had more powerful engines and some upgraded avionics and systems but they were still of the analogue type and similar to those installed on later Neptune models. The P-3B was exported to Australia, Norway and New Zealand, the latter as the P-3K.

The P-3C with substantially updated radar, solid state avionics and systems first flew in September 1968 and deliveries to the USN began in mid 1969. Subsequent Update I, II, II.5 and III versions introduced progressively more sophisticated avionics and computer systems. Exports were made to Australia, Japan (licence built by Kawasaki), South Korea, the Netherlands, Norway and Pakistan while second hand examples went to several other nations. Canada's CP-140 Auroras have the radar, processors and avionics developed for the S-3 Viking shipborne ASW aircraft. Several special missions variants were also developed.

US production ended in 1995 pending further orders with licence production in Japan continuing into 2000. An advanced derivative called the P-7 plus the Upgrade IV and P-3H developments were dropped due to budgetary constraints but in 2000 Lockheed Martin was offering the either new build or converted Orion 21 upgraded with new engines, glass cockpit and other changes.

Photo: P-3C Orion.

Lockheed S-3 Viking

Country of origin: USA.

Type: Four crew carrier based anti submarine warfare.

Powerplants: Two 9275lb (41.2kN) General Electric TF34-GE-2 turbofans.

Dimensions: Wing span 20.93m (68ft 8in); length 16.25m (53ft 4in); height 6.93m (22ft 9in); wing area 55.5m^2 (598sq ft).

Weights: S-3A – empty 10,954kg (24,150lb); max takeoff 21,592kg (47,602lb).

Armament: Internal weapons bay for four torpedoes, mines, bombs or depth charges; two underwing hardpoints for torpedoes, Harpoon ASMs, Maverick ASMs, rocket pods or mines.

Performance: Max speed 450kt (833km/h) at 20,000ft; cruising speed 350kt (649km/h) at low level; low level patrol speed 160kt (296km/h); initial climb 4200ft (1280m)/min; operational ceiling 35,000ft; range with max load 2000nm (3705km); low level loiter endurance 7.5hrs.

Production: 187.

Notes: Investigations into a new carrier based anti submarine, search and strike aircraft to replace the Grumman S-2 Tracker in US Navy service began in 1964 with a Request for Proposals issued in 1966. A joint Lockheed/Vought proposal which became the S-3 Viking was selected in August 1969 ahead of designs from four other manufacturers. The first of eight YS-3A development and evaluation aircraft flew on 21 January 1972.

Vought was responsible for the design and manufacture of the Viking's wings, tail unit, landing gear and engine nacelles. A compact high wing twin jet, the Viking featured an internal weapons bay, four crew members (two pilots, tactical co-ordinator and sensor operator), Univac AYK-10 digital computer, Texas Instruments APS-116 search radar and retractable FLIR pod. Anti submarine warfare systems comprised an extendable magnetic anomaly detector (MAD) boom in the tail and sonobuoys.

Deliveries of the S-3A to the USN began in February 1974, Squadron VS-21 becoming the first operational Viking unit in July 1974. The first carrier deployments took place a year later. Viking production ended in 1978.

Development of the upgraded S-3B was initiated in 1980, this version featuring an improved acoustic processing unit, expanded ESM (electronic support measures) equipment, enhanced radar processing, a new sonobuoy receiver system and the ability to carry the AGM-84 Harpoon anti ship missile. The first converted S-3B flew in September 1984 and almost all of the S-3As were converted to the new standard.

The USN also received four US-3A carrier onboard delivery (COD) conversions from 1976, these stripped of operational equipment and capable of carrying five passengers or freight. A single KS-3A tanker conversion was evaluated but the standard S-3A's 'buddy' refuelling ability was deemed sufficient for service use.

The final major Viking conversion to date is the ES-3A 'Shadow' electronic intelligence gathering (Elint) variant. It first flew in 1989 and 16 conversions were subsequently performed to replace the Douglas EA-3B Skywarrior. The ES-3A equipment fit included various sensors and EW electronics. It was retired in 1998.

Photo: ES-3A 'Shadow'. (USN)

Lockheed F-117A Nighthawk

Country of origin: USA.

Type: Single seat 'stealth' attack aircraft.

Powerplants: Two 10,800lb (48.0kN) General Electric F404-GE-F1D2 turbofans.

Dimensions: Wing span 13.20m (43ft 4in); length 20.09m (65ft 11in); height 3.78m (12 ft 5in); wing area 84.8m^2 (913sq ft).

Weights: Empty 13,381kg (29,500lb); max takeoff 23,814kg (52,500lb).

Armament: Two 907kg (2000lb) laser guided bombs, nuclear bombs or Maverick or HARM ASMs and Sidewinder AAMs in internal weapons bay.

Performance: Max speed 561kt (1039km/h); unrefuelled mission radius 570nm (965km) with full weapons load.

Production: 5 pre-production and 60 production F-117A.

Notes: Lockheed's 'Black Jet', the F-117 Nighthawk was designed and developed by the famed Lockheed 'Skunk Works' in complete secrecy as a stealthy attack fighter and was the winning submission in the XST (Experimental Stealth Technology) or 'Have Blue' competition of 1976-77. The competition was sponsored by the US Defence Advanced Research Projects Agency.

Lockheed was awarded the contract to build two XST prototypes powered by a pair of 2800lb (12.4kN) General Electric CJ610 turbojets. Although smaller, they were similar in overall configuration to the F-117 as it eventually emerged except for having inward canted tailplanes. The first XST flew in December 1977 but both aircraft had been lost in crashes by 1980.

Development of the operational F-117A began in November 1978 under the 'Senior Trend' programme, initial contracts covering five pre-production and 15 production aircraft. The first pre-production aircraft flew on 18 June 1981 and the first of an eventual 60 production F-117As was handed over to the USAF in August 1982. Only 59 of these were taken on strength as one was lost on its maiden flight and not delivered. Initial operational capability was declared in October 1983. The final aircraft was handed over in July 1990 and the name Nighthawk was officially adopted in 1994. The aircraft's unofficial nickname was 'Wobblin Goblin'!

All F-117A flights were undertaken at night for the first five years of service in order to maintain secrecy and it wasn't until November 1988 that the aircraft was officially revealed and day missions began to be flown. The Nighthawk was first used operationally in December 1989 when a single aircraft dropped two 907kg (2000lb) laser guided bombs on the Rio Hato Barrack area in Panama during Operation Just Cause. It has since seen combat in the 1991 Gulf War and over Serbia in 1999.

The F-117A's stealth characteristics derive from its faceted airframe design with the avoidance of straight lines on doors and panels so as to reflect radar in all directions. Radar absorbent materials cover the airframe and the non afterburning F404 engines' exhaust gases are mixed with bypass air and exit through 'slot' type nozzles with protruding lower lips and vertical guide vanes. From there they produce a wide, thin plume and are directed slightly upwards to minimise infrared signature. The F-117A will remain in USAF service until about 2015.

Photo: F-117A Nighthawk.

Lockheed Martin F-16A Fighting Falcon

Country of origin: USA.

Type: Single seat multirole fighter.

Powerplant: One 14,670lb (65.2kN) dry/23,830lb (106.0kN) with afterburner Pratt & Whitney F100-PW-200 or -220 turbofan.

Dimensions: Wing span (without tip AAMs) 9.70m (31ft 10in); length 15.02m (49ft 3½in); height 5.00m (16ft 5in); wing area 27.9m² (300sq ft).

Weights: Empty 7364kg (16,234lb); max takeoff 14,969kg (33,000lb).

Armament: One 20mm rotary cannon in forward fuselage; max 5443kg (12,000lb) ordnance on two wingtip, one centreline, two fuselage and six underwing stations including AAMs, laser guided and free fall bombs, rockets, AGMs, ASMs etc.

Performance: Max short duration dash speed 1160kt (Mach 2.02/2147km/h) at 40,000ft; max sustained speed 1085kt (Mach 1.89/2009km/h) at 40,000ft; max climb over 50,000ft (15,240m)/min; tactical radius hi-lo-hi with 1360kg (3000lb) bomb load 313nm (579km).

Production: 4000 F-16s of all models by May 2000.

Notes: One of the most successful of the current combat aircraft (operated or ordered by some 20 nations) the General Dynamics F-16 Fighting Falcon (nicknamed 'Viper') had its origins in the USAF's Lightweight Fighter (LWF) programme of 1972. The first of two YF-16 prototypes flew on 20 January 1974 and after evaluation against the twin engined Northrop YF-17 was selected for production.

The first of eight pre series F-16As (including a pair of two seater F-16Bs) flew in December 1976 followed by the first production aircraft in August 1978. The initial delivery of 785 F-16A/Bs to the USAF was in January 1979.

The F-16 was the first production fighter to feature fly-by-wire and relaxed stability. Other features include wing/fuselage blending, Westinghouse (now Northrop Grumman) APG-66 radar, and an advanced (for the time) cockpit with sidestick controller and the pilot's seat reclined at 30deg. In June 1975 Norway (78), Denmark (70), Belgium (160) and the Netherlands (213) selected the F-16 to replace their F-104G Starfighters and assembly lines were established in the latter two countries with industrial contributions from all four. The first from this source was handed over in January 1979.

A lower cost export version for 'secondary status' nations powered by a General Electric J79 turbojet was flown as a prototype in October 1980 but not built. Instead, the standard P&W F100 powered model was offered and sold to Egypt (41), Indonesia (12), Israel (75), Pakistan (111), Portugal (20), Singapore (8), South Korea (39), Taiwan (150), Thailand (18) and Venezuela (24).

F-16As from the Block 15 production batch featured enhanced radar capability, the F100-PW-220 engine and structural strengthening. The USAF had 272 Block 15 aircraft converted to ADF (Air Defence Fighter) standards in 1989-91 with ungraded radar and avionics and provision to carry two AIM-7 Sparrow or up to six AIM-9 Sidewinder or AIM-120 air-to-air missiles. Several nations are performing mid life updates on their F-16A/Bs.

Photo: Belgian F-16A.

Lockheed Martin F-16C Fighting Falcon

Country of origin: USA.

Type: Single seat multirole fighter.

Powerplant: One 14,670lb (65.2kN) dry/23,830lb (106.0kN) with afterburner Pratt & Whitney F100-PW-220; 29,100lb (129.4kN) with afterburner F100-PW-229; 28,000lb (124.5kN) with afterburner General Electric F110-GE-100 or 29,588lb with afterburner (131.6kN) F110-GE-129 turbofan.

Dimensions: Wing span (without tip AAMs) 9.70m (31ft 10in); length 15.02m (49ft 3½in); height 5.09m (16ft 8½in); wing area 27.9m² (300sq ft).

Weights: F-16C Block 50 – empty 8581kg (18,917lb); max takeoff 19,187kg (42,300lb).

Armament: One 20mm rotary cannon in forward fuselage; max 5443kg (12,000lb) ordnance on two wingtip, one centreline, two fuselage and six underwing stations including AAMs, laser guided and free fall bombs, rockets, AGMs, ASMs etc.

Performance: Max short duration dash speed 1160kt (Mach 2.02/2147km/h) at 40,000ft; max sustained speed 1085kt (Mach 1.89/2009km/h) at 40,000ft; max speed at sea level 795kt (Mach 1.2/1472km/h); service ceiling over 50,000ft; combat radius hi-lo-lo-hi with two AAMs and 1814kg (2000lb) bomb load 677nm (1254km); max ferry range with drop tanks 2275nm (4214km)

Production: 4000 F-16s of all models by May 2000.

Notes: Various avionics, radar and cockpit changes mark the evolution of the F-16A into the more capable F-16C (and F-16D two seat equivalent), the result being an aircraft with enhanced systems for ground attack and beyond-visual-range intercept missions.

The changes introduced to the F-16C were developed under the Multinational Staged Improvement Programme (MSIP) and include the introduction of a new engine option, the General Electric F110 as an alternative to the P&W F100. General Dynamics' Tactical Military Aircraft Division was sold to Lockheed in December 1992.

The first F-16C was delivered to the USAF on 19 July 1984. Initial production Block 25 F-16Cs introduced improved APG-68 radar, upgraded cockpit with wide angle HUD, compatibility with AGM-65D and AIM-120 missiles and provision for a future increase in maximum takeoff weight.

Subsequent F-16C/D production block models include: the GE F110-100 powered Block 30 and the Block 32 with P&W F100-220; Blocks 40 (GE) and 42 (P&W) with upgraded APG-68(V) radar and LANTIRN (low altitude targeting infrared for night) pods; Blocks 50 and 52 with more powerful F110-GE-129 and F100-PW-229 engine, respectively; and Blocks 50D and 52D with AGM-88 HARM missile capability, these sometimes known as the F-16CJ/DJ.

The latest Block 60 aircraft (ordered by the United Arab Emirates in early 2000) have phased array radar, internal FLIR, advanced ECM, increased weights, conformal fuel tanks and a more powerful engine.

The designations F-16N and TF-16N were applied to 26 Block 30 aircraft modified for aggressor training with the US Navy while the converted F-16XL experimental version flown in 1982 featured a new 'cranked arrow' wing with compound leading edge sweep mated to a lengthened F-16 fuselage.

Photo: F-16C Block 50/52 Fighting Falcon.

Lockheed Martin Boeing F-22A Raptor

Country of origin: USA.

Type: Single seat air superiority fighter.

Powerplants: Two approx 35,000lb (155.7kN) with afterburner Pratt & Whitney F119-PW-100 turbofans.

Dimensions: Wing span 13.56m (44ft 6in); length 18.92m (62ft 1in); height 5.00m (16ft 5in); wing area 78.0m² (840sq ft).

Weights: Estimated – empty 14,515kg (32,000lb); max takeoff 24,948kg (55,000lb).

Armament: One 20mm six barrel rotary cannon; two side weapons bays for two Sidewinder AAMs each; ventral weapons bay for four AIM-120A AMRAAMs or six AIM-120Cs or JDAM GPS guided munitions; four underwing hardpoints for max 2268kg (5000lb) ordnance or fuel tanks.

Performance: Estimated – max speed over 1033kt (Mach 1.8/1913km/h) at altitude; supercruise speed over 803kt (Mach 1.4/1488km/h) at altitude; service ceiling over 50,000ft; unrefuelled range over 1735nm (3213km).

Production: 2 YF-22 prototypes and 4 development F-22As by mid 2000; planned USAF procurement 339.

Notes: The F-22 Raptor is set to become the USAF's next premier air superiority fighter, replacing the McDonnell Douglas (now Boeing) F-15C Eagle. It resulted from the USAF's Advanced Tactical Fighter (ATF) programme of 1983 when seven manufacturers were awarded concept definition contracts. In October 1986 Lockheed (F-22) and Northrop (F-23) were selected to build two prototypes each of their designs, each to be powered by the two competing and newly developed engines, the General Electric F120 and Pratt & Whitney F119 turbofans.

Lockheed teamed with General Dynamics (now part of Lockheed Martin) and Boeing on the ATF project but the original design was then largely abandoned as being technically and competitively unacceptable. A new design was initiated and approved in October 1987. The YF-22 prototype (with F120 engines) first flew on 29 September 1990, a month after the rival YF-23. The second aircraft (with F119s) followed on 30 October 1990 and the F-22/F119 combination was selected as winner of the competition in April 1991.

Now called Raptor, the first F-22A development aircraft with larger wing and tailplanes, smaller fins and reprofiled nose was flown on 7 September 1997, the second in June 1998 and the third in April 2000. The original requirement for 442 F-22s was reduced to 339 due to budgetary constraints and there has been several delays in the programme for the same reason. The two seat F-22B was cancelled in 1996 as an economy measure. The in service date is 2005.

F-22 features include multirole capability, agility, low observability (stealth) characteristics, the ability to cruise at supersonic speeds without afterburner ('supercruise'), a ventral internal weapons bay, two dimensional vectoring nozzles, sidestick controller and triplex fly-by-wire controls. The avionics system integrates data from the APG-77 electronically scanned radar, communications system and radar warning receiver for presentation on the head up display and four colour liquid crystal displays in the cockpit.

Photo: F-22A Raptor development aircraft.

Lockheed Martin X-35 JSF

Country of origin: USA.

Type: Advanced multirole fighter concept demonstrator in conventional takeoff and landing (CTOL), short takeoff/vertical landing (STOVL) and carrier capable versions.

Powerplants: One 35,000lb (155.7kN) class Pratt & Whitney SE611 (F119 derivative) turbofan, additional Allison engine driven lift fan behind the cockpit in STOVL version.

Dimensions: Wing span 10.05m (33ft 0in) for CTOL/STOVL variants and 12.19 (40ft 0in) for USN variant; length 15.47m (50ft 9in); wing area 41.8m² (450sq ft) or 50.2m² (540sq ft) for USN variant.

Weights: Estimated – empty 11,340kg (25,000lb); max takeoff 22,680kg (50,000lb).

Armament: Internal 20mm rotary cannon for USAF aircraft, optional on others; internal weapons bays for max 1814kg (4000lb) AAMs or bombs; external load approx 7000kg (15,430lb).

Performance: Estimated – max speed 918kt (Mach 1.6/1700km/h) at altitude; radius of action 540-600nm (1000-1110km) with specified warload depending on version.

Production: Total planned procurement of 3002 (see below).

Notes: The X-35 concept demonstrator is Lockheed Martin's contender for the highly ambitious US Joint Strike Fighter programme, in competition with the Boeing X-32 (see separate entry) and like that aircraft designed in conventional takeoff, short takeoff/vertical landing and carrier capable variants within the same basic airframe. Britain joined the JSF programme in December 1995 as a 10 per cent partner.

By June 1996 Lockheed Martin, Boeing and McDonnell Douglas had submitted their JSF design proposals, with Boeing and Lockheed Martin then being selected to build two JSF demonstrators each with one to be modified to STOVL configuration. After comparative evaluation, the winner will be decided in 2001. Current planning envisages the USAF taking 1763 JSFs (X-35A), the USMC 609, (X-35B), the USN 480 (X-35C), RAF 90 and RN 60. USAF initial operational capability is planned for 2008.

Lockheed Martin's X-35 effort is headquartered in Forth Worth, Texas, with its Tactical Aircraft Systems division (formerly General Dynamics), with considerable input from its famous Skunk Works unit (which built the two X-35s) and the Marietta based Lockheed Martin Aeronautical Systems (home of the F-22 Raptor). Lockheed Martin's partners on the project are Northrop Grumman and BAE Systems.

The X-35 resembles a scaled down F-22 in broad configuration, with a mid wing, twin outward canted tailfins and internal weapons bays on either side of the fuselage. LM's three JSF variants will share common structural geometries, with the canopy, Raytheon or Northrop Grumman phased array radar, Northrop Grumman IR sensor, subsystems and most of the avionics shared.

The carrier capable model will differ from the basic land aircraft in having a larger area wing and tail and structural strengthening for carrier operations. The STOVL variant will have an Allison designed lift fan driven by the engine and mounted behind the cockpit. The first X-35A recorded its maiden flight on 24 October 2000.

Photo: The first X-35A.

Martin AM Mauler

Country of origin: USA.

Type: Single seat carrier based attack aircraft.

Powerplant: One 2975hp (2218kW) Wright R-3350-4 Cyclone 18-cylinder radial; four bladed propeller.

Dimensions: Wing span 15.24m (50ft 0in); length 12.55m (41ft 2in); height 5.13m (16ft 10in); wing area 46.1m² (496sq ft).

Weights: Empty 6577kg (14,500lb); max takeoff 10,608kg (23,386lb).

Armament: Four 20mm cannon in wings; 15 external hardpoints for typically 2041kg (4500lb) ordnance including bombs, mines and up to 12 5in rocket projectiles; max demonstrated ordnance load 4848kg (10,689lb).

Performance: Max speed 319kt (590km/h) at 11,600ft; cruising speed 164kt (304km/h); initial climb 2780ft (847m)/min; service ceiling 30,500ft; max range 1564nm (2897km).

Production: 2 XBTM-1, 143 AM-1 and 6 AM-1Q, total 151.

Notes: The concept of the single engined carrier based attack aircraft for the US Navy had evolved during World War II with several effective two-three seat designs providing sterling service.

These had traditionally been divided into two roles, the scout/dive bomber aircraft designated SB (such as the Douglas Dauntless and Curtiss Helldiver) and the TB torpedo bombers like the Grumman Avenger.

Towards the end of the war and faced with changing requirements, the US Navy began considering the then radical concept of single seat designs which would combine both roles, the requirement calling for an aircraft with the most powerful available piston engine and carrying a substantial external ordnance load of bombs, rockets and mines.

Martin's response was the Model 210, two prototypes of which were ordered in May 1944 under the designation XBTM-1.

Powered by a 3000hp (2237kW) Pratt & Whitney R-4360-4 Wasp Major 28-cylinder radial, the XBTM-1 featured four 20mm cannon in the wings and no fewer than 15 hardpoints under the wings and fuselage.

The first prototype flew on 26 August 1944 and successful flight trials resulted in the placing of an order for 750 as the BTM-1 in January 1945, this designation subsequently changed to AM-1 and the name 'Mauler' applied. The production Mauler differed from the prototypes in having the Pratt & Whitney R-4360 engine replaced with a Wright R-3350 Cyclone.

The first production AM-1 flew in December 1946 but the end of the war saw the order substantially reduced and in the event only 149 (plus prototypes) were built, six of them as AM-1Q electronic countermeasures aircraft. Production ended in October 1949.

Carrier qualification trials and other testing had meanwhile been conducted during 1947 and the first delivery to a USN operational unit (Attack Squadron VA-17A) was in March 1948. Several other units were equipped with the Mauler during 1948-49 but most aircraft were transferred to Reserve squadrons after production ended so that front line units could standardise on a single type – the hugely successful Douglas AD Skyraider.

Photo: AM-1 Mauler.

Martin P5M Marlin

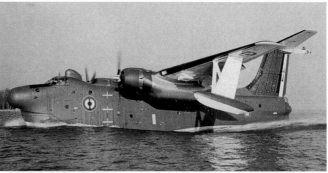

Country of origin: USA.

Type: 9-11 crew maritime patrol and anti submarine flying boat.

Powerplants: P5M-1 – two 3250hp (2423kW) Wright R-3350-30WA Turbo Compound 18-cylinder radials. P5M-2 – two 3450hp (2573kW) R-3350-32WA Turbo Compounds; four bladed propellers.

Dimensions: P5M-2 – wing span 36.02m (118ft 2in); length 30.66m (100ft 7in); height 9.97m (32ft 8½in); wing area 130.6m² (1406sq ft).

Weights: P5M-1 – empty 21,410kg (47,200lb); max takeoff 33,039kg (72,837lb). P5M-2 – empty 22,900kg (50,485lb); max takeoff 38,556kg (85,000lb).

Armament: P5M-1 – two 20mm cannon in radar directed tail turret; up to 3629kg (8000lb) ordnance carried internally in nacelles (torpedoes, bombs or mines) plus up to eight 454kg (1000lb) bombs or mines externally. P5M-2 – guns deleted, same offensive load.

Performance: P5M-2 – max speed 218kt (404km/h) at sea level; cruising speed 130kt (241km/h) at 1000ft; initial climb 1200ft (365m)/min; service ceiling 24,000ft; range 1780nm (3297km).

Production: 160 P5M-1 and 142 P5M-2, total 302.

Notes: The US Navy's last operational flying boat, the P5M Marlin (Martin Model 237) was developed as a successor to the wartime PBM Mariner. It retained some features of the earlier design including the wing and upper hull in combination with a new lower hull of single rather than two step design. The Mariner's two Wright R-2600 Cyclone radials were replaced with more powerful R-3350 Turbo Compounds.

A prototype XP5M-1 was ordered in June 1946, utilising a rebuilt Mariner as its basis and flying for the first time on 30 May 1948. It also differed from its predecessor in having radar operated nose and tail turrets plus a power operated dorsal turret.

It would be July 1950 before a production contract for the P5M-1 was placed, the first example flying on 22 June 1951 and differing from the prototype in having a raised flight deck, the dorsal turret removed and the nose turret replaced by a large radome housing APS-80 search radar.

Deliveries to the US Navy began in April 1952, initially to Squadron VP-44. Subvariants created by conversion included the P5M-1S anti submarine model with magnetic anomaly detection (MAD) equipment plus Julie active and Jezebel passive sonobuoys (80 aircraft); and seven aircraft operated by the US Coast Guard as the P5M-1G, these later re-acquired by the USN and used as trainers as the P5M-1T.

The largely redesigned P5M-2 first flew in August 1953, this featuring a T-tail, lower bow chine line, more powerful engines and uprated equipment. Squadron service began in June 1954 and production continued until late 1960. Ten P5M-2s were delivered to the French Navy and others were upgraded to P5M-2S standards with similar equipment to the P5M-1S. The US Coast Guard received four as the P5M-2G in 1961.

Marlins still in service in 1962 were redesignated P-5A (P5M-1), P-5B (P5M-2) and SP-5B (P5M-2S). The type remained on US Navy strength until 1966.

Photo: A French Navy P5M-2 Marlin.

Martin B-57 Canberra

Country of origin: USA.

Type: Two seat tactical bomber and intruder.

Powerplants: B-57A/B/C/E – two 7220lb (32.1kN) Wright J65-W-5F (Sapphire) turbojets.

Dimensions: B-57A/B/C/E – wing span 19.51m (64ft 0in); length 19.96m (65ft 6in); height 4.75m (15ft 7in); wing area 89.2m² (960sq ft).

Weights: B-57B – empty 12,288kg (27,091lb); max takeoff 26,672kg (58,800lb).

Armament: B-57B – eight 0.50in machine guns or four 20mm cannon in wings; max 2359kg (5200lb) ordnance in weapons bay; four underwing pylons for max 1814kg (4000lb) ordnance.

Performance: B-57B – max speed 506kt (937km/h) at 40,000ft; typical cruise 413kt (765km/h); max climb 6180ft (1883m)/min; service ceiling 48,000ft; max range 2000nm (3705km).

Production: 8 B-57A, 67 RB-57A, 202 B-57B, 38 B-57C, 20 RB-57D, 68 B-57E, 21 RB-57F, total 424.

Notes: American interest in the English Electric Canberra began in 1950 with a USAF requirement for a tactical jet bomber to replace the Douglas A-26 Invader. Following an evaluation 'fly off' against the North American B-45 Tornado and AJ Savage, Avro Canada CF-100 and Martin XB-51 in February 1951, the USAF selected the Canberra for local manufacture by Martin as the B-57. The name 'Canberra' was officially retained but rarely used.

The initial production B-57A and RB-57A (with cameras in the rear bomb bay) were closely modelled on the British Canberra B.2 except that the Rolls-Royce Avons were replaced by Wright J65s, a licence built Armstrong Siddeley Sapphire. The first B-57A flew on 20 July 1953.

The major production B-57B had substantial changes including a new forward fuselage with tandem rather than side-by-side seating under a fighter style canopy, an innovative rotary bomb bay with the stores mounted on the revolving doors, provision for underwing ordnance, guns in the wings, rear fuselage speed brakes and upgraded avionics. First flight was on 28 June 1954 and squadron service began in January 1955. The B-57B served in Vietnam between 1964 and 1974, some converted to B-57G night intruders with forward looking radar, low light TV, infrared sensors and a laser rangefinder.

Other variations on the B-57B theme were the B-57C trainer (later TB-57C) with provision for dual controls and full operational capability retained (first flight December 1954), and the B-57E target tug (first flight April 1956). Specialist versions created by conversion included 25 EB-57E electronic reconnaissance and intercept trainers.

Unarmed high altitude dedicated reconnaissance versions were also produced. The RB-57D of 1955 retained the standard fuselage but had 10,500lb (46.7kN) Pratt & Whitney J57 turbojets and a wing of more than 12m (40ft) greater span. The RB-57F was radically redesigned and had little in common with earlier aircraft. First flown in July 1964 and built by General Dynamics, it had a massive new wing spanning more than 37m (122ft), lengthened fuselage, new tail surfaces and two 18,000lb (80.0kN) Pratt & Whitney TF33 turbofans augmented by two 2900lb (12.9kN) P&W J60s in underwing pods.

Photo: B-57E.

McDonnell FH-1 Phantom

Country of origin: USA.

Type: Single seat carrier based fighter.

Powerplants: Two 1600lb (7.1kN) Westinghouse J30-WE-20 turbojets.

Dimensions: Wing span 12.42m (40ft 9in); length 11.35m (37ft 3in); height 4.32m (14ft 2in); wing area 25.6m² (276sq ft).

Weights: Empty 3031kg (6683lb); max takeoff 5459kg (12,035lb).

Armament: Four 0.50in machine guns in nose.

Performance: Max speed 416kt (771km/h) at sea level; cruising speed 216kt (400km/h); initial climb 4230ft (1289m)/min; service ceiling 34,500ft; normal range 604nm (1118km).

Production: 62.

Notes: The August 1943 decision by the US Navy to ask the only four years old and inexperienced McDonnell Aircraft Corporation to design a new carrier based jet fighter was taken mainly so as not to interrupt the war effort of the established companies. It reaped its rewards in later years as it set the scene for McDonnell to become one of the world's leading combat aircraft manufacturers. It also provided the USN with its first jet fighter.

Early design concepts were somewhat radical, featuring three small Westinghouse turbojets in each wing but the final configuration with two Westinghouse WE-19XB-2B (later J30) turbojets in the wing roots was a rather more conventional and conservative straight winged design which was finalised by the end of 1943. Two prototypes were ordered under the designation XFD-1 and later named Phantom.

The first prototype was ready for its maiden flight by the beginning of January 1945 but only one engine was available. As a result – and remarkably – the maiden flight (a brief hop) was performed with only one engine installed on 2 January, the first proper flight with both engines occurring on 26 January. The second XFD-1 flew in June 1945 and initial carrier trials were performed aboard the USS *Franklin D Roosevelt* in July 1946. These trails marked the first time a US designed jet fighter had operated from an aircraft carrier.

An order for 100 production FD-1s was received in March 1945 but this was cut to 30 when the war ended and subsequently increased again to 60. Production aircraft were delivered as the FH-1, due to McDonnell's US Navy company designator being changed from 'D' (already used by Douglas) to 'H'.

The first FH-1 flew on 28 October 1946 and deliveries to USN Squadron VF-17A (later VF-171) began in July 1947. This was the world's first carrier based jet fighter operational squadron and the sole Navy front line unit to fly the Phantom. Two US Marine Corps squadrons – VMF-122 and VMF-311 – also operated the FH-1.

Front line service ended in July 1950, the Phantom subsequently used for jet pilot indoctrination training by seven Naval Reserve units before being retired in July 1953.

Thus ended the modest career of a modest jet fighter which nevertheless achieved its aims and established McDonnell as a reliable supplier of aircraft to the US military. Later in the 1950s, the name 'Phantom' would be applied to another McDonnell design, the immortal F-4.

Photo: FH-1 Phantom.

McDonnell F2H Banshee

Country of origin: USA.

Type: Single seat carrier based fighter-bomber.

Powerplants: F2H-1 – two 3000lb (13.3kN) Westinghouse J34-WE-22 turbojets. F2H-2/3 – two 3250lb (14.5kN) J34-WE-34. F2H-4 – two 3600lb (16.0kN) J34-WE-38.

Dimensions: F2H-2 wing span over tip tanks 13.66m (44ft 10in); length 12.24m (40ft 2in); height 4.42m (14ft 6in); wing area 27.3m² (294sq ft).

Weights: F2H-2 – empty 5056kg (11,146lb); max takeoff 10,121kg (22,312lb). F2H-3 – empty 5980kg (13,183lb); max takeoff 11,437kg (25,214lb).

Armament: F2H-1 – four 20mm cannon in nose. F2H-2/3 – guns plus two 227kg (500lb) bombs under wings.

Performance: F2H-2 – max speed 462kt (856km/h) at 10,000ft; initial climb 3910ft (1192m)/min; service ceiling 44,800ft; max range 1280nm (2370km). F2H-3 – max speed 504kt (933km/h) at sea level; initial climb 6000ft (1829m)/min; service ceiling 46,600ft; normal range 1017nm (1883km).

Production: 3 XF2D-1, 56 F2H-1, 364 F2H-2, 14 F2H-2N, 58 F2H-2P, 250 F2H-3 and 150 F2H-4, total 895.

Notes: While McDonnell was still developing its first naval jet fighter, the FH-1 Phantom (see previous entry), the US Navy had given the company approval to go ahead with the design of an enlarged version. The formal order for two XF2D-1s was placed in March 1945, the design fundamentally a scaled up and more powerful Phantom. The aircraft's designation was subsequently changed to F2H to avoid confusion with the Douglas company designator.

The first XF2D-1 flew on 11 January 1947 and an initial order for 56 production F2H-1 Banshees was placed in May 1947, these differing from the prototypes in having a slightly longer fuselage and no dihedral on the tailplane. Deliveries to the USN began in August 1948 and operational service with Squadron VF-171 began in March 1949. The Banshee quickly established itself as being reliable and trouble-free.

The F2H-2 Banshee with more powerful engines, a 33cm (13in) longer fuselage to accommodate an extra fuel cell and fixed wing tip tanks entered service in late 1949. It was built in the standard version, the F2H-2N night fighter with radar housed in a lengthened nose, and the F2H-2P photo-reconnaissance model with cameras in the nose.

The F2H-3 dedicated night and all weather fighter was delivered from August 1952, featuring upgraded radar in a larger nose radome (the guns were relocated further aft), a substantially longer fuselage (by more than 2.44m/8ft 0in), considerably increased fuel capacity, higher weights, dihedral tailplane and strengthened structure. Thirty-nine were transferred to the Royal Canadian Navy in 1955 and served until September 1962.

The final Banshee was the F2H-4, an improved version of the -3 with upgraded radar, modified tail surfaces and more powerful engines. Production ended in October 1953. The Banshee saw active service with the USN in Korea and front line service ended in September 1959. Some -3s and -4s flew with Reserve units until 1965, by then redesignated F-2C and -D.

Photo: F2H-2 Banshee.

McDonnell F3H Demon

Country of origin: USA.

Type: Single seat carrier based fighter-bomber.

Powerplant: F3H-2 – one 9500lb (42.7kN) dry/14,250lb (63.4kN) with afterburner Allison J71-A-2E turbojet.

Dimensions: F3H-2 – wing span 10.77m (35ft 4in); length 17.96m (58ft 11in); height 4.44m (14ft 7in); wing area 48.2m² (519sq ft).

Weights: F3H-2 – empty 10,040kg (22,133lb); normal loaded 13,163kg (29,020lb); max takeoff 15,377kg (33,900lb).

Armament: F3H-2 – four 20mm cannon in nose plus up to 2722kg (6000lb) external ordnance including bombs, rockets and Sparrow or Sidewinder AAMs depending on subvariant.

Performance: F3H-2 – max speed (clean) 602kt (1115km/h) at sea level, 543kt (1006km/h) at 35,000ft; initial climb 12,410ft (3782m)/min; service ceiling 42,650ft; range with drop tanks 1190nm (2205km).

Production: 2 XF3H-1, 56 F3H-1N, 142 F3H-2N, 80 F3H-2M and 239 F3H-2, total 519.

Notes: McDonnell's next foray into naval fighter design was the single engined and swept wing (but still subsonic) F3H Demon. It was originally intended as a clear weather fighter but the requirement was changed to include limited all weather capability. The entire project was in serious jeopardy at one stage because of the failure of its original Westinghouse J40 engine.

The first of two prototype XF3H-1 prototypes flew on 7 August 1951 and the first production F3H-1N with upgraded radar on 24 December 1953. These were powered by a 10,500lb (46.7kN) with afterburner J40-WE-8 but due to the failure of the intended more powerful version of the J40, the aircraft were seriously underpowered.

That in combination with high unreliability of the installed engine and some wing torsional strength problems (both causing crashes) resulted in the grounding of the aircraft and the threatened cancellation of the project. Many F3H-1Ns were delivered direct to ground schools as instructional airframes. The last F3H-1N flight was in July 1955.

A reassessment in early 1954 resulted in the F3H-2 models with more powerful (and reliable) Allison J71 engine, a modified wing of greater area and air-to-air missiles supplementing the guns. The first of the new generation Demons flew on 23 April 1955 (converted from an F3H-1N) and 29 other -1Ns were converted to -2N standards with the J71.

New gun and Sidewinder armed F3H-2Ns were also built; other 'Dash 2' variants were the -2M with four Sparrow missiles (the first application for this weapon), and the definitive major production F3H-2 optimised as a strike fighter and capable of carrying up to 2722kg (6000lb) of offensive and defensive ordnance externally.

Demon production ended in November 1959 and despite its shaky start was ultimately successful. The F3H-2 equipped 11 US Navy squadrons before being withdrawn from front line service in September 1964, the final unit to operate the type (VF-161) switching to the F-4 Phantom II. With the introduction of common US military designations in September 1962, the F3H-2 became the F-3B, the F3H-2M the MF-3B and the F3H-2N the F-3C.

Photo: F3H-2 Demon. (Gerard Frawley)

McDonnell F-101A/C Voodoo

Country of origin: USA.

Type: Single seat fighter-bomber.

Powerplants: Two 10,200lb (45.4kN) dry/14,880lb (66.2kN) with afterburner Pratt & Whitney J57-P-13 turbojets.

Dimensions: Wing span 12.09m (39ft 8in); length 20.55m (67ft 5in); height 5.49m (18ft 0in); wing area 34.2m² (368sq ft).

Weights: F-101C – empty 11,919kg (26,277lb); max takeoff 22,185kg (48,908lb).

Armament: Four 20mm cannon in lower forward fuselage; centreline hardpoint for one tactical nuclear bomb, underwing hardpoints for max 1814kg (4000lb) bombs or other ordnance.

Performance: F-101C – max speed 873kt (Mach 1.51/1617km/h) at 35,000ft; cruising speed 478kt (885km/h); max initial climb 33,750ft (10,287m)/min; service ceiling 50,300ft; max combat radius 678nm (1255km).

Production: 807 Voodoos of all models including 77 F-101A, 2 YRF-101A, 35 RF-101A, 47 F-101C and 166 RF-101C.

Notes: McDonnell's first production aircraft for the USAF, the Voodoo originated from a 1945 requirement for a single seat, twin engined long range escort and penetration fighter. The XF-88 was designed to meet this requirement and the first of two prototypes was flown on 20 October 1948. Flight testing revealed it to be seriously underpowered and that in combination with a funding shortage resulted in its cancellation.

A new 1951 requirement for a long range fighter to escort Strategic Air Command's Convair B-36 bombers led to what was officially regarded as merely a revision of the XF-88 design (in reality it was almost completely new) with more than twice as powerful Pratt & Whitney J57 turbojets replacing the original Westinghouse J34s, modified wing, larger fuselage with radar in the nose, increased fuel capacity, new variable geometry intake inner ramps and redesigned T-tail. Even though the SAC requirement lapsed, what became the F-101 Voodoo was ordered by Tactical Air Command. The standard armament of four 20mm cannon was supplemented by Falcon AAMs mounted on rotary weapons bay doors.

The first F-101A flew on 29 September 1954, the initial delivery was to the 27th Tactical Fighter Wing in May 1957 and the last was handed over in November of the same year. It was followed on the production line by the F-101C (first flight 21 August 1957) which had a strengthened wing for low level operations and the ability to carry a tactical nuclear weapon under the fuselage. The last F-101C was delivered in June 1958.

Most single seat Voodoos were built as tactical reconnaissance aircraft with cameras in a lengthened nose. Two F-101A airframes were completed as YRF-101As (first flight 10 May 1956) followed by 35 production RF-101As from May 1957 and 166 RF-101Cs from July 1957.

Subsequently, 29 F-101As and 32 F-101Cs were converted to RF-101G and RF-101H standards, respectively, between 1966 and 1972 for use by the Air National Guard. The tactical reconnaissance Voodoos saw extensive service in Vietnam in the 1960s and 25 RF-101Cs were delivered to Taiwan in 1959, mainly for covert overflights of China.

Photo: F-101A Voodoo.

McDonnell F-101B Voodoo

Country of origin: USA.

Type: Two seat all weather interceptor.

Powerplants: Two 10,700lb (47.6kN) dry/14,990lb (66.7kN) with afterburner Pratt & Whitney J57-P-55 turbojets.

Dimensions: Wing span 12.09m (39ft 8in); length 20.55m (67ft 5in); height 5.49m (18ft 0in); wing area 34.2m² (368sq ft).

Weights: Empty 13,141kg (28,970lb); max takeoff 23,769kg (52,400lb).

Armament: Four AIM-4 Falcon air-air missiles under fuselage, sometimes two AIR-2A Genie unguided nuclear missiles.

Performance: Max speed 950kt (Mach 1.63/1760km/h) at 35,000ft, 622kt (Mach 0.94/1152km/h) at sea level; cruising speed 474kt (879km/h); initial climb 39,250ft (11,963m)/min; service ceiling 52,000ft; combat radius 603nm (1117km); max range (internal fuel) 1320nm (2445km) or 1677nm (2837km) with drop tanks.

Production: 807 Voodoos of all models including 480 F-101B.

Notes: McDonnell began development of a two seat all weather interceptor version of the Voodoo in August 1955 as the F-101B. It combined the wings, tail and centre and rear fuselage of the single seat F-101A/C with a new forward fuselage for two crew members in tandem (pilot and radar operator), Hughes MG-13 fire control radar in the nose and an initial armament of three or four Falcon air-to-air missiles mounted on (and in) the rotary internal weapons bay. The F-101B was also able to carry Genie nuclear unguided missiles, the internal guns were deleted and provision was made for the fitting of flight refuelling equipment.

The F-101B became the major Voodoo production variant. The first one flew on 27 March 1957 and initial deliveries to the USAF were made in early 1959 with the last of 480 handed over in March 1961. Seventeen USAF Air Defence Command squadrons were equipped with the F-101B and although front line use ended in 1971, the Air National Guard continued flying the aircraft until 1983.

F-101B variants created by conversion included 79 F-101Fs with dual controls for operational training (full combat capability was retained); some with only partial dual controls and reduced combat capability became TF-101Bs; and 153 F-101Bs fitted with an improved fire control system and an infrared detection system in place of the flight refuelling equipment were also designated F-101F.

Canada was the only export operator of the two seat Voodoo, receiving 56 F-101Bs (as the CF-101B) between July 1961 and May 1962 and 10 dual control F/CF-101Fs. The surviving 47 CF-101Bs and nine CF-101Fs were swapped for 56 low time ex USAF F-101Bs and 10 F-101Fs with upgraded fire control, systems and avionics in 1970-71.

Twenty-two of the former Canadian aircraft were then modified to RF-101B reconnaissance aircraft (with cameras replacing the fire control system) by Ling-Temco-Vought for use by the Air National Guard. Front line Canadian use of the Voodoo ended in early 1985.

Photo: F-101B Voodoo. (John Sise)

McDonnell Douglas F-4B/J Phantom

Country of origin: USA.

Type: Two seat carrier based fighter-bomber.

Powerplants: F-4B – two 10,900lb (48.5kN) dry/17,000lb (75.6kN) with afterburner General Electric J79-GE-8/8B turbojets. F-4J – two 11,870lb (52.8kN) dry/17,900lb (79.6kN) with afterburner J79-GE-10.

Dimensions: Wing span 11.71m (38ft 5in); length 17.75m (58ft 3in); height 5.00m (16ft 5in); wing area 49.2m^2 (530sq ft).

Weights: F-4B – empty 12,654kg (27,897lb); max takeoff 24,766kg (54,600lb).

Armament: Four or six Sparrow AAMs or four Sparrows and four Sidewinder AAMs; centreline and four underwing hardpoints for max 7258kg (16,000lb) ordnance.

Performance: F-4B – max speed (clean) 1375kt (Mach 2.4/2550km/h) at 48,000ft, 795kt (Mach 1.2/1473km/h) at sea level; initial climb (interceptor) 28,000ft (8534m)/min; low level radius with 2722kg (6000lb) warload 350nm (650km); intercept radius 800nm (1482km); max ferry range 2000nm (3705km).

Production: 5057 Phantoms of all models in USA including 2 YF4H-1, 45 F-4A, 649 F-4B and 522 F-4J.

Notes: The F-4 Phantom II began life in 1954 as a private venture single seat, twin engined naval fighter concept. The US Navy issued McDonnell a specification for an advanced radar equipped and missile armed two seat fleet defence fighter with secondary ground attack capability in April 1955 and after the company revised its original proposals, two prototypes were ordered as the XF4H-1. The first one flew on 27 May 1958 and a production order soon followed.

The first of the initial batch of F4H-1Fs (later F-4A) was delivered to the USN in December 1960, these mainly used for development work and training. The F-4A (and following F-4B) set numerous speed, altitude and time to height records in 1959-62.

The F-4B first flew on 25 March 1961, differing from the F-4A in having more powerful engines, modified intakes, improved radar in a larger nose radome, an infrared detector and a raised cockpit canopy. Deliveries to the USN began in June 1961 and to the Marines a year later. The Phantom's combat debut was in August 1964 when F-4Bs from VF-142 and VF-143 (aboard USS *Constellation*) provided cover for aircraft attacking North Vietnamese torpedo boats.

The second Phantom naval variant was the F-4J with more powerful engines, drooped ailerons and slotted tailplane to reduce approach speeds and upgraded radar, fire control avionics and electrical systems. The first production F-4J flew on 27 May 1966 and deliveries began the following December. The RAF received 15 second hand F-4J(UK)s from August 1984, these incorporating some British equipment (including the Skyflash missile) and remaining in service until early 1991.

The upgrading of 228 F-4Bs to basically F-4J standards from 1972 resulted in the new designation F-4N while a major structural and avionics upgrade of the F-4J between 1977 and 1982 was designated F-4S. This was the last Phantom variant in USN and Marine service, retired in 1989 and 1990, respectively.

Photo: F-4B Phantom.

McDonnell Douglas F-4C/D Phantom

Country of origin: USA.

Type: Two seat multirole fighter.

Powerplants: Two 10,900lb (48.5kN) dry/17,000lb (75.6kN) with afterburner General Electric J79-GE-15 turbojets.

Dimensions: Wing span 11.71m (38ft 5in); length 17.75m (58ft 3in); height 5.00m (16ft 5in); wing area 49.2m^2 (530sq ft).

Weights: Empty 13,154kg (29,000lb); typical loaded (ground attack) 26,968kg (59,435lb).

Armament: Typically four Sparrow and four Sidewinder AAMs; max 7258kg (16,000lb) ordnance including bombs, air-to-ground missiles and rocket pods.

Performance: F-4C (at 24,400kg/53,790lb) – max speed 1188kt (Mach 2.07/2200km/h) at 40,000ft; initial climb 8210ft (2502m)/min; service ceiling 33,500ft; radius of action 250nm (463km). F-4D – max speed (clean) 1290kt (Mach 2.25/2390km/h) at 48,000ft, 760kt (Mach 1.15/1406km/h) at sea level; max climb (mid weight) 28,000ft (8534m)/min; tactical radius with 2722kg (6000lb) bomb load 350nm (648km); max ferry range 2000nm (3705km).

Production: 5057 Phantoms of all models in USA including 583 F-4C, 503 RF-4C and 825 F-4D.

Notes: The early success of the Phantom gave the US Air Force little choice but to take a close look at the aircraft, investigations leading to the unprecedented action of ordering an aircraft which had been designed for carrier operations. The USAF conducted a series of evaluations in 1961-62, comparing the F-4B with other aircraft in its inventory and discovering it to be superior in almost every respect. A large order was placed in March 1962.

The USAF version was initially designated F-110A but this changed to F-4C later in 1962. Intended as a 'minimum change' variant of the F-4B it retained folding wings and an arrester hook (as did all subsequent land based Phantoms) but modifications included changing the flight refuelling system to the USAF's 'flying boom' method, fitting larger and lower pressure tyres with bigger brakes and new avionics appropriate to the USAF's needs.

The first F-4C flew on 27 March 1963 and deliveries to training units began the following November. The first operational unit to receive the F-4C was the 12th TFW in early 1964. F-4Cs recorded the USAF's first two MiG kills of the Vietnam War in July 1965. Spain received 40 ex USAF F-4Cs in 1971-72. The important RF-4C unarmed tactical reconnaissance variant with cameras in a lengthened nose first flew in August 1963 and went on to see active service in Vietnam and the Gulf. After being continually upgraded, it was withdrawn from USAF service in 1995 but remained operational with Spain and South Korea in 2000.

The F-4D was more closely tailored to meet USAF requirements with a substantially updated equipment/avionics and weapons control system fit and the ability to carry a wider range of weapons. The first F-4D flew on 9 December 1965 with deliveries starting in March 1966. It became the mainstay of USAF Phantom operations in Vietnam and although largely used as a bomber also saw considerable air-to-air action. F-4D exports were 32 new examples to Iran in 1968 and 36 ex USAF aircraft to South Korea from 1969.

Photo: F-4C Phantom. (MDC)

McDonnell Douglas F-4E Phantom

McDonnell Douglas Phantom FG.1/FGR.2

Country of origin: USA.

Type: Two seat multirole fighter.

Powerplants: Two 11,870lb (52.8kN) dry/17,900lb (79.6kN) with afterburner General Electric J79-GE-17A turbojets.

Dimensions: Wing span 11.77m (38ft 7½in); length 19.20m (63ft 0in); height 5.00m (16ft 5in); wing area 49.2m² (530sq ft).

Weights: Empty 14,448kg (31,853lb); normal takeoff 26,309kg (58,000lb); max takeoff 28,030kg (61,795lb).

Armament: One 20mm multi barrel rotary cannon under nose; four AAMs semi recessed under fuselage; one centerline and four underwing pylons for max 7257kg (16,000lb) ordnance including drop tanks, AAMs, ASMs, conventional and nuclear bombs, flares, rocket packs, ECM pods or cameras pods.

Performance: Max speed 1244kt (Mach 2.17/2306km/h) at 36,000ft, 790kt (Mach 1.2/1464km/h) at 1000ft; max initial climb (clean) 49,800ft (15,180)m/min; service ceiling (clean) 58,750ft; tactical radius (four AAMs, 1814kg/4000lb bombs) 570nm (1056km); ferry range 1718nm (3184km).

Production: 5057 Phantoms of all models in USA including 1387 F-4E, 150 RF-4E, 175 F-4F, 2 F-4EJ and 14 RF-4EJ. An additional 138 F-4EJs were built in Japan by Mitsubishi.

Notes: The Phantom's lack of a fixed gun had proved to be a disadvantage under some circumstances during operations in Vietnam. The result was the development of the F-4E with a 20mm six barrel Vulcan rotary cannon installed under a lengthened nose. Other changes included the introduction of solid state APQ-120 radar, improved weapons management system, fitting the F-4J's slotted stabilator and more powerful J79-GE-17 engines.

The YF-4E prototype (converted from a YRF-4C) first flew on 7 August 1965 and the first production model in June 1967, two months after McDonnell and Douglas had merged. A major modification which also resulted from Vietnam experience was applied to new production F-4Es from mid 1972 and retrofitted to many aircraft: leading edge wing slats which substantially improved the aircraft's turning ability. F-4E deliveries to the USAF ended in December 1976 and the 5057th and last US built Phantom was an F-4E handed over to South Korea in October 1979.

F-4E variants included the RF-4E tactical reconnaissance model for export, the F-4F for West Germany and the F-4EJ for Japan. Most of these were built by Mitsubishi and the final example was delivered to the JASDF in May 1981, the last Phantom of all.

The F-4G Wild Weasel was an electronic countermeasures conversion of 116 F-4Es for the suppression of enemy weapons and radar guidance systems.

First flown in December 1975 it was armed with precision guided conventional and anti radar AGMs and was used to good effect in the 1991 Gulf War.

The F-4G was retired in 1996 as the last USAF operational Phantom model. Egypt, Germany, Greece, Iran, Israel, Japan, South Korea and Turkey still operated F-4E variants in 2000, many of them with airframe, avionics and equipment upgrades.

Photo: F-4EJ Kai Phantom.

Country of origin: USA.

Type: Two seat multirole fighter.

Powerplants: Two 12,550lb (55.8kN) dry/20,515lb (91.2kN) with afterburner Rolls-Royce Spey Mk.202/203 turbofans.

Dimensions: Wing span 11.71m (38ft 5in); length 17.65m (57ft 11in); height 5.00m (16ft 5in); wing area 49.2m² (530sq ft).

Weights: Empty 14,016kg (30,900lb); max takeoff 26,309kg (58,000lb).

Armament: FGR.2 – one 20mm rotary cannon in centerline pod, four Sparrow III or Sky Flash and four Sidewinder AAMs for air defence; typically 4990kg (11,000lb) air-to-ground ordnance including bombs, rocket pods, Martel ASMs.

Performance: Max speed 1090kt (Mach 1.9/2020km/h) at 36,000ft, 790kt (Mach 1.2/1463km/h) at 1000ft; max climb (clean) 45,600ft (13,900m)/min; combat radius with 2722kg (6000lb) bombs (hi-lo-hi) 478nm (885km); max ferry range 2172nm (4024km).

Production: 5057 Phantoms of all models in USA including 52 FG.1 and 118 FGR.2.

Notes: The decision to purchase Phantoms for the Royal Navy and Royal Air Force was made in 1965 following the abandoning of the Hawker P.1154 supersonic V/STOL aircraft the previous year, this planned to be built in both naval and land based versions. The resulting F-4K (British designation FG.1) for the RN and RAF F-4M (FGR.2) were not powered by the General Electric J79 turbojet, the British Rolls-Royce Spey turbofan substituted instead.

Although based on the US Navy's F-4J, the Spey Phantom had significant differences resulting from the new engine installation, the decision to do so a political one designed to soften the effects of the P.1154 cancellation and its associated job losses. The new engine required substantial structural changes to accommodate the Spey's different dimensions and its 20 per cent increase in required air flow.

A new engine bay, wider inlet ducting, wider fuselage, reshaped lower rear fuselage and larger nozzles were required as well as the need to re-engineer the Spey for supersonic flight and to fit an afterburner. British sourced avionics, systems and equipment was also installed, the result a very high unit cost and a Phantom with inferior performance to the US models.

The first YF-4K flew on 27 June 1966 and the first production FG.1 on 2 November 1966. It featured a double extendable nosewheel leg to assist in launching from small British carriers and drooped ailerons to reduce landing speeds. The FG.1 served with only one front line Fleet Air Arm squadron (No 892 aboard HMAS Ark Royal), the service receiving 24 of the 52 aircraft and the remainder going to the RAF. The survivors were transferred to the RAF with the end of conventional RN carrier operations in 1978.

The first YF-4M flew on 17 February 1967 and the first production FGR.2 on 26 December 1967. Deliveries began in August 1968 and the first operational squadron to receive the aircraft was No 6 in May 1969. The multirole FGR.2 lacked some of the FG.1's naval features but had upgraded fire control radar and avionics plus enhanced weapons carrying capability. It remained in service until 1992.

Photo: Phantom FGR.2.

McDonnell Douglas F-15A/C Eagle

Country of origin: USA.

Type: Single seat air superiority fighter.

Powerplants: F-15A – two 14,870lb (66.1kN) dry/23,830lb (106.0kN) with afterburner Pratt & Whitney F100-PW-100 turbofans. F-15C – two 14,590lb (64.9kN) dry/23,770lb (105.7kN) with afterburner F100-PW-220.

Dimensions: Wing span 13.04m (42ft 9¹/₂in); length 19.43m (63ft 9in); height 5.63m (18ft 5¹/₂in); wing area 56.5m² (608sq ft).

Weights: F-15C – empty equipped 12,973kg (28,600lb); max takeoff 30,845kg (68,000lb).

Armament: One 20mm rotary cannon in starboard wing root; max external ordnance load 7257kg (16,000lb); typical combat air patrol fit four AIM-7 Sparrow on fuselage stations and two AIM-9 Sidewinder or AIM-120 AAMs on each wing pylon.

Performance: F-15C – max short endurance dash speed 1458kt (Mach 2.54/2700km/h) at 40,000ft; max initial climb over 50,000ft (15,240m)/min; service ceiling 63,000ft; combat radius (intercept mission) 1060nm (1963km); max ferry range with external and conformal tanks 3100nm (5742km).

Production: 1513 Eagles of all models by 2000 including 384 F-15A, 61 F-15B, 473 F-15C, 85 F-15D, 175 F-15J (most by Mitsubishi) and 12 F-15DJ.

Notes: Designed as an uncompromised air superiority fighter, the F-15 resulted from a 1965 USAF study , the project receiving some impetus in the late 1960s when information about new Soviet fighters (especially the MiG-25) became available.

The FX requirement which came from the study took some lessons from Vietnam experience and called for a fighter with a thrust to weight ratio in excess of unity and one that could out-turn any adversary. The F-15's Pratt & Whitney F100 turbofans were also new and other features included Hughes APG-63 radar, a wing of large area to help meet the manoeuvrability requirements and advanced (for the time) cockpit displays including HUD.

McDonnell Douglas' design was chosen ahead of proposals from Fairchild-Republic and North American Rockwell and the first of 20 development aircraft (18 single seat F-15As and two combat capable F-15B two seaters) flew on 27 July 1972. Service entry with the USAF was in November 1974. Nineteen F-15As and two F-15Bs were exported to Israel which subsequently received a further 13 and two, respectively, from USAF stocks.

Production switched to the improved F-15C (first flight 26 February 1979) and two seat D from June 1979, this with upgraded avionics, F100-PW-220 engines and the ability to carry conformal fuel tanks. The USAF received 409 F-15Cs and 61 F-15Ds while exports were made to Israel (18 and eight) and Saudi Arabia (46 and 16) these later supplemented by 20 F-15Cs and four F-15Ds.

Licence manufacture was undertaken in Japan by Mitsubishi for the JASDF between 1981 and 1992. After receiving two F-15Js built by the parent company and eight in knocked down form for local assembly, Mitsubishi manufactured a further 165 for the Japanese Air Self Defence Force. McDonnell Douglas supplied an additional 12 F-15DJ two seaters.

Photo: F-15A Eagle. (MDC)

McDonnell Douglas (Boeing) F-15E Eagle

Country of origin: USA.

Type: Two seat strike fighter.

Powerplants: Two 14,590lb (64.9kN) dry/23,770lb (105.7kN) with afterburner Pratt & Whitney F100-PW-220 or 17,800lb (79.2kN) dry/29,100lb (129.4kN) with afterburner F100-PW-229 turbofans.

Dimensions: Wing span 13.04m (42ft 9¹/₂in); length 19.43m (63ft 9in); height 5.63m (18ft 5¹/₂in); wing area 56.5m² (608sq ft).

Weights: Operating empty 14,515kg (32,000lb); max takeoff 36,742kg (81,000lb).

Armament: One 20mm rotary cannon in starboard wing root; max load 11,113kg (24,500lb) of AAMs, conventional and laser/optically guided bombs, AGMs, cluster bombs, JDAM etc on centreline and two wing stations plus tangential stations carriers on conformal fuel tanks.

Performance: Max dash speed 1458kt (Mach 2.54/2700km/h); max sustained speed 1319kt (Mach 2.3) at 40,000ft; cruising speed 495kt (917km/h); combat radius 686nm (1271km); max range 2400nm (4445km).

Production: 1513 Eagles of all models by 2000 including 226 F-15E, 72 F-15S and 25 F-15I.

Notes: McDonnell Douglas (Boeing from 1997) had long promoted the bomb carrying capabilities of the F-15 but no US official requirement for a strike version existed until the early 1980s when a replacement for the General Dynamics F-111 was sought under the Enhanced Tactical Fighter (ETF) programme. The two crew (pilot and weapons systems operator) F-15E 'Strike Eagle' was selected over the General Dynamics F-16XL in February 1984.

The F-15E is capable of flying deep air-to-ground interdiction missions by day or night while at the same time defending itself. Compared to the F-15A/C models it features a 60 per cent structural redesign allowing substantially increased operating weights and a 50 per cent increase in maximum ordnance load. Early aircraft had the F-15C's F100-PW-220 engines but those built after August 1991 had more powerful F100-PW-229s. Synthetic aperture ground mapping radar, multifunction HUDs, target designation pods, FLIR, terrain following radar and permanent conformal fuel tanks with tangential stores stations are also fitted.

A prototype Strike Eagle modified from an F-15B was followed by the first production F-15E on 11 December 1986. The USAF ordered a total of 226, the main batch delivered between 1988 and 1994 with some attrition replacements following later in the decade. USAF F-15Es saw service during the 1991 Gulf War and over Serbia and Kosova in 1999.

Saudi Arabia's 72 F-15S versions feature downgraded avionics and simplified radar without ground mapping capability. The first one flew in June 1995 and deliveries were completed in 1999. The 25 Israeli F-15Is delivered between 1997 and 1999 differed from the standard F-15E in having locally developed electronic warfare suites.

Although Eagle production temporarily ended in 2000, both the F-15C and E were still being marketed with the prospect of additional orders from Israel and Saudi Arabia and possibly South Korea, while an order for three from the USAF kept the line active while negotiations for these sales were continuing.

Photo: F-15E Strike Eagle. (MDC)

McDonnell Douglas F/A-18A/C Hornet

Country of origin: USA.

Type: Single seat carrier or land based multirole fighter.

Powerplants: F/A-18A and early C – two 10,600lb (47.1kN) dry/16,000lb (71.1kN) with afterburner General Electric F404-GE-400 turbofans. Later C – two 17,700lb (78.7kN) with afterburner F404-GE-402.

Dimensions: Wing span 11.43m (37ft 6in); length 17.07m (56ft 0in); height 4.66m (15ft 3½in); wing area 37.2m² (400sq ft).

Weights: Empty (C) 10,810kg (23,832lb); max takeoff (A/C) 25,402kg (56,000lb).

Armament: One 20mm rotary cannon in nose; nine external hardpoints for max 7030kg (15,500lb) ordnance including AAMs, AGMs, ASMs, anti radiation missiles, conventional or laser guided bombs.

Performance: Max speed over 1033kt (Mach 1.8/1914km/h) at 37,000ft; max initial climb (clean) 60,000ft (18,288m)/min; combat ceiling over 50,000ft; combat radius (intercept mission) 400nm (740km) or 575nm (1065km) for attack mission; max ferry range 2000nm (3705km).

Production: 1478 F/A-18A/B/C/D Hornets ordered by 2000.

Notes: The US Congress cancelled the US Navy's lightweight multirole fighter programme in August 1974 and instead recommended that the service should study developments of the General Dynamics YF-16 and Northrop YF-17 which were designed to contest the USAF's lightweight fighter competition. The F-16 won that contest but both aircraft then vied for the USN order, Northrop teaming with McDonnell Douglas and GD with Vought.

The MD/Northrop team was selected to develop its enlarged YF-17 proposal in May 1975 with the former as the prime contractor and the latter as main sub contractor. Initial plans were for the aircraft to built in fighter (F-18) and ground attack (A-18) versions but the two roles were combined into a single airframe as the F/A-18 Hornet. The first of 11 development aircraft flew on 18 November 1978, features including fly-by-wire controls, HUD and HOTAS, multimode APG-65 radar, powered folding wing tips and two GE F404 turbofans.

The two seater version was initially dubbed TF-18A and then F/A-18B, the first production F/A-18A flew in April 1980 and operational status (initially with the USMC) was achieved in January 1983. The USN/MC eventually received 380 F/A-18As and 41 Bs while exports were made to Australia (75 mainly locally assembled), Canada (138) and Spain (72), all operating from land. Spain also received 24 ex USN F/A-18s.

The improved F/A-18C first flew in production form in September 1987. The two seat equivalent was designated F/A-18D and differences include improved avionics, a new central computer and greater weapons options. F/A-18C/Ds delivered after November 1989 feature all weather and night attack capability, uprated F404-GE-402 engines were installed from October 1992 and improved APG-73 radar from May 1994.

Apart from the USN/MC, F/A-18Cs and Ds have been purchased by Kuwait (40), Finland (64, most assembled locally), Switzerland (34), Thailand (8) and Malaysia (8). Total US Navy/Marine Corps procurement of the A-D models Hornets was 1028.

Photo: F/A-18C Hornet. (Paul Merritt)

McDonnell Douglas (Boeing) FA-18E Super Hornet

Country of origin: USA.

Type: Single seat carrier based multirole fighter.

Powerplants: Two 22,000lb (97.8kN) with afterburner General Electric F414-GE-400 turbofans.

Dimensions: Wing span (over missiles) 13.63m (44ft 8½in); length 18.31m (60ft 1in); height 4.88m (16ft 0in); wing area 46.5m² (500sq ft).

Weights: Empty 13,903kg (30,650lb); takeoff for attack mission 29,938kg (66,000lb).

Armament: One 20mm rotary cannon in nose; six underwing, one centreline, two fuselage side and two wingtip hardpoints for max 7938kg (17,500lb) ordnance including AAMs, AGMs, ASMs, anti radiation missiles, conventional and laser guided bombs.

Performance: Max speed over 1033kt (Mach 1.8/1913km/h) at 36,000ft; combat ceiling over 50,000ft; attack mission radius of action 660nm (1222km); fighter escort radius 400nm (740km); hi-lo-lo-hi interdiction radius with 1814kg (4000lb) bomb load and four AAMs 462nm (855km).

Production: 7 development and 22 production Super Hornets by mid 2000; 284 ordered against USN requirement for 548 by July 2000.

Notes: McDonnell Douglas (Boeing since 1997) proposed an enlarged and more capable Hornet as a successor to the cancelled General Dynamics/McDonnell Douglas A-12 Avenger in 1991. The proposals created sufficient interest for the awarding in June 1992 of a $US3.7bn contract covering engineering and manufacturing development of the F/A-18E (single seat) and F (two seat) versions and the construction of seven development aircraft.

The first F/A-18E was rolled out in September 1995 (at which time the name 'Super Hornet' was announced) and flew for the first time on 29 November 1995. The second E followed in December and the first two seat F/A-18F in April 1996. The final development aircraft was flown in February 1997 and the first production model the following year. Twenty-two production Super Hornets had been delivered by May 2000 with initial deliveries to the US Navy evaluation squadron VX-9 beginning in late 1998.

The Super Hornet was declared operational in February 2000 with squadron VF-115 becoming the first USN front line unit to fly the aircraft later in the same year. Initial carrier deployment is scheduled for June 2002 aboard the USS *Abraham Lincoln*.

The Super Hornet is significantly larger than the original models: overall length is 1.24m (4ft 1in) greater; wing span increased by 1.29m (4ft 3in) and its area by 25 per cent. The wing leading edge extensions are increased in size, as are the horizontal tail surfaces. Internal fuel capacity is increased by 40 per cent and the intakes are redesigned to provide the extra air flow required for the more powerful General Electric F414 engines. The Super Hornet's avionics suite is initially similar to the F/A-18C/D's but with some detail upgrades.

The US Navy originally wanted to purchase up to 1000 Super Hornets but that figure has been revised down to 548. The US Navy awarded Boeing a multi year contract for the production of 222 Super Hornets in June 2000, bringing the total to 284 aircraft. The new contract covered the purchase of 36 aircraft in fiscal year 2000, 42 in 2001 and 48 in each of the following three years.

Photo: The fourth development F/A-18E Super Hornet. (MDC)

McDonnell Douglas/BAe Harrier II

Countries of origin: USA and United Kingdom.

Type: Single seat V/STOL attack fighter.

Powerplant: AV-8B – one 21,450lb (95.4kN) Rolls-Royce F402-RR-406A (Pegasus 11 Mk.21) or 23,800lb (105.9kN) F402-RR-408A (Pegasus 11 Mk.61) vectored thrust turbofan. GR.5/7 – 21,550lb (95.8kN) Pegasus 11 Mk.105.

Dimensions: AV-8B/GR.5 – wing span 9.25m (30ft 4in); length 14.12m (46ft 4in); height 3.56m (11ft 8in); wing area 21.4m² (230sq ft) or 22.6m² (243sq ft) with larger leading edge extensions. GR.7 – length 14.53m (47ft 8in).

Weights: AV-8B – empty 6337kg (13,970lb); max takeoff (STO) 14,062kg (31,000lb).

Armament: AV-8B – optional one 25mm five barrel cannon in ventral pod; seven stores pylons for max 6003kg (13,234lb) ordnance with -408A engine. GR.7 – optional two 25mm cannon in ventral pod; nine stores pylons for max 4900kg (10,800lb) ordnance.

Performance: AV-8B – max speed 585kt (1083km/h) at sea level; initial climb 14,715ft (4485m)/min; combat radius (hi-lo-hi) with 1588kg (3500lb) bomb load and drop tanks 595nm (1102km); max ferry range 1965nm (3640km).

Production: 431 Harrier IIs of all models comprising 244 AV-8B, 51 AV-8B Plus, 62 GR.5, 34 GR.7, 27 TAV-8B and 13 T.10.

Notes: Hawker Siddeley (later British Aerospace) and McDonnell Douglas began investigations into a 'big wing' Harrier in 1973 for service with the US Marine Corps but the British government withdrew its support in 1975. The companies continued working on the idea and in October 1976 the concept was revived as the Harrier II with US and UK government support.

The new aircraft had a larger wing of supercritical section and with leading edge root extensions. It was constructed largely of carbonfibre composites and had two additional hardpoints. Other features included a raised cockpit, upgraded avionics and systems, increased weights and more powerful versions of the Pegasus vectored thrust turbofan. The result was a Harrier with considerably improved combat capabilities.

The new wing was first flown on an AV-8A Harrier on 9 November 1978 as the YAV-8B. The first true AV-8B Harrier II flew on 5 November 1981 and deliveries to the USMC began in January 1984. The two seat operational trainer version is designated TAV-8B. The AV-8B Night Attack version with FLIR and pilot night vision goggles was introduced from the 167th aircraft in 1989 and the AV-8B Harrier II Plus (first flight 22 September 1992) with APG-65 radar has been built new for the USMC (with 72 others are being converted), and for the Italian (16 plus 2 trainers) Spanish (8/1) Navies. Spain also received 12 standard AV-8Bs.

The RAF's Harrier GR.5 first flew on 30 April 1985 and entered service in July 1987. The FLIR equipped night attack GR.7 (first flight May 1990) followed. In addition to new build GR.7s, all the GR.5s have been upgraded. The two seat equivalent is the T.10.

The Harrier II has seen active service in the Gulf War and over the former Yugoslavia and Kosova. The final new build example for the RAF (a T.10) was delivered in October 1995 and the last AV-8B (for the Italian Navy) in December 1997.

Photo: AV-8B Harrier Night Attack. (MDC)

Mikoyan-Gurevich MiG-9

Country of origin: Soviet Union.

Type: Single seat ground attack fighter.

Powerplants: MiG-9F – two 1760lb (7.8kN) Lyulka RD-20 (BMW 003A) turbojets. MiG-9FF – two 2205lb (9.8kN) Lyulka RD-21 turbojets.

Dimensions: Wing span 10.00m (33ft 10in); length 9.83m (32ft 3in); height 3.22m (10ft 7in); wing area 18.2m² (196sq ft).

Weights: MiG-9F – 3540kg (7804lb); max takeoff 5500kg (12,125lb). MiG-9FF – empty 3471kg (7652lb); max takeoff 5117kg (11,281lb).

Armament: One 37mm cannon in intake splitter bulkhead and two 23mm cannon in lower nose.

Performance: MiG-9F – max speed 492kt (911km/h) at 14,800ft, 466kt (864km/h) at sea level; time to 16,400ft 4.3min; service ceiling 42,650ft; max range 594nm (1100km). MiG-9FF – max speed 512kt (949km/h) at sea level; time to 16,400ft 2.9min.

Production: 604 of all models including about 80 MiG-9UTI.

Notes: The first Soviet jet fighter of wholly indigenous design, the MiG-9 (or I-300 as it was designated by the military) benefited greatly from the acquisition of German data at the end of WWII. At the time, the Soviet Union was lagging well behind the west in jet engine development and despite the acquisition of the German data would not start to catch up until the British Government later decided to help by supplying Rolls-Royce engine technology.

Initial studies for this twin engined fighter centred around a configuration very similar to the Messerschmitt Me 262 with underwing jets, an example of which had been captured in late 1944. MiG dropped this concept in 1945 and instead went with the definitive I-300/MiG-9 configuration of unswept wings and a spilt nose intake feeding the two RD-20 jet engines mounted side by side in the fuselage. The RD-20 was simply a copy of the BMW 003A.

Fourteen months after its design was initiated, the MiG-9 performed a brief 'hop' on 19 April 1946 and its first true flight five days later. It crashed on its 19th flight when a root fairing detached and hit the tail but second and third prototypes were flown in August 1946. These were followed by 10 pre series aircraft (as the I-301) from October 1946 and two tandem two seat operational trainer versions (I-301T, later MiG-9UTI) first flown in August 1947.

The MiG-9 had several problems which needed to be solved before it could enter service including airframe vibration at high speeds and a tendency for the engines to flame out when the nose mounted guns were fired due to gas ingestion. This was not an uncommon problem for several of the early jet fighters including most famously the Hawker Hunter.

The MiG-9 entered Soviet service in 1947 and was used mainly in the ground attack role, It remained in production until 1948 and NATO applied the codename 'Fargo'. There were several variants including the basic MiG-9F with RD-20 engines, MiG-9FR (I-308) with pressurised cockpit and afterburning RD-21 (originally RD-20F) engines, MiG-9FF with RD-21s, and MiG-9FP (I-302, first flight July 1947) with relocated nose armament in an attempt to beat the ingestion problem. One was completed with a single Rolls-Royce Nene engine but reportedly never flown.

Photo: Production MiG-9.

Mikoyan-Gurevich MiG-15

Country of origin: Soviet Union.

Type: Single seat fighter.

Powerplant: One 5000lb (22.2kN) Klimov RD-45 or RD-45F (Nene) turbojet.

Dimensions: Wing span 10.13m (33ft 3in); length 10.16m (33ft 4in); height 3.70m (12ft 2in); wing area 20.6m² (222sq ft).

Weights: Empty 3382kg (7465lb); loaded (clean) 4806kg (10,595lb); max takeoff 5260kg (11,596lb).

Armament: One 37mm and two 23mm cannon in lower nose.

Performance: Max speed 567kt (1050km/h) at sea level, 557kt (1033km/h) at 16,400ft; initial climb (clean) 8260ft (2520m)/min; service ceiling 49,870ft; range (internal fuel) 766nm (1419km); range with drop tanks 1036nm (1919km).

Production: At least 7500 MiG-15s of all models, possibly up to 12,000 including production in Czechoslovakia, Poland and China.

Notes: The West was shaken out of its complacent attitude to Soviet fighter capabilities over Korea in November 1950 with the unexpected and very effective appearance of the hitherto unknown MiG-15. It went on to be built in very large numbers in the USSR, Czechoslovakia, Poland and China, and was operated by nearly 40 Soviet aligned nations.

Until late 1946, the Soviet Union lagged well behind the West in jet engine development but all that changed when the socialist British Government of the time decided to send examples of the Rolls-Royce Nene and Derwent to its comrades in the USSR. It was manna from heaven, the engines were quickly copied and Soviet jet powerplant technology leapt forward.

The MiG-15 began life in 1946 under the internal designation I-310 and was designed around the Nene, the local copy of which (reverse engineered by Vladimir Klimov) was called the RD-45. The first prototype first flew on 30 December 1947 and the second on 27 May 1948. A production order was placed in March 1948 and the first production example flew in December 1948. The NATO codename 'Fagot' was applied and production of this original series lasted just over a year before the improved MiG-15bis (see next entry) took over.

As noted above, the MiG-15's combat debut was over Korea in late 1950 following the entry of China into the war. Although the aircraft involved carried Chinese markings they were being flown by Soviet pilots, a practice which continued throughout the conflict. Chinese pilots also flew the new fighter over Korea.

The tandem two seat MiG-15UTI (NATO codename 'Midget') first flew in June 1949 and went on to become the most built and longest serving MiG-15 variant. Production outlasted the single seaters and by 2000 several small African nations still flew it.

Foreign production of the original MiG-15 fighter was undertaken in Czechoslovakia (853 as the S-102 and 2012 CS-102 UTI equivalents); Poland (227 Lim-1 fighters); and China, which acquired a licence to manufacture the MiG-15 but the technology transfer process took so long to complete it was decided to go straight to the MiG-17. Complete MiG-15UTI trainers were built in large numbers, however, as the JJ-2.

Photo: Polish built MiG-15UTI.

Mikoyan-Gurevich MiG-15bis

Country of origin: Soviet Union.

Type: Single seat fighter-bomber.

Powerplant: One 5950lb (26.5kN) Klimov VK-1A turbojet.

Dimensions: Wing span 10.13m (33ft 3in); length 10.16m (33ft 4in); height 3.70m (12 ft 2in); wing area 20.6m² (222sq ft).

Weights: Empty 3681kg (8115lb); normal loaded 5070kg (11,177lb); max takeoff 6045kg (13,327lb).

Armament: One 37mm and two 23mm cannon in lower nose; two underwing hardpoints for max 500kg (1102lb) ordnance including bombs or rocket pods.

Performance: Max speed 581kt (1075km/h) at sea level, 565kt (1046km/h) at 10,000ft; max climb 10,100ft (3078m)/min; service ceiling 50,855ft; range (internal fuel) 718nm (1329km); max range with drop tanks 1360nm (2519km).

Production: Estimated at least 7500 MiG-15s of all models, possibly up to 12,000 including production in Poland, Czechoslovakia and China.

Notes: The original production version of the basic MiG-15 was built for only about a year before it was replaced by the improved MiG-15bis, the definitive and most produced single seat fighter variant.

The performance improvements the MiG-15bis demonstrated over the original were largely due to the efforts of engine designer Vladimir Klimov and his team, who developed the poorly manufactured basic RD-45/Nene copy into a more powerful, substantially redesigned and reliable (by Soviet standards of the time) engine. The upgraded powerplant was designated the VK-1, the initials in honour of its designer.

The MiG-15bis was developed under the designation Project SD and featured several changes over the original including the more powerful engine (which required a revised internal structure to accommodate its slightly greater dimensions), increased internal fuel capacity, larger airbrakes, wider chord ailerons, perforated flaps (part of an overall weight reduction programme), modified wing spars, increased elevator balance, the incorporation of narrow trim tabs on the wing trailing edges, improved aileron boost and a faster firing 37mm cannon.

The first SD flew in July 1949 and mass production as the MiG-15bis was initiated in early 1950. The first few aircraft featured the original RD-45 engine but the VK-1 and other improvements were quickly incorporated. Production in the USSR ended in 1953.

Manufacture of the MiG-15bis was also undertaken in Czechoslovakia (620 as the S-103 1954-56) and Poland (500 as the Lim-2 1954-56). As noted in the previous entry, China acquired a licence to build the MiG-15 but the technology transfer process took so long to complete it was decided to go directly to the MiG-17. Despite this, a few were completed from a combination of locally manufactured and imported parts and components purchased to support the large number of Soviet built MiG-15s in Chinese service as the J-2.

Several smaller nations still flew the MiG-15bis or its licence built equivalents into the 1990s but by 2000 Albania was the only operator of the single seater with 13 in service.

Photo: MiG-15bis.

Mikoyan-Gurevich MiG-17/F

Country of origin: Soviet Union.

Type: Single seat fighter-bomber.

Powerplant: MiG-17F – one 5950lb (26.5kN) dry/7450lb (33.1kN) with afterburner Klimov VK-1F turbojet.

Dimensions: MiG-17F – wing span 9.40m (30ft 10in); length 11.10m (36ft 5in); height 3.73m (12ft 3in); wing area 22.6m² (243sq ft).

Weights: MiG-17F – empty 3930kg (8664lb); normal loaded 5352kg (11,800lb); max takeoff 6286kg (13,858lb).

Armament: One 37mm and two 23mm cannon in lower nose; two underwing hardpoints for max 500kg (1102lb) ordnance.

Performance: Max speed 618kt (1144km/h) at 9800ft; initial climb 12,795ft (3900m)/min; service ceiling with afterburner 54,460ft; range (internal fuel) 367nm (679km); max ferry range 903nm (1673km).

Production: Over 8000 MiG-17s of all versions in Soviet Union and Poland plus over 1800 in China.

Notes: Studies into what eventually became the MiG-17 began in early 1950 under the Soviet military designation I-330 and Project SI by MiG. The aircraft was a natural progression from the MiG-15, the initial aim being to increase the earlier aircraft's limiting Mach number (which was restricted to 0.92 due to some high speed handling and stability problems) by fitting a thinner wing of increased sweep and area. The fuselage was lengthened, the tail surfaces modified and in the initial version, the MiG-15's non afterburning 5950lb (26.5kN) Klimov VK-1A engine retained.

The prototype (converted from a MiG-15) first flew on 1 February 1950 and achieved Mach 1.03 in a dive a few weeks later. Codenamed 'Fresco-A' by NATO, the basic day fighter MiG-17 was ordered into production in September 1951 and achieved operational capability in October 1952. It was built only until early 1953.

It was followed by the MiG-17F ('Fresco-C'), another day fighter but powered by the afterburning VK-1F engine. Otherwise fundamentally similar to the original version apart from minor modifications, the MiG-17F was first flown as a converted prototype on 29 September 1951.

It was ordered into quantity production from late 1952 and continued to be built in the Soviet Union until 1958 as the major production version of the series.

The MiG-17F was also built in Poland (477 as the Lim-5 1956-60) and China (about 800 as the J-5 from 1956). China also developed the only two seat trainer version of the MiG-17 as the JJ-5 with 1061 built between 1966 and 1986.

MiG-17s and their licence built derivatives served with 38 nations and have been involved in several conflicts including Vietnam, Pakistan versus India (twice), the various Arab-Israeli wars, Uganda versus Tanzania, Mozambique, Afghanistan and many other local conflicts.

The Vietnam War produced several North Vietnamese MiG-17 'aces' including the legendary Colonel Toon, who shot down 13 American aircraft before finally being brought down himself by a Phantom.

Photo: East German MiG-17F. (MAP)

Mikoyan-Gurevich MiG-17P

Country of origin: Soviet Union.

Type: Single seat limited all weather fighter.

Powerplant: MiG-17P – one 5950lb (26.5kN) Klimov VK-1A turbojet. MiG-17PF/PFU – one 5950lb (26.5kN) dry/7450lb (33.1kN) with afterburner Klimov VK-1F turbojet.

Dimensions: Wing span 9.40m (30ft 10in); length 11.43m (37ft 6in); height 3.80m (12 ft 3in); wing area 22.6m² (243sq ft).

Weights: P- empty 4154kg (9168lb); max takeoff 6280kg (13,845lb). PF – empty 4182kg (9220lb); max takeoff 6552kg (14,444lb).

Armament: PF – three 23mm cannon in lower nose. PFU – guns deleted; four AA-1 air-to-air missiles under wings.

Performance: P – max speed 602kt (1115km/h) at 9800ft; initial climb 7283ft (2220m)/min; range (clean) 695nm (1175km). PF – max speed 606kt (1123km/h) at 16,000ft, 560kt (1038km/h) at 38,500ft; time to 32,100ft 4.6min; service ceiling with afterburner 52,300ft; range (internal fuel) 540nm (1000km); max range with external tanks 934nm (1730km).

Production: Over 8000 MiG-17s of all versions in Soviet Union and Poland plus over 1800 in China.

Notes: The second 'family' of MiG-17s was also the first radar equipped all weather interceptor to enter series production for the *Voenno-Vozdushnye Sily* (VVS – Military Aviation Forces). It was designated MiG-17P, the suffix denoting *Poiskovyi* – 'search'.

Development began via a modified experimental version of the MiG-15bis designated SP-5 and fitted with *Izumrud* (Emerald) dual antennae radar (with separate search and tracking functions), the search antenna in a protruding 'lip' radome above the intake and the tracking unit in a small radome mounted on the intake splitter plate. The prototype MiG-17P was created by grafting an SP-5 nose onto a standard MiG-17. First flight was in 1952.

The MiG-17P entered limited production later in 1952 with a non afterburning VK-1A turbojet but was quickly superceded by the MiG-17PF (first flight October 1952, NATO codename 'Fresco-D') with the afterburning VK-1F. The MiG-17PF was continuously upgraded with improved radar and other modifications. It was also built in Poland as the Lim-5P (129 in 1959-60) and China as the J-5A, the first Chinese example not flying until November 1964 due to the non supply of some equipment and drawings from the Soviet Union.

The MiG-17PFU ('Fresco-E') was built in relatively small numbers but it was significant in being the Soviet Union's (and Europe's) first fighter armed solely with air-to-air missiles, in this case four AA-1 *Alkari* beam riding weapons. The missiles were mounted on underwing rails and the guns were removed. The PFU first flew in 1954 and retained the PF's VK-1F engine but had improved *Imzumrud-2* radar and a semi active guidance system. Many MiG-17PFs in Soviet service were upgraded to a similar standard.

By 2000, MiG-17s were still operated by Cuba (18), Guinea-Bissau (3), Guinea Republic (4), Madagascar (4), Mali (5) and Syria (30) while Chinese built J-5s and JJ-5s were flown by Albania (19), China (1000) and Sudan (5).

Photo: MiG-17PF. (Keith Myers)

Mikoyan-Gurevich MiG-19S

Country of origin: Soviet Union.

Type: Single seat day fighter.

Powerplants: Two 5732lb (25.5kN) dry/7165lb (31.9kN) with afterburner Tumansky RD-9B turbojets or (later aircraft) two 7277lb (32.4kN) with afterburner RD-9FB turbojets.

Dimensions: Wing span 9.19m (30ft 2in); length 12.60m (41ft 4in); height 3.88m (12ft 9in); wing area 25.0m² (269sq ft).

Weights: Empty 5172kg (11,402lb); max takeoff 8662kg (19,096lb).

Armament: Three 30mm cannon in nose and wing roots; max 500kg (1102lb) ordnance under wings.

Performance: Max speed 784kt (Mach 1.34/1452km/h) at 32,800ft; initial climb 22,640ft (6900m)/min; service ceiling 56,150ft; range (internal fuel) 750nm (1390km); range with external fuel 1080nm (2000km).

Production: Approximately 2500 MiG-19s of all versions in Soviet Union (plus about 3000 Shenyang J-6 in China, see separate entry).

Notes: The Soviet Union's first production fighter capable of supersonic speeds in level flight, the MiG-19 could be regarded as the last of the 'conventional' MiGs, combining a highly swept (58deg) wing with two afterburning engines.

The MiG-19's production life was relatively brief in the Soviet Union, ending – some say prematurely – in 1959 in favour of the MiG-21. As a result, most development was undertaken in China where the aircraft was built as the Shenyang J-6 (see separate entry), remaining in production until the mid 1980s and widely exported. The NATO reporting name was 'Farmer'.

The MiG-19 was developed via the experimental I-360 prototype first flown on 24 May 1952. The designation SM-9 was applied to the prototypes of the initial day fighter version, the first of these flying on 5 January 1954. The SM-9 was ordered into production almost immediately as the MiG-19, well before official trails had begun. The first production aircraft were delivered in March 1955 but demonstrated some serious handling problems including inadequate control effectiveness at supersonic speeds.

This was solved by replacing the original conventional tailplane (with elevators) with a slab type, all flying horizontal tail, fitting anti flutter masses on the tips, installing a ventral airbrake to supplement the existing side fuselage units, and a spoiler system interlinked with the ailerons was incorporated. As the MiG-19S ('Farmer-C'), service with the VVS began in mid 1956, the aircraft a simple clear weather fighter with no radar ranging equipment and only a gyroscopic gunsight for weapons aiming. No missiles were carried and the three 30mm cannon were mounted one in each wing root and one in the starboard side nose.

The MiG-19S was manufactured under licence in Czechoslovakia as the S.105 until 1963 (103 built) and some Soviet aligned nations received the aircraft.

Experimental or limited production variants included the MiG-19SV high altitude interceptor with a reduced armament of only two 30mm cannon and a slightly larger wing. The SV reached an altitude of 68,045ft in December 1956.

Photo: Czech built S.105, equivalent to the MiG-19S.

Mikoyan-Gurevich MiG-19P

Country of origin: Soviet Union.

Type: Single seat limited all weather fighter.

Powerplants: Two 5732lb (25.5kN) dry/7165lb (31.9kN) with afterburner Tumansky RD-9B turbojets.

Dimensions: Wing span 9.19m (30ft 2in); length 13.25m (43ft 5½in); height 3.88m (12ft 9in); wing area 25.0m² (269sq ft).

Weights: MiG-19PM – empty 5200kg (11,464lb); loaded (clean) 7730kg (17,041lb); max takeoff 9100kg (20,062lb).

Armament: MiG-19PF – two 30mm cannon in wing roots. MiG-19PM – four K-5M beam riding air-to-air missiles under wings, guns deleted.

Performance: MiG-19PM – max speed 675kt (Mach 1.15/1250km/h) at 32,800ft, 610kt (Mach 1.06/1130km/h) at 49,200ft, 634kt (Mach 0.96/1175km/h) at sea level with dry power; time to 49,200ft 4.8min; service ceiling 53,900ft; range (internal fuel) 540nm (1000km); range with external fuel 1031nm (1910km).

Production: Approximately 2500 MiG-19s of all versions in Soviet Union (plus approximately 3000 Shenyang J-6 in China, see separate entry).

Notes: Recognising the operational limitations of the purely day fighter and gun armed MiG-19S, the Mikoyan-Gurevich design bureau began development of a MiG-19 variant with limited all weather capability at an early stage under the internal designation SM-7 and MiG-19P for the production version.

Compared to the original versions, the MiG-19P had its gun armament reduced to a pair of 30mm cannon in the wing roots and RP-1 *Izumrud* (Emerald) radar installed in a modified nose. *Izumrud* was a dual antennae radar (with separate search and tracking functions), the search antenna in a protruding 'lip' radome above the intake and the tracking unit in a small radome mounted on the intake splitter plate.

The aerodynamic modifications (including the all flying tailplane) which had been developed for the MiG-19S were incorporated. The 'P' in the designation stands for *Poiskovyi* – search.

The converted SM-7 prototype first flew on 28 August 1954 and the MiG-19P was ordered by both the Soviet Air Force and Navy, entering service in 1956. The original gun armed version is also known as the MiG-19PF and 'Farmer-D' by NATO.

Further development resulted in the missile armed MiG-21PM (*Modifikatsirovanny* – modification) with *Izumrud-2* radar, the guns deleted and four first generation, beam riding K-5M Alkali air-to-air missiles mounted under the wings. The prototype SM-7/M flew in January 1956 and in its production form the MiG-19PM replaced the P/PF on the assembly lines.

With the arrival of the MiG-21 into Soviet service from 1959, the MiG-19's star began to wane. Production in the USSR ended in the same year but the Czechoslovakian S-105 was built until 1961. The Chinese F-6 derivative was only at the start of its career at the time and was manufactured for a further quarter of a century. In 2000, it remained the most numerous fighter in Chinese service by a very substantial margin.

Photo: MiG-19PM.

Mikoyan-Gurevich MiG-21F

Country of origin: Soviet Union.

Type: Single seat fighter.

Powerplant: One 9500lb (42.2kN) dry/12,655lb (56.3kN) with after-burner Tumansky R-11F-300 turbojet.

Dimensions: Wing span 7.15m (23ft 5$^{1}/_{2}$in); length 13.46m (44ft 2in); height 4.10m (13ft 5$^{1}/_{2}$in); wing area 23.0m^2 (248sq ft).

Weights: Empty 4980kg (13,183lb); max takeoff 8625kg (19,015lb).

Armament: One or two 30mm cannon in lower fuselage; two under-wing pylons for two K-13 or K-5A AAMs or rocket pods.

Performance: MiG-21F-13 – max speed 1148kt (Mach 2.0/2126km/h) at 42,600ft, 594kt (Mach 0.9/1100km/h) at sea level; time to 32,800ft 3.2min; service ceiling 60,900ft; range (clean) 702nm (1300km); range with external fuel 902nm (1525km).

Production: 10,158 MiG-21s of all versions in USSR, 195 in Czecho-slovakia and 651 in India.

Notes: One of the most important and widely operated combat aircraft of any era, the MiG-21 has been flown by well over 40 nations and manufactured not only in the Soviet Union but also in China (as the F-7), India (by Hindustan Aeronautics Ltd) and Czechoslovakia.

By 2000, no fewer than 20 countries still had the MiG-21 in service, some of them taking advantage of the several upgrades which are available, most of these incorporating Western avionics. NATO allo-cated the MiG-21 the codename 'Fishbed'.

The MiG-21 grew out of experience in the Korean War, where it was realised that a higher power-to-weight ratio was necessary for effec-tive air combat. Development began in 1953 to meet a Soviet require-ment for a lightweight, short range and easily constructed and maintained supersonic day interceptor.

Development was pursued along two lines via prototypes of different configurations: the Ye-2 (first flight 14 February 1955) with swept wings and the Ye-4 (16 June 1955) with a delta wing, both also featuring slab type horizontal tail surfaces. The tailed delta configura-tion was selected for production and six Ye-6 prototypes which were close in specification to the initial production MiG-21F were built in 1958-59.

The MiG-21F ('Fishbed-B') entered production in 1959, this featuring a forward opening single piece canopy, narrow chord fin, two internal 30mm cannon and range finding radar. It was replaced in production in 1960 (from the 115th aircraft) by the MiG-21F-13 ('Fishbed-C') with *Kvant* (Quantum) radar, a broader chord fin, the ability to carry either two K-5A 'Alkali' or K-13 'Atoll' AAMs and fully variable afterburner. Some were subsequently fitted with an infrared search and track sys-tem for night operations. The designation MiG-21F-12 was applied to aircraft delivered to Finland from 1963, the first non Warsaw Pact nation to use the aircraft.

The MiG-21F-13 was manufactured in the Soviet Union until 1965 and also in Czechoslovakia, where 195 were built between 1962 and 1972. Chinese production as the Chengdu F-7 (see sepa-rate entry) started in 1964. The tandem two seat MiG-21U ('Mon-gol') conversion trainer based on the MiG-21F-13 first flew in October 1960.

Photo: MiG-21F.

Mikoyan-Gurevich MiG-21P

Country of origin: Soviet Union.

Type: Single seat limited all weather fighter.

Powerplant: One 9500lb (42.2kN) dry/12,655lb (56.3kN) with after-burner Tumansky R-11F-300 or 13,490lb (60.0kN) with afterburner R-11F2-300 turbojet.

Dimensions: Wing span 7.15m (23ft 5$^{1}/_{2}$in); length 14.10m (46ft 3in); height 4.10m (13ft 5$^{1}/_{2}$in); wing area 23.0m^2 (248sq ft).

Weights: MiG-21PF – empty 5256kg (11,587lb); max takeoff 9080kg (20,018lb). MiG-21PFM – empty 5180kg (11,420lb); takeoff (clean) 7750kg (17,085lb).

Armament: MiG-21P – two K-13 AAMs under wings. MiG-21PF/PFM – one twin barrel 23mm cannon in ventral pack; two AAMs or AGMs under wings.

Performance: MiG-21PF – max speed 1174kt (Mach 2.05/2175km/h) at 40,100ft, 594kt (Mach 0.9/1100km/h) at sea level; time to 32,000ft 2.7min; service ceiling 60,900ft; range (clean) 837nm (1550km); range with external fuel 1000nm (1850km).

Production: 10,158 MiG-21s of all versions in USSR, 195 in Czecho-slovakia and 651 in India.

Notes: As has been the case with the MiG-17 and -19, a second genera-tion of MiG-21s was produced incorporating limited all weather capability. As the MiG-21P, this family of fighters initially discarded guns in favour of a pair of K-13 air-to-air missiles mounted on pylons under the wings.

The MiG-21P retained the R-11F-300 engine of its predecessor but also featured an enlarged dorsal spine housing additional fuel, a longer nose with a larger diameter intake (for a bigger intake shock cone accommodating TsD-30T airborne intercept radar), and modified main undercarriage and speed brakes. The pitot tube was moved from below to above the nose.

Two prototypes designated Ye-7/1 and Ye-7/2 were flown on 10 August 1958 and 18 January 1960, respectively, with series production of the MiG-21P starting in mid 1960. It was replaced in 1962 by the MiG-21PF (for *Forsirovanny* – boosted) 'Fishbed-D' with more powerful R-11-F2-300 engine and improved RP-21 *Sapfir* (Sapphire) radar. Later models had a modified fin and rudder and more advanced RP-21M radar. Production ended in 1964 after Warsaw Pact members had been supplied along with other nations sympathetic to the Soviet cause in Asia and the Middle East. Cuba was also a recipient.

Other MiG-21P variants were the MiG-21FL for export with less sophisticated R-2L radar (195 built in India by HAL 1966-1974 and others in the USSR between 1965 and 1968); and the MiG-21PFM ('Fishbed-F') introduced in 1964 with a ventral gun pod for a 23mm twin barrel cannon, provision for air-to-ground weaponry, broader chord fin and a new two piece canopy design with fixed windscreen and an opening section which hinged to starboard. The MiG-21PFS was the export equivalent and was manufactured between 1966 and 1968.

The designation MiG-21PFV was applied to a version of the MiG-21FL developed specifically for North Vietnam and operations in the hot and humid climate of the region. Although the aircraft was effective during the Vietnam War, its pilots generally preferred the MiG-17 with its greater agility and built in gun armament.

Photo: MiG-21P. (Bruce Malcolm)

Mikoyan-Gurevich MiG-21S/M

Country of origin: Soviet Union.

Type: Single seat limited all weather fighter.

Powerplant: One 9340lb (41.5kN) dry/14,550lb (64.7kN) with afterburner Tumansky R-13-300 turbojet.

Dimensions: Wing span 7.15m (23ft 5¹/₂in); length 14.10m (46ft 3in); height 4.10m (13ft 5¹/₂in); wing area 23.0m² (248sq ft)

Weights: MiG-21MF – empty 5843kg (12,881lb); max takeoff 9800kg (21,605lb). MiG-21SMT – empty 5700kg (12,566lb); max takeoff 10,100kg (22,266lb).

Armament: MiG-21MF – one twin barrel 23mm cannon in ventral pack; four underwing pylons for max 1500kg (3307lb) ordnance including AAMs, bombs and rocket pods.

Performance: MiG-21MF – max speed 1177kt (Mach 2.05/2180km/h) at 39,400ft, 700kt (Mach 1.06/1296km/h) at sea level; max initial climb 58,000ft (17,677m)/min; service ceiling 57,750ft; range (clean) 594nm (1100km); range with external fuel 972nm (1800km).

Production: 10,158 MiG-21s of all versions in USSR, 195 in Czechoslovakia and 651 in India.

Notes: The third generation of MiG-21s (NATO reporting name 'Fishbed-J') was developed in the mid 1960s, the fundamental concept behind the aircraft to increase range and weapons carrying options.

This was achieved by incorporating ever larger fuselage dorsal spines for additional fuel, two extra underwing hardpoints and the mounting of a semi internal 23mm twin barrel cannon on the centreline in later models. As the Americans were discovering in Vietnam, the Soviets also realised that a fixed gun was essential in air-to-air combat because missiles alone could not always do the job.

The first of this new generation was the MiG-21S built between 1965 and 1968 for the Soviet Air Force. It was an interim version featuring the MiG-21P's R-11-F2-300 engine and gun pod (instead of the definitive fixed arrangement) in combination with the extra fuel capacity plus upgraded RP-22S *Sapfir* radar and an improved gunsight. A reconnaissance version (MiG-21R) was built between 1965 and 1971.

The MiG-21SM (1968-74) switched to the more powerful R-13-300 engine and had the fixed gun and additional hardpoints, while its export equivalent was the MiG-21M (1968-71) which reverted to the R-11 powerplant and had earlier generation RP-21MA radar. It was delivered to Warsaw Pact and other Soviet aligned countries and was also built under licence by HAL in India (160 aircraft) between 1973 and 1981.

The MiG-21MF (1970-74) combined all the 'new generation' features with increased armament options and some lightened structural parts (titanium alloy instead of steel). It subsequently saw considerable combat including in Afghanistan, the Iraq-Iran War, the Gulf War and Yugoslavia. The MiG-21MT (only 15 built) had a further increase in fuel capacity in a broader dorsal spine and the MiG-21SMT 'Fishbed-K' with still more fuel in a further enlarged dorsal spine was built in 1971-72. The SMT was used exclusively by the Soviets and was reportedly disliked by pilots because the new spine spoilt the aircraft's flight characteristics.

Photo: MiG-21MF. (Paul Merritt)

Mikoyan-Gurevich MiG-21bis

Country of origin: Soviet Union.

Type: Single seat multirole fighter.

Powerplant: One 9039lb (40.2kN) dry/15,652lb (69.6kN) with afterburner Tumansky R-25-300 turbojet.

Dimensions: Wing span 7.15m (23ft 5¹/₂in); length 14.71m (48ft 3in); height 4.10m (13ft 5¹/₂in); wing area 23.0m² (248sq ft).

Weights: Empty 5843kg (12,881lb); normal loaded 8700kg (19,180lb); max takeoff 10,470kg (23,082lb).

Armament: One 23mm twin barrel cannon in ventral pack; one centreline and four underwing hardpoints for max 2000kg (4409lb) ordnance including AA-2 'Atoll' or AA-8 'Aphid' AAMs, bombs and rocket pods.

Performance: Max speed 1176kt (Mach 2.05/2178km/h) at 42,600ft, 700kt (Mach 1.06/1296km/h) at sea level; max climb (at mid weight) 45,275ft (1380m)/min; time to 55,800ft 8.5min; service ceiling 57,400ft; range (internal fuel) 600nm (1110km); range with external fuel 1026nm (1900km).

Production: 10,158 MiG-21s of all versions in USSR, 195 in Czechoslovakia and 651 in India.

Notes: The final evolution of the new production MiG-21, the MiG-21bis (NATO reporting name 'Fishbed-L') embodied experience gained by earlier versions of the aircraft in several conflicts including Vietnam and various Arab-Israeli wars. Development work began in early 1971, the aim being to produce a more complete multirole combat aircraft.

Intended to fill both air-to-air and air-to-ground missions, the MiG-21bis featured upgrades and modernisation of most aspects of its specification including the use of lighter titanium instead of steel in some airframe components, cockpit instrumentation similar to that of the MiG-23, upgraded radar, avionics and navigational equipment, a wider dorsal spine fairing with additional fuel, a more powerful Tumansky R-25-300 turbojet with improved afterburner, increased weights and greater weapons carrying capability.

Built in relatively modest numbers compared to earlier MiG-21 versions (about 500), -21bis deliveries to the VVS began in February 1972 and Soviet production ended in 1974. Some were exported to Warsaw Pact countries (and to Finland) while of the overall total, 296 were assembled in India by HAL from kits between 1978 and 1987. The final variant was the MiG-21bis-SAU 'Fishbed-N', manufactured in small numbers at the end of the Soviet MiG-21 production run in 1974 and differing from the standard MiG-21bis in having an upgraded avionics fit.

With large numbers of MiG-21bis and other later generation aircraft still in service with some 20 nations by 2000, several upgrades have been marketed with airframe and engine refurbishment and the installation of modern radar, cockpits, avionics and weapons capability.

These include the Israeli Aircraft Industries MiG-21-2000 (first flight May 1995), the MiG-MAPO MiG-21-93 (also first flown in May 1995, India placed an order for 100 in 1993); and the Elbit/Aerostar MiG-21 Lancer for Romania.

Photo: Indian Air Force MiG-21bis.

Mikoyan-Gurevich MiG-23

Country of origin: Soviet Union.

Type: Single seat multirole fighter.

Powerplant: MiG-23ML – one 18,850lb (83.8kN) dry/28,660lb (127.5kN) with afterburner Soyuz/Khachaturov R-35-300 turbojet.

Dimensions: MiG-23ML – wing span (fully extended) 13.97m (45ft 10in) or 7.78m (25ft 6in) fully swept; length (excl nose probe) 15.88m (52ft 1in); height 4.82m (15ft 10in); wing area 37.3m² (401sq ft) extended or 34.2m² (368sq ft) swept.

Weights: MiG-23ML – empty 10,200kg (22,485lb); max takeoff 17,800kg (39,250lb).

Armament: MiG-23ML – one twin barrel 23mm cannon; five external hardpoints (one centreline, two underfuselage and two underwing) for max 2000kg (4410lb) ordnance.

Production: 5047 MiG-23s of all versions.

Performance: MiG-23ML – max speed 1349kt (Mach 2.35/2500km/h) at altitude, 729kt (Mach 1.1/1350km/h) at sea level; max climb 47,250ft (14,400m)/min; service ceiling 59,055ft; range (internal fuel) 1050nm (1945km); range with external fuel 1520nm (2815km); combat radius with 2000kg (4410lb) ordnance 378nm (700km).

Notes: From the mid 1970s and into the 1980s the MiG-23 (NATO reporting name 'Flogger') was the Soviet Union's most capable tactical fighter. The MiG-23 was developed to replace the MiG-21, with improvements in overall performance and in particular short field performance.

Two Mikoyan designed prototypes were built, the swept wing 23-01 'Faithless' and the swing wing (with three positions of sweep) 23-11. The latter first flew on 10 June 1967 and was ordered into production as the MiG-23S powered by a 22,046lb (98.1kN) with afterburner Khachaturov R-27F2M-300 turbojet.

The MiG-23M ('Flogger-B', first flight June 1972) was the first model to attain large scale production and the first with the specially designed Sapfir-23 pulse doppler radar in a larger nose radome. It also featured a more powerful Khachaturov R-29-300 turbojet plus infrared search and track (IRST) and R-23 missile compatibility. The reduced specification MiG-23MS ('Flogger-E') for export was similar but for its R-27F2M-300 engine, while the further downgraded MiG-23MF was for non Warsaw Pact nations.

Subsequent fighter MiG-23s were the lightened MiG-23ML ('Flogger-G') with less fuel, no dorsal fin extension and more powerful R-35-300 turbojet, the similarly powered MiG-23P interceptor with automatic guidance to a target by ground controllers and the MiG-23MLD ('Flogger-K') with aerodynamic changes. The MiG-23UB ('Flogger-C') is the two seat conversion trainer version first flown in May 1969.

Other MiG-23 variants were also built specifically for ground attack, the first of these the MiG-23B (first flight August 1970) with a pointed nose lacking radar and a 25,350lb (112.7kN) with afterburner Lyulka AL-21F-300 turbojet. The improved MiG-23BN ('Flogger-F') reverted to the R-29 engine. Further improved MiG-23 attack variants were the MiG-23BK and MiG-23BM, both of which used the MiG-27's nav/attack system. MiG-23 production ended in 1986 and by 2000 it remained in service with 16 nations.

Photo: MiG-23MF. (Sebastian Zacharias)

Mikoyan MiG-27

Country of origin: Soviet Union.

Type: Single seat ground attack aircraft.

Powerplant: One 17,637lb (78.5kN) dry/25,353lb (112.8kN) with afterburner Soyuz/Khachaturov R-29B-300 turbojet.

Dimensions: Wing span (fully extended) 13.97m (45ft 10in) or 7.78m (25ft 6in) fully swept; length 17.08m (56ft 0in); height 5.00m (16ft 5in); wing area 37.4m² (402sq ft) extended or 34.2m² (368sq ft) swept.

Weights: MiG-27 – operating empty 12,100kg (26,675lb); max takeoff 20,300kg (44,753lb).

Armament: One 30mm multi barrel cannon; max external weapons load of over 4000kg (8820lb) including laser, TV and electro optically guided ASMs and PGMs, bombs and rockets.

Performance: Max speed 1017kt (Mach 1.77/1885km/h) at 36,200ft, 728kt (Mach 1.1/1350km/h) at sea level; max initial climb 39,370ft (12,000m)/min; service ceiling 45,930ft; combat radius with two ASMs and three drop tanks lo-lo-lo 292nm (540km); radius with two ASMs (internal fuel) 120nm (222km); ferry range with drop tanks 1350nm (2500km).

Production: Approximately 910 of all models comprising 550 MiG-27, 214 MiG-27K and about 150 MiG-27M.

Notes: The MiG-27 is a direct development of the MiG-23 optimised for strike and ground attack and retains the NATO reporting name 'Flogger'. The MiG-27 designation originally applied to a range of Mikoyan design studies aimed to meet a requirement for a modern day Shturmovik that was eventually met by the Sukhoi Su-25. Instead, the MiG-27 is the definitive strike/ground attack member of the MiG-23/27 family.

The ground attack MiG-23s, as described in the previous entry, were regarded as interim aircraft in that role pending the arrival of the optimised MiG-27. Compared with the MiG-23, the MiG-27 features simplified fixed instead of variable ramp air intakes (the MiG-23's were designed for maximum top end performance) and a simplified two stage afterburner nozzle on the engines. An extra external hardpoint and strengthened main undercarriage permit the carriage of over 4000kg (8820lb) of ordnance.

A distinctive feature is the duckbill nose (which it shares with ground attack MiG-23s) which houses a laser rangefinder and other sensors. The MiG-27 also has advanced nav/attack systems allowing all weather operations, and can be used in the tactical reconnaissance role carrying reconnaissance pods.

Development work on the MiG-27 began in 1969 and the prototype (as the MiG-23B) first flew on 20 August 1970. A series of 24 MiG-23Bs was built in 1971-72 and the aircraft entered Soviet service in 1973 under the new designation MiG-27 ('Flogger-D'). The initial production model was soon followed by the MiG-27K and M models ('Flogger-J') with uprated avionics and weapons control/targeting systems. Soviet production ended in 1983.

India was the only MiG-27 customer outside the Soviet Union/CIS, where it was built under licence by HAL under the name MiG-27M Bahadur (Valiant) from 1986. Mikoyan's designation for the Indian aircraft is MiG-27L.

Photo: HAL built MiG-27M Bahadur. (Sebastian Zacharias)

Mikoyan MiG-25

Country of origin: Soviet Union.

Type: Single seat interceptor and reconnaissance aircraft.

Powerplants: MiG-25P – two 16,534lb (73.5kN) dry/22,509lb (100.1kN) with afterburner Soyuz/Tumansky R-15B-300 turbojets. MiG-25PD etc – two 19,400lb (86.3kN) dry/24,690lb (109.8kN) R-15BD-300 turbojets.

Dimensions: Wing span 14.02m (46ft 0in); length 23.82m (78ft 2in); height 6.10m (20ft 0in); wing area 61.4m² (660.9sq ft).

Weights: Normal loaded with four R-40 AAMs and max internal fuel 36,720kg (80,952lb).

Armament: MiG-25P/PD etc – four underwing hardpoints for max 4000kg (9635lb) ordnance including AAMs. MiG-25BM – four Kh-58 (AS-11 'Kilter') anti radiation missiles.

Performance: MiG-25P – max speed 1620kt (Mach 2.82/3000km/h) at 42,600ft, 648kt (Mach 0.98/1200km/h) at sea level; time to 65,615ft 8.9min; service ceiling 67,915ft; range (internal fuel) 934nm (1730km). MiG-25RB – range with four missiles and drop tank 1296nm (2400km).

Production: 1186 of all models.

Notes: The MiG-25 (NATO codename 'Foxbat') high altitude, high speed interceptor was initially developed to counter the Mach 3 North American XB-70 Valkyrie bomber under development in the US in the late 1950s and early 1960s. Although the XB-70 programme was cancelled in 1961 (apart from research flying), work on the Soviet Union's new high speed interceptor and reconnaissance platform continued. The two main design considerations for the aircraft were speed and high altitude performance, these attained at the expense of manoeuvrability.

The design of the MiG-25 was a considerable feat for the time, given that it had to withstand the high temperatures and stresses of sustained very high speed flight. The airframe was made mainly of nickel steel, with some titanium used in areas such as leading edges.

The first MiG-25 prototype to fly was the Ye-155R-1 reconnaissance version on 6 March 1964. The interceptor Ye-166P-1 followed on 9 September 1964. Under the designations Ye-266 and Ye-266M, two MiG-25s set several speed and altitude records, many of which still stand. Deliveries of the initial production MiG-25P interceptor to the VVS began in April 1972 with service entry achieved the following year.

Subsequent interceptor variants were the MiG-25PD 'Foxbat-E' (first flight 19 November 1977) with new look down/shoot down radar and more powerful engines; and the MiG-25PDS, a conversion of MiG-29Ps undertaken from 1979. The MiG-25U 'Foxbat-C' two seat conversion trainer has separate stepped cockpits.

Reconnaissance versions were the initial MiG-25R which was soon replaced by the MiG-25RB 'Foxbat-B' with ground attack capability. Other variants (MiG-25RBS, BSh, RBV, RBK and RBF) differed in their operational equipment and were mainly conversions. The MiG-25BM ('Foxbat-F') is a dedicated defence suppression variant armed with four AS-11 'Kilter' anti radiation missiles. Series production ended in 1982 followed by the small batch of MiG-25BMs built in 1985. MiG-25s were supplied to Algeria, India, Iraq, Libya and Syria.

Photo: MiG-25P.

Mikoyan MiG-31

Country of origin: Soviet Union/Russia.

Type: Two seat long range interceptor.

Powerplants: MiG-31 – two 20,944lb (93.1kN) dry/34,172lb (152.0kN) with afterburner Aviadvigatel (Soloviev) D-30F-6 turbofans.

Dimensions: Wing span 13.46m (44ft 2in); length 22.68m (75ft 5in); height 6.15m (20ft 2in); wing area 61.6m² (663sq ft).

Weights: MiG-31 – empty 21,820kg (48,104lb); max takeoff 46,200kg (101,852lb).

Armament: MiG-31 – one 23mm six barrel cannon; four underfuselage pylons for R-33 (AA-9 'Amos') long range AAMs; four underwing pylons for R-40T (AA-6 'Acrid') and R-60 (AA-8 'Aphid') AAMs.

Performance: MiG-31 – max speed 1620kt (Mach 2.83/3000km/h) at 57,400ft; max speed 810kt (Mach1.22/1500km/h) at sea level; time to 32,810ft 7.9min; service ceiling 67,585ft; combat radius with four AAMs (internal fuel) 648nm (1200km) or 756nm (1400km) with drop tanks; max ferry range 1782nm (3300km).

Production: Approximately 400 by 2000.

Notes: The first MiG to emerge from the redesignated Mikoyan OKB (Mikhail Gurevich having retired), the very large and heavy MiG-31 two seat long range interceptor was designed mainly to counter low flying strike aircraft and cruise missiles.

Development began in the 1972, the design based on the MiG-25. The Ye-155MP prototype first flew on 16 September 1975 followed by the first pre-production MiG-31 (NATO reporting name 'Foxhound-A') in December 1976. State acceptance trails were completed in December 1981 and regular service began in 1983.

While the MiG-31's airframe is based on the MiG-25, it is in many ways a new aircraft powered by afterburning turbofan engines (instead of turbojets) and with revised airframe construction comprising nickel steel, light alloy and titanium.

The MiG-31 was the first production aircraft to feature an electronically scanned phased array radar, the SBI 16 Zalson ('Flash Dance') which can track up to 10 targets and engage four simultaneously. Via datalink, the MiG-31 can be controlled automatically by a ground controller.

Other changes include the addition of a retractable flight refuelling probe on later production aircraft, an internal gun and tandem main undercarriage.

Production models are the basic MiG-31 and the MiG-31B with radar, ECM and EW upgrades. Strike (MiG-31F), defence suppression (MiG-31BM) and export (MiG-31E and FE) variants have also been proposed, while two anti satellite MiG-31Ds were built in 1986.

The improved MiG-31M first flew in December 1985, this featuring a Phazotron phased array radar, retractable infrared search and track (IRST) equipment, no gun, two extra centreline hardpoints, R-37 (a derivative of the R-33) and R-77 (AA-12) AAM compatibility, increased weights, more powerful D-30F-6M engines and three colour CRTs in the rear cockpit. Very low rate production was being maintained at the end of the 1990s, by which time only about 10 MiG-31Ms had been completed due to a lack of funding.

Photo: MiG-31M. (Doug Mackay)

Mikoyan MiG-29

Country of origin: Soviet Union/Russia.

Type: Single seat air superiority and attack fighter.

Powerplants: MiG-29/29S – two 11,100lb (49.4kN) dry/18,300lb (81.4kN) with afterburner Klimov/Sarkisov RD-33 turbofans.

Dimensions: Span 11.36m (37ft 3in); length (incl nose probe) 17.32m (56ft 10in); height 4.73m (15ft 6in); wing area 38.0m² (409sq ft).

Weights: MiG-29S – operating empty 10,900kg (24,030lb); max take-off 19,700kg (43,430lb).

Armament: MiG-29S – one 30mm cannon; six underwing hardpoints for max 3000kg (6614lb) ordnance including R-27, R-73 and R-77 AAMs plus rockets and bombs.

Performance: MiG-29S – max speed 1320kt (Mach 2.3/2445km/h) at 39,400ft, 810kt (Mach 1.22/1500km/h) at sea level; max climb 64,960ft (19,800m)/min; ceiling 59,060ft; range (internal fuel) 772nm (1430km); range with external fuel 1565nm (3000km).

Production: Approximately 1600 MiG-29s of all models by 2000.

Notes: The highly capable MiG-29 (NATO reporting name 'Fulcrum') is Russia's most important tactical fighter and has been exported to 15 nations. Initial development began in 1969 to meet a Soviet requirement for a heavy fighter, this evolving into an agile 'lightweight' fighter to replace a range of aircraft in Frontal Aviation service including the MiG-21, MiG-23 and Su-15. The preliminary design was accepted in 1974.

The first of 14 prototypes flew on 6 October 1977 and the first production aircraft in May 1982. Initial deliveries were in July 1983 and service entry in 1984. The prototype MiG-29UB two seat trainer version had meanwhile flown in April 1981.

The MiG-29 features excellent high angle of attack performance and low speed handling, plus a thrust-to-weight ratio greater than unity when used as an interceptor. It also features RP-29 pulse doppler look down/shoot down radar and an IRST unit which allows it to passively detect, track and engage other aircraft, while a helmet mounted sight can cue IR guided AAMs to off boresight targets. For operations from primitive airfields, doors seal the main intakes to protect the engines from foreign object damage (FOD) during start-up and taxying, with air drawn from louvred intakes in the wing roots. The intake doors open on takeoff.

The basic MiG-29 'Fulcrum-A' was joined in production by the 'Fulcrum-C' with a larger dorsal spine containing extra fuel and active ECM equipment. It was built only for the USSR/Russia and forms the basis of the MiG-29S (first flight December 1990) with a modified flight control system, improved Phazotron N019M radar, compatibility with the advanced Vympel R-77 (AA-12) radar guided AAM and greater weapons load. The S is offered for export as the MiG-29SE (and SD export upgrade of the 'Fulcrum-A'). The MiG-29SM has enhanced ASM capability.

The MiG-29SMT is an upgrade of the basic MiG-29 incorporating improvements developed for the MiG-29M, including twin liquid crystal displays, upgraded HUD and N019MP radar. It also features an enlarged spine with more fuel. The Russian Air Force plans to upgrade 200 MiG-29s to SMT standards.

Photo: A Luftwaffe MiG-29.

Mikoyan MiG-29M and MiG-33

Country of origin: Soviet Union/Russia.

Type: Single seat multirole fighter.

Powerplants: MiG-29M – two 19,400lb (86.3kN) with afterburner Klimov/Sarkisov RD-33K turbofans.

Dimensions: MiG-29M – wing span 11.36m (37ft 3in); length (incl nose probe) 17.37m (57ft 0in); height 4.73m (15ft 6in); wing area 38.0m² (409sq ft).

Weights: MiG-29M – normal loaded 16,800kg (37,037lb); max takeoff 22,000kg (48,500lb).

Armament: MiG-29M – one 30mm cannon; one underfuselage and eight underwing hardpoints for max 4500kg (9920lb) ordnance including AAMs, laser or TV guided ASMs, radar homing ASMs, TV guided and conventional bombs and rockets.

Performance: MiG-29M – max speed 1320kt (Mach 2.3/2445km/h) above 36,000ft, 810kt (Mach 1.22/1500km/h) at sea level; max climb 64,960ft (19,800m)/min; service ceiling 55,775ft; air combat mission radius 675nm (1250km); range (internal fuel) 1188nm (2200km); ferry range 1728nm (3200km).

Production: Approximately 1600 MiG-29s of all models by 2000 including 6 MiG-29M and 2 MiG-29K prototypes.

Notes: The MiG-29M is an enhanced multirole version of the MiG-29, development beginning in 1982. The first of six prototypes (powered by the standard MiG-29's RD-33 engines rather than the intended RD-33Ks) flew on 25 April 1986 while the first with the more powerful RD-33K powerplants followed in late 1989. Funding limitations have prevented the Russian Air Force ordering the MiG-29M into production. The designation MiG-29ME was to have applied to export aircraft but these are now covered by the MiG-33 appellation.

The MiG-29M features significant changes over the basic MiG-29 including substantially increased internal fuel capacity in a bulged dorsal spine (different to that of the 'Fulcrum-C'), a smaller cannon ammunition magazine and deletion of the overwing air intakes with retractable meshed intake FOD doors fitted instead. The MiG-29M's chaff and flare dispensers are housed in the spine rather than in the extended fins of earlier models, while the M also features modified leading edge root extensions, ailerons and tailplane.

Internally, the MiG-29M has an analogue fly-by-wire flight control system, a slightly aft centre of gravity for relaxed stability, new Phazotron N-010 Zhuk radar with vastly improved processing capabilities and new operating modes expanding air-to-ground capabilities, and a revised cockpit with two CRT displays and HOTAS controls. It can also fire a wider range of advanced AAMs and ASMs. After a period of inactivity, the MiG-29M restarted trials in 1995 but mainly to support the next generation MiG-35 programme.

The carrier capable MiG-29K was based on the MiG-29M but dropped in favour of a Sukhoi Su-27 variant. It first flew in July 1988 but after several inactive years was reflown in September 1996 in anticipation of India purchasing the carrier *Admiral Gorshkov*. Mikoyan has also failed to interest the Russian Air Force in the larger MiG-35 development, this with a Phazotron RP-35 phased array radar, more powerful engines and thrust vectoring.

Photo: MiG-29ME. (Alex Radetski)

Mil Mi-24/25/35

Country of origin: Soviet Union/Russia.

Type: Armed assault/attack helicopter.

Powerplants: Mi-24P/V – two 2225shp (1659kW) Klimov/Isotov TV3-117/117VM turboshafts; five bladed main rotor.

Dimensions: Mi-24P/V – main rotor diameter 17.30m (56ft 9in); fuselage length 17.51m (57ft 5in); height to top of rotor head 4.44m (13ft 1in); main rotor disc area 235.1m² (2530sq ft).

Weights: Mi-24V – empty 8340kg (18,386lb); max takeoff 11,500kg (25,353lb).

Armament: One 12.7mm four barrel machine gun or twin 23mm cannon in undernose turret; two anti tank missiles on each stub wing endplate; four underwing hardpoints for max 1200kg (2645kg) rockets and guns.

Performance: Mi-24P/V – max speed 181kt (335km/h); cruising speed 151kt (280km/h); economical cruising speed 117kt (217km/h); initial climb 2460ft (750m)/min; service ceiling 15,090ft; hovering ceiling OGE 6560ft; range with standard fuel 243nm (450km); ferry range 607nm (1124km); combat radius with max military load 85nm (157km); radius with two external fuel tanks 120nm (222km); radius with four tanks 155nm (287km).

Production: More than 2500 of all versions by 2000 including approx 240 Mi-24A, 350 Mi-24D, 1000 Mi-24V, 25 Mi-24VP, 620 Mi-24P, 152 Mi-24R, 163 Mi-24K.

Notes: Mil's battle proven 'Devil's Chariot' is unique in that it was designed from scratch as a combined armed assault/attack helicopter, although the latter is its primary role. Up to eight troops or four stretchers can be accommodated in the main cabin in addition to a pilot and weapons operator seated in tandem. The Mi-24 is based on the dynamic systems of the Mi-8/Mi-17 transport helicopters and its NATO reporting name is 'Hind'.

Development began in 1967 with a Soviet competition for a combat-transport helicopter. Two designs were considered, the Kamov Ka-25F and Mil V-24. The latter was selected in May 1968 and the prototype V-24 first flew 19 September 1969 followed by the first production Mi-24 in November 1970. Service entry was in 1973.

Early production 'Hind-A', 'Hind-B' and 'Hind-C' versions (the latter the training Mi-24U) feature a glasshouse style cockpit for the pilot and weapons operator which offered poor visibility and protection. The Mi-24D 'Hind-D' of 1973 and export Mi-25 introduced the definitive stepped and armoured cockpits, plus a four barrel 12.7mm machine gun in an undernose turret and undernose missile guidance and electro optical pods.

The similar and major production Mi-24V 'Hind-E' (Mi-35 for export) was built between 1976 and 1986 and introduced stub wing endplates for anti armour missiles and a HUD for the pilot. The Mi-24VP introduced a twin barrel 23mm cannon on the starboard fuselage side as operational experience in Afghanistan found the original gun ineffective against some targets.

The Mi-24P 'Hind-F' (and export Mi-35P) has a twin 30mm cannon. It was manufactured between 1981 and 1989. Other variants include the Mi-24R nuclear, biological and chemical reconnaissance sampling model and Mi-24K unarmed artillery spotter/reconnaissance version. Proposed upgrades are being developed as the Mi-35M.

Photo: A Czech Mi-24V. (Bruce Malcolm)

Mil Mi-28

Country of origin: Soviet Union/Russia.

Type: Two seat attack helicopter.

Powerplants: Mi-28A – two 2200shp (1640kW) Klimov TV3-117VMA turboshafts. Mi-28N – two 2500shp (1864kW) TV3-117VMA-SB3 turboshafts; five bladed main rotor.

Dimensions: Main rotor diameter 17.20m (56ft 5in); fuselage length 17.01m (55ft 9in); height to top of rotor head 3.83m (12ft 7in); main rotor disc area 232.3m² (2501sq ft).

Weights: Mi-28N – empty equipped 8095kg (17,846lb); normal takeoff 10,700kg (23,598lb); max takeoff 12,100kg (26,675lb).

Armament: One 30mm cannon in undernose turret; four underwing hardpoints for max 2000kg (4409lb) ordnance including two rocket pods and up to 16 9P149 Shturm C (AT-6 'Spiral') radio guided tube launched anti armour missiles; also gun packs, minelaying containers, submunitions dispensers and tube launched AAMs.

Performance: Mi-28N – max speed 173kt (320km/h); max cruising speed 146kt (270km/h); max climb 2677ft (816m)/min; service ceiling 19,030ft; hovering ceiling OGE 11,810ft; range (internal fuel) 243nm (450km); ferry range with auxiliary fuel 534nm (989km); combat radius with standard fuel 108nm (200km).

Production: 5 prototypes/demonstrators only by 2000.

Notes: Manoeuvrable, well armed, armoured and fast, the Mi-28 (NATO reporting name 'Havoc') is Mil's first dedicated two seat attack helicopter, developed in competition with the Kamov Ka-50 to meet a long standing Russian Army requirement for a new generation combat helicopter which dates back to December 1976.

Mil's initial design was accepted by the Soviet Sate Commission in June 1981 and the first of three prototypes performed its maiden hovering flight on 10 November 1982. Its initial 'circle' flight followed on 19 December.

The Mi-28 has tandem stepped cockpits with energy absorbing crew seats, an undernose turret containing a 30mm cannon, stub wings with two hardpoints on each and twin TV3 turboshafts, this engine also powering the Ka-50, plus Mil's Mi-17 and Mi-24. The original three bladed tail rotor unit was replaced by a four bladed X-shape unit, similar to that on the AH-64 Apache. The cockpits feature ceramic and titanium armour, while the entire airframe is designed to absorb and survive small arms fire. Countermeasures are carried in stub wing pods. The thimble nose radome contains a missile guidance radar, beneath are two fixed infrared sensors.

The Mi-28N is an improved night/all weather development featuring a mast mounted millimetre wave radar, a FLIR ball turret under the nose radome, low light TV, night vision compatible cockpit lighting, uprated engines and swept main rotor tips. Intended as the principal production version, development was launched in December 1988. The first of so far two Mi-28Ns performed its first hovering flight on 14 November 1996 and initial conventional flight on 26 April 1997.

No orders had been placed for the Mi-28 by mid 2000, although it has been evaluated by Sweden and a licence production agreement with Iraq was signed in 1990 but abandoned.

Photo: Mi-28N. (Sebastian Zacharias)

Mitsubishi F-1

Country of origin: Japan.

Type: Single seat close support/ground attack fighter.

Powerplants: Two 5115lb (22.8kN) dry/7305lb (32.5kN) with afterburner Ishikawajima-Harima TF40-IHI-801A (licence built Rolls-Royce Turboméca Adour Mk 801) turbofans.

Dimensions: Wing span 7.88m (25ft 10in); length 17.32m (56ft 10in); height 4.48m (14ft 8^1/$_2$in); wing area 21.2m^2 (228sq ft).

Weights: Empty 6358kg (14,017lb); max takeoff 13,700kg (30,203lb).

Armament: One Vulcan 20mm multi barrel cannon in lower forward fuselage; one centreline and four underwing hardpoints for max 2720kg (6000lb) ordnance including bombs, rocket pods or fuel tanks; AIM-9L Sidewinder or Mitsubishi AAM-1 AAMs on wingtip and outboard underwing hardpoints; ASM-1 radar guided anti ship missile on each inboard underwing pylon.

Performance: Max speed 918kt (Mach 1.6/1700km/h) at 40,000ft; max initial climb 35,000ft (10,668m)/min; service ceiling 50,000ft; combat radius with eight 227kg (500lb) bombs hi-lo-hi 190nm (352km); combat radius with two ASM-1 anti ship missiles and two drop tanks hi-lo-hi 300nm (555km).

Production: 77.

Notes: Based on the Mitsubishi T-2 advanced trainer, the F-1 is the first supersonic combat aircraft designed and built in Japan and the country's first indigenous pure combat aircraft since World War II.

The Japan Air Self Defence Force (JASDF) ordered development of a single seat ground attack (with secondary air combat capability) version of the Mitsubishi T-2 under the provisional designation FS-T2-Kai in 1972. The second and third XT-2 prototypes were converted to act as prototypes for the F-1, and the first of these flying in its new guise on 3 June 1975 with the second following four days later.

The F-1 prototypes were largely unchanged from the T-2 except that the faired over rear cockpit contained a fire control system and test equipment. In mid 1975 they were delivered to the JASDF's Air Proving Wing at Gifu for a year of service testing.

Following the successful completion of service trials the F-1 designation was adopted and the type ordered into production. The 77 production F-1s were delivered between September 1977 and March 1987, replacing the JASDF's fleet of elderly F-86 Sabres.

The only major external change which differentiates the F-1 from the T-2 is the faired over second cockpit which contains the bombing computer, inertial navigation system and radar warning system. From 1982 the Mitsubishi J/AWG-12 search and ranging radar replaced the earlier J/AWG-11, introducing compatibility with the radar guided ASM-1 anti ship air-to-surface missile.

Since being armed with this weapon the F-1 has been primarily tasked with anti shipping strike duties. The aircraft is also cleared to fire the AIM-9L Sidewinder.

Other avionics and equipment upgrades were performed in 1991-93 to allow the F-1 to remain in service until 2000, when replacement by the multirole Mitsubishi F-2 (a development of the Lockheed Martin F-16) was scheduled to begin.

Photo: Mitsubishi F-1.

Mitsubishi F-2

Countries of origin: Japan and the USA.

Type: Ground attack and maritime strike fighter.

Powerplants: One 17,200lb (76.5kN) dry/29,00lb (129.0kN) with afterburner General Electric F110-GE-129 turbofan.

Dimensions: Wing span 11.13m (36ft 6in); length overall 15.52m (50ft 11in); height 4.96m (16ft 3in); wing area 34.8m^2 (375sq ft).

Weights: Empty 9527kg (21,003lb); max takeoff 22,100kg (48,721lb).

Armament: One Vulcan 20mm multi barrel cannon; 13 underfuselage, underwing and wing tip hardpoints for max 9000kg (19,840lb) ordnance including AIM-9L Sidewinders or Mitsubishi AAM-3 AAMs on wingtip rails, radar guided Mitsubishi ASM-1 or ASM-2 anti ship missiles, AIM-7M Sparrow AAMs etc.

Performance: F-2A (estimated) – max speed 1148kt (Mach 2.0/2126km/h) at altitude, 660kt (Mach 1.0/1223km/h) at sea level; combat radius (anti ship mission) more than 448nm (830km).

Production: 4 prototypes plus planned acquisition of 83 F-2A and 47 F-2B by JASDF.

Notes: The highly expensive Mitsubishi F-2 is a significant Japanese development of the Lockheed Martin F-16C to replace the F-1 for maritime strike, ground attack and counter air missions. Following on from the success of the T-2 trainer and F-1 fighter, Japan originally planned to develop an all new aircraft to meet the F-1 replacement requirement.

In the early 1980s, Japan's Technical Research and Development Institute had been studying designs for a new fighter for the Japan Air Self Defence Force. However the USA exerted considerable pressure on Japan to continue to buy US weapons and to reduce the large trade imbalance between the two countries. Thus plans to develop an indigenous fighter were dropped in 1987 with the Japan Defence Agency (JDA) instead compromising on developing an existing US fighter with considerable US industrial participation.

In October 1987, the General Dynamics F-16 was selected to form the basis of a Japanese developed aircraft. Mitsubishi was appointed prime contractor for what was called the FS-X programme in November 1988, while the General Electric F110-GE-129 was selected as its powerplant in December 1990. Four FS-X prototypes were built, the first of these flying on 7 October 7 1995. The FS-X was redesignated F-2 in December of that year.

Compared with the F-16 the F-2 features a 25 per cent larger wing constructed of co-cured composites, a longer fuselage, redesigned cockpit canopy, a Mitsubishi Electric developed active phased array radar and Japanese avionics including the integrated electronic warfare system, liquid crystal displays and a HUD. It also has a Japanese developed fly-by-wire flight control system because of the USA's refusal to release F-16 fly-by-wire software source codes.

The JASDF originally required 141 FS-Xs, including some two seat TFS-X conversion trainers, although funding cuts and spiralling development costs (over $US3bn) saw this number reduced to around 80. The JDA now plans to acquire 83 F-2A fighters and 47 F-2B conversion trainers. Problems with cracking of the composite wing have delayed first deliveries, until late 2000.

Photo: One of the prototype F-2B two seaters. (Lockheed Martin)

Myasishchev M-4 and M-6

Country of origin: Soviet Union.

Type: Six crew strategic bomber.

Powerplants: M-4 – four 20,943lb (93.1kN) Mikulin AM-3D turbojets. M-6 – four 28,660lb (127.5kN) Dobrynin VD-7B turbojets.

Dimensions: M-4 – wing span 50.48m (165ft 7½in); length 47.19m (154ft 10in); height 14.10m (46ft 3in); wing area 309.0m² (3326sq ft).

Weights: M-4 – max takeoff 165,000kg (363,757lb). M-6 empty 82,000kg (180,776lb); normal loaded 140,000kg (308,642lb); max takeoff 190,000kg (418,870lb).

Armament: M-4 – two 23mm cannon in each of four remotely controlled barbettes; max 9000kg (19,840kg) of free fall bombs. M-6 – usually two-six 23mm cannon in one-three remotely controlled barbettes; bomb load over 10,000kg (22,045lb).

Performance: M-4 – max speed 540kt (1000km/h) at 39,000ft; long range cruise 451kt (837km/h); max range 5775nm (10,700km). M-6 – max speed 491kt (910km/h) at 36,000ft; range 5097nm (9440km).

Production: Approximately 200.

Notes: The Soviet Union's first operational four jet strategic bomber, the M-4/M-6 family (NATO reporting name 'Bison') enjoyed a lengthy but largely anonymous career, in later years mainly as maritime reconnaissance and tanker aircraft.

Development began in 1949 in response to intelligence information that Boeing was developing what would become the B-52 Stratofortress, at that stage still three years away from first flight. The M-4 was a large, shoulder wing jet with 37deg sweep on the inner leading edges and powered by four Mikulin AM-3 turbojets mounted in the wings near the roots. Other features were bicycle landing gear with outriggers at the tips and remotely controlled barbettes housing 23mm cannon. The circular section fuselage included a large weapons bay for free fall bombs.

The prototype M-4 first flew on 20 January 1953 (10 months after the B-52) and made its first public appearance in May 1954 as part of a flypast over Moscow. Called 'Bison-A' by NATO, the original version was found to be underpowered and required the aircraft to fly with a reduced fuel load, thus making it impossible to meet its mission requirements.

A redesign resulted in the M-6, this featuring much more powerful Dobrynin VD-7 turbojets, a revised wing and tailplane and the fitting of radar under the nose. Designated 3M in Soviet service, deliveries began in late 1955 and squadron service in May 1956. Production ended in 1959.

Subsequent modified versions include the 'Bison-B' and 'C' (3MS/3MS2) mainly for the Soviet Navy in the reconnaissance/ECM/tanker roles. Various radar and avionics upgrades were installed over the years, as was a fixed flight refuelling probe.

Never able to fully meet its design role as a strategic bomber (and usurped by the turboprop Tupolev Tu-95 'Bear'), 'Bisons' were nevertheless regularly employed on probing missions over the Arctic, Atlantic, Pacific and elsewhere, usually flying at either very low or very high altitudes. About 40 aircraft remained in service until the early 1990s as tankers.

Photo: Myasishchev M-4.

Nanchang Q-5/A-5

Country of origin: China.

Type: Single seat close air support fighter-bomber.

Powerplants: Two 5732lb (25.5kN) dry/7165lb (31.9kN) with afterburner Shenyang WP6 turbojets.

Dimensions: Wing span 9.70m (31ft 10in); length (excl nose probe) 15.42m (50ft 7in); height 4.50m (14ft 9in); wing area 27.95m² (301sq ft).

Weights: A-5C – empty 6495kg (14,319lb); loaded (clean) 9530kg (21,010lb); max takeoff 12,000kg (26,455lb).

Armament: Q-5 II/A-5C – two 23mm cannon in wing roots; four underfuselage and six underwing hardpoints for max 2000kg (4410lb) ordnance including bombs, rockets, air-to-surface and air-to-air missiles. Chinese aircraft can carry a 5-20kT nuclear bomb.

Performance: A-5C – max speed 643kt (Mach 1.12/1190km/h) at 36,000ft, 653kt (Mach 0.99/1210km/h) at sea level; max climb 20,275ft (6180m)/min; service ceiling 52,000ft; range with max internal and external fuel 1080nm (2000km); combat radius with max external stores 324nm (600km) hi-lo-hi or 216nm (400km) lo-lo-lo.

Production: Approximately 1300.

Notes: The Nanchang Q-5 (*Qiangjiji-5* – 'Attack Aircraft 5' or A-5 for export) is a close air support/ground attack fighter developed from China's MiG-19 copy. Development of the Q-5 (NATO reporting name 'Fantan') began in 1958, with Shenyang undertaking initial work and mock-up construction and assisting Nanchang (now Hongdu) with subsequent detail design.

Prototype construction began in May 1960, although China's Cultural Revolution intervened and the programme was cancelled in 1961 only to be reinstated in 1963. First flight was on 4 June 1965, subsequent testing revealing the need for a number of modifications to the armament, hydraulic and other systems. The first of two prototypes with the required changes flew in late 1969 and production aircraft were delivered from 1970.

The Q-5 retained the Shenyang J-6/MiG-19's rear fuselage and powerplants but featured a stretched area ruled main fuselage with an internal weapons bay, side mounted air intakes, a new conical nose and larger wings with reduced sweep. Initial production was of the basic Q-5 followed by the longer range Q-5 I with extra fuel in place of the internal bomb bay. Chinese Navy Q-5 Is may be fitted with a radar and can carry C-801 anti ship missiles and torpedoes. The Q-5 IA gained two extra underwing hardpoints and the Q-5 II a radar warning receiver.

The A-5C was developed for Pakistan and is based on the Q-5 I but with upgraded Western avionics and compatibility with Western weapons including the Sidewinder AAM. The export A-5K Kong Yun (Cloud) with Thomson-CSF laser rangefinder was cancelled in 1990.

The A-5M is also intended for export and features improved engines and Alenia avionics based on those in the AMX, including a ranging radar, INS, HUD and RWR. It first flew in October 1988, but none were sold and development was abandoned. In 2000, A-5s served with China (at least 700 with limited production continuing), Bangladesh (12), Myanmar (22), North Korea (40) and Pakistan (60).

Photo: Nanchang A-5C. (Sebastian Zacharias)

North American F-82 Twin Mustang

Country of origin: USA.

Type: Two seat escort and night fighter.

Powerplants: F-82E/F/G – two 1600hp (1193kW) Allison V-1710-143/ 145 V12s; four bladed propellers.

Dimensions: F-82G – wing span 15.72m (51ft 7in); length 12.86m (42ft 2$\frac{1}{2}$in); height 4.22m (13ft 10in); wing area 37.9m^2 (408sq ft). F-82E – length 11.92m (39ft 1$\frac{1}{2}$in).

Weights: F-82E – empty 6765kg (14,914lb); normal loaded 11,278kg (24,864lb). F-82G – empty 7256kg (15,997lb); loaded 11,744kg (25,891lb).

Armament: Six 0.50in machine guns in centre wing section; up to 1814kg (4000lb) bombs or rockets under wings.

Performance: F-82G – max speed 396kt (734km/h) at 21,000ft; cruising speed 248kt (460km/h); initial climb 3770ft (1149m)/min; service ceiling 38,900ft; combat radius 882nm (1633km) at low level; max range 1946nm (3605km).

Production: 2 XP-82, 1 XP-82A, 20 P-82B, 100 P-82E, 100 P-82F, 50 P-82G and 14 P-82H, total 287.

Notes: Despite the P-51 Mustang's exceptional range for a single engined fighter, a requirement existed in 1944 for an escort fighter with even greater range so that Allied bombers could be accompanied to the farthest reaches of the Third Reich, Czechoslovakia, Poland and Northern Italy. Greater range was also required in the Pacific, this leading to development of the P-82 (F-82 from June 1948) Twin Mustang. Too late to see service in WWII, the Twin Mustang was subsequently developed into a night fighter and saw combat in Korea.

On the surface, the design allowed a substantial increase in fuel capacity by simply joining two lengthened Mustang fuselages with a new centre wing and tailplane. The engineering involved was a little more complicated than that, but the basic concept remained. The command pilot was housed in the port fuselage section and a second pilot in the starboard. Six 0.50in machine guns were mounted in the new centre section and ordnance could be carried under the wings. Counter-rotating propellers were fitted.

Two XP-82 prototypes with Packard Merlin engines and one XP-82A with Allison V-1710s were ordered, the first XP-82 flying on 6 July 1945 and the others later in the year. The USAAF ordered 500 Merlin powered P-82Bs but the contract was cancelled in early 1946 after only 20 had been built. Two were converted to P-82C and D night fighter prototypes with SCR720 radar in a large nacelle under the centre section and the starboard cockpit was modified to house a radar operator.

Subsequent production models were all Allison powered: the F-82E long range escort fighter which served with Strategic Air Command 1948-50 and the radar equipped F-82F and G night fighters operated by Air Defence Command between 1947 and 1953. The designation F-82H was applied to 14 Fs and Gs 'winterised' on the production line for operations in Alaska.

Three F-82G squadrons operated in Korea, two aircraft of the 68th FS credited with the destruction of a pair of Yak-9s on 27 June 1950, the first USAF 'kills' of the Korean War.

Photo: F-82B Twin Mustang.

North American B-45 Tornado

Country of origin: USA.

Type: Four crew medium bomber.

Powerplants: B-45A – four 4000lb (17.8kN) Allison J35-11 or 5200lb (23.1kN) General Electric J47-GE-9 turbojets. B-45C – four 5200lb (23.1kN) dry/6000lb (26.7kN) with water injection General Electric J47-GE-13/15 turbojets.

Dimensions: B-45A/C – wing span 27.14m (89ft 0$\frac{1}{2}$in); length 22.95m (75ft 3$\frac{1}{2}$in); height 7.67m (25ft 2in); wing area 109.2m^2 (1175sq ft).

Weights: B-45A – empty equipped 21,671kg (47,775lb); max takeoff 42,069kg (92,745lb). B-45C – empty 22,182kg (48,903lb); max takeoff 51,235kg (112,952lb).

Armament: Two 0.50in machine guns in tail turret; max bomb load 9979kg (22,000lb).

Performance: B-45A – max speed 495kt (917km/h) at sea level; normal range 1190nm (2205km); B-45C – max speed 503kt (932km/h) at sea level; cruising speed 396kt (734km/h); initial climb 5800ft (1768m)/min; service ceiling 43,200ft; max range 1660nm (3074km).

Production: 3 XB-45, 96 B-45A, 10 B-45C and 33 RB-45C, total 142.

Notes: Like many of its pioneering jet combat aircraft contemporaries, the B-45 Tornado combined piston engined airframe technology with the new engines, was underpowered and lacked range. Despite this and the fact it was built only in relatively small numbers, the B-45 was an important step in the development of tactical and strategic jet bombers. It achieved several 'firsts' – the USA's first four jet bomber, its first combat capable jet bomber, the first to be modified for reconnaissance missions, and the first aircraft to drop bombs at over 500mph (805km/h).

The Tornado was developed to meet a 1944 specification, three prototype XB-45s being ordered in 1945. A conventional, shoulder mounted straight wing design with dihedral tailplane (to clear the jet efflux), the Tornado's four jets were grouped in pairs in nacelles under the wings. Crew compliment was four – two pilots in tandem under a fighter style canopy, bombardier in the nose and a rear gunner. Bombs were carried in an internal weapons bay.

The prototype XB-45 first flew on 17 March 1945 powered by Allison built General Electric J35 turbojets, this engine also fitted to the first 22 production B-45As before switching to the definitive and more powerful GE J47 for the remaining 74. Service entry was in November 1948. The B-45B was an unbuilt projected variant with upgraded radar and fire control systems and the final bomber variant, the B-45C, had a strengthened airframe for higher weights, water injected engines for a power boost on takeoff and tip tanks. Only 10 were delivered from late 1949 and the bomber Tornado versions remained in service until 1958.

Thirty-three B-45Cs were completed as RB-45C reconnaissance aircraft with 12 cameras in four positions and photo-flash bombs carried in the weapons bay, a lengthened nose plus additional fuel. Delivered between June 1950 and October 1951, the RB-45Cs saw active service over Korea with the 91st SRW. A number of USAF RB-45Cs flew in RAF colours in the mid 1950s for use on highly secret covert flights over Eastern Europe and the Soviet Union. Tornado conversions included 14 TB-45A target tugs and DB-45A/C drone director aircraft.

Photo: B-45A Tornado.

North American AJ Savage

Country of origin: USA.

Type: Three seat carrier based strike and reconnaissance.

Powerplants: Two 2400hp (1790kW) Pratt & Whitney R-2800-44W or -48W Double Wasp 18-cylinder radials driving four bladed propellers; one 4600lb (20.5kN) Allison J33-A-19 or -10 auxiliary turbojet.

Dimensions: AJ-2 – wing span 21.77m (71ft 5in); length 19.23m (63ft 1in); height 6.63m (21ft 5in).

Weights: AJ-2 – empty 12,500kg (27,558lb); max takeoff 24,948kg (55,000lb).

Armament: Two 20mm cannon; max bomb load 5443kg (12,000lb).

Performance: AJ-2 – max speed 369kt (683km/h); cruising speed 252kt (466km/h); initial climb 2700ft (823m)/min; combat radius 973nm (1803km); max range 2607nm (4828km).

Production: 3 XAJ-1, 55 AJ-1, 55 AJ-2 and 30 AJ-2P, total 143.

Notes: The first naval combat aircraft designed to carry an atomic bomb and for a time the world's largest carrier based aircraft, the Savage was developed (as the North American NA-146) to meet a US Navy requirement for a high performance attack bomber capable of carrying a nuclear weapon.

In order to meet the specification's demands a large aircraft was required, this in turn dictating the need for an unusual composite powerplants configuration – a pair of Pratt & Whitney R-2800 Double Wasp radials as the primary engines augmented by an auxiliary Allison J33 turbojet in the lower rear fuselage.

This third engine was intended to provide a high speed 'dash' capability during the attack phase of the aircraft's operation and for extra boost on takeoff when required.

Other features included shoulder mounted folding wings, tricycle undercarriage, wing tip fuel tanks and (on the first models) dihedral tailplanes.

The Savage was ordered in June 1946, the first of three XAJ-1 prototypes flying on 3 July 1948. These were followed by 55 initial production AJ-1s, the first one flying in May 1949.

Deliveries to US Navy squadron VC-5 began in September 1949 and the first carrier landings were performed aboard USS *Constellation* in August 1950.

The AJ-2 first flew on 19 February 1953, this upgraded model featuring revised versions of the same powerplants, increased fuel capacity, systems modifications, a taller fin and no tailplane dihedral.

Preceding the AJ-2 bomber was the was the photo-reconnaissance AJ-2P (first flight 6 March 1952) equipped with 18 cameras for day and night photography at high and low altitudes, photo-flash bombs in the weapons bay, automatic control of most of the cameras, the associated electronics equipment in a modified nose and additional fuel capacity. Four US Navy combat squadrons were still operating the AJ-2 in 1958 and these received AJ-2Ps.

A number of AJ-1s and AJ-2s were converted to flight refuelling tankers with a hose-and-reel unit installed in the weapons bay. The few Savages still in service in September 1962 when all USAF and USN aircraft designations were combined into the existing Air Force system were redesignated A-2A (AJ-1) and A-2B (AJ-2).

Photo: AJ-2 Savage tanker. (USN)

North American FJ-1 Fury

Country of origin: USA.

Type: Single seat carrier based fighter.

Powerplant: XFJ-1 – one 3820lb (17.0kN) General Electric J35-GE-2 turbojet. FJ-1 – one 4000lb (17.8kN) Allison (General Electric) J35-A-2 turbojet.

Dimensions: Wing span 11.63m (38ft 2in); length 10.49m (34ft 5in); height 4.52m (14ft 10in); wing area 20.5m² (221sq ft).

Weights: Empty 4011kg (8843lb); max takeoff 7076kg (15,600lb).

Armament: Six 0.50in machine guns in nose.

Performance: Max speed 475kt (880km/h) at 9000ft; initial climb 3300ft (1006m)/min; service ceiling 32,000ft; normal range 843nm (1560km); ferry range 1300nm (2408km).

Production: 3 XFJ-1 and 30 FJ-1, total 33.

Notes: A significant aircraft in North American Aviation's history, the FJ-1 Fury was the company's first gas turbine powered aircraft, the first of a long line of jet fighters produced by the company and progenitor of the world beating F-86 Sabre family.

Although built only in small numbers for the US Navy, the original straight wing FJ-1 Fury was (along with the USN's similarly conservative McDonnell FH-1 Phantom and Vought F6U Pirate – see separate entries) part of the important and necessary transition period between piston engined fighters and the swept wing jets which would follow.

A US Navy contract for the building of three XFJ-1 prototypes was awarded to North American on 1 January 1945, the company designation being NA-134. Designed around the General Electric J35 axial flow turbojet, NAA chose a simple configuration with a nose intake and straight through airflow to the engine in the rear fuselage.

This necessitated putting the cockpit above the intake ducting and resulted in a short and stumpy looking fuselage. The armament of six 0.50in machine guns was installed on the sides of the nose. Fuel was housed in the fuselage and in tip tanks on production aircraft.

The first XFJ-1 Fury flew on 27 November 1946, by which time the US Navy had ordered an additional 100 production FJ-1s but this was cut to only 30 by the time deliveries began in March 1948. Production aircraft were powered by J35-A-2 engines built by Allison.

The Fury was quickly overtaken by the rapid pace of jet fighter development and remained in front line USN service for only 14 months before being relegated to Naval Reserve units. The only operational squadron to fly the aircraft was VF-5A (later VF-51) operating aboard the carrier USS *Boxer*.

The first carrier landings were performed on 10 March 1948 and VF-5A became the first jet fighter unit to go to sea under operational conditions. The FJ-1 also had another claim to fame for a brief time in 1947 when one of the prototypes achieved a speed of Mach 0.87, the fastest by any US fighter to that point.

The later FJ-2, -3 and -4 Fury models (see separate entries) were naval developments of the Sabre and despite their designation similarity with the original aircraft, had little in common with it apart from being the result of the evolutionary process the FJ-1 had started.

Photo: FJ-1 Fury.

North American F-86A/E Sabre

Country of origin: USA.

Type: Single seat fighter-bomber.

Powerplant: One 5200lb (23.1kN) General Electric J47-GE-7/13 turbojet.

Dimensions: Wing span 11.31m (37ft 1½in); length 11.43m (37ft 6in); height 4.49m (14ft 9in); wing area 26.7m² (288sq ft).

Weights: F-86A – empty 4780kg (10,538lb); max takeoff 7359kg (16,223lb). F-86E – empty 4919kg (10,844lb); max takeoff 8077kg (17,806lb).

Armament: Six 0.50in machine guns in nose; max 454kg (2000lb) bombs or 15 5in rockets under wings.

Performance: F-86E – max speed 579kt (1072km/h) at sea level, 522kt (966km/h) at 35,000ft; initial climb 7250ft (2210m)/min; service ceiling 47,200ft; combat radius 380nm (704km); max range with drop tanks 1060nm (1965km).

Production: 6756 Sabres of all versions in USA including 3 XP-86, 554 F-86A and 336 F-86E.

Notes: The most produced Western combat aircraft of the post war era, the Sabre was the first swept wing fighter to enter production and service with the USAF, its design benefiting from captured German data. Features included slatted wings swept at 35deg, a nose intake, swept tail surfaces, conventional elevators on the early models and a pressurised cockpit.

The various Sabre versions were operated by the air forces of 38 nations and a naval variant (the FJ Fury) was also developed for the US Navy and Marine Corps. Sabres flew with 150 USAF front line squadrons and 57 Air National Guard units between 1948 and 1970. The fourth production F-86A set a new world's air speed record of 670.981mph (1079.8km/h) in September 1948.

The XP-86 prototype powered by a 3750lb (16.7kN) Allison J35 turbojet first flew on 1 October 1947 and the first production F-86A with a more powerful General Electric J47 on 20 May 1948 against an initial USAF order for 221. Service entry was in February 1949 and in December 1950 the first Sabres were deployed to Korea to counter the MiG-15. The first combat between the two adversaries took place on the 17th of that month, Lt-Col Bruce Hinton of the 4th FIW downing the first of 792 MiG-15s claimed by Sabre pilots during the conflict.

The F-86A was replaced on the production line by the F-86E from December 1950, the first example having flown on 23 September. A relatively simple evolution of the A, the F-86E differed from its predecessor mainly in having an all-flying tailplane with linked elevators, and power boost for the tail controls with artificial 'feel' incorporated. This new system eliminated many of the effects of compressibility and provided generally better control responses.

F-86Es were built in four production blocks until April 1952 when the further improved F-86F came on line. Changes introduced during the production run were minor and included fitting an optically ground and armoured flat windscreen instead of the previous 'V' shaped unit. Production of the Sabre in Canada by Canadair (see separate entry) was based on the F-86E and 60 Mk.2s from that source were delivered to the USAF as the F-86E-6 for use in Korea.

Photo: F-86A Sabre. (Bruce Malcolm)

North American F-86F Sabre

Country of origin: USA.

Type: Single seat fighter-bomber.

Powerplant: One 5910lb (26.3kN) General Electric J47-GE-27 turbojet.

Dimensions: F-86F-1/35 – wing span 11.31m (37ft 1½in); length 11.44m (37ft 6½in); height 4.49m (14ft 9in); wing area 28.1m² (303sq ft). F-86F-40 – wing span 11.92m (39ft 1½in); wing area 29.1m² (313sq ft).

Weights: F-86F-25 – empty 4967kg (10,950lb); normal loaded 7648kg (16,860lb); max takeoff 9234kg (20,357lb).

Armament: Six 0.50in machine guns in nose; four underwing hardpoints for drop tanks or two 454kg (1000lb) bombs on inner points, or 16 5in rockets.

Performance: F-86F-25 – max speed 604kt (1118km/h) at sea level, 530kt (981km/h) at 35,000ft; cruising speed 423-452kt (782-838km/h); initial climb 9300ft (2835m); service ceiling 48,000ft; combat radius with 907kg (2000lb) bombs 275nm (509km); range (internal fuel) 683nm (1263km); max ferry range 1327nm (2458km).

Production: 6756 Sabres of all versions in USA including 2539 F-86F of which 300 assembled in Japan by Mitsubishi.

Notes: The final US development of the basic day fighter Sabre, the F-86F embodied a number of refinements resulting from combat experience against the MiG-15 in Korea. These centred around the installation of a more powerful version of the J47 engine and replacement of the original slatted wing with the so-called '6-3' wing without slats for enhanced manoeuvrability. The new wing got its name because the fixed leading edge was extended by six inches at the root and three inches at the tip. It was introduced about one-third of the way through the F-86F production run.

The first F-86F was flown on 19 March 1952, production beginning immediately with over 2200 produced by the parent company between then and December 1956. Of these, many new and ex USAF aircraft were supplied to Argentina, Japan, Iraq, Norway, Pakistan, Peru, the Philippines, Portugal, South Africa, South Korea, Spain, Thailand, Turkey, Taiwan and Venezuela. An additional 300 aircraft were assembled in Japan by Mitsubishi in 1956-61, some of these converted to RF-86F photo-reconnaissance aircraft. Many other nations operated second and third hand F-86Fs, some of them into the 1980s. Bolivia kept some until 1996!

Upgrades introduced to the F-86F during its production run include the '6-3' wing (as mentioned above) plus the 'dual store' wing with additional hardpoints. Yet another revised wing was introduced to the last (Block 40) production batch with extended span and reinstatement of the leading edge slats. This was intended to restore the original slatted wing's handling docility at low speeds and to reduce stalling speeds. A tandem two seat trainer version (the TF-86F) was developed in 1953 but only two prototypes were flown.

The F-86F began to reach USAF units in Korea during 1952, joining the Es already there and making a substantial contribution to the Sabre's ascendency over the MiG-15 in that conflict to the tune of a claimed 10 to 1 kill/loss ratio.

Photo: Japan Air Self Defence Force F-86F Sabre.

North American F-86D/K/L Sabre

Country of origin: USA.

Type: Single seat all weather fighter.

Powerplant: One 5425lb (24.1kN) dry/7500lb (33.4kN) with afterburner General Electric J47-GE-17B or 5550lb (24.7kN) dry/7650lb (34.0kN) with afterburner J47-GE-33 turbojet.

Dimensions: Wing span 11.31m (37ft 1½in); length 12.27m (40ft 3in); height 4.57m (15ft 0in); wing area 26.7m² (288sq ft).

Weights: F-86D-45 – empty 6132kg (13,518lb); max takeoff 9060kg (19,975lb).

Armament: F-86D/L – 24 2.75in (70mm) Mighty Mouse FFAR rockets in retractable ventral tray. F-86K – four 20mm cannon in nose; two Sidewinder AAMs on some aircraft.

Performance: F-86D-45 – max speed 603kt (1115km/h) at sea level, 536kt (991km/h) at 40,000ft; typical cruise 478kt (885km/h); initial climb 12,150ft (3703m)/min; service ceiling 49,750ft; combat radius (clean) 287nm (531km); ferry range 889nm (1645km).

Production: 6756 Sabres of all versions in USA including 2 YF-86D, 2504 F-86D and 341 F-86K; 981 F-86L conversions.

Notes: Popularly known as the 'Sabre Dog', the F-86D all weather fighter was the first major redesign of the basic aircraft to attain production, having only 25 per cent commonality (mainly the wings and undercarriage) with the F-86A. Such were the changes that the aircraft was initially designated F-95A before F-86D was settled on for political (ie funding) reasons.

Intended to intercept Soviet bombers, the F-86D was the first single seat all weather (or 'night') fighter and the first in regular service to dispense with guns in favour of missiles, in this case 24 2.75in Mighty Mouse FFAR (folding fin aircraft rocket) weapons mounted in a lower fuselage retractable tray.

The heart of the F-86D was its complicated, heavy and notoriously unreliable fire control system – it was all vacuum tubes in those days – comprising a Hughes AN/APG-36 radar, E-4 fire control system and an AN/APA-84 computer. It was very effective once the 'bugs' had been ironed out, but this took some time. Compared to previous Sabres, the F-86D featured a completely new fuselage, hydraulically powered flight controls and an afterburning version of the J47 engine.

The first YF-86D flew on 22 December 1949 and although deliveries to the USAF began in December 1951 it would be April 1953 before full operational status would be achieved due to the fire control system's problems. The last of over 2500 was delivered in September 1956. Nearly 1000 were converted to F-86L standards in 1956-60, this involving major avionics and fire control system upgrades including installation of a ground-air datalink.

The F-86K (first flight July 1954) was a simplified version of the D intended for supply to NATO nations under the Mutual Defence Assistance Program (MDAP) and fitted with guns instead of rockets and lower specification avionics. North American built 120 complete aircraft for Norway and the Netherlands while 221 assembled by Fiat from May 1955 were delivered to Italy, France and West Germany. USAF service of the F-86D/L ended in 1960 and the Air National Guard retired its last aircraft in 1965.

Photo: F-86K Sabre. (NAA)

North American F-86H Sabre

Country of origin: USA.

Type: Single seat fighter-bomber.

Powerplant: One 8920lb (39.7kN) General Electric J73-GE-3D turbojet.

Dimensions: Wing span 11.92m (39ft 1½in); length 11.84m (38ft 10in); height 4.57m (15ft 0in); wing area 29.1m² (313sq ft).

Weights: Empty 6276kg (13,836lb); combat weight 8475kg (18,683lb); max takeoff 11,020kg (24,295lb).

Armament: Four 20mm cannon in nose; underwing hardpoints for two 454kg (1000lb) bombs, two 340kg (750lb) napalm bombs, eight 5in rockets or one 544kg (1200lb) 100kT atomic bomb; early aircraft with six 0.50in machine guns in nose.

Performance: Max speed 602kt (1115km/h) at sea level, 537kt (995km/h) at 35,000ft; typical cruise 480kt (888km/h); max climb 12,900ft (3932m)/min; combat radius with 907kg (2000lb) warload 350nm (648km); max ferry range 1575nm (2917km).

Production: 6756 Sabres of all versions in USA including 1 YF-86H and 474 F-86H.

Notes: The final US production version of the Sabre and the first version designed from the start as a fighter-bomber, the F-86H was substantially different from previous models.

New features included the much more powerful General Electric J73 turbojet (the F-86H was its only production application), a substantially redesigned and deeper fuselage to accommodate the new engine, and in aircraft from number 114 onwards, a four cannon fixed armament instead of the previous six machine guns.

The new engine was larger and heavier than its predecessor and demanded considerably greater airflow, this resulting in the necessity for a fuselage which was 15cm (6in) deeper than before. Other physical changes included the fitting of a rear hinging clamshell (instead of sliding) canopy, a larger tailplane with no dihedral, strengthened undercarriage with a longer nosewheel leg and increased fuel capacity.

The first aircraft retained the F-86E's slatted wing but all but the last few production aircraft had the extended fixed leading edge (the '6-3' wing) which had been introduced during the F-86F's production run. The final 10 F-86Hs had the extended span and slatted wing which had appeared on the last batch of F-86Fs.

Four underwing hardpoints allowed the carriage of a variety of weapons including conventional bombs, napalm bombs, 5in rockets or a 100 kiloton atomic bomb, or 'special store' as the US military has always euphemistically described these weapons. Operational equipment included the LABS low altitude bombing system, this allowing accurate delivery of the nuclear weapon by computing its 'lob bombing' release point.

The YF-86H prototype flew on 30 April 1953, this followed by another test aircraft and 473 production models, the first of which flew on 4 September 1953. Deliveries to the USAF began in January 1954 and the last was handed over in August 1955. The F-86H equipped five USAF fighter-bomber wings but by mid 1958 all had been replaced by the F-100 Super Sabre and transferred to the Air National Guard. The last was retired in 1970.

Photo: F-86H Sabre. (NAA)

North American FJ-2/3 Fury

Country of origin: USA.

Type: Single seat carrier based fighter.

Powerplant: FJ-2 – one 6000lb (26.7kN) General Electric J47-GE-2 turbojet. FJ-3 – one 7700lb (34.2kN) Wright J65-W-16A (Armstrong Siddeley Sapphire) turbojet.

Dimensions: FJ-2 – wing span 11.31m (37ft 1½in); length 11.45m (37ft 7in); height 4.14m (13ft 7in); wing area 26.7m² (288sq ft). FJ-3 – height 4.16m (13ft 8in); wing area 28.1m² (302sq ft).

Weights: FJ-2 – empty 5353kg (11,802lb); max takeoff 8523kg (18,790lb). FJ-3 – empty 5536kg (12,205lb); loaded (clean) 7797kg (17,189lb).

Armament: FJ-2 – four 20mm cannon in nose; later capability for two Sidewinder AAMs under wings. FJ-3 – guns plus later capability for two Sidewinder AAMs or bombs and rocket packs under wings.

Performance: FJ-2 – max speed 587kt (1088km/h) at sea level, 523kt (969km/h) at 35,000ft; initial climb 7230ft (2204m)/min; combat ceiling 46,800ft; normal range 860nm (1593km). FJ-3 – max speed 592kt (1096km/h) at sea level, 541kt (1002km/h) at 35,000ft; initial climb 8450ft (2575m)/min; max ferry range 1550nm (2872km).

Production: 1115 Furies of all versions including 2 XFJ-2, 1 XFJ-2B, 200 FJ-2 and 538 FJ-3.

Notes: Despite its name and designation, the FJ-2 Fury bore no design relationship to the earlier FJ-1 (which see), being fundamentally a navalised version of the slatted wing F-86E Sabre. The decision to keep the FJ designation and name was mainly due to political (ie funding) issues.

The three XFJ-2 prototypes were converted from F-86E airframes by fitting vee-frame arrester hooks, catapult attachment points and a lengthened nosewheel to set the aircraft at the correct angle of attack for a carrier launch.

Production FJ-2s gained hydraulically folding wings, an all flying tailplane, a more powerful J47-GE-2 engine and four cannon gun armament instead of the Sabre's six machine guns. The first XFJ-2 flew on 27 December 1951 and deliveries against an order for 300 (reduced to 200 with the end of Korean War) began to the first of six USMC fighter units in January 1954.

A need for improved performance resulted in development of the FJ-3 powered by the Wright J65, a licence built version of the British Armstrong Siddeley Sapphire. With 28 per cent more thrust than the FJ-2's J47 at virtually no cost in weight (although some redesign of the intake area was necessary), the FJ-3 was able to operate at higher weights and therefore offer greater operational flexibility.

The prototype XFJ-3 (converted from an FJ-2) first flew on 3 July 1953 and the first true FJ-3 on 11 December 1953. Deliveries began in September 1954 and production ended in August 1956, the FJ-3 eventually equipping 20 USN and six USMC fighter squadrons.

Some modifications were introduced during the production run including replacing the original slatted wing leading edges with extended fixed leading edges (this also permitting a fuel capacity increase) and adding two more underwing hardpoints. Eighty were modified to carry a pair of Sidewinder AAMs under the designation FJ-3M. Surviving FJ-3/3Ms were redesignated F-1C in 1962.

Photo: XFJ-2 Fury prototype.

North American FJ-4 Fury

Country of origin: USA.

Type: Single seat carrier based strike fighter.

Powerplant: One 7700lb (34.2kN) Wright J65-W-16A (Armstrong Siddeley Sapphire) turbojet.

Dimensions: Wing span 11.91m (39ft 1in); length 11.07m (36ft 4in); height 4.24m (13ft 11in); wing area 31.5m² (339sq ft).

Weights: FJ-4B – empty 6251kg (13,780lb); normal loaded 9131kg (20,130lb); max overload 11,794kg (26,000lb).

Armament: Four 20mm cannon in nose; four (FJ-4) or six (FJ-4B) underwing hardpoints for combinations of drop tanks, 227kg (500lb) or 454kg (1000lb) bombs, rocket pods, Sidewinder AAMs, Bullpup radar guided AGMs or an atomic weapon.

Performance: FJ-4B – max speed 591kt (1094km/h) at sea level, 549kt (1017km/h) at 35,000ft; typical cruise 464kt (859km/h); initial climb 7660ft (2335m)/min; service ceiling 46,800ft; max range (internal fuel) 1290nm (2390km); range with two drop tanks 1755nm (3250km); ferry range with max external fuel 2346nm (4345km).

Production: 1115 Furies of all versions including 152 FJ-4 and 222 FJ-4B.

Notes: Despite its designation, the final Fury variant – the FJ-4 – represented a complete structural redesign compared with the FJ-2 and -3. One of the few common components was the Wright J65 (Sapphire) engine and the result was a highly competent attack fighter with genuine multirole capability.

The deeper and completely recontoured fuselage featured a prominent dorsal spine running from the rear of the redesigned canopy to the base of the taller fin; the new wing of greater span was thinner with revised control surfaces, drooped leading edges and a different folding point; the main undercarriage was of a revised lever suspension design with a wider track; the tail surfaces were thinner and enlarged; and internal fuel capacity was increased by 50 per cent.

The first FJ-4 was flown on 28 October 1954 and the first production example in February 1955. The US Marine Corps flew the FJ-4 exclusively, VMF-451 the first squadron to receive the new Fury. Three other USMC units also took delivery of the FJ-4 between then and March 1957 as a replacement for the FJ-2.

The improved FJ-4B had meanwhile recorded its first flight on 4 December 1956, this ultimate Fury variant a true attack fighter equally capable of air defence or strike roles. Compared to the basic FJ-4 it had a strengthened wing with six (rather than four) hardpoints and the ability to carry Bullpup air-to-surface missiles on five of them plus a guidance pod on the sixth. It could also carry a tactical nuclear weapon and was capable of 'buddy' flight refuelling.

The FJ-4B flew with ten Navy and three Marine Corps attack squadrons and the last was delivered in May 1958. Front line service began to wind down in 1959 and by late 1962 aircraft still operational were in the hands of Naval Reserve units. By then, surviving FJ-4s and FJ-4Bs had been redesignated F-1E and AF-1E, respectively, in line with the general reorganisation of USN designations into the USAF system.

Photo: FJ-4B Fury.

North American F-100A/C Super Sabre

Country of origin: USA.

Type: F-100A – single seat fighter. F-100C – single seat fighter-bomber.

Powerplant: F-100A – one 9700lb (43.1kN) dry/14,800lb (65.8kN) with afterburner Pratt & Whitney J57-P-7 turbojet. F-100C – one 10,200lb (45.4kN) dry/16,000lb (71.2kN) with afterburner J57-P-21 turbojet.

Dimensions: Wing span 11.82m (38ft 9½in); length 14.35m (47ft 1in); height 4.67m (15ft 3in); wing area 35.8m² (385sq ft).

Weights: F-100A – empty 8249kg (18,185lb); max takeoff 13,109kg (28,899lb). F-100C – empty 8741kg (19,270lb); max takeoff 14,794kg (32,615lb).

Armament: F-100A – four 20mm cannon in lower nose; two 454kg (1000lb) bombs under wings. F-100C – guns plus six underwing hardpoints for max 2268kg (5000lb) ordnance.

Performance: F-100C – max speed 794kt (Mach 1.37/1470km/h) at 35,000ft, typical cruise 515kt (954km/h); initial climb 19,000ft (5790m)/min; service ceiling 38,700ft; range (clean) 497nm (920km); max ferry range 1698nm (3145km).

Production: 2294 Super Sabres of all versions including 2 YF-100A, 203 F-100A and 476 F-100B.

Notes: One of the first fighters capable of supersonic performance in level flight, the F-100 Super Sabre began life in 1950 as a North American Aviation private venture evolution of the F-86 called the Sabre 45, denoting the design's wing sweep in degrees. The concept developed into an all new design, features including an oval nose intake for the J57 turbojet, low set slab tailplane, rear hinged clamshell canopy and extensive use of titanium in the structure, an aviation first. The USAF ordered two YF-100A prototypes and 32 production F-100s in early 1952.

The first YF-100A flew on 25 May 1953 and the first production F-100A on 29 October 1953. The first YF-100A set a new world's air speed record of 755.149mph (1215.26km/h) on the same day. USAF operational service began in September 1954.

Early production Super Sabres differed from the prototypes in having a shorter fin and broader chord rudder. Serious roll control problems at high speeds resulted in several crashes and the grounding of the aircraft for three months from November 1954. A taller fin was developed and retrofitted to the early examples. Six F-100As were later converted to unarmed RF-100As with five cameras.

F-100A production ended in April 1955 in favour of the F-100C fighter-bomber with a strengthened 'wet' wing with increased fuel capacity and incorporating six hardpoints for drop tanks and ordnance, a more powerful engine, increased weights and provision for flight refueling. It first flew on 17 January 1955 with the last of 476 delivered in July 1956. An F-100C set the first supersonic (and high altitude) world's air speed record in August 1955, achieving 822.135mph (1323.06km/h) or Mach 1.25.

Nationalist China (Taiwan) received 118 ex USAF F-100As (modified to near 'D' standards) and four RF-100As in 1959-60 and Turkey received 92 ex USAF F-100Cs.

Photo: F-100C Super Sabre.

North American F-100D/F Super Sabre

Country of origin: USA.

Type: F-100D – single seat fighter-bomber. F-100F – two seat operational trainer/fighter-bomber.

Powerplant: One 10,200lb (45.4kN) dry/16,000lb (71.2kN) with afterburner Pratt & Whitney J57-P-21/21A turbojet.

Dimensions: F-100D – wing span 11.82m (38ft 9½in); length 14.45m (47ft 5in); height 4.94m (16ft 2½in); wing area 37.2m² (400sq ft). F-100F – length 16.00m (52ft 6in).

Weights: F-100D – empty 9526kg (21,000lb); max takeoff 17,258kg (38,048lb).

Armament: Four 20mm cannon in lower nose; six underwing hardpoints for max 3193kg (7040lb) ordnance. F-100F – two 20mm cannon plus ordnance.

Performance: F-100D – max speed 775kt (Mach 1.34/1435km/h) at 35,000ft; typical cruise 512kt (948km/h); initial climb 18,000ft (5486m)/min; service ceiling 39,600ft; range (clean) 464nm (859km); max ferry range 1733nm (3210km).

Production: 2294 Super Sabres of all versions including 1274 F-100D and 339 F-100F.

Notes: Development of the Super Sabre continued with the major production F-100D, another single seater further optimised for the air-to-ground role with substantially increased external ordnance carrying capability. A taller fin and rudder, wider wing root chord providing a wing area increase, upgraded avionics (including a supersonic autopilot) and weapons control system, and flaps added to the inboard wing trailing edges were other new features. The F-100C's J57-P-21 engine was retained and air-to-air capability was also enhanced through the ability to carry four Sidewinder missiles.

The first F-100D was flown on 24 January 1956 and despite USAF plans to keep the aircraft in service for a relatively short time (Air National Guard units began receiving it as early as April 1958), the USA's commitments in Vietnam saw the Super Sabre's front line career substantially lengthened by its involvement in the conflict.

The F-100F was a tandem two seater version of the D, the crew members accommodated in a lengthened forward fuselage under a single long canopy. The F was intended to be a conversion and combat trainer while retaining full operational capabilities. The first two seater was converted from an F-100C and flown on 6 August 1956 as the TF-100C.

The first production F-100F flew on 7 March 1957 and manufacture continued until October 1959. Apart from the changes necessitated by the extra seat, the major difference between the F-100D and F was that the latter had two (rather than four) cannon in the nose.

Numerous modification programmes were developed for the F-100D/F as a result of combat experience in Vietnam including the conversion of seven to the USAF's first 'Wild Weasel' anti radar detect and attack aircraft armed with Shrike anti radar missiles.

Nearly 300 were converted to QF-100D/F pilotless target drones by Sperry and Tracor/Flight Systems from 1979, the same year Air National Guard use of the Super Sabre ended. F-100Ds and Fs were also supplied to France (100), Denmark (72) and Turkey (181) under the USA's Military Assistance Program.

Photo: F-100D Super Sabre.

North American A-5 Vigilante

North American/Rockwell OV-10 Bronco

Country of origin: USA.

Type: A-5A – two seat carrier based attack bomber. RA-5C – two seat reconnaissance.

Powerplants: A-5A – two 16,150lb (71.8kN) with afterburner General Electric J79-GE-2/4 or 10,800lb (48.0kN) dry/17,000lb (75.6kN) with afterburner J79-GE-8 turbojets. RA-5C – J79-GE-8s or 17,860lb (79.4kN) with afterburner J79-GE-10 turbojets.

Dimensions: Wing span 16.15m (53ft); length 23.32m (76ft 6in); height 5.92m (19ft 5in); wing area 70.0m² (754sq ft).

Weights: A-5A – empty 15,581kg (34,350lb); normal takeoff 27,670kg (61,000lb). RA-5C – empty 17,009kg (37,498lb); max takeoff 36,101kg (79,588lb).

Armament: A-5A – normally one B28 or other nuclear or conventional weapons internally.

Performance: A-5A – max speed (clean) 1205kt (Mach 2.1/2232km/h) at 40,000ft; high altitude combat radius with external fuel 956nm (1770km). RA-5C – max speed 1205kt (Mach 2.1/2232km/h) at 40,000ft; long range cruise 486kt (900km/h); normal range 2300nm (4260km).

Production: 2 XA3J-1, 57 A-5A, 6 YA-5C, and 79 RA-5C; 43 A-5As converted to RA-5Cs and 14 A-5B completed as RA-5Cs.

Notes: An advanced, effective and highly innovative combat aircraft, the Vigilante enjoyed only a brief career in its design role of carrier based attack bomber before the US Navy lost its strategic bombing role. Subsequently, it proved to be a highly capable reconnaissance aircraft used extensively in the Vietnam War with little fanfare.

The design originated in 1955 to meet a US Navy requirement for a large supersonic all weather attack bomber. Two prototypes were ordered in August 1956 under the designation YA3J-1. From 1962 the aircraft was redesignated A-5. Among the many 'firsts' included in the Vigilante's design were fully variable geometry intakes for the two J79 engines, multimode radar and a digital computer. The lateral control system dispensed with ailerons and used a combination of spoilers, differential 'tailerons' ('slab' tailplanes, another first) and all moving 'slab' fin/rudder. A linear bomb bay was fitted, the weapon ejected rearwards between the two jetpipes. Structural and aerodynamic design innovations were plentiful.

The first XA3J-1 flew on 31 August 1958 with deliveries of the A3J-1 (A-5A) starting in 1960. The first operational unit (VAH-7) began receiving its first aircraft in June 1961. Manufacture of the first batch of improved A-5Bs with extra fuel in a dorsal 'saddle' (or conformal) tank, larger flaps, additional underwing hardpoints and full boundary layer control was underway when the USN lost its strategic bombing role. These features were incorporated into the A3J-3P (RA-5C) reconnaissance aircraft which had its photographic and electronic surveillance equipment in the space previously occupied by the bomb bay.

Six A-5Bs were completed as the YA-5C (Limited) – first flight 29 April 1962 – and the first RA-5C flew on 30 June 1962. Production was in two separate batches with the last aircraft delivered in October 1970. Forty-three A-5As were converted to RA-5Cs and 14 A-5Bs were completed to the same standard. Nine USN operational squadrons flew the RA-5C, the last one relinquishing its Vigilantes in 1979.

Photo: RA-5C Vigilante.

Country of origin: USA.

Type: Two seat light attack/COIN/FAC aircraft

Powerplants: OV-10A – two 715ehp (533kW) Garrett AiResearch T76-G-416/417 turboprops; three bladed propellers. OV-10D – two 1040shp (775kW) T76-G-420/421.

Dimensions: OV-10A – wing span 12.19m (40ft 0in); length 12.67m (41ft 7in); height 4.62m (15ft 2in); wing area 27.0m² (291sq ft). OV-10D – length 13.41m (44ft 0in).

Weights: OV-10A – empty equipped 3162kg (6970lb); max takeoff 6552kg (14,444lb).

Armament: Four 7.62mm machine guns on underfuselage sponsons; two underwing, one centreline and four sponson hardpoints for max 1633kg (3600lb) ordnance including light bombs, rockets and gun pods.

Performance: OV-10A – max speed 244kt (452km/h); initial climb 2600ft (1097m)/min; service ceiling 24,000ft; combat radius with max ordnance 198nm (367km); ferry range with external fuel 1200nm (2222km). OV-10D – max speed 250kt (463km/h); initial climb 3020ft (920m)/min; service ceiling 30,000ft.

Production: 7 YOV-10A, 271 OV-10A, 18 OV-10B, 32 OV-10C, 16 OV-10E and 16 OV-10F, total 360.

Notes: The OV-10 resulted from the US Marines sponsored Light Armed Reconnaissance Aircraft (LARA) programme to find a multirole utility aircraft that could perform reconnaissance and light attack missions. North American's NA-300 design was selected in August 1964 and seven YOV-10A prototypes were ordered for evaluation, the first one flying on 16 July 1965.

The Bronco's 'pod and twin boom' configuration accommodated a crew of two in tandem under a large canopy with room in the rear fuselage for five troops or two stretchers. Power was from two Garrett T76s (military equivalent of the TPE331) although one YOV-10 was powered by P&WC T74s (PT6s). Early testing revealed the need to increase the original wing span by no less than 3.05m (10ft 0in).

The first production OV-10A flew on 6 August 1967 followed by deliveries to the USAF (157) and Marines (114). Many saw operational service in Vietnam from 1968 where they were used for forward air control (FAC) and counter insurgency (COIN). The OV-10B designation applied to Broncos delivered to Germany from 1970 for target towing, while Germany's OV-10B(Z)s were fitted with a J85 auxiliary turbojet mounted above the fuselage.

In 2000, the Royal Thai Air Force continued to operate 19 survivors of 32 OV-10Cs delivered from 1971, while Venezuela took delivery of 16 OV-10Es and later ex USAF OV-10As. The OV-10C, OV-10E and Indonesia's OV-10Fs are similar to the OV-10A.

Seventeen OV-10As were converted to OV-10D standards in 1979-80 for the US Marines, the result of the US Navy sponsored OV-10D NOGS (Night Observation/Gunship System) programme to give the Bronco an all weather capability. The OV-10D featured more powerful engines, an undernose turret containing a FLIR, laser designator and automatic video tracker, and extra underwing hardpoints. It saw service during the Gulf War of 1991 and was retired shortly afterwards. the OV-10A having been withdrawn the previous year.

Photo: OV-10D Bronco.

Northrop XB-35 and YB-49

Country of origin: USA.

Type: 15 crew (XB-35) or seven crew (YB-49) strategic bombers.

Powerplants: XB-35 – four 3000hp (2237kW) Pratt & Whitney R-4360-17/21 Wasp Major 28-cylinder radials; six or eight bladed pusher contraprops or single props. YB-49 – eight 4000lb (17.8kN) Allison J35-A-5 turbojets.

Dimensions: Wing span 52.42m (172ft 0in); length 16.18m (53ft 1in); height 6.12m (20ft 1in); wing area 371.6m² (4000sq ft).

Weights: XB-35 – empty 40,624kg (89,560lb); max takeoff 94,802kg (209,000lb). YB-49 – empty 39,962kg (88,100lb); max takeoff 96,617kg (213,000lb).

Armament: XB-35 proposed – 20 0.50in machine guns in seven remotely controlled turrets; max bomb load 9072kg (20,000lb). YB-49 – max bomb load 13,608kg (30,000lb).

Performance: XB-35 – max speed 340kt (629km/h) at 35,000ft; service ceiling 40,000ft; max range 2172nm (4024km). YB-49 – max speed 428kt (793km/h); cruising speed 364kt (674km/h); service ceiling 40,700ft; range with 7258kg (16,000lb) bomb load 2742nm (5078km).

Production: 2 XB-35s and 13 YB-35s; 2 completed YB-49s and 1 converted to YRB-49A.

Notes: 'Jack' Northrop had, throughout his aircraft designing career, been convinced that the flying wing was the way to go to achieve efficiency, reasoning that if everything except the wing was left out of a design, both weight and drag could be saved. Northrop designed and built several small 'all wing' designs from the late 1920s, his early efforts culminating in the giant XB-35 strategic bomber, development of which began in 1941 with USAAF approval.

Four one-third scale proof of concept aircraft (the N9M series) with 18.3m (60ft) wing spans were flown from December 1942 and the first of two XB-35 prototypes on 25 June 1946. It was quite an aircraft, with an enormous for the time 52.42m (172ft 0in) wing span (coincidentally exactly the same as today's B-2), four Pratt & Whitney Wasp Major radials driving counter-rotating pusher propellers and innovative split aileron flight controls called 'Decelerons'. The USAAF ordered 200 B-35s but these were cancelled.

Thirteen others were built as YB-35s but at Northrop's suggestion, two of these were completed as YB-49s with the piston engines and their troublesome propellers replaced by eight 4000lb (17.8kN) Allison J35 turbojets buried in the wings. The first YB-49 flew on 21 October 1947 and the second in January 1948. This was lost five months later when it broke up during high speed diving tests, design limits having been exceeded. The Muroc Lake flight test centre in California was renamed Edwards Air Force Base in honour of the aircraft's skipper, Capt Glen Edwards.

Despite this, the USAF announced an order for 30 RB-49A reconnaissance bombers in the same month plus the conversion of 10 YB-35s to a similar standard with four 5600lb (24.9kN) J35-A-21s in the wings and two more underslung in pods. Northrop was unhappy that the aircraft were to be built by rival Convair, but the contracts were cancelled due to budgetary constraints and only one YRB-49A conversion was performed, first flying on 4 May 1950.

Photo: YB-49.

Northrop F-89 Scorpion

Country of origin: USA.

Type: Two seat all weather fighter.

Powerplants: F-89A – two 5000lb (22.2kN) dry/6800lb (30.2kN) with afterburner Allison J35-A-21 turbojets. F-89B/C/D/H/J – two 5400lb (24.0kN) dry/7400lb (32.9kN) with afterburner J35-A-33/35/35A/41/47 turbojets.

Dimensions: F-89C – wing span (over tip tanks) 17.07m (56ft 0in); length 16.28m (53ft 5in); height 5.33m (17ft 6in); wing area 56.3m² (606sq ft). F-89D – wing span (over tip tanks/pods) 18.20m (59ft 8½in); length 16.39m (53ft 9½in).

Weights: F-89C – empty 11,145kg (24,570lb); normal loaded 16,941kg (37,348lb). F-89D – empty 11,428kg (25,194lb); max takeoff 19,160kg (42,241lb).

Armament: F-89A/B/C – six 20mm cannon in nose. F-89D/H – 104 2.75in (70mm) folding fin air rockets (FFARs) in wingtip pods. F-89H – six Falcon AAMs and 42 FFARs in wingtip pods. F-89J – Two Genie unguided nuclear rockets and four Falcon AAMs under wings plus FFARs.

Performance: F-89C – max speed 565kt (1046km/h) at sea level, 488kt (904km/h) at 40,000ft; initial climb 12,300ft (3749m)/min; max range 786nm (1456km). F-89D – max speed 552kt (1023km/h) at 10,600ft, 454kt (842km/h) at 46,500ft; initial climb 7440ft (2268m)/min; service ceiling 49,200ft; max ferry range 1188nm (2200km).

Production: 1 XF-89, 1 YF-89, 18 F-89A, 30 F-89B, 164 F-89C, 682 F-89D and 156 F-89H, total 1052.

Notes: The F-89 Scorpion all weather fighter resulted from a December 1945 Northrop proposal for a P-61 Black Widow replacement. The design was accepted by the USAAF and a development contract was issued in May 1946. Features included removable tip tanks and six 20mm cannon along with an airborne intercept (AI) radar in the nose.

Two prototypes were ordered in December 1946 and the first of them (designated XF-89) flew on 16 August 1948 followed by the second (YF-89) on 1 February 1949. Deliveries of F-89A Scorpions to Air Defense Command began in July 1950 but only 18 were built before production switched to the F-89B with avionics and equipment changes. The F-89C (first flight 25 October 1951) had further upgrades including changes to the tailplane to cure a flutter problem. Progressively more powerful engines had meanwhile been introduced. Several crashes due to structural failures led to the Scorpion's grounding in 1952, necessitating some redesign of the wing's internal structure.

The major production F-89D (first flight 23 October by a converted prototype) introduced a fundamental change in armament with the guns deleted and replaced by 52 2.75in FFAR rockets in each of the larger wingtip pods, which also contained fuel. Squadron service began in early 1954 and in March 1956 the F-89D was joined by the final production F-89H with tip pods redesigned to carry Falcon AAMs and FFARs. Final delivery was later in the same year.

The F-89J was a conversion of 350 F-89Ds in 1956-58 to carry Genie unguided nuclear tipped rockets and Falcon AAMs under the wings. The final Scorpions were retired from active USAF service in 1960 but the Air National Guard operated some until 1969.

Photo: F-89D Scorpion.

Northrop F-5A Freedom Fighter

Country of origin: USA.

Type: Single seat lightweight multirole fighter.

Powerplants: Two 2720lb (12.1kN) dry/4080lb (18.2kN) with after-burner General Electric J85-GE-13 turbojets.

Dimensions: Wing span over tip tanks 7.87m (25ft 10in); span without tip tanks 7.70m (25ft 3in); length 14.38m (47ft 2in); height 4.01m (13ft 2in); wing area 15.8m² (170sq ft).

Weights: Empty equipped 3667kg (8085lb); max takeoff 9375kg (20,677lb).

Armament: Two 20mm cannon in nose; four underwing hardpoints for max 1995kg (4400lb) ordnance including bombs, rockets and AAMs; Sidewinders on wingtip stations.

Performance: Max speed 804kt (Mach 1.4/1488km/h) at 36,090ft, 635kt (Mach 0.96/1176km/h) at sea level; max climb 28,700ft (8748m)/min; service ceiling 50,500ft; combat radius with 480kg (1060lb) warload hi-lo-hi 485nm (898km); radius with 1995kg (4400lb) load hi-lo-hi 170nm (315km); ferry range 1400nm (2593km).

Production: 2626 F-5s of all versions (incl licence production) including 799 F-5A, 107 RF-5A and 293 F-5B (plus 1187 T-38 Talon).

Notes: The US adopted Northrop's N-156F lightweight fighter as the F-5 Freedom Fighter to supply to friendly European and Asian nations under the Military Assistance Program (MAP). Northrop designed its first lightweight jet fighter in 1952, the delta winged and single engined N-102 Fang. While the USAF rejected the Fang, its interest in a light-weight fighter was aroused and in 1954 it conducted a study into the concept of a compact yet high performance fighter that could be supplied under MAP. This prompted Northrop to design the N-156 powered by two afterburning General Electric J85 turbojets.

US official interest was initially in the two seat N-156T which be-came the T-38 Talon (first flight 10 April 1959), while Northrop contin-ued development of the single seat N-156F as a private venture. Three prototypes were then funded by the US Department of Defence in May 1958, the first of these flying on 30 July 1959. As the F-5A Freedom Fighter, the N-156F was selected for MAP supply and the first produc-tion standard aircraft flew in October 1963. A two seat conversion trainer variant, the F-5B, first flew in February 1964.

Although F-5 production was intended for the MAP and not the USAF itself, the 4503rd Tactical Fighter Squadron operated 'borrowed' aircraft in Vietnam for combat evaluation, these aircraft designated F-5C (sin-gle seaters) and F-5D (two seaters) and flying more than 3500 sorties. Over a dozen MAP customers received F-5A/Bs. Canadair built 240 under licence with uprated engines and a flight refuelling probe as the CF-5A and CF-5D for Canada and NF-5A/B for the Netherlands, while Spain's CASA assembled 70. The RF-5A reconnaissance variant had four cameras in a reprofiled nose. F-5A/B production ended in June 1972.

Several countries have upgraded their F-5A/B fleets, including Canada, Venezuela and Norway. Canada's upgrade was comprehensive but its CF-5s had been retired by 1996 and offered for sale with Botswana purchasing 13. Other F-5A/B operators in 2000 were Brazil, Greece, Morocco, the Philippines, Saudi Arabia, South Korea, Spain, Thailand and Turkey.

Photo: Canadair built NF-5A of the 'Turkish Stars' display team. (D Fraser)

Northrop F-5E Tiger II

Country of origin: USA.

Type: Single seat lightweight multirole fighter.

Powerplants: Two 3500lb (15.6kN) dry/5000lb (22.2kN) with after-burner General Electric J85-GE-21B turbojets.

Dimensions: Wing span (without tip mounted AAMs) 8.13m (26ft 8in); length 14.45m (47ft 5in); height 4.08m (13ft 4¹/₂in); wing area 17.3m² (186sq ft).

Weights: Empty 4350kg (9558lb); max takeoff 11,187kg (24,664lb).

Armament: Two 20mm cannon in nose; two wingtip, one centreline and four underwing hardpoints for max 3175kg (7000lb) ordnance including Sidewinder AAMs, bombs, rockets, cluster bombs and ASMs.

Performance: Max speed 940kt (Mach 1.63/1741km/h) at 36,090ft, 654kt (Mach 0.99/1211km/h) at sea level; max climb 34,300ft (10,455m)/min; service ceiling 51,800ft; combat radius with two Sidewinder AAMs 760nm (1407km); max ferry range 2010nm (3723km).

Production: 2626 F-5s of all versions (including licence production) including 1171 F-5E, 12 RF-5E and 244 F-5F.

Notes: Northrop's F-5E Tiger II was selected as the USA's International Fighter Aircraft (IFA) competition winner for a lightweight fighter for export, the USAF having begun considering a successor to the F-5A in 1968 to continue the Military Assistance Program.

Northrop began work on an improved F-5 as a private venture, this resulting in the first flight of a converted F-5A prototype powered by two GE J85-GE-21 turbojets in March 1969. This aircraft was submit-ted for the IFA competition and announced the winner in further devel-oped form as the F-5E Tiger II in November 1970 after being evaluated against other US fighters including versions of the F-8 Crusader, F-104 Starfighter and F-4 Phantom.

Compared with the F-5A, the F-5E Tiger II featured more powerful engines, larger wings with leading edge root extensions, a wider and reprofiled fuselage, additional internal fuel, permanent wingtip AAM stations and more modern and capable avionics and systems. The first F-5E flew on 11 August 1972 and the first F-5F two seater on 25 September 1974. The RF-5E Tigereye reconnaissance version had four cameras in a modified nose section.

The F-5E/F series was delivered to 24 nations between 1976 and 1986 with licence production undertaken in Taiwan, South Korea and Switzerland. The USAF and USN used it for 'aggressor' training. Several upgrades involving new radar, avionics and systems have been offered, including by IAI which upgraded Chilean aircraft and by Northrop Grumman.

The ultimate F-5 development was the F-5G, or F-20 Tigershark, powered by a single 17,000lb (75.6kN) with afterburner General Electric F404 turbofan for substantially higher performance and fitted with upgraded radar, avionics and cockpit, plus structural and aerodynamic enhancements. The first of three privately funded pro-totypes flew on 30 August 1982 but the relaxation of export restric-tions on the F-16 and selection of the F-16 as the USAF's new air defence fighter badly damaged sales prospects and the F-20 was cancelled in 1986.

Photo: F-5E Tiger.

Northrop Grumman B-2 Spirit

Country of origin: USA.

Type: 2-3 crew low observable strategic bomber

Powerplants: Four 17,300lb (77.0kN) General Electric F118-GE-110 turbofans.

Dimensions: Wing span 52.43m (172ft 0in); length 21.03m (69ft 0in); height 5.18m (17ft 0in); wing area approx 477.5m² (5140sq ft).

Weights: Empty 69,718kg (153,700lb); typical takeoff 152,636kg (336,500lb).

Armament: Two side by side internal weapons bays for max 18,144kg (40,000lb) ordnance; two rotary launcher assemblies (RLAs), one in each bomb bay to carry 16 AGM-129 ACMs or 16 B61 tactical/strategic or B83 strategic freefall nuclear bombs; alternative loads include 80 227kg (500lb) bombs, 16 JDAMs or 16 GAMs.

Performance: Max speed approx 459kt (850km/h) above 36,000ft, 495kt (917km/h) at sea level; max cruise 448kt (829km/h) at 37,000ft; economical cruise 300-320kt (555-593km/h); service ceiling 50,000ft; range with 16,920kg (37,300lb) warload 6300nm (11,670km) hi-hi-hi or 4400nm (8150km) hi-lo-hi; range with 10,886kg (24,000lb) warload 6600nm (12,225km) hi-hi-hi or 4500nm (8335km) hi-lo-hi.

Production: 21.

Notes: Highly controversial for its more than $US45bn development and production costs, the B-2 Spirit strategic penetration stealth bomber was designed from the outset to be near invisible to radar. The Advanced Technology Bomber (ATB) programme for a new strategic bomber incorporating low observable or stealth technology was launched in 1978, and a Northrop design was selected in June 1981.

Only the existence of the programme and that the aircraft was a flying wing design had been officially recognised until the B-2 was publicly rolled out in November 1988. First flight was on 17 July 1989. The USAF originally planned to acquire 133 B-2s, although its cost and the end of the Cold War has seen this figure reduced to only 21 including the prototype.

The B-2A's flying wing design harks back to Northrop's revolutionary post war XB-35 and XB-49 (which see), and features a 'double W' trailing edge with eight flying control surfaces. The flying wing design has an inherently low radar cross section, and the airframe is largely constructed of graphite/epoxy, which forms a honeycomb radar absorbent structure. Exterior surfaces are designed to minimise radar returns and heat radiation.

Other features include four General Electric F118-GE-110 turbofans (modified and non afterburning versions of the F110), fly-by-wire flight controls, two side by side internal weapons bays, a Raytheon APQ-181 low probability of intercept radar (for terrain following and last minute target position updates) behind two dielectric panels beneath the nose, and an estimated internal fuel capacity of up to 90 tonnes. Initial operational capability was achieved in April 1997.

B-2 production ended in 1997, with all aircraft upgraded to full Block 30 standards (within enhanced weapons capability and avionics) by mid 2000. The B-2 made its combat debut in the Kosovo campaign in 1999 flying non stop missions from the USA and dropping a total of 454 tonnes of GPS guided bombs.

Photo: B-2A Spirit. (Northrop)

Panavia Tornado IDS

Countries of origin: United Kingdom, Germany and Italy.

Type: Two seat strike/ground attack aircraft.

Powerplants: Two 9100lb (40.5kN) dry/16,075lb (71.5kN) with afterburner Turbo-Union RB199-34R Mk 103 turbofans.

Dimensions: Wing span 13.91m (45ft 7½in) fully extended or 8.60m (28ft 2½in) fully swept; length 16.72m (54ft 9½in); height 5.95m (19ft 6in); wing area 26.6m² (286sq ft).

Weights: Empty 14,000kg (30,864lb); max takeoff 28,000kg (61,7280lb).

Armament: Two 27mm cannon; three underfuselage and four underwing hardpoints for max 9000kg (19,841lb) ordnance including AAMs, conventional and laser guided bombs, anti radiation missiles, nuclear bombs, area denial weapons and anti ship missiles.

Performance: Max speed 1263kt (Mach 2.2/2339km/h) clean or 1033kt (Mach 1.8/1914km/h) with weapons above 36,000ft; interdiction combat radius 600nm (1112km) lo-lo-lo or 800nm (1482km) hi-lo-lo-hi; combat radius (maritime attack hi-lo-lo-hi) 700nm (1296km); ferry range 2100nm (3890km).

Production: 986 Tornados of all versions incl 789 IDS variants.

Notes: A veteran of combat over Iraq and Kosovo/Yugoslavia, the Tornado is western Europe's most important strike aircraft. It resulted from a late 1960s study for a strike aircraft conducted by Belgium, Germany, Italy, the Netherlands and the UK. Belgium and the Netherlands subsequently withdrew. The Panavia consortium was formed in March 1969 to develop the aircraft, initially dubbed the MRCA (Multi Role Combat Aircraft).

The Tornado features variable geometry wings, two Turbo-Union RB199 engines (developed specifically by a consortium of Rolls-Royce, MTU and FiatAvio), a Texas Instruments radar with terrain following and ground mapping, fly-by-wire and digital INS.

The IDS (interdiction/strike) version was the first to be developed, the first of nine prototypes flying on 14 August 1974. Production aircraft were delivered from June 1979, initially to Britain and Germany with Italy's first aircraft following in September 1981. IDS deliveries were: Germany 357 (210 IDS and 35 ECR versions for the Luftwaffe, 112 IDS for the navy); Italy 99; RAF 228 and Saudi Arabia 96. The last (Saudi) Tornado was delivered in 1998.

UK aircraft were designated GR.1 and featured a laser rangefinder in an undernose pod, while their engines were downrated to extend life. Twelve GR.1As are used for reconnaissance and are fitted with a BAe SLIR (side looking infrared) and Vinten IR linescan. The 24 converted GR.1Bs are used for maritime strike and can carry up to five Sea Eagle anti ship missiles. The GR.4 upgrade (involving 142 GR.1s) comprises a new HUD, undernose FLIR, new avionics and ECM. Redeliveries began in October 1997.

Italy and Germany are upgrading their IDS aircraft under the MLI (Mid Life Improvement) programme with FLIR, ECM and new avionics. The Tornado ECR (Electronic Combat Reconnaissance) for Germany and Italy is a dedicated Suppression of Enemy Air Defence (SEAD) variant of the IDS fitted with an Emitter Location System (ELS) and can fire the AGM-88 HARM. Guns are not fitted to the ECRs.

Photo: Luftwaffe Tornado IDS. (Luftwaffe)

Panavia Tornado ADV

Countries of origin: United Kingdom, Germany and Italy.

Type: Two seat air defence fighter/interceptor.

Powerplants: Two 9100lb (40.5kN) dry/16,520lb (73.5kN) with afterburner Turbo-Union RB199-34R Mk 104 turbofans.

Dimensions: Wing span 13.91m (45ft 7¹/₂in) fully extended or 8.60m (28ft 2¹/₂in) fully swept; length 18.62m (61ft 1in); height 5.95m (19ft 6in); wing area 26.6m² (286sq ft).

Weights: Empty 14,500kg (31,966lb); max takeoff 28,000kg (61,728lb).

Armament: One 27mm cannon; four underfuselage Skyflash AAMs and two AIM-9L Sidewinders on each underwing pylon; Italian aircraft modified to carry Alenia Aspide AAMs under fuselage.

Performance: Max speed (clean) 1263kt (Mach 2.2/2339km/h) at 40,000ft, 792kt (Mach 1.2/1468km/h) at sea level; time to 30,000ft less than 2min; service ceiling approx 60,000ft; point intercept combat radius 200nm (370km) supersonic or 900nm (1667km) subsonic; combat air patrol endurance 3hrs at 300nm (555km) from base.

Production: 986 Tornados of all versions including 3 prototypes and 194 production ADV.

History: A fighter version of the Tornado had always been part of the aircraft's planning, and a feasibility study of an Air Defence Variant (ADV) was first conducted before the Panavia consortium was formally established. The Tornado ADV was subsequently selected to meet the UK's 1971 requirement for an air defence fighter armed with the BAe Skyflash medium range air-to-air missile and fitted with an advanced radar. Formal development of the Tornado ADV was authorised in March 1976.

The first of three ADV prototypes flew on 27 October 1979 with the first delivery to the RAF occurring in November 1985. Compared with the Tornado IDS, the ADV features a lengthened fuselage allowing the carriage of four Skyflash missiles in semi recessed stations under the fuselage and increased internal fuel capacity.

The ADV features GEC-Marconi Foxhunter radar, which was designed to track up to 20 targets while scanning, with a search range of up to 100nm (185km). Development of the radar was troubled and early production Tornado F.2s and F.3s were fitted with units which did not meet the full RAF requirement. Full specification Foxhunters were available from 1989, while all radars are being upgraded to an improved standard with a new data processor.

The RAF ordered 170 Tornado ADVs, the first 18 of which were delivered to an interim F.2 standard with RB199 Mk.103 engines (as fitted to the Tornado IDS), while the definitive F.3 features the more powerful RB199 Mk 104. The F.2s have been retired from service. About 100 F.3s are being modified to carry ASRAAM and AIM-120 missiles. The last Tornado F.3 was delivered to the RAF in March 1993.

Saudi Arabia is the only Tornado ADV export customer, with 24 delivered from February 1989. Saudi and RAF Tornados ADVs flew combat air patrols during the Gulf War, but without seeing any action. Italy began leasing 24 RAF Tornado F.3s from 1995 (modified to fire the Alenia Aspide AAM) to bolster its fighter force pending the delivery of the Eurofighter.

Photo: Saudi Tornado ADV. (BAe)

Republic F-84B/C/D Thunderjet

Country of origin: USA.

Type: Single seat fighter-bomber.

Powerplant: One 4000lb (17.8kN) Allison J35-A-15C/13C turbojet.

Dimensions: Wing span 11.10m (36ft 5in); length 11.40m (37ft 5in); height 3.91m (12ft 10in); wing area 24.1m² (260sq ft).

Weights: F-84B – empty 4326kg (9538lb); max takeoff 8931kg (19,689lb). F-84D – empty 4472kg (9860lb); max takeoff 9106kg (20,076lb).

Armament: Four 0.50in machine guns in nose and two in wings; 32 5in (12.7cm) rockets or two 454kg (1000lb) bombs under wings.

Performance: F-84B – max speed 510kt (945km/h) at 4000ft; initial climb 4210ft (1283m)/min; service ceiling 40,750ft; range with drop tanks 1114nm (2063km). F-84D – max speed 510kt (945km/h); initial climb 4060ft (1237m)/min; range with drop tanks 1041nm (1928km).

Production: 4457 Thunderjets of all versions including 3 XP-84, 15 YP-84A, 226 F-84B, 191 F-84C and 154 F-84D.

Notes: Conceived in 1944 as a jet successor to the P-47 Thunderbolt, the F-84 Thunderjet was the last subsonic straight winged fighter to see operational service with the USAF. Regarded as lacking the necessary agility to be a pure fighter, it was developed as a fighter-bomber, seeing extensive service in the Korean War, often in the escort role. It was also the first single seat fighter-bomber capable of carrying a tactical nuclear weapon.

Designed around the General Electric TG-180 (J35) turbojet under the company designation AP-23, the Thunderjet was a simple 'straight though airflow' design with nose intake. Three XP-84 prototypes were ordered in November 1944 and 100 pre series/production aircraft in January 1945. The first XP-84 flew on 28 February 1946. The third XP-84 had an Allison built J35, this powering all subsequent Thunderjets.

The first of 15 pre series YP-84As (YF-84A from mid 1948) was delivered to the USAF in February 1947, these differing from the prototypes in having six (rather than four) guns and provision for tip tanks. The F-84B (delivered from August 1947) was the first operational model with guns which fired at a higher rate and provision for underwing rockets. The F-84C (May 1948) was similar but for a new electrical system and a different but similarly rated J35 variant.

Both the F-84B and C were retired from USAF front line service by the end of 1952, replaced by the F-84D with thicker wing and aileron skins, modified undercarriage with mechanical instead of hydraulic compression linkages, a 'winterised' fuel system, jettisonable instead of retractable ordnance racks, and lightweight fuel cells. F-84D deliveries began in November 1948 and ended in April 1949.

The F-84D and F-84E (see next entry) were the first Thunderjet variants to serve in Korea, aircraft of the USAF's 27th Fighter Escort Group flying their initial combat missions of the war on 6 December 1950. A further 102 F-84Ds were sent to Korea in 1952 as replacements for the F-84Es which had been lost. F-84Ds were subsequently flown by the Air National Guard and retired in 1957.

Photo: F-84B Thunderjet. (Keith Myers)

Republic F-84E/G Thunderjet

Country of origin: USA.

Type: Single seat fighter-bomber.

Powerplant: F-84E – one 5000lb (22.2kN) Allison J35-A-17D turbojet. F-84G – one 5600lb (24.9kN) Allison J35-A-29 turbojet.

Dimensions: Wing span 11.10m (36ft 5in); length 11.61m (38ft 1in); height 3.83m (12ft 7in); wing area 24.1m² (260sq ft).

Weights: F-84E – empty 4987kg (10,995lb); max takeoff 10,189kg (22,463lb). F-84G – empty 5033kg (11,095lb); max takeoff 10,671kg (23,525lb).

Armament: Four 0.50in machine guns in nose and two in wings; max 2041kg (4500lb) external ordnance including bombs, rockets and drop tanks.

Performance: F-84G – max speed 540kt (1000km/h) at sea level, 500kt (925km/h) at 20,000ft; initial climb 4050ft (1234m)/min; time to 35,000ft 9.4min; service ceiling 40,500ft; range (internal fuel) 582nm (1078km); max ferry range 1738nm (3219km).

Production: 4457 Thunderjets of all versions including 843 F-84E and 3025 F-84G.

Notes: The F-84D Thunderjet was regarded as an interim type by the USAF pending introduction of the extensively revised F-84E, the first example of which was flown on 18 May 1949.

Compared to its predecessor, the E featured a more powerful J35-A-17 engine, radar gunsight, improved tip tanks which were more suitable for combat use, increased internal fuel capacity, a modified fuel system allowing the carriage of drop tanks on the underwing bomb shackles, increased weights, a strengthened wing structure for a greater ordnance load and a slightly lengthened fuselage intended to provide more cockpit space. The F-84E also had provision for the attachment of Jet Assisted Takeoff (JATO) rockets.

The F-84E (along with the D) was the first Thunderjet variant sent to Korea from late 1950 and although the aircraft had been used by Tactical Air Command mainly as a fighter-bomber, the aircraft was initially assigned to B-29 Superfortress escort duties in Korea where it was quickly found to be no match for the MiG-15 in air-to-air combat. Ground attack operations made up the bulk of the Thunderjet's operations in Korea later in the war. The last F-84E was delivered in June 1951 and of the 843 built, 100 went to NATO countries, mainly France. The Air National Guard retired the F-84E in 1959.

The final Thunderjet variant was the F-84G, developed mainly due to delays with the swept wing F-84F Thunderstreak (see next entry). Delivered from mid 1951, the F-84G featured a further increase in power, flight refuelling equipment with the receptacle in the port wing leading edge (it was the first production fighter with this feature), an autopilot and provision to carry a tactical nuclear weapon as the first single seater with this capability.

The F-84G was built in larger numbers than any other Thunderjet variant and of the 3025 manufactured up to July 1953, no fewer than 2236 were delivered to foreign nations under the Mutual Defence Assistance Program (MDAP). Recipients were Denmark, France, Iran, Italy, the Netherlands, Norway, Portugal, Taiwan, Thailand and Yugoslavia. Portugal was the last Thunderjet operator, phasing out its F-84Gs in 1976.

Photo: F-84E Thunderjet.

Republic F-84F Thunderstreak

Country of origin: USA.

Type: Single seat fighter-bomber.

Powerplant: One 7220lb (32.1kN) Wright J65-W-3 (Armstrong Siddeley Sapphire) or 7800lb (34.7kN) J65-W-7 turbojet.

Dimensions: Wing span 10.24m (33ft 7¼in); length 13.23m (43ft 4¾in); height 4.57m (15ft 0in); wing area 30.2m² (325sq ft).

Weights: Empty 6189kg (13,645lb); normal loaded 12,156kg (26,800lb); max overload 12,700kg (28,000lb).

Armament: Four 0.50in machine guns in nose and two in wings; four underwing hardpoints for max 2722kg (6000lb) ordnance.

Performance: Max speed 604kt (1119km/h) at sea level, 572kt (1059km/h) at 20,000ft; initial climb 8200ft (2500m)/min; service ceiling 46,000ft; range (clean) 800nm (1480km); max ferry range 1860nm (3445km).

Production: 3 YF-84F, 2713 F-84F (2476 by Republic, 237 by General Motors) and 715 RF-84F, total 3431.

Notes: Republic began development of a swept wing version of the F-84 Thunderjet in 1949, the intention being to produce a new fighter-bomber with a high degree of commonality with the earlier versions by simply mating swept wings and tail surfaces to an F-84E fuselage. It was never as simple as that, the necessary redesign making what became the F-84F Thunderstreak a largely new aircraft designed around the much more powerful Wright J65 (licence built Armstrong Siddeley Sapphire) turbojet.

The new engine installation required a deeper and structurally redesigned fuselage to accommodate the larger air intake capacity needed to feed the Sapphire and the cockpit, canopy and upper fuselage were also completely new. The designation F-96A was originally applied until after the first aircraft flew and was subsequently changed to F-84F.

The first of three YF-84F prototypes (with a standard F-84E fuselage) flew on 3 June 1950 powered by an Allison J35; the second (first flight 14 February 1951) and subsequent aircraft were all powered by the J65/Sapphire and had the new fuselage design. The first production F-84F was flown on 22 November 1952 and deliveries to the USAF began in January 1954. Running changes included the introduction of an all flying tailplane during the production run and the more powerful J65-W-7 engine in the final batch. Production ended in 1958.

The J65-W-7 was also installed in the RF-84F Thunderflash tactical reconnaissance version with cameras in the nose and the engine intakes relocated to the wing roots, this configuration having been tested on the third YF-84F but rejected for the fighter versions. The first RF-84F flew in February 1952 and deliveries started in March 1954.

The USAF's Tactical Air Command transferred its last F-84F to the Air National Guard in June 1964, the ANG operating some until late 1971 and a few RFs until 1972. Over 1300 F-84Fs and nearly 400 RF-84Fs were supplied to NATO nations including Belgium, France, Italy, Germany and the Netherlands. Greece and Turkey operated second hand examples well into the 1970s.

Photo: F-84F Thunderjet.

Republic F-105B Thunderchief

Country of origin: USA.

Type: Single seat fighter-bomber.

Powerplant: One 16,000lb (71.2kN) dry/23,500lb (104.5kN) with afterburner Pratt & Whitney J75-P-5 or 16,100lb (71.6kN) dry/24,500lb (109.0kN) with afterburner J75-P-19 turbojet.

Dimensions: Wing span 10.64m (34ft 11in); length 19.23m (63ft 1in); height 5.99m (19ft 8in); wing area 35.8m² (385sq ft).

Weights: Empty 11,728kg (25,855lb); max takeoff 23,587kg (52,000lb).

Armament: One 20mm multi barrel cannon in nose; internal weapons bay for max 3629kg (8000lb) ordnance (although usually occupied by fuel tank) and one centreline and four underwing hardpoints for max 5443kg (12,000lb) ordnance.

Performance: Max speed 1204kt (Mach 2.1/2230km/h) at 36,000ft, 750kt (Mach 1.13/1390km/h) at sea level; max initial climb 35,000ft (10,668m/min); service ceiling 50,000ft; max ferry range 1936nm (3586km).

Production: 833 Thunderchiefs of all versions including 2 YF-105A, 75 F-105B and 3 JF-105B.

Notes: Developed as a supersonic successor to the F-84F Thunderstreak, the F-105 Thunderchief is regarded as one of the best tactical fighter-bombers of any era. USAF Tactical Air Command's primary strike aircraft during the 1960s and '70s, the 'Thud' was deployed to Vietnam just after the last example left the production line where it was extensively used as a bomber including bearing the brunt of operations into the North. By the 1970s it was capable of delivering no fewer than 6700 combinations of weapons including all US tactical missiles and bombs.

Development began during the Korean War as a private venture and the design that emerged was of a large and heavy single seater capable of Mach 2 and carrying up to 5443kg (12,000lb) of ordnance, both externally and in a fuselage weapons bay. Originally, the intended primary mission was to deliver a tactical nuclear weapon carried in the internal bay, but in practice the bay was rarely used (for any weapon) and a fuel tank was usually installed instead.

A single engined configuration was chosen, this necessitating fitting the most powerful available powerplant, the Pratt & Whitney J75 turbojet. Other features included low speed ailerons and high speed spoilers for roll control, full span leading edge flaps, provision for flight refuelling and an automatic flight control system.

After some contract changes and cuts in planned numbers due to the end of the Korean War, the first of two YF-105A prototypes flew on 22 October 1955, the aircraft exceeding Mach 1 during the sortie. It and the second YF-105A were both powered by a 15,000lb (66.7kN) with afterburner Pratt & Whitney J57 engine due to the J75 not being ready. The first F-105B with the J75, new forward swept variable geometry intakes and modified fuselage flew on 24 May 1957 and first delivery to the USAF was a year later. Three were completed as RF-105Bs (later JF-105B) tactical photo-reconnaissance aircraft with cameras in the nose.

F-105B production ended in 1960 in favour of the F-105D, the 'Bravo' model equipping only two squadrons of the 4th Tactical Fighter Wing which kept them until 1964 when they were swapped for Ds and passed onto the Air National Guard.

Photo: F-105B Thunderchief.

Republic F-105D/F Thunderchief

Country of origin: USA.

Type: Single seat (F-105D) fighter-bomber or two seat (F-105F) operational mission trainer and fighter-bomber.

Powerplant: One 17,200lb (76.5kN) dry/26,500lb (117.9kN) with afterburner and water injection Pratt & Whitney J75-P-19W turbojet.

Dimensions: F-105D – wing span 10.64m (34ft 11in); length 19.63m (64ft 5in); height 5.99m (19ft 8in); wing area 35.8m² (385sq ft). F-105F – length 21.22m (69ft 7½in); height 6.15m (20ft 2in).

Weights: F-105D – empty 12,474kg (27,500lb); max takeoff 23,967kg (52,838lb).

Armament: One 20mm multi barrel cannon in nose; max 6350kg (14,000lb) ordnance.

Performance: F-105D – max speed 1192kt (Mach 2.08/2208km/h) at 36,000ft, 726kt (Mach 1.1/1345km/h) at sea level; max initial climb 34,500ft (10,515m)/min; service ceiling 42,000ft; combat radius with 2900kg (6392lb) bomb load 622nm (1152km); ferry range 1917nm (3550km).

Production: 833 Thunderchiefs of all versions including 610 F-105D and 143 F-105F.

Notes: The F-105D was the definitive single seat version of the Thunderchief and had numerous modifications over its predecessor. These included the fitting of a more powerful J75-P-19W engine with water injection, modified intake ducting, strengthened structure and undercarriage, new search and ranging radar in a longer nose and enhanced all weather capability through a General Electric FC-5 fully integrated flight and fire control system.

The first F-105D flew on 9 June 1959, first delivery to the USAF was in September 1960 and after sorting out some problems, regular squadron service began in mid 1961. Successive production batches introduced equipment and avionics upgrades with earlier aircraft modified to the later standards.

The two seat F-105 was intended as a mission trainer with full combat capability, featuring a lengthened fuselage for tandem seating and taller fin. The first F-105F flew on 11 June 1963 and entered service the following December. From 1965, 86 F-105Fs were converted to 'Wild Weasel' anti radar detect and strike aircraft armed with Standard anti radiation missiles. The installation of AGM-78B missiles and other upgraded equipment resulted in the new designation F-105G. Wild Weasel Thunderchiefs were first deployed to Vietnam in mid 1966.

The last F-105F was handed over to the USAF in January 1965, shortly before the 'Thud' began operations over North Vietnam as the major part of the 'Rolling Thunder' bombing campaign. Between then and November 1968, some 350 Thunderchiefs were lost in combat or to operational accidents. Thunderchief single seater operations in Vietnam ended in November 1970 when the 355th TFW's F-105Ds returned to the USA, but the two seaters remained for a time flying Wild Weasel and other missions.

After Vietnam, the Thunderchief was gradually phased out of USAF front line service and passed onto Air National Guard and Air Force Reserve units. ANG use of the F-105F ended in 1983 while the last Reserve unit with the F-105D relinquished its Thuds in February 1984.

Photo: F-105G Wild Weasel.

Rockwell B-1B Lancer

Country of origin: USA.

Type: Four crew strategic bomber.

Powerplants: Four 17,000lb (75.6kN) dry/30,780lb (136.9kN) with afterburner General Electric F101-GE-102 turbofans.

Dimensions: Wing span 41.66m (136ft 8in) fully extended or 23.84m (78ft 2³/₄in) fully swept; length 44.42m (145ft 9in); height 10.24m (33ft 7in); wing area 181.1m² (1950sq ft).

Weights: Operating empty 87,091kg (192,000lb); max takeoff 216,367kg (477,000lb).

Armament: Max internal weapons load of 34,020kg (75,000lb) in three weapons bays, normal load 19,050-29,030kg (42,000-64,000lb) including B-61 and B-83 thermonuclear bombs or on rotary launchers up to eight AGM-86B ALCMs; 24 AGM-69A short range attack missiles (SRAM-As); 12 B-28, 28 B-61 or 28 B-93 free fall nuclear bombs; up to 84 500lb (227kg) Mk 82 conventional bombs and CBU-87/-89/-97 cluster bombs. Upgrade to carry JDAMs, JSOWs and JASSMs being carried out.

Performance: Max speed 717kt (Mach 1.25/1329km/h) at high altitude, low level penetration speed over 520kt (963km/h); service ceiling over 50,000ft; range approx 6480nm (12,000km).

Production: 4 B-1A and 100 B-1B, total 104.

Notes: The USA's most numerically important strategic bomber, the B-1 had to endure criticisms of its high cost, cancellation, reinstatement, a 20 year gestation period and early operational serviceability problems. The B-1 resulted from the USAF's Advanced Manned Strategic Aircraft (AMSA or, as it became known, 'America's Most Studied Airplane') programme of 1965 to find a low altitude supersonic penetration nuclear bomber to replace the Boeing B-52.

A North American Rockwell design was eventually selected for further development in 1970. The first of four B-1A prototypes first flew on 23 December 1974 but in 1977 new US President Jimmy Carter cancelled planned B-1A production (the USAF hoped to acquire 244) but test flying continued. The B-1 was resurrected in 1981 when Ronald Reagan was installed as US President and 100 revised production aircraft, designated B-1B, were ordered.

Compared with the B-1A, the B-1B Lancer (first flight 18 October 1984) features improved avionics and systems, incorporation of some low observable features such as RAM coatings, optional weapons bay fuel tanks, external underfuselage hardpoints for fuel and weapons, ejection seats rather than a crew escape capsule, fixed rather than variable air inlets (limiting top speed to Mach 1.25 rather than the B-1A's Mach 2.3) with ducting masking the engines from radar.

The B-1B's primary mission remained low level penetration, its offensive systems based around the APG-164 radar for navigation and terrain following, with a low observable phased array antenna. The core of the defensive systems is the Eaton ALQ-161 upgradable ECM suite. The last B-1B was delivered in April 1988. Upgrades are being undertaken to equip the Lancer with precision conventional weapons. The B-1B was used operationally over Iraq in 1998 and Kosovo/Serbia in 1999, but not during the Gulf War, allegedly because its crews were "not proficient in conventional ordnance delivery".

Photo: B-1B Lancer. (Bill Lines)

Saab 21

Country of origin: Sweden.

Type: Single seat fighter.

Powerplant: 21A – one 1475hp (1100kW) Daimler-Benz DB605B inverted V12; three bladed propeller. 21RA – one 3000lb (13.3kN) de Havilland Goblin II turbojet. 21RB – one 3305lb (14.7kN) SFA built Goblin III.

Dimensions: 21A – wing span 11.61m (38ft 1in); length 10.44m (34ft 3in); height 4.00m (13ft 1¹/₂in); wing area 22.2m² (239sq ft). 21R – wing span 11.38m (37ft 4in); length 10.56m (34ft 8in); height 2.94m (9ft 8in); wing area 22.3m² (240sq ft).

Weights: 21A – empty 3250kg (7165lb); max takeoff 4413kg (9730lb). 21RB – empty 3112kg (6861lb); max takeoff 5033kg (11,096lb).

Armament: 21A – one 20mm cannon in nose and four 13.2mm machine guns (two in nose, two in wings). 21B – guns plus external pack of eight 8mm machine guns or eight 14.5cm rockets.

Performance: 21B – max speed 346kt (640km/h); initial climb 2955ft (900m)/min; max range 810nm (1500km). 21RB – max speed 432kt (800km/h); initial climb 3346ft (1020m)/min; service ceiling 39,370ft; range 388nm (720km).

Production: 300 J21A and 60 J21R.

Notes: A rarity in that it was produced in both piston and jet engined forms, the conceptually innovative Saab 21 was developed during WWII as a fighter for Swedish service. Its 'pod and twin booms' configuration was highly unusual for a single engined combat aircraft, with the propulsion provided by a Daimler-Benz DB605 inverted V12 engine mounted in the rear of the fuselage pod and driving a pusher propeller. The 21 was also the world's second operational fighter to be fitted with an ejection seat, behind the Heinkel He 219.

The first of three prototypes flew on 30 July 1943 and deliveries of production aircraft (as the J 21A) to the Flygvapnet began in July 1945 with production continuing until January 1949. Variants were the initial J 21A-1, J 21A-2 with minor changes and A 21-3 optimised for the attack role.

The decision to adapt the J 21 to jet power was taken in 1945, the de Havilland Goblin the chosen powerplant. Four J 21A-1 airframes were converted as prototypes, the first of them flying as the Saab 21R on 10 March 1947. About 50 per cent airframe commonality was retained from the original piston engined version, changes including moving the tailplane to the top of the redesigned twin fins to clear the jet efflux, shortening the undercarriage (propeller clearance was no longer a problem), fitting a wider rear fuselage pod to accommodate the jet engine and strengthening the structure to cope with higher speeds.

The 21R entered Swedish service in early 1950 but was disappointing, having a low critical Mach number, poor manoeuvrability and a very short endurance. The original order was cut from 120 to 60 comprising 30 each of the J 21RA with British built Goblin II and J 21RB with a more powerful Svenska Flygmotor built Goblin III. They had short careers as fighters, being quickly converted to A 21R attack aircraft, but even that career was short lived and the type was withdrawn from service during 1954.

Photo: Saab J 21A-1.

Saab 29

Country of origin: Sweden.

Type: Single seat fighter-bomber.

Powerplant: 29A-C – one 5005lb (22.2kN) Svenska Flygmotor RM2 (de Havilland Ghost) turbojet. 29D-F – one 6173lb (27.5kN) with afterburner RM2B.

Dimensions: Wing span 11.00m (36ft 1in); length 10.13m (33ft 2½in); height 3.75m (12ft 3½in); wing area 24.1m² (259sq ft).

Weights: 29A – empty 4300kg (9479lb); max takeoff 6060kg (13,360lb). 29F – empty 4845kg (10,681lb); max takeoff 8375kg (18,463lb).

Armament: Four 20mm cannon in nose; two Sidewinder AAMs on J 29F; max 500kg (1102lb) underwing ordnance on ground attack versions.

Performance: 29A – max speed 572kt (1060km/h) at low level; initial climb 7500ft (2286m)/min; service ceiling 45,000ft; range (internal fuel) 704nm (1304km); max ferry range 1457nm (2700km). 29F – max speed 572kt (1060km/h) at low level; initial climb 11,810ft (3600m)/min; service ceiling 50,850ft; max ferry range 1458nm (2700km).

Production: 661 of all versions.

Notes: The first of Saab's long line of advanced and versatile multirole jet fighters and Europe's first swept wing jet fighter to attain service, the Saab 29's portly appearance quickly earned it the universally accepted nickname 'Tunnan', meaning 'barrel'.

Design work began in 1945 and was completed the following year, chief design engineer Lars Brising coming up with a nose intake configuration with exhaust exiting below the tail surfaces, a wing with 25 degrees of sweep and power provided by a de Havilland Ghost centrifugal flow turbojet built under licence by Svenska Flygmotor (SFA) as the RM2.

The first of three prototypes flew on 1 September 1948 and deliveries of the initial production J 29A fighter (224 built) began in May 1951. Subsequent early versions were the J 29B (first flight March 1953, 360 built) with provision to carry external ordnance and drop tanks and the unarmed reconnaissance S 29C (first flight June 1953) of which 76 were delivered.

Even as the 'Tunnan' was entering service it was realised that the RM2/Ghost powerplant was obsolescent. SFA set about extending its usefulness by designing an afterburner which would boost power by about 20 per cent. As the RM2B, the new engine was tested on a small batch of Saab 29Ds from March 1954 and fitted to 29 modified earlier aircraft as the J 29E, these also featuring a revised wing with 'sawtooth' leading edge.

Both these features were incorporated in the final production 29F which was built in J 29F fighter and A 29F ground attack versions. The J 29F was later upgraded to carry a pair of Sidewinder air-to-air missiles under the wings and more than 300 earlier models were modified to F standards in the late 1950s. The reconnaissance S 29Cs were also fitted with the new wing.

Production ended in March 1956 but despite a gradual decline in numbers over nearly two decades, the last 29 were not retired from *Flygvapnet* service until August 1976. Austria purchased 30 ex Swedish J 29Fs in two batches between 1961 and 1964, these remaining in service until 1970-72.

Photo: Saab J 29A.

Saab 32 Lansen

Country of origin: Sweden.

Type: Two seat attack and all weather fighter.

Powerplant: 32A/C – one 7628kg (33.9kN) dry/10,362lb (46.1kN) with afterburner Svenska Flygmotor RM5A2 (Rolls-Royce Avon 100) turbojet. 32B – 10,560lb (47.0kN) dry/15,190lb (67.6kN) with afterburner RM6A (Avon 200) turbojet.

Dimensions: Wing span 13.00m (42ft 7¾in); length 14.95m (49ft 0¾in); height 4.65m (15ft 3in); wing area 37.4m² (403sq ft).

Weights: 32A – empty 7438kg (16,398lb); max takeoff 13,000kg (28,660lb). 32B – empty 7983kg (17,600lb); max takeoff 13,500kg (29,762lb).

Armament: 32A – four 20mm cannon in nose; four underwing pylons for max 1360kg (3000lb) ordnance including bombs, rockets and ASMs. 32B – four 30mm cannon and four Sidewinder AAMs.

Performance: 32A – max speed 601kt (1114km/h) at sea level; initial climb 11,810ft (3600m)/min; service ceiling 49,200ft; range with max bomb load and drop tanks 956nm (1770km); ferry range 1738nm (3219km). 32B – max speed 533kt (988km/h) at 36,000ft; max climb 19,685ft (6000m)/min; service ceiling 52,500ft; range 1080nm (2000km).

Production: 450 of all versions including 280 A 32A and 140 J 32B.

Notes: A true multirole fighter which preceded similarly versatile aircraft from the rest of Western Europe by several years, the Lansen (Lance) was developed to fill three specific missions: all weather attack, night and all weather interception and reconnaissance. All Lansen variants were two seaters and all were powered by licence built versions of the afterburning Rolls-Royce Avon. Supersonic in a dive, the Lansen quickly developed a good reputation for its ease of flying, low maintenance burden and accurate weapons delivery.

Go ahead for the Saab 32 was given in December 1948 and four prototypes ordered. The first of them flew on 3 November 1952. The first production model was the A 32A all weather attack version powered by an RM5A2 (Avon 100) engine. The first production examples were delivered to the *Flygvapnet* in December 1955 and deliveries continued until May 1958 when it was replaced on the production line by the J 32B all weather and night fighter. The S 32C dedicated reconnaissance version was based on the A 32A and first flown on 26 March 1957.

The first J 32B flew on 7 January 1957 and deliveries began in July 1958. This was the final Lansen variant built with the last example delivered in May 1960. Apart from the necessary armament changes due to its role, the J 32B differed from the A 32A in having the more powerful RM6A (Avon 200) engine with larger air intakes, new avionics, new interception radar, 30mm instead of 20mm cannon and structural modifications to allow for the different manoeuvring loads imposed by air combat.

The J 32B was retired from front line service in 1973 but two converted versions (J 32D target tug and J 32E electronic warfare 'aggressor' training aircraft) were not withdrawn until 1997. The S 32C and A 32A remained on strength well into the 1970s. Surprisingly given its capabilities, no new or second hand Lansens were exported.

Photo: Saab J 32E conversion. (Paul Merritt)

Saab 35 Draken

Country of origin: Sweden.

Type: Single seat multirole fighter.

Powerplant: 35A/B – one 10,780lb (47.9kN) dry/14,407lb (64.1kN) with afterburner Volvo Flygmotor RM6B (Rolls-Royce Avon Mk.48A) turbojet. 35D/E/F/J/X – one 12,790lb (56.9kN) dry/17,650lb (78.5kN) with afterburner RM6C (Avon Mk.60) turbojet.

Dimensions: Wing span 9.40m (30ft 10in); length 15.35m (50ft 4in); height 3.89m (12ft 9in); wing area 49.2m² (530sq ft).

Weights: 35X – empty 8250kg (18,188lb); max takeoff 16,000kg (35,273lb).

Armament: 35X – one or two 30mm cannon in wing/s; four underwing and two underfuselage hardpoints for max 2722kg (6000lb) ordnance including rockets, bombs and AAMs.

Performance: 35X – max speed (clean) 1148kt (Mach 2.0/2126km/h) at 36,000ft; max climb 34,450ft (10,500m)/min; time to 36,000ft 2.6min; combat radius (internal fuel) hi-lo-hi 343nm (635km) or 541nm (1003km) with drop tanks; max ferry range 1755nm (3250km).

Production: 3 prototypes, 89 J 35A, 72 J 35B, 120 J 35D, 30 S 35E, 230 J 35F, 20 35XD, 20 RF35, 11 TF35, 12 35XS, total 607.

Notes: The remarkable Draken (Dragon) was developed to meet a demanding 1949 Swedish Air Force requirement for an advanced high performance interceptor to replace the Saab J 29. Among that requirement's specifications was a speed of at least Mach 1.5 and the ability to use existing airfields.

Saab's design team used an unusual double delta wing to provide the required performance and to have much shorter airfield length requirements than contemporaries such as the Mirage III. The double delta wing configuration was successfully test flown on the Saab 201 research aircraft before the first of three Draken prototypes (powered by a British built Avon) flew for the first time on 25 October 1955.

Initial production J 35A fighters were powered by the locally built RM6B (Avon Mk.48A) engine and delivered to the Swedish Air Force from December 1959. Of the 89 built, 25 were later converted to SK 35C tandem two seat conversion trainers. The J 35B (first flight November 1959, delivered from 1961) featured Saab's S7 fire control radar and a lengthened rear fuselage, while the J 35D (first flight December 1960) was powered by an uprated RM6C turbojet, as were all subsequent Drakens. The camera equipped S35E first flew in June 1963.

The final Swedish fighter Draken, the J 35F, represented a big advance and introduced a Hughes weapon system comprising a pulse doppler radar, automatic fire control system and Falcon AAMs. The J 35F-II has a Hughes infrared sensor. Sixty-six J 35Fs were upgraded to J 35J standards from 1987 and the last Swedish Drakens were retired in 1999.

The export 35X based on the J 35F was sold to Denmark as the 35XD and delivered 1970-72 (20 as the F-35 fighter, 20 reconnaissance R-35s and 11 TF-35 trainers); and Finland which bought 12 J 35XS and later ex 35 Swedish aircraft. Finland retired the last of its Drakens in August 2000, leaving Austria as the sole operator. Austria's 24 35OEs were rebuilt and upgraded ex Swedish J 35Ds, 24 of which were delivered 1987-89.

Photo: Saab J 35F Draken.

Saab 37 Viggen

Country of origin: Sweden.

Type: Single seat multirole fighter.

Powerplant: AJ 37 – one 14,750lb (65.6kN) dry/26,000lb (115.6kN) with afterburner Volvo Flygmotor RM8A turbofan. JA 37 – one 16,200lb (72.0kN) dry/28,110lb (125.0kN) with afterburner RM8B turbofan.

Dimensions: Wing span 10.60m (34ft 9¹/₂in); length (excl nose probe) 15.59m (51ft 2in); height 5.90m (19ft 4¹/₂in); wing area 46.0m² (495sq ft).

Weights: JA-37 – normal loaded 16,800kg (37,037lb); max takeoff 20,000kg (44,092lb).

Armament: JA 37 – one 30mm cannon in permanent underfuselage pack; four underwing and three underfuselage hardpoints for Sidewinder, Skyflash or AIM-120s AAMs.

Performance: JA 37 – max speed 1205kt (Mach 2.1/2232km/h) at 36,000ft, 790kt (Mach 1.2/1463km/h) at sea level; time to 32,800ft 1.6min; service ceiling 59,055ft; low altitude combat radius 270nm (500km); range (internal fuel) 1080nm (2000km). AJ 37 – tactical radius (hi-lo-hi) over 540nm (1000km).

Production: 7 prototypes, 110 AJ 37, 26 SF 37, 26 SH 37, 18 SK 37 and 149 JA 37, total 336.

Notes: The Viggen (Thunderbolt) was developed as the airborne component of Sweden's System 37 air defence network and to replace the Saab Lansen. Design considerations included Mach 2 performance at altitude, supersonic flight at low level and exceptional STOL performance.

To meet these requirements Saab utilised the then unconventional canard delta configuration. First flight was on 8 February 1967. The canards or foreplanes are fixed but have trailing edge flaps. The wing arrangement not only gives good agility but also excellent takeoff performance, allowing operations from damaged runways or sections of freeway. The Volvo Flygmotor RM8 engine is a licence built Pratt & Whitney JT8D, much modified to incorporate afterburning and an automatic thrust reverser, activated when the nosewheel oleo is compressed.

Initial production was of the AJ 37 Viggen (first delivered June 1971) optimised for ground attack but with a secondary interception role. It featured Ericsson PS-37/A radar, Saab digital nav/attack computer and HUD. The SF 37 (first flight May 1973) and SH 37 (first delivery June 1975) were reconnaissance variants, the latter with radar optimised for maritime reconnaissance with a secondary maritime strike role. The Sk 37 is the two seater trainer version.

Final production was of the extensively revamped JA 37 interceptor with an Ericsson PS-46/A multimode, doppler, look down/shoot down radar, Sky Flash and Sidewinder missile armament, an uprated RM8B engine and new avionics. The first production JA 37 flew on 4 November 1977 with deliveries starting in 1979. The last JA 37 was delivered in June 1990.

About 100 AJ, SH and SF 37s were modified to multirole AJS 37 standard with expanded weaponry and some new avionics, while from 2000, 65 JA 37s are being modified to JA 37Ds with upgraded radar, avionics and cockpit displays plus AIM-120 missile compatibility. With the arrival of the JAS 39 Gripen, the AJS 37 Viggens were withdrawn from regular service in April 2000 while the first JA 37s were also being retired.

Photo: JA 37 Viggen. (Paul Merritt)

Saab JAS 39 Gripen

Country of origin: Sweden.

Type: Single seat multirole fighter.

Powerplant: One 12,150lb (54.0kN) dry/18,110lb (80.5kN) with after-burner Volvo Aero Corporation RM12 (licence built General Electric F404) turbofan.

Dimensions: JAS 39A – wing span 8.40m (27ft 7in); length 14.10m (46ft 3in); height 4.50m (14ft 9in); wing area 30.0m² (323sq ft).

Weights: JAS 39A – operating empty 6622kg (14,600lb); max takeoff approx 14,000kg (30,864lb).

Armament: One 27mm cannon; two wingtip stations for AAMs; one centreline and four underwing hardpoints for rockets, cluster bomb dispensers, air-to-air, air-to-surface or anti shipping missiles; max ordnance 4500kg (9920lb).

Performance: Max speed over 1148kt (Mach 2.0/2126km/h) above 36,000ft; combat radius with max load approx 432nm (800km); unrefuelled range 1620nm (3000km).

Production: 5 prototypes and about 85 production Gripens by mid 2000.

Notes: Saab's sixth jet fighter, the (relatively) light weight and genuinely multirole Gripen (Griffin) is marketed as the first 'new generation' production combat aircraft. It was developed to replace the Swedish Air Force's Viggens and remaining Drakens.

Definition studies began in 1980, while Swedish Government programme approval and development funding (for five prototypes and 30 production aircraft) was given in June 1982. The IG JAS (Industry Group JAS) teaming of Saab, Volvo Aero Corporation, Ericsson and FFV Aerotech had meanwhile been formed in 1981 to develop and build the new aircraft.

From the outset it was recognised that the growing cost of new fighters meant the new design would be smaller than the Viggen and that it would be powered by a single engine. The General Electric F404 turbofan was selected for local development and production as the Volvo RM12, while other design features include a canard delta configuration, lateral instability with fly-by-wire, an Ericsson/GMAv PS-05/A pulse doppler multimode look down/shoot down radar with multiple target track-while-scan and ground mapping capabilities, and a modern cockpit with three multifunction displays, a wide angle HUD and HOTAS controls. Thirty per cent of the Gripen by weight is made of composites.

The first prototype flew on 9 December 1988 but crashed the following February due to fly-by-wire software problems. Four other prototypes were flown between May 1990 and October 1991, the first production aircraft in September 1992. First delivery was in June 1993 and official commissioning into Swedish service was in June 1996. The first Gripen squadron was declared operational in 1997, while deliveries are due to continue to 2007.

Two versions are in production for Sweden: the single seat JAS 39A fighter (176 on order) and JAS 39B two seater (28) which first flew on 29 April 1996. Future deliveries could be to JAS 39C/D standards with helmet mounted sight and IRST, and improved radar and EW. A phased array radar upgrade is also planned from around 2010. Saab is pursuing Gripen export sales in partnership with part owner BAE Systems with South Africa the launch export customer.

Photo: JAS 39 Grippen.

SEPECAT Jaguar

Countries of origin: United Kingdom and France.

Type: Single seat strike.

Powerplants: GR.1 – two 4620lb (20.5kN dry/7140lb (31.7kN) with afterburner Rolls-Royce Turboméca Adour Mk.103 turbofans. GR.1A/International – two 5320lb (23.7kN) dry/ 8040lb (35.8kN) with afterburner Adour Mk.104/804.

Dimensions: GR.1A – wing span 8.69m (28ft 6in); length (excl nose probe) 15.52m (50ft 11in); height 4.89m (16ft 0½in); wing area 24.1m² (260sq ft).

Weights: GR.1A – empty equipped 7700kg (16,975lb); max takeoff 15,700kg (34,612lb).

Armament: GR.1A – two 30mm cannon; two above wing pylons (for AAMs only), one centreline and four underwing hardpoints for max 4536kg (10,000lb) ordnance.

Performance: GR.1A – max speed 918kt (Mach 1.6/1700km/h) at 36,000ft; 726kt (Mach 1.1/1345km/h) at sea level; service ceiling 45,930ft; combat radius with internal fuel and 1814kg (4000lb) load 432nm (800km) hi-lo-hi or 324nm (600km) lo-lo-lo; combat radius with external fuel 760nm (1408km) hi-lo-hi or 495nm (917km) lo-lo-lo.

Production: 8 prototypes and 497 production Jaguars of all models plus 108 in India by HAL.

Notes: The world's first binational combat aircraft, the Jaguar was the result of a joint British/French requirement for an advanced jet trainer, the British originally specifying a supersonic aircraft and the French a subsonic and inexpensive trainer/attack aircraft.

After settling on a supersonic design, the programme was initiated in May 1965, the SEPECAT (*Société Européene de Production de l'Avion Ecole de Combat et d'Appui Tactique*) consortium of Breguet (design leader) and the British Aircraft Corporation (BAC) established in 1966 to build the aircraft, while Rolls-Royce and Turboméca teamed to develop the Adour turbofan engine.

The first of eight prototypes (a French two seater) first flew on 8 September 1968 and the first British aircraft (a single seater) on 12 October 1969. Deliveries to France began in May 1972 and to Britain in March 1974.

The 203 Jaguars delivered to the RAF comprised 165 GR.1 (Jaguar S) single seaters and 38 two seat T.2s (Jaguar B). The GR.1 (since upgraded to GR.1A standard with Adour Mk 104s) features an advanced nav/attack system and laser rangefinder in a chisel shaped nose. A further upgrade features laser designation pod compatibility, helmet mounted sight, improved ECM, a towed decoy system, new LCD screen in the cockpit and more powerful Adour Mk 106s.

France took delivery of 160 single seat Jaguar As and 40 Jaguar E trainers, these fitted with a less advanced nav/attack system and DEFA rather than Aden cannon. Some had an undernose laser rangefinder and others carry a laser designator pod for the AS.30L missile.

The Jaguar International with more powerful engines and provision for two overwing AAMs was marketed and built by BAe and first flew on 19 August 1976. Based on the GR.1, it was sold to Ecuador (12), Nigeria (18), Oman (24) and India (40) with a further 108 built in India by HAL as the Shamsher from 1982 with low rate production continuing in 2000. British and French production ended in 1985.

Photo: Jaguar GR.1A. (RAF)

Shenyang J-6/F-6

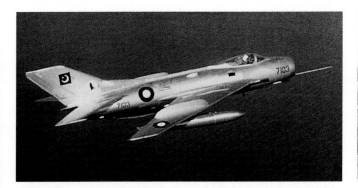

Countries of origin: China and Soviet Union.

Type: Single seat interceptor and ground attack fighter.

Powerplant: Two 5732lb (25.5kN) dry/7167lb (31.9kN) with afterburner Shenyang WP-6 (Tumansky R-9BF) turbojets.

Dimensions: Wing span 9.19m (30ft 2in); length 12.60m (41ft 4in); height 3.86m (12ft 8in); wing area 25.0m² (269sq ft).

Weights: Empty equipped 5760kg (12,700lb); normal loaded 7600kg (16,755lb); max takeoff 8700kg (19,180lb).

Armament: Three 30mm cannon in nose and wing roots; four underwing hardpoints for max 500kg (1102lb) ordnance including bombs, rockets and AAMs (Sidewinders on Pakistani aircraft).

Performance: Max speed 783kt (Mach 1.34/1450km/h) at 32,800ft; cruising speed 513kt (950km/h); max climb 22,638ft (6900m)/min; service ceiling 58,725ft; combat radius with external fuel 370nm (685km); normal range 750nm (1390km); ferry range 1188nm (1366km).

Production: Approximately 3000.

Notes: The Chinese built versions of the MiG-19 were manufactured in larger numbers than the original and widely exported. Manufacture of the J-6 lasted nearly three decades longer than the MiG-19 which was quickly superseded by the MiG-21.

The MiG-19 was selected for licence production in China initially by both the Shenyang and Nanchang Aircraft factories, the agreement signed in January 1958, about the same time production was ending in the Soviet Union.

The Chinese version was designated J-6 (or F-6 for export) the first true locally built aircraft (based on the MiG-19S clear weather fighter) flying on 30 September 1959. Soviet built aircraft had meanwhile been supplied in knocked down form before the deterioration of relations between the two countries. The first one to be assembled (a MiG-19P all weather fighter version) flew on 17 December 1958.

Production was at first sporadic and the build quality poor, but became more regular and of a better quality from 1966, by which time the J-6 had become the standard fighter in Chinese service. Equivalents to the MiG-19S (J-6) and MiG-19P (J-6A/B, including with locally developed air intercept radar) were built along with new versions including the J-6C improved multirole day fighter, JZ-6 high altitude reconnaissance aircraft and JJ-6 two seat fighter trainer with lengthened fuselage for tandem seating. This was the only two seat MiG-19 variant to achieve production. Production is believed to have ended in 1986.

The aircraft was exported as the F-6 (and two seat FT-6) and in 2000 it was still operated by Albania (32), Bangladesh (10), China (approx 650), Egypt (45), North Korea (120), Pakistan (95), Tanzania (10) and Zambia (12).

China offered the F-6 to Pakistan immediately after the Indo-Pakistani war of 1965 with deliveries of the first batch of 40 starting the following year. Pakistan eventually acquired 135, most of which were modified to carry two AIM-9 Sidewinder air-to-air missiles under the wings.

Photo: Pakistani Shenyang F-6.

Shenyang J-8/F-8

Country of origin: China.

Type: Single seat fighter-bomber.

Powerplants: J-8 II – two 9590lb (42.7kN) dry/14,815lb (65.9kN) with afterburner Liyang (Guizhou) WP13A II turbojets.

Dimensions: J-8 II – wing span 9.34m (30ft 8in); length 21.59m (70ft 10in); height 5.41m (17ft 9in); wing area 42.2m² (454sq ft).

Weights: J-8 II – empty 9820kg (21,649lb); max takeoff 17,800kg (39,242lb).

Armament: J-8 II – one 23mm cannon in underfuselage blister fairing; one centreline and six underwing hardpoints for PL-2B infrared guided AAMs, PL-7 medium range semi active radar guided AAMs, unguided air-to-air rockets, air-to-ground rockets and bombs.

Performance: J-8 II – max speed 1262kt (Mach 2.2/2338km/h) at 36,000ft; max initial climb 39,370ft (12,000m)/min; service ceiling 65,615ft; combat radius 432nm (800km); ferry range 1188nm (2200km).

Production: Estimated at approximately 150 of all versions.

Notes: China's J-8 and J-8 II interceptors have suffered from protracted and fitful development. The J-8 (NATO reporting name 'Finback') resulted from a 1964 requirement for a new interceptor with improved performance compared to the MiG-21. The resulting aircraft was a twin engined tailed delta with a nose air intake, ranging radar in the intake centrebody and a single piece forward opening canopy.

The first of two prototypes flew for the first time on 5 July 1969. Because of the upheaval of China's Cultural Revolution, initial production was not authorised until 1979 and first deliveries were nearly six years later. Only small numbers of J-8s were built, although an estimated 100 improved J-8 Is were delivered from 1985. The J-8 I featured a Sichuan SR-4 radar in an enlarged intake centrebody, conferring some all weather capability, plus some aerodynamic changes. First flight was on 24 April 1981.

Development of the much improved J-8 II began in 1981 and it first flew on 12 June 1984. The J-8 II introduced lateral air intakes (similar in configuration to the MiG-23) and a nose mounted radar. It features a ventral folding fin which extends after takeoff and conventional two piece canopy, and has a secondary ground attack role capability. Low rate production was continuing in 2000 and the aircraft is offered for export as the F-8 II.

The Peace Pearl program to fit the J-8 II with US avionics (integrated by Grumman) including the APG-66 radar and US ejection seat, HUD and INS, as well as a bubble canopy with a frameless windscreen, was suspended following the 1989 Tiananmen Square massacre. Two J-8 IIs had been delivered to Grumman in the US for conversion but were returned to China unmodified in 1993.

Shenyang is currently working on the F-8 IIM which is intended for export. It features more powerful 15,432lb (68.6kN) with afterburner WP13B turbojets, a Russian Phazotron Zhuk-8 II pulse Doppler radar and a modernised cockpit with a HUD, HOTAS controls, multifunction displays, INS and GPS. First flight was on 31 March 1996.

Photo: Shenyang F-8 II.

Singapore Aerospace Super Skyhawk

Countries of origin: USA and Singapore.

Type: Single seat ground attack.

Powerplant: One 10,800lb (48.0kN) General Electric F404-GE-100D turbofan.

Dimensions: Wing span 8.38m (27ft 6in); length 12.71m (41ft 8½in); height 4.57m (15ft 0in); wing area 24.1m² (260sq ft).

Weights: Operating empty 4649kg (10,250lb), max takeoff 10,206kg (22,500lb).

Armament: Two 20mm cannon in wing roots; one centreline and four underwing hardpoints for rockets, bombs, AIM-9 AAMs, AGM-65 ASMs and gun pods.

Performance: Max speed 609kt (1128km/h) at sea level; max cruising speed 445kt (824km/h) at 30,000ft; economical cruising speed 424kt (785km/h) at 35,000ft; max initial climb 10,913ft (3326m)/min; combat ceiling 40,000ft; range with max warload 625nm (1158km); range with max internal and external fuel 2046nm (3790km).

Production: 52 conversions.

Notes: Singapore's programme to upgrade the A-4 with a non after-burning General Electric F404-GE-100D turbofan and modern avionics has resulted in a Skyhawk variant with enhanced capabilities compared to the standard models.

The Republic of Singapore Air Force joined the ranks of McDonnell Douglas A-4 Skyhawk operators in 1970 when the first of 40 refurbished ex USN A-4Bs were delivered (as the A-4S). Lockheed upgraded the first eight aircraft, with the remainder modified locally by Singapore Aerospace.

The upgrade to A-4S standards involved installing a more powerful Wright J65-W-20 turbojet, spoilers and new nav/attack system. The two seat TA-4S Skyhawk conversion is unique in its installation of separate tandem cockpits. Further ex US Navy Skyhawks were delivered (16 A-4Bs in 1983 and 70 A-4Cs in 1980) and while most of these were broken down for spares, enough were converted to A-4S standards to allow the formation of an additional squadron.

In 1984 Singapore elected to further upgrade its Skyhawks to extend their service lives rather than replace them. Phase one of Singapore Aerospace's two phase Super Skyhawk program was developed with the assistance of Grumman and General Electric and involved installing the F404 turbofan, strengthening the structure to accommodate the new and heavier engine and modifying the air intakes.

The 27 per cent more powerful F404 provides a 15 per cent higher dash speed, 35 per cent greater climb rate, 40 per cent better level acceleration and enhanced takeoff performance and sustained turn rate. The first F404 powered Skyhawk first flew on 19 September 1986, with production conversions of 52 A-4S Skyhawks to GE powered A-4S-1 standards completed in 1989.

The second phase of the programme was the Ferranti (now part of BAE Systems) developed avionics upgrade. Features include a Mil Std 1553B databus, head-up display, multifunction display, mission computer and ring laser gyro INS. Phase II began in 1991 and the upgraded aircraft were designated A-4SU. The first squadron equipped with fully modified Super Skyhawks became operational in 1992.

Photo: A-4SU Super Skyhawk. (Paul Merritt)

Shin Meiwa PS-1

Country of origin: Japan.

Type: 10 crew maritime patrol and ASW flying boat.

Powerplants: Four 3060ehp (2282kW) Ishikawajima built General Electric T64-IHI-10 turboprops; three bladed propellers.

Dimensions: Wing span 33.14m (108ft 9in); length 33.50m (109ft 11in); height 9.71m (31ft 10½in); wing area 135.8m² (1462sq ft).

Weights: Empty equipped 26,309kg (58,000lb); max takeoff 45,000kg (99,206lb).

Armament: Four 150kg (330lb) anti submarine bombs in upper deck weapons compartment; two homing torpedoes under wings; hardpoints under wingtips for six 5in (12.7cm) rockets.

Performance: Max speed 295kt (547km/h) at 5000ft; normal cruise 230kt (426km/h); initial climb 2264m (690m)/min; service ceiling 29,530ft; normal range 1170nm (2168km); max ferry range 2560nm (4740km); max endurance 15 hours.

Production: 2 prototypes and 23 production PS-1 plus 15 US-1.

Notes: The Kawanishi Aircraft Company was responsible for Japan's two major flying boats of World War II (the H6K 'Mavis' and H8K 'Emily') and returned to that area of activity in the 1960s with the PS-1 maritime patrol and anti submarine flying boat. Kawanishi had been reconstituted as the Shin Meiwa Industry Company in 1949, becoming a major overhaul centre for Japanese and US military and commercial aircraft. It was renamed ShinMaywa in 1992.

Shin Meiwa was awarded a Japan Maritime Self Defence Force (JMSDF) contract in 1966 to complete design and development of the new flying boat under the company designation SS-2. Two prototypes were flown on 5 October 1967 and 14 June 1968. They were delivered to the JMSDF's 51st Flight Test Squadron for evaluation and given the military designation PS-1. Two pre-production PS-1s were delivered in 1972 with production deliveries beginning the following year. A total of 23 was taken on charge by the JMSDF, the 31st Koko-tai (Air Group) at Iwakuni the initial operator.

PS-1 design features include a single step hull, fixed strut mounted floats under the outer wings, T-tail, retractable beaching undercarriage and four General Electric T64 turboprops built under licence by Ishikawajima. A fifth powerplant – a 1400shp (1043kW) Ishikawajima/GE T58 gas turbine – was mounted in the fuselage to provide compressed air for the PS-1's boundary layer control system.

Shin Meiwa began work on an amphibian derivative of the PS-1 in 1970 under the company designation SS-2A. Development was protracted due to difficulties in incorporating the retractable undercarriage, the main wheels finally housed in side fuselage fairings with the tyres exposed. The SS-2A's first flight (from water) was on 16 October 1974 and its first land takeoff was on 3 December 1974.

Ordered into production as the US-1 search and rescue aircraft, the amphibian was stripped of all the operational equipment and armament associated with the ASW role, fuel capacity was increased and loading ramps and doors incorporated. The initial production run of 12 US-1s was completed in 1988 followed by another three in the early 1990s.

Photo: Shin Meiwa PS-1.

Soko Jastreb

Country of origin: Yugoslavia.

Type: Single seat light strike.

Powerplant: One 3000lb (13.3kN) Rolls-Royce Viper 531 turbojet.

Dimensions: Wing span over tip tanks 11.68m (38ft 4in); wing span with tip tanks removed 10.56m (34ft 8in); length 10.88m (35ft 8½in); height 3.64m (11ft 11½in); wing area 19.4m² (209sq ft).

Weights: Empty equipped 2820kg (6217lb); loaded (basic strike mission) 3969kg (8750lb); loaded with max ordnance 4364kg (9620lb); max takeoff 5287kg (11,655lb).

Armament: R-1 – three 12.7mm (0.50in) machine guns in nose; eight underwing hardpoints for two bombs of up to 250kg (551lb) each on inner pylons; 12 or 16 57mm rockets, two multiple containers each with three 50kg (110lb) bombs, bomblet containers, napalm bombs or single 127mm rockets on outer pylons. RJ-1 – four underwing hardpoints only.

Performance: Max speed 443kt (820km/h) at 19,700ft; max cruise 400kt (740km/h) at 16,400ft; max climb 4135ft (1260m)/min; service ceiling 39,375ft; typical strike mission radius 260nm (482km); max range 820nm (1518km).

Production: Approximately 250 of all versions.

Notes: The Soko J-1 Jastreb (Hawk) was developed from the G-2A Galeb basic jet trainer as a single seat light attack version of the two seater. The basic configuration and structure of the two aircraft are similar, but the Jastreb has some local strengthening and a more powerful version of the Viper turbojet installed as well as additional underwing hardpoints.

The Jastreb's single crew member is accommodated in the normal forward cockpit position with the rear cockpit replaced by an equipment bay covered by a metal fairing/access panel. Three, rather than two 12.7mm (0.50in) machine guns are installed in the nose.

The Galeb (Seagull) was the first jet powered aircraft of local design to enter service with the Yugoslav Air Force. Development began in 1957 and the first of two prototypes flew in May 1961. The first production model flew in February 1963 and deliveries to the Yugoslav Air Force began in 1965.

More than 300 Galebs were built for Yugoslavia, Libya and Zambia, production ending in 1980. Design features include unswept wings with tip tanks, lightweight Folland ejection seats, sideways hinging cockpit transparencies and underwing hardpoints for light ordnance.

The Jastreb first flew in 1967 or 1968 (the precise date is not publically recorded) and initial deliveries to the Yugoslav Air Force were in 1970. Five variants were produced between then and the end of production in 1978: the Jastreb J-1 standard attack version for the former Yugoslav Air Force; J-1E export attack version sold to Libya and Zambia (and also built for Yugoslavia); RJ-1 armed tactical reconnaissance version for Yugoslavia and RJ-1E export equivalent sold to Zambia; and TJ-1 operational and pilot proficiency trainer, combining the Galeb's tandem two seat fuselage with the Jastreb's wings and powerplant.

In 2000, Jastrebs remained in service with Bosnia-Herzegovina, Croatia, Libya, Yugoslavia and Zambia.

Photo: J-1E Jastreb.

Soko Orao and Avioane IAR-93

Countries of origin: Yugoslavia/Bosnia-Herzegovina and Romania.

Type: Single seat ground attack.

Powerplants: IAR-93B – two 4000lb (17.8kN) dry/5000lb (22.2kN) with afterburner Turbomecanica/Orao licence built Rolls-Royce Viper Mk.633-47 turbojets.

Dimensions: Wing span 9.30m (30ft 6in); length single seater (incl nose probe) 14.90m (48ft 10½in); length two seater (incl nose probe) 15.38m (50ft 5½in); height 4.52m (14ft 10in); wing area 26.0m² (280sq ft).

Weights: IAR-93B – empty equipped 5750kg (12,676lb); max takeoff 10,900kg (24,030lb).

Armament: IAR-93 – one 23mm twin barrel cannon in lower forward fuselage; one centreline and four underwing hardpoints for max 2100kg (4630lb) ordnance including rockets, bombs, gun pods, air-to-ground and air-to-air missiles.

Performance: IAR-93B – max speed 586kt (1085km/h) at sea level; max cruise 587kt (1087km/h) at 15,240ft; max initial climb 12,800ft (3900m)/min; service ceiling 44,625ft; combat radius with four rocket launchers and 5min over target lo-lo-lo 140nm (260km); radius with two rocket launchers, six 100kg (220lb) bombs and one drop tank with 10min over target hi-lo-hi 243nm (450km); radius with four 250kg (551lb) bombs and one drop tank with 5min over target hi-hi-hi 285nm (530km).

Production: 218 of all versions in Romania and 144 in Yugoslavia.

Notes: The J-22 Orao (Eagle) and IAR-93 were the results of a joint collaboration between the aircraft industries of the former Yugoslavia and Romania to meet requirements for a ground attack fighter. A team of Romanian and Yugoslav designers began work on the J-22/IAR-93 in 1970 under the project name YuRom, an acronym for the participating nations.

Planning called for the new aircraft to be built in single seat ground attack and two seat advanced and conversion trainer variants, with service entry scheduled for 1977. Both countries built single seat prototypes, both of which made their first flights on 31 October 1974. Similarly, two two-seaters (one built in each country), had their maiden flights on 29 January 1977. After 30 pre-series prototypes were built (15 in each country), series production began in Romania (with IAv Craiova, now Avioane) in 1979 and with Soko in Yugoslavia in 1980.

Romanian IAR-93s and Yugoslav Oraos are generally similar with mainly armament and equipment variations. Romanian production models comprised the initial non afterburning single and two seat IAR-93A (26 single seaters and 10 two seaters), and the single and two seater IAR-93B with afterburning engines (first flight 1985, 165 built), this delayed due to development problems with the afterburner.

Yugoslav Orao variants are the non afterburning Orao 1 (17 built), which was considered underpowered and was relegated to reconnaissance duties as the IJ-22 (two two-seaters were designated INJ-22), the NJ-22 production two seat reconnaissance variant (35 built, some with afterburning) and the J-22 Orao production single seater (most without afterburning).

Soko built 75 J-22s at Mostar in Bosnia until 1992 when the factory was abandoned and the jigs transferred to UTVA within the new Yugoslav state. Further work ceased in 1996.

Photo: IAR-93.

Sud-Ouest Vautour

Country of origin: France.

Type: IIA – single seat tactical fighter. IIN – two seat all weather fighter. IIB – two seat medium bomber.

Powerplants: Two 7716lb (34.3kN) Snecma Atar 101E-3 or (later IINs) 8157lb (36.3kN) Atar 101E-5 turbojets.

Dimensions: Wing span 15.10m (49ft 6½in); length 15.79m (51ft 10in); height 4.94m (16ft 2½in); wing area 45.0m² (484sq ft).

Weights: IIB – empty 10,580kg (23,325lb); max takeoff 20,700kg (45,635lb). IIN – empty 10,932kg (24,100lb); max takeoff 20,700kg (45,635lb).

Armament: IIN – four 30mm cannon in nose; retractable fuselage pack for 104 68mm rockets and four underwing pylons for rocket pods or AAMs. IIB – internal bay for one nuclear weapon or max 2040kg (4500lb) conventional bombs; underwing hardpoints for max 1814kg (4000lb) ordnance; max total combined load 2400kg (5291lb).

Performance: IIN – max speed 626kt (1160km/h) at sea level, 513kt (950km/h) at 40,000ft; max climb 11,810ft (3600m)/min; service ceiling 49,000ft; max range (internal fuel) 1650nm (3055km); max ferry range 3215nm (5955km). IIB – max speed 540kt (1100km/h) at sea level; combat radius with 1995kg (4400lb) bomb load 713nm (1320km) hi-lo-hi.

Production: 3 prototypes, six pre-production, 30 IIA, 40 IIB and 70 IIN, total 149.

Notes: Conceived in 1951 as a multi role combat aircraft to meet an *Armée de l'Air* requirement, the SO.4050 Vautour (Vulture) was planned in three versions for different roles: Vautour A (*Attaque*) close support/attack aircraft; Vautour B (*Bombardement*) bomber with nuclear weapon capability; and Vautour N (*Nuit*) night/all weather fighter. The A was a single seater and the other pair tandem two seaters, the A and N had solid noses (the latter with radar) and a fixed armament of four 30mm cannon, while the glazed nose B had an internal weapons bay, as did the A.

The design that emerged was of a mid wing aircraft with swept wings and tail surfaces, tandem main undercarriage retracting into the fuselage and two Atar turbojets in large nacelles under the wings. Outrigger undercarriage units retracted into the nacelles.

Three prototypes (one of each version) were flown on 16 October 1952 (N), 16 December 1953 (A) and 5 December 1954 (B). Orders were placed for 140 aircraft under the designations Vautour IIN, IIA and IIB. Six pre series aircraft were flown from March 1955 and the first production model on 30 April 1956. Service entry was the following year.

The Vautour IIA never entered regular French service, most of the 30 built instead supplied to Israel. The IIB and IIN enjoyed successful careers with the *Armée de l'Air*, retirement of the IIB beginning in 1966 and the IIN in 1973. Late production aircraft were fitted with a slab tailplane, resulting in the new designations II-1N and IIB-1N.

Israel also received seven ex French Vautour IINs in 1958-59, from 1963 they had their radar removed and were used in the attack role alongside the IIAs. By the early 1970s some French IINs were being converted to electronic warfare (EW) aircraft fitted with ECM receivers and jammers. Some were subsequently transferred to Israel.

Photo: Vautour IIB.

Sukhoi Su-7

Country of origin: Soviet Union.

Type: Su-7B – single seat ground attack fighter.

Powerplant: Su-7B – one 20,944lb (93.2kN) with afterburner Lyulka AL-7F turbojet. Su-7BM – one 15,432lb (68.6kN) dry/22,288lb (99.1kN) with afterburner Lyulka AL-7F-1 turbojet.

Dimensions: Su-7B – wing span 8.93m (29ft 3½in); length (excl nose probe) 16.60m (54ft 5½in); height 4.70m (15ft 5in); wing area 30.0m² (323sq ft).

Weights: Su-7BM – empty 8328kg (18,360lb); max takeoff 13,440kg (29,630lb). Su-7BMK – empty 8636kg (19,040lb); max takeoff 14,800kg (32,628lb).

Armament: Su-7B/BM/BMK – two 30mm cannon in wing roots; four underwing pylons for typically two 500kg (1102lb) and two 750kg (1653lb) bombs, or rocket pods.

Performance: Su-7BM – max speed 918kt (Mach 1.6/1700km/h) at 39,370ft, 621kt (Mach 0.94/1150km/h) at sea level; max climb 29,525ft (9000m)/min; service ceiling 49,200ft; tactical radius hi-lo-hi with 1500kg (3307lb) warload and two drop tanks 248nm (460km); max range with drop tanks 782nm (1448km).

Production: No accurate figures available, probably about 1500.

Notes: After building several jet and mixed powerplant experimental and prototype aircraft in the immediate post war years, Pavel Sukhoi's design bureau was closed down in November 1949 due to a reorganisation of the Soviet industry. It was reopened in May 1953 to develop two new combat aircraft, the S-1 swept wing (60 degrees) tactical air superiority fighter and T-3 tailed delta missile armed all weather fighter. The S-1 became the Su-7 and the T-3 evolved into the Su-9/11 series (see next entry).

Powered by a single Lyulka AL-7 turbojet, the S-1 prototype flew on 8 September 1955 followed by the revised S-2 with modified fuselage and other changes. From 1957 the aircraft went into limited production as the Su-7 air-to-air fighter, sufficient being built to equip an air regiment for evaluation purposes and entering service in early 1959.

It was then decided to revise the Su-7 as a primarily ground attack fighter, the S-2 taken as the basis and given structural and equipment modifications appropriate to the new role. The prototype was designated S-22 by the company (first flight April 1959) and the production designation was Su-7B. NATO applied the name 'Fitter-A' to the first production model which entered service in early 1960.

This was followed in 1961 by the Su-7BM ('Fitter-B') with the definitive AL-7F-1 powerplant, the Su-7BKL with modified undercarriage for rough field operations and final Su-7BMK with further modified undercarriage, upgraded avionics and increased weapons carrying capability. The Su-7U and Su-7UM/UMK were tandem two seat conversion trainers with the NATO reporting name 'Moujik'. Su-7B production ended in the early 1970s.

The Su-7B was exported to Afghanistan, Algeria, Czechoslovakia, Egypt, Hungary, India, Iraq, North Korea, Poland, Romania, Syria, Vietnam and South Yemen. Soviet front line service ended in 1986 but Algeria and Iraq operated the Su-7B well into the 1990s. North Korea still had some in service in 2000.

Photo: Sukhoi Su-7BMK.

Sukhoi Su-9 and Su-11

Country of origin: Soviet Union.

Type: Single seat all weather fighters.

Powerplant: Su-9 – one 20,944lb (93.2kN) with afterburner Lyulka AL-7F turbojet. Su-11 – one 15,432lb (68.6kN) dry/22,288lb (99.1kN) with afterburner Lyulka AL-7F-1 turbojet.

Dimensions: Su-11 – wing span 8.43m (27ft 8in); length (excl nose probe) 17.37m (57ft 0in); height 4.88m (16ft 0in); wing area 26.2m² (282sq ft).

Weights: Su-11 – empty 9100kg (20,062lb); normal loaded 12,247kg (27,000lb); max takeoff 14,000kg (30,864lb).

Armament: Two AA-3 'Anab' air-to-air missiles (one infrared homing and one radar homing) under wings; optional cannon pack on centreline hardpoint.

Performance: Su-11 – max speed (clean) 1034kt (Mach 1.8/1915km/h) at 39,370ft, 625kt (Mach 0.95/1160km/h) at sea level; max speed with AAMs and drop tanks 686kt (Mach 1.2/1270km/h) at 36,000ft; initial climb 27,000ft (8230m)/min; service ceiling 55,000ft; combat radius (subsonic intercept mission, internal fuel) 243nm (450km); range with drop tanks 955nm (1770km).

Production: Approximately 1000 Su-9s and 1000 Su-11s.

Notes: Developed in parallel with the swept wing S-1/S-2/Su-7 family of day and ground attack fighters (see previous entry), the tailed delta Su-9 all weather fighter (NATO reporting name 'Fishpot') began life as a series of prototypes powered by an afterburning AL-7F turbojet and featuring radar mounted in a radome above the circular nose intake. Under the Sukhoi design bureau designation T-3, the first aircraft flew on 26 May 1956 followed by two other prototypes (PT-7 and PT-8) with modifications. A further evolution called the T-4 flew in 1957.

The production Su-9 was a direct development of the T-4, retaining the delta wing with 57 degrees sweep, tail surfaces and AL-7F engine plus the radar housed in an intake centrebody shock cone. Series production of the Su-9 'Fishpot B' was launched 1959 as a pure interceptor armed with air-to-air missiles under the wings. The tandem two seat conversion trainer variant was designated Su-9U and 'Maiden' by NATO.

Further development resulted in the Su-11 'Fishpot C', basically an upgraded Su-7 with more powerful AL-7F-1 engine, enhanced capability *Uragan*-5B (Hurricane) radar, a lengthened and recontoured forward fuselage with reshaped and enlarged intake to allow greater airflow, and the AA-3 'Anab' air-to-missile usually carried in both infrared and semi active radar homing forms. The Su-11 was regarded by the Soviets as an interim all weather fighter pending the introduction of the Su-15 'Flagon' (see next entry).

The Su-11 succeeded the Su-9 in production from 1966, and partly replaced it in service with both aircraft operating side-by-side until their numbers began to decline. Production of the Su-11 ended in the early 1970s and although a combined total 300-400 Su-9s and -11s remained in service by 1981, they had been withdrawn from Soviet service within three or four years. None were exported and a few were converted to radio controlled target drones.

Photo: Sukhoi Su-9.

Sukhoi Su-15

Country of origin: Soviet Union.

Type: Single seat all weather interceptor.

Powerplants: Two 9340lb (41.5kN) dry/14,550lb (64.7kN) with afterburner Tumansky R-13F-300 or 11,600lb (51.6kN) dry/15,870lb (70.6kN) with afterburner R-13F2-300 turbojets.

Dimensions: Su-15TM (estimated) wing span 9.14m (30ft 0in); length (excl nose probe) 19.81m (65ft 0in); height 5.08m (16ft 8in); wing area 35.8m² (385sq ft).

Weights: Su-15TM (estimated) empty 11,000kg (24,250lb); max takeoff 18,000kg (39,682lb).

Armament: Typically two AA-3 'Anab' AAMs (one infrared homing and one radar homing) and two AA-8 'Aphid' short range AAMs under wings; gun pods or fuel tanks under fuselage.

Performance: Su-15TM (estimated) – max speed 1204kt (Mach 2.1/2230km/h) at 39,370ft with underwing missiles or 1320kt (Mach 2.3/2445km/h) clean; max climb 35,000ft (10,668m)/min; time to 36,000ft 2.5min; service ceiling 65,000ft; combat radius (internal fuel) 390nm (722km) or 540nm (1000km) with two drop tanks.

Production: Approximately 1500.

Notes: Developed to meet a requirement for a high performance all weather interceptor to replace the Sukhoi Su-11, the Su-15 in its original form combined the Su-11's plain 57 degree delta wing with a new and larger fuselage housing a pair of Tumansky R-11 turbojets. Horizontal tail surfaces were retained, radar was housed in an elongated solid nose, lateral engine intakes were fitted and armament was planned at two air-to-air missiles under the wings.

Sukhoi's designation for the aircraft was the T-58 and production Su-15s were given the reporting name 'Flagon' by NATO. The first T-58 prototype flew on 30 May 1962 followed by the similar pre series Su-15 'Flagon-A' with *Oriol*-D radar, two AA-3 'Anab' missiles and two 13,668lb (60.8kN) with afterburner R-11F2S-300 engines.

The NATO name 'Flagon-B' was allocated to an experimental variant, the Tu-15VD (*vertikal'nye dvigateli* – vertical engines) built as a V/STOL technology demonstrator with three Koliesov RD-36 lift engines in the fuselage. The first production version, the Su-15T 'Flagon-D' (T for *Taifun* – the type of radar fitted) delivered in 1969 was built in only small numbers (about 10 due to the failure of the radar) but established the basic configuration of following Su-15s in having cranked wing leading edges with the outer sweepback reduced to 47 degrees. The Su-15UT 'Flagon-C' was a tandem two seat conversion trainer based on the Su-15T.

The major production variant was the Su-15TM 'Flagon-E' from 1972 with increased span cranked wings, improved *Taifun*-M radar, R-13F engine and additional wing pylons. The standard Su-15TM was replaced late in the production run by the Su-15bis 'Flagon-F' which differed mainly in having a reshaped radome and more powerful engines. Su-15 production ended in the late 1970s but some remained in service well into the 1990s.

An Su-15TM achieved notoriety in September 1983 when it shot down a Korean Air Lines Boeing 747 north-west of Japan killing all 263 on board. The Soviets claimed they thought it was a USAF RC-135 intelligence gathering aircraft.

Photo: Sukhoi Su-15TM.

Sukhoi Su-17/20/22

Country of origin: Soviet Union.

Type: Single seat ground attack/strike fighter.

Powerplant: Su-17M-4/Su-22M-4 – one 17,200lb (76.5kN) dry/ 24,800lb (110.3kN) with afterburner Lyulka AL-21F-3 turbojet.

Dimensions: Wing span 3.68m (44ft 11in) fully extended or 10.03m (32ft 11in) fully swept; length (excl nose probes) 15.87m (52ft 1in); height 5.13m (16ft 10in); wing area 38.5m² (414sq ft).

Weights: Su- 22M-4 – empty equipped 10,767kg (23,737lb); max takeoff 19,500kg (42,990lb).

Armament: Two 30mm cannon in wing roots; five underfuselage and four underwing hardpoints for max 4000kg (8818lb) ordnance including bombs, gun pods, rockets, AAMs or ASMs.

Performance: Su-22M-4 – max speed (clean) 1200kt (Mach 2.09/ 2222km/h) above 36,000ft, 752kt (Mach 1.14/1394km/h) at sea level or 673kt (Mach 1.02/1247km/h) with external stores; max initial climb 45,275ft (13,800m)/min; service ceiling 49,865ft; range with external fuel at altitude 1242nm (2300km) or 755nm (1400km) at low altitude.

Production: Estimated at over 3000 of all models.

Notes: The swing wing and widely used Su-17 was the result of efforts to improve the Su-7 'Fitter-A's payload-range and takeoff performance. The Su-17's variable geometry wing design is unusual in that each one pivots midway along its span rather than at the root. The prototype for the Su-17, designated S-22I or Su-7IG (*Izmenyaemaya Geometriya* – variable geometry) and codenamed 'Fitter-B' by NATO, first flew on 2 August 1966. The first basically similar Lyulka AL-7 powered 'improved Fitter-B' pre-series Su-17 flew in 1968.

Initial production was of the Su-17M 'Fitter-C' with ranging radar, a 24,800lb (110.3kN) with afterburner AL-21F-3 turbojet and a new nav/ attack system. It was exported as the Su-20 and additional small numbers of reconnaissance pod carrying Su-17Rs and Su-20Rs were built.

The improved Su-17M-2 with lengthened nose and Su-17M-2D (both 'Fitter-D') were built from 1974 and introduced a fixed intake centrebody carrying a laser rangefinder and doppler radar in an undernose pod. The 'Fitter-D' was exported as the Su-22 'Fitter-F' and powered by a 25,350lb (112.7kN) with afterburner Tumansky R-29 turbojet. Tandem two seat operational trainer versions are the Su-22U 'Fitter-E', Su-17UM-3 'Fitter G' and Su-17UM-3K (also 'Fitter G') with either Tumansky or Lyulka engines .

Later single seaters were the Su-17M-3 'Fitter-H' and M-4 'Fitter K' built 1980-1990 with a deeper dorsal spine, upgraded avionics and modified tail. The M-3 also had an internal doppler radar. Export equivalents were the Su-22M-3 'Fitter J' with either Lyulka or Tumansky engines or the Lyulka powered Su-22M-4. Sukhoi and Sextant offered the Su-22M-5 upgrade with a HUD, HOTAS, twin multifunction displays, FLIR, new radar and mission computer.

By 2000, Su-17 variants and their export equivalents were operated by Angola, Azerbaijan, Bulgaria, Czech Republic, Georgia, Iraq, Libya, Peru, Poland, Russia, Slovakia, Syria, Turkmenistan, Ukraine, Vietnam and Yemen.

Photo: Sukhoi Su-22M-4. (Sebastian Zacharia)

Sukhoi Su-24

Country of origin: Soviet Union.

Type: Two seat tactical bomber/strike.

Powerplants: Su-24M – two 17,196lb (76.5kN) dry/24,692lb (109.8kN) with afterburner Saturn/Lyulka AL-21F-3A turbojets.

Dimensions: Su-24M – wing span 17.64m (57ft 10½in) fully extended or 10.37m (34ft 0in) fully swept; length (incl nose probe) 24.54m (80ft 6in); height 6.19m (20ft 4in); wing area 55.2m² (594sq ft) extended or 51.0m² (549sq ft) swept.

Weights: Su-24M – operating empty 22,320kg (49,206lb); max takeoff 39,700kg (87,523lb).

Armament: One 23mm cannon; nine external stores stations for max 8000kg (17,637lb) ordnance including nuclear, conventional or laser guided bombs, AGMs and AAMs.

Performance: Su-24M – max speed (clean) 1250kt (Mach 2.18/ 2315km/h) above 36,000ft, 759kt (Mach 1.15/1405km/h) at sea level; max initial rate of climb 29,525ft (9686m)/min; service ceiling 54,135ft; combat radius lo-lo-hi with 2500kg (5510lb) bombs 513nm (950km); combat radius hi-lo-hi with external fuel and 3000kg (6614lb) bombs 567nm (1050km); unrefuelled range at high altitude 1350nm (2500km).

Production: Approximately 1200.

History: The Su-24 (NATO name 'Fencer') tactical bomber and strike aircraft was developed to replace Il-28 and Yak-28 medium bombers. Sukhoi originally planned to meet the new bomber requirement with its delta wing T-6 with four RD-36-35 auxiliary lift jets to improve takeoff performance. A T-6-1 prototype first flew on 2 July 1967, but the jet lift configuration was abandoned in favour of using swing wings to achieve the desired field performance.

A variable geometry T-6-2IG prototype (without lift jets) therefore flew for the first time on 17 January 1970. The T-6-2IG was put into production as the Su-24, the first example leaving the factory in December 1971. The Su-24 was officially commissioned into Soviet service in February 1975.

The basic Su-24 was built in three variants which NATO designated 'Fencer-A', 'Fencer-B' and 'Fencer-C'. The original 'Fencer-A' served only with a trials unit; the 'Fencer-B' was the first regular production variant with a redesigned rear fuselage; and the 'Fencer-C' had improved avionics.

The Su-24M 'Fencer-D' was the major production strike/bomber development, first flown on 24 June 1977 and entering service in early 1980. It featured a modified nav/attack system, new weapons options, a retractable flight refuelling probe, a longer nose for new avionics including a Kaira laser/TV weapons guidance system and wing root fences. The Su-24MK export equivalent was built from 1988 and supplied to Algeria, Iran, Libya and Syria.

The Su-24MR 'Fencer-E' reconnaissance variant has a Shtik side looking radar in a shortened nose (with dielectric panels), infrared and TV sensors, a panoramic camera in the nose and an oblique camera in the lower fuselage. The Su-24MR can also carry various reconnaissance and Elint pods. The final Su-24 variant was the EW, jammer and Sigint Su-24MP 'Fencer-F' of which only 12 are thought to have been built. Su-24M production ended in 1992.

Photo: Su-24 'Fencer-C'.

Sukhoi Su-25

Country of origin: Soviet Union/Russia.

Type: Single seat close support/ground attack aircraft.

Powerplants: Two 9039lb (40.2kN) Soyuz/Tumansky R-95Sh or 9920lb (44.2kN) R-195 turbojets.

Dimensions: Su-25K – wing span 14.36m (47ft 1½in); length 15.53m (50ft 11½in); height 4.80m (15ft 9in); wing area 33.7m² (363sq ft).

Weights: Su-25K – empty 9500kg (20,944lb), max takeoff 14,600-17,600kg (32,187-38,800lb).

Armament: Su-25K – one 30mm twin barrel cannon on lower port side forward fuselage; eight underwing hardpoints for max 4400kg (9700lb) ordnance including laser guided rocket boosted bombs, ASMs, rockets, bombs, cluster bombs, gun pods and AAMs.

Performance: Su-25K – max speed 526kt (974km/h) at sea level; max attack speed (air brakes open) 372kt (689km/h); service ceiling 22,950ft clean or 16,400ft with max weapons load; range with 4400kg (9700lb) warload and two external fuel tanks 405nm (750km) at sea level or 675nm (1250km) at altitude; max range with drop tanks 10000nm (1850km).

Production: More than 700.

Notes: The Su-25 ('Frogfoot' to NATO) was designed specifically for close air support missions in conjunction with ground forces as a kind of modern equivalent to the Ilyushin Il-2 *Shturmovik* of WWII fame. Development began in 1968 and a prototype – designated T-8-1 – first flew on 22 February 1975 powered by twin Tumansky RD-9Bs (non afterburning developments of the MiG-19's engines).

The first Soviet Su-25 unit was declared operational in February 1981 and early combat operations in Afghanistan a few months later resulted in a number of changes and modifications. These included the incorporation of bolt on chaff/flare dispensers, engine exhaust IR signature suppressors and titanium shielding between the engines.

The Su-25 features titanium cockpit armour and wingtip pod airbrakes. Its engines can run on kerosene, diesel or petrol if necessary while the aircraft can deploy its own ground support and maintenance equipment in four underwing pods.

The basic Su-25 and export Su-25K (both 'Frogfoot-A') account for most Su-25 production. The Su-25UB and export Su-25UBK (both 'Frogfoot-B') are two seat conversion trainers with ground attack capability. The Su-25UT, later Su-28 (both also 'Frogfoot-B'), was offered as a dedicated advanced trainer. Ten carrier capable two seat Su-25UTGs (with arrester hook and strengthened undercarriage) were built for carrier trials aboard the *Admiral Kuznetsov* in 1989-90. The Su-25BM is a single seat target tug powered by the more powerful and lower IR signature R-195 engine also fitted to some other later production Su-25s.

The Su-25TM (Su-39 to Sukhoi) is a dedicated anti tank variant based on the two seaters but with the rear cockpit faired over for extra fuel and avionics including a new nav system, plus a chaff/flare dispenser in the base of the tail and a laser rangefinder and TV camera in the nose. Only pre-series Su-25TMs have been built, but a requirement for 12 upgraded incomplete airframes remains. Su-25 production ended in 1992 and 13 nations operated it in 2000.

Photo: A Czech Su-25K. (Sebastian Zacharias)

Sukhoi Su-27/30/33

Country of origin: Soviet Union/Russia.

Type: Single or two seat air superiority/multirole/carrier based fighter.

Powerplants: Su-27 – two 17,857lb (79.4kN) dry/27,557lb (122.6kN) with afterburner Saturn/Lyulka AL-31F turbofans.

Dimensions: Su-27 – wing span 14.70m (48ft 3in); length (excl nose probe) 21.94m (72ft 0in); height 5.93m (19ft 6in); wing area 62.0m² (667sq ft).

Weights: Su-27 – empty 16,380kg (36,111lb); max takeoff 33,000kg (72,751lb).

Armament: Su-27/30 – one 30mm cannon in starboard wing leading edge extension; ten hardpoints for AAMs or normally 4000kg (8818lb) ordnance. Su-33 – cannon and 12 hardpoints for max 6500kg (14,330lb) ordnance.

Performance: Su-27 – max speed 1241kt (Mach 2.17/2300km/h) at altitude, 756kt (Mach 1.14/1400km/h) at sea level; max climb 60,040ft (18,300m)/min; service ceiling 59,055ft; max range (clean) 2008nm (3720km); range with 10 AAMs 1512nm (2800km).

Production: Over 800 Su-27s, about 80 Su-30s and 40 Su-33s by 2000.

Notes: The formidable Su-27 boasts long range without external tanks, a large missile armament and superb manoeuvrability. It was designed as an agile all weather interceptor and bomber escort with a secondary ground attack capability. Development was originally inspired by the McDonnell Douglas F-15 Eagle.

Design work began in 1969, resulting in the first flight of a prototype designated T-10-1 on 20 May 1977. Designated 'Flanker-A' by NATO, the T-10-1 and subsequent prototypes exhibited serious control problems which necessitated a substantial redesign. As the T-10S-1, the revised aircraft first flew on 20 April 1981 and closely resembled production Su-27s.

Su-27 design features include a blended wing/fuselage, widely separated AL-31 turbofans, all moving tailplanes, a large F-15 style airbrake, leading edge slats, an infrared search and track and laser rangefinder set which allows passive target detection and engagement, fly-by-wire, HUD and Zhuk look down/shoot down and track-while-scan radar. Initial operational capability was achieved in December 1984.

The Su-27 'Flanker-B' is a single seat air defence fighter and can carry wingtip EW pods. The similar export multirole Su-27SK can carry a 4000kg (8820lb) bomb load; the Su-27SMK has two extra hardpoints and an 8000kg (17,636lb) maximum weapons load; and the Su-27UB 'Flanker-C' and export UBK are tandem two seat operational trainers.

The two seat Su-30 (or Su-27PU) air defence fighter is designed for up to 10 hour missions and can provide targeting information for other Su-27s by datalink. The Su-30M and export Su-30MK are multirole variants, the latter ordered by India with canards, thrust vectoring, Sextant avionics and Israeli EW when fully upgraded. The Su-30 first flew in December 1989 and the first production example in April 1992.

The Russian Navy operates the carrier capable Su-33 'Flanker-D' air defence fighter from the carrier *Admiral Kuznetsov*. First flown as the Su-27K in August 1987, features include folding wings, canards, strengthened undercarriage, refuelling probe and arrester hook.

Photo: Sukhoi Su-30MK/Su-27PU. (Sebastian Zacharias)

Sukhoi Su-35/37

Country of origin: Soviet Union/Russia.

Type: Single seat multirole fighter.

Powerplants: Su-35 – two 28,218lb (125.5kN) with afterburner Saturn/Lyulka AL-35F turbofans. Su-37 – two 31,970lb (142.2kN) with afterburner AL-37FU thrust vectoring turbofans.

Dimensions: Su-35/37 – wing span 14.71m (48ft 3in); length 22.17m (72ft 9in); height 6.43m (21ft 1in); wing area 62.0m² (667sq ft).

Weights: Su-35 – operating empty 18,400kg (40,564lb); normal loaded 25,670kg (56,592lb); max takeoff 34,000kg (74,956lb). Su-37 – max takeoff 34,000kg (56,592lb).

Armament: Su-35 – one 30mm cannon in starboard wing leading edge extension; 12 external hardpoints for max 8000kg (17,637lb) ordnance including AAMs, ASMs, infrared and laser guided rockets, laser guided bombs, and television guided bombs.

Performance: Su-35 – max speed 1350kt (Mach 2.35/2500km/h) above 36,000ft, 756kt (Mach 1.14/1400km/h) at sea level; max climb 45,275ft (13,800m)/min; service ceiling 58,400ft; range at low altitude 750nm (1390km); range (internal fuel) 1781nm (3300km) at high altitude; range with one flight refuelling over 3510nm (6500km).

Production: 11 Su-35 prototypes/pre-production; prototype Su-37 only.

Notes: Development of advanced and more capable Su-27 variants began in the mid 1980s, design aims including improved manoeuvrability, upgraded avionics and enhanced multirole capability.

A development Su-27 fitted with canards first flew in May 1985, while the first prototype for what would become the Su-35, the T-10S-70, first flew on 28 June 1988. It was followed by 10 other prototypes and pre-production aircraft. For a time the improved Su-27 was designated Su-27M but has since been changed to Su-35.

Changes over the basic Su-27 are numerous: canard foreplanes were added; power is from two upgraded Saturn AL-35F (or AL-31MF) turbofans; and flight control is provided by a digital fly-by-wire system with quadruplex redundancy (the Su-27's fly-by-wire system is analogue). The reprofiled nose houses a multimode Phazotron N011 Zhuk 27 radar with a larger diameter flat plate antenna. It has a search range of 55nm (100km), can track 24 targets simultaneously and has terrain following/avoidance, while a phased array upgrade has been under development.

The tailcone houses a rearwards facing Ryazan radar. A new infrared search and track (IRST) set has been repositioned on the nose. The EFIS cockpit features three colour CRTs and a HUD. Other features are a retractable flight refuelling probe, taller squared off fins each containing an auxiliary fuel tank and twin nosewheels. Some have large ECM wingtip pods.

The Su-37 first flew on 2 April 1996 and is a further improvement of the Su-35 with increased armament options and two dimensional thrust vectoring nozzles operated through the fly-by-wire flight control system, this resulting in extraordinary manoeuvrability. The Russian Air Force had hoped to introduce the Su-35 into service in the late 1990s, but these plans did not come to fruition due to budgetary constraints.

Photo: Sukhoi Su-35.

Sukhoi Su-27IB

Country of origin: Russia.

Type: Two seat tactical interdiction and strike.

Powerplants: Two 16,875lb (75.1kN) dry/27,560kb (122.6kN) with afterburner Saturn/Lyulka AL-31F turbofans.

Dimensions: Wing span 14.70m (48ft 3in); length 23.34m (76ft 7in); height 6.50m (21ft 4in); wing area 62.0m² (667sq ft).

Weights: Max takeoff 45,000kg (99,206lb).

Armament: One 30mm cannon in forward starboard fuselage; two wingtip stations for self defence AAMs; 10 other underfuselage and underwing hardpoints for max 8000kg (17,637lb) ordnance including AAMs, laser guided bombs and ASMs.

Performance: Max speed 1025kt (Mach 1.79/1900km/h) at 36,000ft, 702kt (Mach 1.06/1300km/h) at sea level; service ceiling 45,930ft; low level combat radius (internal fuel and 4000kg/8818lb warload) 324nm (600km); ferry range 2430nm (4500km).

Production: 7 by mid 2000.

Notes: The Su-27IB is a side-by-side two seat development of the Su-27 fighter intended for long range strike and to replace older types such as the Su-17, MiG-27 and Su-24. When the Su-27IB (or Su-34 to Sukhoi) was publicly revealed in 1991, some confusion surrounded its intended role, with the first prototype variously identified as an aircraft carrier trainer designated Su-27KU (*Korabelnii Uchebno* – shipborne trainer) and a strike fighter as the Su-27IB (*Istrebitel Bombardirovschik* – fighter-bomber).

It is now clear that two distinct variants of the aircraft had been proposed, the air force Su-27IB fighter-bomber and the Su-32FN (Sukhoi's designation), a shore based long range maritime strike fighter intended to replace Russian Naval Aviation Su-24s.

Features of the Su-27IB (first flight 13 April 1990) include the side-by-side seating, twin nosewheels, tandem main undercarriage units, canards, a Leninetz phased array multifunction radar with terrain following/avoidance, rearwards facing radar in the tailcone (as on the Su-35), retractable flight refuelling probe, broader chord vertical tail surfaces, three multifunction displays in the cockpit and modern avionics.

Access to the cockpit is via an integral ladder aft of the nosewheel, while behind the two crew seats in the humped fuselage is a small galley and toilet. The crew sits on Z-36 zero/zero ejection seats and the cockpit is protected by titanium armour. The future of the Su-27IB is unclear, a lack of funding inhibiting production although it is believed more are being built.

The Su-32FN as proposed was similar but with a maritime search radar, sonobuoy launcher, MAD, laser rangefinder, wingtip ECM pods and seven LCD screen EFIS cockpit. The Su-32FN program was suspended in 1997 with none built.

The carrier trainer concept has been resurrected, as in 1999 Sukhoi had begun flight testing the externally similar Su-27KUB side-by-side two seat Flanker variant intended for carrier conversion training for pilots who will fly the Su-33 in Russian Navy service. Despite superficial similarities, the Su-27KUB is not based on the Su-27IB.

Photo: Sukhoi Su-27IB/Su-32FN. (Paul Merritt)

Supermarine Spitfire F.22 and F.24

Country of origin: United Kingdom,

Type: Single seat fighter-bomber.

Powerplant: One 2050hp (1529kW) Rolls-Royce Griffon 61 or 65 V12; five bladed propeller.

Dimensions: Wing span 11.25m (36ft 11in); length 10.03m (32ft 11in); height 4.11m (13ft 6in); wing area 22.6m² (244sq ft).

Weights: F.22 – empty 3248kg (7160lb); normal loaded 4490kg (9900lb); max overload 5148kg (11,350lb). F.24 – max overload 5511kg (12,150lb).

Armament: F.22 – four 20mm cannon in wings plus provision for one 227kg (500lb) bomb under fuselage and two 227kg (500lb) bombs under wings. F.24 – additional provision for eight underwing rockets.

Performance: F.22 – max speed 391kt (724km/h) at 19,500ft, 318kt (589km/h) at sea level; max climb 5100ft (1554m)/min; service ceiling 43,500ft; max range (internal fuel) 504nm (933km); range with drop tanks 838nm (1553km). F.24 – max range with internal fuel 738nm (1368km).

Production: 20,351 Spitfires of all versions including 288 F.22 and 54 F.24.

Notes: The Spitfire F.22 and F.24 were the final developments of the famous line, based on the F.21 with its completely new wing of revised aerofoil section and planform. The F.21 had entered limited service in March 1945 following a problematic development period. External differences between the F.22/24 and the F.21 were the incorporation of the 'rear view' fuselage with bubble canopy and, in all but the first few F.22s, larger vertical and horizontal tail surfaces.

The first F.22 flew in November 1944 and at one stage 627 were on order. Contract cutbacks in 1945 saw this number drastically reduced but 288 were ultimately built. The first production F.22 flew in March 1945 but entry to operational service was slow, the aircraft flying with only one regular RAF squadron (No 73) from Malta in 1947-48 before re-equipping with de Havilland Vampires, while seven Royal Auxiliary Air Force squadrons operated the type between 1947 and 1951 before they also re-equipped with jets.

The Spitfire F.24 first flew in February 1946 (converted from an F.22) and production aircraft began appearing in February 1946, early aircraft converted on the production line from F.22s. The final F.24 (and the last Spitfire) was delivered in February 1948, although some more Seafires were still to come. The Spitfire F.24 differed from the F.22 in having short barrel Hispano Mk.V cannon (instead of Mk.II) in later aircraft, electrical rather than pneumatic gun firing, additional fuel tanks in the rear fuselage and the ability to carry underwing rocket projectiles.

No 80 Squadron was the only RAF operational unit to fly the F.24, receiving its first aircraft in January 1948 in Germany and relinquishing them in December 1951 when based in Hong Kong. Egypt received 20 refurbished ex RAF Spitfire F.22s in 1950 and Syria 10 in 1950. Eight F.24s were transferred to the Hong Kong Auxiliary Air Force in December 1951. Earlier mainly ex RAF Spitfire versions were operated post war by Belgium, Burma, Czechoslovakia, Denmark, France, Greece, India, Eire, Israel, Italy, the Netherlands, Norway, Portugal, South Africa, Thailand, Turkey and Yugoslavia. Some of them saw action, notably Israel's and Egypt's.

Photo: Spitfire F.22.

Supermarine Seafire 45/46/47

Country of origin: United Kingdom.

Type: Single seat carrier based fighter-bomber.

Powerplant: 45/46 – one 2050hp (1529kW) Rolls-Royce Griffon 61 V12; five bladed propeller. 47 – one 2145hp (1599kW) Griffon 87 or 2350hp (1752kW) Griffon 88; six bladed counter-rotating propellers.

Dimensions: 45/46/47 – wing span 11.25m (36ft 11in); wing area 22.6m² (244sq ft). 45 – length 9.96m (32ft 8in). 46/47 – length 10.46m (34ft 4in); height 3.88m (12ft 9in).

Weights: 45 – empty 3220kg (7100lb); max takeoff 4536kg (10,000lb). 46 – empty 3402kg (7500lb); max takeoff 5171kg (11,400lb). 47 – empty – 3459kg (7625lb); max takeoff 5783kg (12,750lb).

Armament: Four 20mm cannon in wings; provision for underwing 113kg (250lb) bombs or depth charges; or eight rockets in Mk.46/47.

Performance: 45 – max speed 387kt (718km/h) at 20,500ft; max climb 5300ft (1615m)/min; service ceiling 43,000ft; range 504nm (933km). 47 – max speed 393kt (727km/h) at 20,500ft, 308kt (568km/h) at sea level; initial climb 4800ft (1463m)/min; time to 20,000ft 4.9min; service ceiling 43,100ft; max range with drop tank 817nm (1513km).

Production: 2408 Seafires of all versions including 50 Mk.45, 24 Mk.46 and 90 Mk.47.

Notes: The three final Seafire variants equated to navalised versions of the last three Spitfire models – the Seafire 45 (first flight August 1944) to the Spitfire 21, Seafire 46 (first flight 8 September 1944) to Spitfire 22, and Seafire 47 (first flight 25 April 1946) to Spitfire 24, except in the case of the latter a more powerful Griffon 87 or 88 engine driving counter-rotating propellers was fitted. A small number of Seafire 45/46s were also tested with this engine/propeller combination

All three utilised the new wing and four cannon armament which had first been applied to the Spitfire 21, the Seafire 45 and 46 retaining the non folding wing of their land based counterparts which made them unsuitable for use from several aircraft carriers. The Seafire 47 introduced single fold wings, manually operated in early aircraft and then hydraulically actuated.

Externally, the Seafire 45 retained the standard canopy and broad chord fin and rudder of the Spitfire 21 while the Mks.46 and 47 had bubble canopies and the enlarged Spiteful type vertical and horizontal tail surfaces of the Spitfire 22/24. 'Sting' hooks were fitted and the Mk.47 introduced a 24 rather than 12 volt electrical system. All three were built in standard fighter 'F' and fighter-reconnaissance 'FR' versions with rear fuselage camera. Most Mk.47s were completed to FR.47 standards.

Only the F/FR.47 entered front line Fleet Air Arm squadron service and then with just two units. No 800 Squadron's Mk.47s were the only of its type to see action. Based aboard HMS *Triumph* but operating from land in Singapore, they conducted rocket attacks against communist terrorists in late 1949 before spending a three months tour of duty (from July 1950) flying ground attack sorties from *Triumph* during the Korean War. The final Seafire FR.47 was also the last of the Spitfire/Seafire line, delivered in January 1949.

Photo: Seafire FR.47.

Supermarine Attacker

Country of origin: United Kingdom.

Type: Single seat carrier based fighter-bomber.

Powerplant: F/FB.1 – one 5000lb (22.2kN) Rolls-Royce Nene Mk.101 turbojet. FB.2 – one 5000lb (22.2kN) Nene Mk.102 turbojet.

Dimensions: Wing span 11.25m (36ft 11in); length 11.43m (37ft 6in); height 3.02m (9ft 11in); wing area 21.0m² (226sq ft).

Weights: F.1 – empty 3826kg (8434lb); max takeoff 5539kg (12,211lb). FB.2 – empty 4495kg (9910lb); max overload 7870kg (17,350lb).

Armament: F.1 – four 20mm cannon in wings. FB.1/2 – guns plus two 454kg (1000lb) bombs or four 27kg (60lb) rockets under wings.

Performance: FB.2 – max speed 513kt (950km/h) at sea level, 467kt (866km/h) at 30,000ft; time to 30,000ft 6.7min; service ceiling 45,000ft; range with standard fuel 513nm (950km); range with overload tank 1034nm (1915km).

Production: 3 prototypes, 52 F.1, 8 FB.1, 85 FB.2 and 36 for Pakistan, total 184.

Notes: Originally conceived in 1944 as a land based jet fighter for the RAF, the Supermarine Type 392's design combined the new laminar flow wing which was being developed for the unsuccessful Spiteful piston engined fighter (intended as a successor to the Spitfire) with a new fuselage and tail plus the Rolls-Royce RB.41 (later Nene) centrifugal flow turbojet.

The undercarriage was also taken from the Spiteful, resulting in a tailwheel configuration – unusual for a jet aircraft. The wing retained the Spiteful's four cannon armament but the radiators for its Griffon piston engine were naturally removed and replaced by fuel tanks.

Three prototypes were ordered in August 1944 but development was slower than anticipated due to delays in laminar flow wing research, with low speed handling problems proving difficult to solve. As the RAF had begun to lose interest in the aircraft, it was decided that the last two prototypes would be navalised.

The first prototype flew on 27 July 1946 and the second on 17 June 1947 (the name 'Attacker' applied on the same day), this differing in having longer stroke undercarriage, smaller fin, enlarged tailplane, increased fuel capacity, arrester hook and an ejection seat. Folding wings would not appear until the production versions were built. By then, the RAF was no longer a prospective customer and the aircraft was ordered only for the Royal Navy Fleet Air Arm.

The first production Attacker F.1 flew on 5 May 1950 and operational service began in August 1951 with No 800 Squadron FAA. Subsequent versions were the FB.1 fighter-bomber with provision for underwing ordnance and the FB.2 which differed mainly in its Nene Mk.102 engine with a throttle acceleration control unit to prevent flameout if the throttle was opened quickly, such as when performing a go-around. The Attacker served with only two FAA front line squadrons and had been relegated to Volunteer Reserve units by 1954 and retired two years later.

The only export was to the Pakistan Air Force, which received 36 'denavalised' aircraft between 1951 and 1953 for operation from land. These lacked the folding wings and arrester gear of the Royal Navy's aircraft but were otherwise similar to the Attacker F.1.

Photo: Attacker F.1.

Supermarine Swift

Country of origin: United Kingdom.

Type: Single seat interceptor and tactical reconnaissance.

Powerplant: FR.5 – one 7500lb (33.3kN) dry/9500lb (42.2kN) with afterburner Rolls-Royce Avon Mk.108 turbojet.

Dimensions: FR.5 – wing span 9.85m (32ft 4in); length 12.88m (42ft 3in); height 4.11m (13ft 6in); wing area 30.5m² (328sq ft).

Weights: FR.5 – empty 6094kg (13,435lb); max takeoff 9831kg (21,673lb).

Armament: Two 30mm cannon in lower forward fuselage; provision for underwing ordnance.

Performance: FR.5 – Max speed 620kt (1147km/h) at sea level; time to 40,000ft 4.7min; service ceiling 45,800ft; range 547nm (1014km).

Production: 2 Type 541 prototypes, 18 F.1, 17 F.2, 25 F.3, 6 F.4, 94 FR.5 and 14 F.7, total 176.

Notes: Only briefly used in its intended role as an interceptor before being declared unsuitable as a result of suffering sometimes severe handling deficiencies, the Swift is usually dismissed as a failure, especially when compared to its more illustrious contemporary the Hawker Hunter.

By the time the Swift was sorted out it proved to be effective in the low level tactical reconnaissance role and what is often forgotten is that the Hunter also had serious early problems – such as a wholly inadequate fuel capacity and the inability to fire its guns for fear of causing an engine flameout.

The Swift did get one up on the Hunter in September 1953 when an F.4 flown by Mike Lithgow set a new world's air speed record of 737.7mph (1186.8km/h), beating the mark set by a Hunter only three weeks earlier.

The Swift resulted from a series of evolutionary prototypes starting with the Nene powered and tailwheel equipped Type 510 (first flight 29 December 1948) which was basically a swept wing Attacker. The Type 528 was similar, this subsequently fitted with an afterburning Nene, lengthened nose and tricycle undercarriage as the Type 535, flying in this form on 23 August 1950 and serving as the basis for the Swift. The 535 achieved some fame as the fictional 'Prometheus' fighter in the film *Sound Barrier*, starring alongside Nigel Patrick and Ralph Richardson.

The true Swift prototypes were the two Avon powered Type 541s, the first of them flying on 1 August 1951. The production Swift F.1 powered by a 7500lb (33.3kN) non afterburning Avon 105 first flew on 25 August 1952 and entered limited RAF service in February 1954. The F.2 with four rather than two guns and increased wing chord (which caused severe pitch up problems) followed, then the F.3 with afterburning Avon (which didn't work at altitude) and F.4 with variable incidence tailplane. By then, the decision had been made to abandon the Swift as an interceptor and large orders were cancelled.

Only the FR.5 tactical reconnaissance version with cameras in a lengthened nose and dogtooth wing leading edges was built in any numbers. It first flew in May 1955 and successfully operated with two RAF Germany squadrons until 1961. Production ended in 1957. The Swift F.7 with radar, four Blue Sky (Fireflash) AAMs and extended span wings was built but did not enter service despite showing that finally, the design had been properly sorted – but too late.

Photo: Swift FR.5. (Bill Lines)

Supermarine Scimitar F.1

Country of origin: United Kingdom.

Type: Single seat carrier based strike fighter.

Powerplants: Two 11,250lb (50.0kN) Rolls-Royce Avon Mk.202 turbojets.

Dimensions: Wing span 11.33m (37ft 2in); length 16.84m (55ft 3in); height 5.28m (17ft 4in); wing area 45.0m² (485sq ft).

Weights: Empty 10,869kg (23,962lb); max takeoff 15,513kg (34,200lb).

Armament: Four 20mm cannon in lower forward fuselage; provision for one tactical nuclear weapon under wing; four underwing hardpoints for four 454kg (100lb) bombs, four Sidewinder air-to-air missiles or four Bullpup air-to-surface missiles.

Performance: Max speed 640kt (Mach 0.97/1186km/h) at sea level, 587kt (Mach 0.98/1088km/h) at 30,000ft; initial climb 20,000ft (6096m)/min; time to 45,000ft 6.7min; service ceiling 46,000ft; max range 1236nm (2288km).

Production: 3 Type 544 prototypes and 76 Scimitar F.1.

Notes: The last aircraft to carry the famous 'Supermarine' name, the Scimitar naval strike fighter resulted from a long gestation period involving a series of evolutionary prototypes beginning in 1945 with design of the Type 505. This large, straight winged and V-tailed aircraft powered by two Rolls-Royce Avons was intended to test Royal Navy interest in the use of 'undercarriageless' aircraft operating from aircraft carriers with flexible deck 'carpets', the aircraft landing on its belly. Not surprisingly, this idea was abandoned (after being tested by a DH Vampire) and the 505 was flown in August 1951 with conventional undercarriage.

Development of the basic design as a conventional naval fighter led to the similar Type 529 prototype flying in August 1952 and then the Type 525 with swept wings and conventional tail (first flight 27 April 1954), this becoming in effect the prototype for what would become the Scimitar. Three pre series aircraft were built as the Type 544 (first flight 19 January 1956) with dogtooth wing leading edges, all moving tailplane, area ruled fuselage, lengthened nose and blown flaps. Provision was made for an armament of four 20mm cannon mounted in the lower forward fuselage and for external ordnance.

As the Scimitar F.1, the aircraft would be capable of high subsonic speeds in level flight and, as its normal operating environment would be at very low altitude, manufacturing techniques such as using high tensile steel spars, chemically etched skins, rear fuselage titanium heat shields and synthetic bonding were employed to resist the very high stresses on the airframe.

The first Scimitar F.1 flew on 11 January 1957 with operational service starting in June 1958 with the Fleet Air Arm's No 803 Squadron. The initial embarkation was aboard HMS *Victorious* three months later. Three other squadrons operated the Scimitar but 803 was the final front line operator, disbanding in October 1966. The last aircraft were retired in 1969.

The Scimitar was a useful aircraft but regarded as an interim strike type pending arrival of the all weather Buccaneer. Modifications incorporated during service included clearance to carry an increasingly wide range of weapons including the Sidewinder AAM, Bullpup ASM and a 'Target Marker Bomb', the euphemism employed for a nuclear weapon.

Photo: Scimitar F.1.

Tupolev Tu-4

Country of origin: Soviet Union.

Type: Heavy bomber.

Powerplants: Four 2200hp (1640kW) Shvetsov ASh-73TK 18-cylinder two row radials; four bladed propellers.

Dimensions: Wing span 43.08m (142ft 4in); length 30.19m (99ft 0¹/₂in); height 8.46m (27ft 9in); wing area 161.6m² (1740sq ft).

Weights: Empty equipped 35,270kg (77,755lb); max takeoff 66,000kg (145,502lb).

Armament: Five twin 12.7mm machine guns or 23mm cannon in turrets; max bomb load 4000kg (8818kg).

Performance: Max speed 301kt (558km/h) at 20,000ft; cruising speed 200-280kt (370-518km/h); service ceiling 36,750ft; range 2754nm (5100km).

Production: 847.

Notes: The old Soviet Union was never too modest to copy the West's technology and reproduce it without the benefit of a licence. The Boeing B-29 Superfortress was subject to such an 'arrangement' following the emergency diversion of three USAAF aircraft to an area near Vladivostok in 1944. These aircraft had been engaged on operations over Japanese targets and the first of them landed on Soviet soil in July 1944 after running short of fuel.

The Soviet Government interned the B-29s and handed them over to the Tupolev design bureau which immediately set about copying the aircraft under the designation Tu-4. The NATO reporting name 'Bull' was later applied. The advanced technology incorporated in the B-29 gave the Soviet aircraft industry a wealth of useful information about systems, structures and radar. The unexpected arrival of the three aircraft was very timely as it coincided with the USSR gaining access to the West's atomic bomb technology.

This and the subsequent 'Cold War' era was one in which everything Soviet was regarded by themselves as the best, anything from the West was rubbish and anything worthwhile had been invented in Russia. This is well illustrated by a Russian book on the Tu-4 which fails to mention – even once – the B-29 from which the design was stolen!

Powered by four Shvetsov ASh-73 radial engines (themselves based on the B-29's Wright R-3350s), the first Tu-4 flew on 3 July 1947, series production ending in 1952. There were some internal differences between the Tu-4 and B-29, the Soviet aircraft lacking the US aircraft's integral fuel tanks and the pressurised tunnel which linked the forward and midships crew compartments.

About 100 Tu-4s were supplied to China in 1951 to equip that country's newly established strategic bombing force. China also converted at least two aircraft with 4000shp (2985kW) Ivchenko AI-20 turboprops from an Antonov An-12 transport. Tupolev developed a 72 passenger airliner version of the Tu-4 (the Tu-70 'Cart') with low wings and new fuselage with cabin windows and a stepped windscreen, but this did not enter production.

The Tu-4 was a very important part of the development of Soviet strategic aircraft as it served as the starting point for a long line which culminated in the Tu-95 and Tu-142 'Bear' series of turboprop powered bomber/reconnaissance aircraft plus the Tu-114 airliner.

Photo: Tupolev Tu-4.

Tupolev Tu-14

Country of origin: Soviet Union.

Type: Three crew torpedo bomber.

Powerplants: Two 5955lb (26.5kN) Klimov VK-1 turbojets.

Dimensions: Wing span 21.69m (71ft 2in); length 21.95m (72ft 0in); wing area 67.3m² (725sq ft).

Weights: Empty 14,930kg (32,914lb); max takeoff 25,350kg (55,886lb).

Armament: Six 23mm cannon in tail, nose and dorsal pairs; two Type 45-36-A torpedoes or 3000kg (6614lb) bombs in bomb bay.

Performance: Max speed 456kt (845km/h) at 16,400ft; 432kt (800km/h) at sea level; service ceiling 36,745ft; range 1550nm (2870km).

Production: 88.

Notes: The first Tupolev jet bomber to be manufactured in substantial numbers, the Tu-14 (NATO reporting name 'Bosun') followed several projects and prototypes. The first Tupolev jet bomber was a twinjet conversion of the wartime Tu-2 piston engined medium bomber.

One of the designs which followed was the Tu-12, the first Soviet jet bomber to achieve production, albeit in extremely limited numbers. Powered by two 5000lb (22.2kN) Rolls-Royce Nenes, the Tu-12 was a mid wing medium bomber with the engines underslung in large nacelles into which the main undercarriage retracted. Fitted with twin tail fins, it first flew in June 1947 and it is believed that a handful was built and these never served with operational units.

The Tu-14 began under the Tupolev design bureau designation Type 81 and followed a series of designs which dated back to the Tu-12 and included the Type 73 trijet (an unsuccessful competitor to the Ilyushin Il-28) and its Type 78 derivative of 1948.

The twin engined Type 81 retained most of the major features of its predecessors but had the tail mounted third engine eliminated (allowing the fitting of defensive armament at the rear with a pressurised compartment for the gunner) and was powered by two Klimov VK-1 turbojets.

There were many other detail changes relating to armament and avionics and despite some lack of official enthusiasm, a production run of 500 was authorised in 1950 under the Soviet military designation Tu-14 as a land based medium bomber for the *Aviatsiya-Voenno Morskikh Flota* (A-VMF – Naval Air Fleet).

The Tu-14's role was changed before any had been delivered when it was decided to modify and deploy it as a torpedo carrier, still for service with the A-VMF. The new designation Type 81T (Tu-14T in service) was applied and numerous modifications incorporated to cater for the new primary armament of two Type 45-36-A torpedoes and revised defensive armament. Bomb carrying capability was retained.

The Tu-14T entered service in February 1951 and remained in front line service until about 1961 with some aircraft continuing to fly in secondary roles well into the 1970s. Also in February 1951 was the first flight of the Tu-14R reconnaissance variant with increased fuel capacity and cameras in the weapons bay, but it was not put into production.

Photo: Tupolev Tu-14T.

Tupolev Tu-16

Country of origin: Soviet Union.

Type: Six-nine crew medium range strategic and anti shipping bomber.

Powerplants: Two 19,285lb (85.8kN) Mikulin AM-3M or 20,950lb (93.2kN) AM-3M-500 turbojets.

Dimensions: Tu-16A – wing span 32.93m (108ft 0½in); length 34.80m (114ft 2in); height 10.82m (35ft 6in); wing area 164.6m² (1772sq ft).

Weights: Tu-16A – empty 40,300kg (88,445lb); max takeoff 75,800kg (167,107lb).

Armament: Tu-16A – one fixed 23mm cannon in forward fuselage plus two each in dorsal, ventral and tail barbettes; max weapons load 9000kg (19,840lb). Tu-16K (depending on subvariant) – one AS-2 'Kipper' anti shipping standoff missile semi recessed in weapons bay, or two AS-5 'Kelt' or AS-6 'Kingfish' standoff missiles under wings.

Performance: Tu-16A – max speed 558kt (1033km/h) 32,800ft; service ceiling 40,000ft; range with 3800kg (8377lb) ordnance 2780nm (5150km). Tu-16K-10 – max speed 566kt (1050km/h) at 19,700ft; service ceiling 49,200ft; range with 3000kg (6614lb) warload 3888nm (7200km).

Production: 1508 of all versions in Soviet Union.

Notes: One of the more important Soviet combat aircraft over several decades of service, the twin engined Tu-16 medium strategic bomber was built in substantial numbers for the Soviet Air Force and Navy and was exported to Egypt, Iraq and Indonesia. Licence production was also undertaken in China as the Xian H-6.

The prototype first flew on 27 April 1952 under the design bureau designation Tu-88 but was substantially overweight. A redesign and slight delay resulted in the more acceptable second prototype flying in early 1953. As the Tu-16A (NATO reporting name 'Badger-A'), the new bomber entered service in 1955 armed with conventional or nuclear free fall weapons.

Numerous variants followed between then and the end of production in 1964, combat versions which went into service including the Tu-16KS ('Badger-B', first flight 1954) with underwing ASMs; Tu-16K-10 ('Badger-C', 1958) with a semi recessed AS-2 standoff missile under the belly; Tu-16K-11 and -16 ('Badger-G', 1959) with upgraded underwing standoff missiles; and Tu-16K-26 ('Badger-G' Mod, 1959) modified to carry two AS-5 missiles underwing.

Numerous reconnaissance, electronic intelligence gathering and electronic countermeasures variants were also built either new or by conversion. A dedicated aerial refuelling model was also produced. It was the Elint/ECM versions of the Tu-16 which remained longest in Soviet (and then Russian/Ukraine) service, well into the 1990s.

China acquired a licence to manufacture the Tu-16 in 1957, two pattern aircraft arriving in dismantled form two years later. The first of these flew on 27 September 1959 but deteriorating relations between China and the USSR forced China to 'reverse engineer' the aircraft. The engines were also copied. Progress was painfully slow but the first Xian H-6 finally flew on 24 December 1968. Production was initiated and about 120 had been built by the mid 1990s. The H-6 was offered for export and a few are believed to have been delivered to Iraq. An improved version with increased wing span and weights was developed as the H-6D.

Photo: Tupolev Tu-16s.

Tupolev Tu-95 and Tu-142

Country of origin: Soviet Union/Russia.

Type: Tu-95 – seven crew strategic bomber. Tu-142 – 11-13 crew maritime patrol.

Powerplants: Four 14,795ehp (11,0353W) KKBM Kuznetsov NK-12MV turboprops; eight bladed counter-rotating propellers.

Dimensions: Tu-95MS – wing span 50.04m (164ft 2in); length 49.13m (161ft 2in); height 13.30m (43ft 8in); wing area 289.9m² (3120sq ft).

Weights: Tu-95MS – empty 94,400kg (208,116lb); max takeoff 185,000kg (407,849lb).

Armament: Tu-95MS – up to six Kh-55 (AS-15A 'Kent') cruise missiles on rotary launcher in bomb bay. Tu-95MS16 – additional 10 Kh-55s under wings.

Performance: Tu-95MS – max speed 499kt (924km/h) at 25,000ft; 350kt (648km/h) at sea level; cruising speed 384kt (711km/h); ceiling 39,370ft; combat radius with 11,340kg (25,000lb) payload 3456nm (6400km).

Production: 174 Tu-95s and approx 225 Tu-142s.

Notes: Development of the very large (for the time) Tu-95 (NATO reporting name 'Bear') began in July 1951 around the enormously powerful Kuznetsov NK-12 turboprop and the fuselage cross section originally introduced on the Tu-4 'Bull', the USSR's unlicenced copy of the Boeing B-29 Superfortress.

At the time, it was considered that turboprops offered the best compromise between speed and fuel efficiency. The engines, eight bladed counter-rotating propellers, swept wings (unique for a propeller driven aircraft) and enormous fuel capacity give the Tu-95 jet like speeds and intercontinental range. The prototype Tu-95 first flew on 12 November 1952.

Initial production was of the Tu-95M 'Bear-A' freefall nuclear bomber which has long been withdrawn from use. Some were converted as Tu-95U crew trainers. Tu-95Ms were also converted to Kh-20 (AS-3 'Kangaroo') cruise missile launching Tu-95K-20 'Bear-B' standards with a nose mounted radar. The Tu-95KD was similar but had a flight refuelling probe, as did the Tu-95KM 'Bear-C' as well as Elint antennae and some reconnaissance sensors.

The Tu-95K-22 'Bear-G' had a revised radome profile and carried two Kh-22 (AS-4 'Kitchen') missiles, one under each wing root. The final bomber variant was the Tu-95MS 'Bear-H', developed to carry the Kh-55 (AS-15A 'Kent' cruise missile and first flown in August 1979. Tu-95 series production originally ended in 1969 but was reinstated between 1982 and 1992 for the MS.

Surplus Tu-95M bombers were converted to maritime reconnaissance Tu-95RT 'Bear-D' and Tu-95MR 'Bear-E' configurations. The Tu-95RT has an undernose radome and was used for missile mid course guidance and reconnaissance duties, while the Tu-95MR has cameras in the bomb bay. The Tu-142 is a dedicated ASW platform based on the Tu-95 and first flown in June 1968. The Tu-142 'Bear-F' features a slight fuselage stretch and a maritime search radar in a ventral radome. It carries sonobuoys, torpedoes and mines. The later Tu-142M 'Bear-F Mod 2' introduced a Magnetic Anomaly Detector (MAD) on top of the tail. The Tu-142MR 'Bear-J' is used as a submarine communications relay. Production ended in 1994.

Photo: Tupolev Tu-95MS. (Paul Merritt)

Tupolev Tu-28P/Tu-128

Country of origin: Soviet Union.

Type: Two seat long range interceptor.

Powerplants: Two 16,370lb (72.8kN) dry/22,046lb (98.1kN) with afterburner Lyulka AK-7F-2 turbojets.

Dimensions: (Estimated) wing span 18.10m (59ft 4¹/₂in); length 30.00m (98ft 5in).

Weights: (Estimated) empty equipped 25,960kg (57,231lb); max takeoff 45,000kg (99,206lb).

Armament: Two infrared and two semi active radar homing Bisnovat R-4 (AA-5 'Ash') air-to-air missiles.

Performance: Max speed (with four AAMs) 900kt (Mach 1.57/ 1667km/h) at 39,400ft; service ceiling 65,600ft; combat radius (high altitude patrol, allowance for supersonic intercept) 678nm (1255km); max fuel range 2700nm (5000km).

Production: 199.

Notes: Surprisingly little detail is known about the Tupolev Tu-28 (or Tu-128 as it was dubbed by the US Department of Defense), the largest and heaviest interceptor to have achieved service status. To provide a comparison, its overall length and maximum weight are close to that of the BAC One-Eleven, Fokker 100 and BAe 146-200 airliners.

Allocated the reporting name 'Fiddler' by NATO, the Tu-28 was developed in the 1950s as a dedicated long range interceptor optimised for high altitude and long endurance work. It was intended to intercept Western bombers long before they could reach their targets, or in the case of those armed with standoff missiles, before the missiles could be launched.

An advanced, supersonic design with two crew members seated in tandem, the production standard Tu-28P ('Fiddler-B') was armed with four of the large delta winged AA-5 'Ash' air-to-air missiles mounted under the wings. Two of them were usually infrared homing versions and the others semi active radar homing. A large ogival nose radome carried a substantial I-band radar known to NATO as 'Big Nose'. Other features included a wide track main undercarriage with four wheel bogies retracting into fairings built into the wing trailing edges and shoulder mounted intakes for the two afterburning AL-7F turbojets.

The Tu-28 was indirectly descended from the Tu-98 prototype of the mid 1950s. First flight was originally noted as 1957-58 although it is now known to be 18 March 1961 with production deliveries beginning in late 1966. Previously, an in service date of around 1961 was considered to be correct and it was in July of that year that the aircraft was first publicly seen during the Tushino Aviation Day flypast.

The two early aircraft seen on that date were dubbed 'Fiddler-A' by NATO and carried two missiles and had a large bulged fairing under the fuselage, this assumed by some observers to be some kind of early warning radar.

The 'Fiddler-B' served with Soviet *Voyska PVO* home defence regiments for a quarter of a century. By the early 1980s it still equipped a handful of regiments but its numbers steadily declined after that until it was finally replaced in service by the MiG-31 in the early 1990s. By 1993 it was thought that only 20 or so remained on Russian strength.

Photo: Tupolev Tu-28P.

Tupolev Tu-22

Country of origin: Soviet Union/Russia.

Type: Three seat strategic bomber/electronic warfare aircraft.

Powerplants: Two 27,560lb (122.6kN) dry/36,375lb (161.8kN) with afterburner Dobrynin RD-7ND turbojets.

Dimensions: Wing span 23.50m (77ft 1in); length 42.60m (139ft 9in); height 9.98m (32ft 9in); wing area 162.0m² (1744sq ft).

Weights: Tu-22K – empty 38,100kg (83,995lb); normal loaded 85,000kg (187,390lb); max takeoff 92,000kg (202,822lb); max takeoff with rocket assistance 94,000kg (207,231lb).

Armament: One 23mm radar directed cannon in tail; weapons bay for max 8000kg (17,637lb) bombs. Tu-22K can alternatively carry a single Kh-22 (AS-4 'Kitchen') supersonic cruise missile semi recessed in weapons bay.

Performance: Tu-22K – max speed 872kt (Mach 1.52/1616km/h) at 40,000ft, 478kt (885km/h) at sea level; service ceiling 43,635ft; combat radius hi-lo-hi with a 216nm (400km) full throttle dash 1188nm (2200km); max range with internal fuel 2645nm (4900km); max ferry range 3050nm (5650km).

Production: 313.

Notes: The Tu-22 was Russia's first successful attempt at fielding a supersonic bomber. The Tu-22 (NATO reporting name 'Blinder') dates from a 1956 study to build a supersonic bomber capable of penetrating then modern air defences and carrying a payload similar to the subsonic Tu-16. The new aircraft (Tupolev's own designation was Tu-105) flew for the first time in September 1959. The Tu-22 remained unknown in the West until two years later when 10 aircraft participated in the Tushino Aviation Day flypast.

The Tu-22's most unusual feature was the position of the engines at the base of the fin, which had the dual benefits of leaving the fuselage free for fuel (and without the need for long inlet ducts) and giving the two engines (mounted side by side) largely undisturbed airflow. The lips of the intakes moved forward for takeoff creating a gap through which extra air was drawn.

The area ruled fuselage housed a bombing/navigation radar in the nose, a crew of three with the navigator in the lower forward fuselage with the pilot and radio operator/gunner in tandem behind him, an internal weapons bay, and a radar controlled 23mm cannon in the tail for self defence. The large and highly swept wing (70deg at the root and 52deg at the tip) features pods into which the main undercarriage units retract.

Initial production was of the Tu-22 'Blinder-A' conventional and nuclear bomber but the major version of the production run (which ended in 1971-72) was about 150 Tu-22K 'Blinder-Cs' capable of carrying the Kh-22 cruise missile. The Tu-22K also featured an enlarged radome for the new multimode radar.

The Tu-22U 'Blinder-D' trainer had a raised second cockpit aft of the normal cockpit, while about 60 reconnaissance Tu-22R 'Blinder-C's were built, fitted with a range of sensors. Most surviving Tu-22s in Russian service have been converted as Tu-22PD 'Blinder-E' EW jammers. In 2000 the Tu-22 was also still operated by Libya and the Ukraine.

Photo: Tupolev Tu-22s.

Tupolev Tu-22M

Country of origin: Soviet Union.

Type: Four crew strategic and maritime strike/reconnaissance bomber.

Powerplants: Tu-22M-1/2 – two 44,090lb (196.1kN) with afterburner Kuznetsov NK-20 turbofans. Tu-22M-3 – two 55,115lb (245.2kN) with afterburner Kuznetsov NK-25 turbofans.

Dimensions: Tu-22M-3 – wing span 34.28m (112ft 6in) fully extended or 23.290m (76ft 5in) fully swept; length overall 42.46m (139ft 4in), height 11.05m (36ft 3in); wing area 183.6m² (1976sq ft) extended or 175.8m² (1892sq ft) swept.

Weights: Tu-22M-3 – empty 54,000kg (119,050lb); max takeoff 124,000kg (273,370lb); rocket assisted max takeoff 126,400kg (278,660lb).

Armament: One 23mm twin barrel cannon in tail; max 24,000kg (52,910lb) conventional bombs or mines in bomb bay, or six Kh-15P (AS-16 'Kickback') ASMs on a bomb bay rotary launcher plus four under wings; or three Kh-22 (AS-4 'Kitchen') ASMs, one semi recessed under fuselage and one on each underwing hardpoint.

Performance: Tu-22M-3 – max speed 1080kt (Mach 1.88/2000km/h) at altitude, 567kt (Mach 0.86/1050km/h) at low level; cruising speed 486kt (900km/h); service ceiling 45,930ft; subsonic combat radius with 12,000kg (26,455lb) warload lo-lo-lo 900nm (1665km) or 1300nm (2410km) hi-lo-hi; supersonic radius with one cruise missile 1188nm (2200km) hi-hi-hi.

Production: 578 of all versions.

Notes: The Tu-22M was originally conceived as a swing wing development of the Tu-22 but evolved into an essentially new aircraft, despite the designation similarity with the earlier aircraft. Only some fuselage, tail and systems components were common. Tupolev began serious design work on its variable geometry Tu-22 project in late 1962 and the substantially modified design was accepted in 1967.

Apart from the swing wings (which had a sweep range of 20-65deg), the other key change was the powerplants, two Kuznetsov NK-20 afterburning turbofans mounted in the rear of the fuselage and fed by two intakes with variable splitter plates. The nose was redesigned, while new six wheel main undercarriage units retracted into the fuselage.

The first Tu-22M-0 prototype first flew on 30 August 1968, although the West did not identify the new bomber until September 1969, the NATO reporting name 'Backfire-A' was applied. The first pre-production Tu-22M flew on 28 July 1971 and the major production version, the Tu-22M-2 'Backfire B' (with a new nav/attack radar and avionics plus a defensive gun in the tail) on 7 May 1973. Development was slow, with deliveries to operational units not starting until 1975.

Some 283 Tu-22M-2s were built before production switched to the Tu-22M-3 'Backfire-C' (277 built), this first flying on 20 June 1977. The Tu-22M-3 is powered by two increased thrust NK-25 turbofans fed by new wedge shaped air inlets, and introduced a new multimode radar in a reprofiled nose and has increased weights. The Tu-22MR is a reconnaissance version (12 converted for the Russian Navy) and the Tu-22MP a one-off EW/escort jammer.

Production ended in 1993. Russia had about 250 Tu-22Ms in service by 2000 and the Ukraine about 70.

Photo: Tupolev Tu-22M-3. (Paul Merritt)

Tupolev Tu-160

Country of origin: Soviet Union/Russia.

Type: Four crew strategic bomber.

Powerplants: Four 30,865lb (137.3kN) dry/55,115lb (245.2kN) with afterburner Samara/Trud NK-231 turbofans.

Dimensions: Wing span 55.70m (182ft 9in) extended or 35.60m (116ft 9¹/₂in) swept; length 54.10m (177ft 6in); height 13.10m (43ft 0in); wing area 232.0m² (2497sq ft).

Weights: Empty 117,000kg (257,936lb); normal takeoff 267,600kg (589,947lb); max takeoff 275,000kg (606,261lb).

Armament: Two tandem internal weapons bays for theoretical max 40,000kg (88,183lb) load comprising freefall bombs or ASMs. One rotary launcher in each bay to for six Kh-55MS (AS-15 'Kent') ALCMs or 12 Kh-15P (AS-16 'Kickback') SRAMs.

Performance: Normal max speed 1080kt (Mach 1.88/2000km/h) above 36,000ft, 556kt (1030km/h) at sea level; cruising speed 518kt (960km/h) at 45,000ft; max climb 13,780ft (4200m)/min; service ceiling 52,494ft; radius of action at Mach 1.5 1080nm (2000km); subsonic range with six ALCMs 6642nm (12,300km).

Production: Estimated at 40-50.

Notes: The Tu-160 (NATO reporting name 'Blackjack') is the heaviest and most powerful bomber ever built and was developed as a direct response to the Rockwell B-1A, although the original requirement for a supersonic strategic bomber dated back a few years earlier.

Tupolev began design work of its all new 'Aircraft 70' under the leadership of V I Bliznuk in 1973. Although the B-1A was cancelled in 1977 (the less capable B-1B substituted instead), design and development work on the new Tupolev bomber continued, resulting in the first prototype flying on 19 December 1981 and the second in October 1984. Production of 100 Tu-160s was authorised in 1985 although only 40-50 were built before the line closed in 1992.

The Tu-160 is similar in overall configuration to the B-1, but is much larger. The four NK-231 afterburning turbofans are the most powerful engines fitted to a combat aircraft and are mounted in pairs under the inner fixed wings. Variable geometry air inlets designed for high speeds are incorporated as is a retractable flight refuelling probe.

The variable geometry wings have full span leading edge slats and double slotted trailing edge flaps and can be set at three sweep positions – 20deg, 35deg and 65deg. The airframe is free of any protuberances except for a small video camera window for the pilots. The nav/attack radar is believed to have a terrain following function, while the Tu-160 has a comprehensive ECM jamming system. The four crew sit on individual ejection seats and the pilots have fighter style sticks and a fly-by-wire flight control system is fitted.

By 2000, only five airworthy Tu-160s were operated by Russia and 19 by the Ukraine, eight of which were being transferred to Russian control. In 2000 it was thought they would be joined by others in storage at the factory. The Tu-160SK is a commercial variant being offered as a launch vehicle for the Burlak-Diana satellite launching rocket. Three demilitarised ex Ukrainian aircraft were sold in the US in 1999 for use as satellite launchers.

Photo: Tupolev Tu-160. (Robert Meerding)

Vickers Valiant

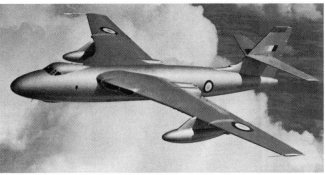

Country of origin: United Kingdom.

Type: Five-seven crew strategic reconnaissance/tanker/bomber.

Powerplants: Four 9500lb (42.2kN) Rolls-Royce Avon RA.14 or 10,050lb (44.7kN) Avon RA.28 Mk.204 turbojets.

Dimensions: Wing span 34.85m (114ft 4in); length 32.99m (108ft 3in); height 9.80m (32ft 2in); wing area 219.4m² (2362sq ft).

Weights: B(K).1 – empty 34,420kg (75,881lb); normal loaded 63,504kg (140,000lb); max takeoff 79,380kg (175,000lb).

Armament: One 4536kg (10,000lb) Blue Danube nuclear weapon or up to 21 454kg (1000lb) conventional bombs.

Performance: B(K).1 – max speed 493kt (912km/h) at 30,000ft, 360kt (666km/h) structural limit at sea level; max cruise 480kt (890km/h) at 30,000ft; economical cruise 430kt (796km/h); initial climb 4000ft (1219m)/min; service ceiling 54,000ft; range with 4536kg (10,000lb) warload 3000nm (5556km); max range with underwing tanks 4500nm (8335km).

Production: 2 prototypes, 36 B.1, 11 B(PR).1, 13 B(PR)K.1, 44 B(K).1 and 1 B.2, total 107.

Notes: The first of the RAF's 'V-Bomber' strategic nuclear force, the Valiant resulted from a 1945 operational requirement for a bomber capable of evading enemy defences by high speed and high altitude and then delivering a thermonuclear weapon. This evolved into a January 1947 specification for a bomber capable of carrying a 4536kg (10,000lb) 'special weapon' (atomic bomb) or equivalent load of conventional bombs over a distance of 3600 statute miles (5793km).

The first of two Vickers Type 660 and 667 prototypes flew on 18 May 1951 by which time an initial production order for 25 had been placed. The aircraft was named Valiant the following month. The first of five pre-production Valiant B.1s (Type 674) flew on 22 September 1953 and operational service began in February 1955, the aircraft eventually equipping 10 RAF front line squadrons. Four of them flew combat missions during the 1956 Suez Crisis, bombing Egyptian airfields from Malta. A Valiant also dropped Britain's first atomic bomb over Maralinga, South Australia in October 1956.

Four variants were produced: the basic B.1 bomber; B(PR).1 strategic reconnaissance version; B(PR)K.1 multirole bomber/reconnaissance/flight refuelling tanker; and B(K).1 bomber/tanker. Production ended in August 1957. Vickers flew a single prototype of the B.2 low level night pathfinder in September 1954, this featuring a substantially redesigned structure for low altitude and high speed missions and new four wheel bogie main undercarriage which retracted rearwards into streamlined bodies aft of the wings.

The B.2 was not proceeded with, ironically as it turned out because from the early 1960s the Valiant was operated at low altitudes, an environment for which it was not designed. Speed was limited due to structural considerations but in December 1964 the discovery of serious stress induced fatigue cracks in the wing main spars of many aircraft resulted in the RAF's entire Valiant force being grounded within two months. With the cost of repairs prohibitive, they were scrapped *en masse*.

Photo: Valiant B.1.

Vought F6U-1 Pirate

Country of origin: USA.

Type: Single seat carrier based fighter.

Powerplant: One 3150lb (14.0kN) dry/4225lb (18.8kN) with afterburner Westinghouse J34-WE-30 turbojet.

Dimensions: Wing span (without tip tanks) 10.00m (32ft 10in); length 11.45m (37ft 7in); height 3.94m (12ft 11in); wing area 18.9m² (203sq ft).

Weights: Empty 3320kg (7320lb); max takeoff 5851kg (12,900lb).

Armament: Four 20mm cannon in nose.

Performance: Max speed 518kt (959km/h) at sea level, 478kt (885km/h) at 31,000ft; cruising speed 375kt (695km/h); initial climb 8060ft (2456m)/min; time to 30,000ft 5.4min; service ceiling 46,300ft; range with tip tanks 1017nm (1883km).

Production: 3 XF6U-1, 30 F6U-1, total 33.

Notes: Although built only in small numbers for the US Navy and regarded as unsuccessful, the F6U Pirate was (along with the USN's similarly conservative McDonnell FH-1 Phantom and North American FJ-1 Fury – see separate entries) part of the important and necessary transition period between piston engined fighters and the swept wing jets that would follow.

The Pirate was Vought's first jet and resulted from a September 1944 proposal issued by the USN's BuAer for a single seat carrier based fighter. Vought responded with its V-340 design and three prototypes were ordered in December 1944 under the designation XF6U-1.

A conventional straight wing design, the aircraft had some interesting construction features, namely Vought's patented 'Metalite' skinning, this comprising two thin sheets of aluminium sandwiching a balsa wood core. Also used on the vertical tail and intake ducts was 'Fabrilite', a fibreglass and balsa sandwich.

The first XF6U-1 flew on 2 October 1946, powered by a non afterburning 3000lb (13.3kN) thrust Westinghouse J34-WE-22 turbojet. Several unsatisfactory handling characteristics were immediately apparent and the aircraft was also underpowered. Numerous modifications were introduced in attempts to improve handling, mainly with the tail surfaces which went through several redesigns. Although the original cruciform tail configuration was retained, the tailplanes were increased in area, the fin made notably taller and auxiliary fin surfaces were attached to the tailplanes near the tips.

Production F6U-1s incorporated the new tail surfaces and a redesigned rear fuselage with a longer jetpipe for the Solar A-103A afterburner which was fitted to the J34 engine in an attempt to overcome the lack of power.

The first production F6U-1 Pirate flew on 5 March 1949 but only 30 were built and most of these were assigned to a development squadron. Operational service was never achieved. The Pirate programme was cancelled in October 1950, the USN reporting to Vought: "The F6U-1 had proven so sub-marginal in performance that combat utilisation is not feasible". Some ended their days used in arrester gear and barrier trials and as technical training airframes. Average flight time was only 31 hours per aircraft.

Photo: F6U-1 Pirate.

Vought F7U Cutlass

Country of origin: USA.

Type: Single seat carrier based fighter.

Powerplant: F7U-1 – two 3600lb (16.0kN) dry/4250lb (18.9kN) with afterburner Westinghouse J34-WE-32 turbojets. F7U-3 – two 4600lb (20.5kN) dry/6100lb (27.1kN) with afterburner Westinghouse J46-WE-8A turbojets.

Dimensions: F7U-3 – wing span 11.78m (38ft 8in); length 13.49m (44ft 3in); height 4.46m (14ft 7¹/₂in); wing area 46.1m² (496sq ft).

Weights: F7U-3 – empty 8283kg (18,262lb); max takeoff 14,353kg (31,642lb).

Armament: F7U-3 – four 20mm cannon; four underwing hardpoints for max 907kg (2000lb) ordnance or four Sparrow air-to-air missiles on F7U-3M.

Performance: F7U-3 – max speed 605kt (1120km/h) at sea level, 591kt (1095km/h) at 10,000ft; initial climb 11,150ft (3398m)/min; service ceiling 40,000ft; range (internal fuel) 573nm (1062km).

Production: 3 XF7U-1, 14 F7U-1, 180 F7U-3, 98 F7U-3M and 12 F7U-3P, total 307.

Notes: Highly unconventional in its configuration, the Cutlass's design drew heavily from data on tailless designs retrieved from Germany in 1945, especially the work performed by the Arado company. As the Vought V-346, the aircraft was designed to meet a June 1945 US Navy requirement for a single seat carrier based fighter capable of achieving a maximum speed of 600mph (965km/h) at 40,000ft. Unfortunately, the Cutlass is probably best remembered for the number of crashes it suffered.

Three prototypes were ordered as the XF7U-1 in June 1946, design features including a very low aspect ratio swept wing with no horizontal tail surfaces and twin fins and rudders mounted on the outer edges of the wing centre section. Elevons combined the functions of elevators and ailerons and the whole leading edge was fitted with slats. Power was from two afterburning Westinghouse J34 turbojets.

The first XF7U-1 flew on 29 September 1948 but crashed a few weeks later after a loss of control, the second and third aircraft suffering similar fates. They were followed by 14 pre series F7U-1s, the first of these flying on 1 March 1950. The F7U-2 with major changes was cancelled after 88 had been ordered due to problems with the J34 engine, development instead concentrating on the further improved F7U-3 with J46 powerplants.

First flown on 20 December 1951, the F7U-3 was substantially different to its predecessor with new engines, new fins, redesigned fuselage and cockpit area, strengthened structure (the F7U-1 was pronounced not strong enough for carrier operations), new undercarriage and numerous other modifications. Only the wing remained pretty much as before.

The F7U-3 entered service in 1954 and flew with four US Navy operational squadrons. Subvariants were the F7U-3M armed with four Sparrow beam riding AAMs and the unarmed camera equipped F7U-3P. Production ended in August 1955 and the Cutlass was progressively withdrawn from service in 1956-57, although the last F7U-3P wasn't retired until March 1959. In the meantime, more than a quarter of the fleet had been lost in accidents.

Photo: F7U-3 Cutlass.

Vought F-8 Crusader

Country of origin: USA.

Type: Single seat carrier based fighter.

Powerplants: F-8E – one 10,700lb (47.6kN) dry/18,000lb (80.1kN) with afterburning Pratt & Whitney J57-P-20A turbojet.

Dimensions: F-8E – wing span 10.87m (35ft 8in); length 16.61m (54ft 6in); height 4.80m (15ft 9in); wing area 32.5m² (350sq ft).

Weights: F-8E – empty 8090kg (17,836lb); max takeoff 15,422kg (34,000lb).

Armament: F-8E – four 20mm cannon in forward fuselage; two underwing and four side fuselage hardpoints for max 2268kg (5000lb) ordnance including Sidewinder AAMs, bombs, two Bullpup ASMs or 24 Zuni ASMs.

Performance: F-8E – max speed 1033kt (Mach 1.8/1914km/h) at 36,000ft, 662kt (Mach 1.0/1226km/h) at sea level; max initial climb 27,200ft (8290m)/min; service ceiling 58,000ft; combat radius 520nm (963km); ferry range 1215nm (2250km).

Production: 2 XF8U-1, 318 F8U-1 (F-8A), 144 RF8U-1P (RF-8A), 130 F8U-1E (F-8B), 1 TF-8A, 2 XF8U-2, 187 F8U-2 (F-8C), 152 F8U-2N (F-8D), 286 F-8E and 42 F-8E(FN), total 1264.

Notes: The F-8 Crusader was the US Navy's first supersonic day interceptor and resulted from Vought's V-383 proposal to meet a 1952 requirement for a supersonic fighter but with low landing speed (below 100kt/185km/h) and powered by a Pratt & Whitney J57 turbojet. Vought's design was selected for development ahead of seven others and the first prototype (designated XF8U-1) flew for the first time on 25 March 1955.

The Crusader's most unusual feature was its high mounted variable incidence wing, which rotated to a higher angle of attack for takeoff to increase lift and for landing to increase drag and pilot visibility. Folding wings, all moving tailplanes and fire control radar were also fitted.

Initial production was of the F8U-1 (F-8A from 1962) first flown in September 1955 and entering USN service in March 1957. Then followed the more powerful and limited all weather F8U-1E/F-8B; the reconnaissance F8U-1P/RF-8A; F8U-2/F-8C with four fuselage side missile rails and further increase in power, and the limited all weather F8U-2N/F-8D. The final production model was the multirole F8U-2NE/F-8E (in production 1961-65) with an APQ-94 fire control radar and increased weapons load of 2265kg (5000lb) including Bullpup ASMs.

Rebuilds and upgrades to extend many F-8s' service lives saw F-8Ds become F-8Hs, F-8Es become F-8Js, F-8Cs become F-8Ks, and F-8Bs upgraded as F-8Ls. USN and USMC Crusaders were extensively operated in Vietnam and responsible for 18 confirmed MiG 'kills'. Replacement began in 1972 but the last wasn't retired until 1982.

France's *Aéronavale* was the only other customer for new Crusaders, receiving 42 F-8E(FN)s for operation from the carriers *Foch* and *Clemenceau*. The F-8E(FN) differed from the basic F-8E in having blown flaps and other high lift devices to allow it to operate from the smaller French carriers plus provision to carry French weapons. The last F-8E(FN)s were retired in December 1999. The Philippines received 25 ex USN F-8Hs (as F-8Ps) in 1978 and operated them until 1988.

Photo: F-8E(FN) Crusader. (Paul Merritt)

Vought A-7 Corsair II

Country of origin: USA.

Type: Single seat carrier and land based attack.

Powerplants: A-7E – One 15,000lb (66.7kN) Allison TF41-A-2 (Rolls-Royce Spey) turbofan.

Dimensions: A-7E – Wing span 11.80m (38ft 9in); span wings folded 7.24m (23ft 9in); length 14.06m (46ft 2in); height 4.90m (16ft 1in); wing area 34.8m² (375sq ft).

Weights: A-7E – Empty 8668kg (19,111lb); max takeoff 19,050kg (42,000lb).

Armament: One 20mm rotary cannon in port side forward fuselage; two side fuselage (for Sidewinder AAMs) and six underwing hardpoints for 6804kg (15,000lb) ordnance.

Performance: A-7E – max speed 600kt (1112km/h) at sea level; max climb 12,640ft (3853m)/min; service ceiling 43,000ft; typical tactical radius 426-608nm (789-1127km); max range (internal fuel) 1981nm (3671km); ferry range (external fuel) 2485nm (4604km).

Production: 199 A-7A, 196 A-7B, 67 A-7C, 5 YA-7D, 454 A-7D, 535 A-7E, 60 A-7H, 5 TA-7H, and 30 A-7K, total 1551.

Notes: The A-7 Corsair resulted from the US Navy's May 1963 VAL (light attack aircraft) specification to find an attack aircraft with roughly twice the payload of the A-4 Skyhawk, for an in service date of 1967. Vought's proposal was selected ahead of those from North American, Douglas and Grumman, and seven development aircraft plus 35 production A-7As were ordered in March 1964.

Vought's design looked like a shortened version of the F-8 Crusader fighter but was subsonic and in reality a completely new design optimised for the carriage of air-to-ground ordnance. It lacked the Crusader's variable incidence wing and had less sweep back. Power was from a non afterburning 11,350lb (50.5kN) thrust Pratt & Whitney TF30-P-6 turbofan. The first A-7A flew on 27 September 1965, initial deliveries to USN training squadrons were in October 1966 and deliveries to operational units began in February 1967. The A-7B (first flight February 1968) had a more powerful 12,200lb (54.3kN) thrust TF30-P-8 engine.

The USAF ordered its own version of the A-7 in 1966 to fill a requirement for a tactical attack aircraft. The USAF's A-7D introduced the Allison TF41 turbofan, a licence built development of the Rolls-Royce Spey. First flight was on 5 April 1968 and initial delivery in December 1968. The first 67 aircraft were powered by the TF30 due to production problems with the TF41 and redesignated A-7C to avoid confusion. The USN's improved A-7E (first flight November 1968) was also powered by the TF41, the tandem two seat TA-4C was a conversion of 65 A-7B/Cs, and the USAF's two seat A-7K was a new build version based on the A-7D first flown in November 1980. The final Corsair II – an A-7E – was delivered in March 1981.

USAF and especially USN Corsairs were used widely during the Vietnam War, while USN aircraft were also flown in the Gulf War. Both services had retired their A-7s by 1993. The first Corsair II export customer was Greece, which ordered 60 new A-7Hs and five TA-7Hs for delivery from late 1975. Portugal's 20 A-7Ps are refurbished ex USN A-7As delivered from 1981, while Thailand acquired 18 ex USN A-7Es for service with its Navy in the land based maritime strike role.

Photo: A-7E Corsair.

Westland Wyvern

Country of origin: United Kingdom.

Type: Single seat carrier based torpedo and strike fighter.

Powerplant: S.4 – one 4110ehp (3065kW) Armstrong Siddeley Python ASP.3 Mk.101 turboprop; eight bladed counter-rotating propellers.

Dimensions: S.4 – wing span 13.41m (44ft 0in); length 12.80m (42ft 0in); height 4.57m (15ft 0in); wing area 33.0m² (355sq ft).

Weights: S.4 – empty 7080kg (15,608lb); max takeoff 11,113kg (24,500lb).

Armament: S.4 – four 20mm cannon in wings; one centreline and two underwing hardpoints for one 18in (45.7cm) torpedo, three 454kg (1000lb) bombs or 16 60lb (27kg) rockets.

Performance: Max speed 333kt (616km/h) at sea level; initial climb 2350ft (716m)/min; service ceiling 28,000ft; range with two drop tanks 791nm (1465km).

Production: 6 prototypes, 10 TF.1 (of which 4 unflown), 3 Mk.2 prototypes, 13 TF.2, 1 T.3, 94 S.4, total 127.

Notes: Westland's last fixed wing design to achieve production, development of what would become the Wyvern naval strike fighter began in early 1944 as a day fighter, torpedo carrier and fighter-bomber under the company designation P.10. A specification was written around Westland's proposals and in November 1944 six prototypes were ordered, four of them the naval variant and two land based versions for the RAF. RAF interest had disappeared before the first prototype had flown.

Larger and heavier than any previous British single engined naval fighter, the Wyvern prototypes were powered by a single 3500hp (2610kW) Rolls-Royce Eagle 24-cylinder H-configuration piston engine driving eight bladed contraprops. The first prototype flew on 16 December 1946, the other five prototypes and 10 Eagle powered pre series Wyvern TF.1s following. Only six of the TF.1s were flown despite having been built, because the decision had already been made to concentrate on a 'Mk.2' Wyvern with turboprop engine.

Three turboprop powered Wyvern Mk.2 prototypes were ordered, two powered by the Armstrong Siddeley Python (first flight 22 March 1949) and one with the 4500shp (3355kW) Rolls-Royce Clyde (first flight 18 January 1949). Twenty pre series Python powered Wyvern TF.2s were ordered in 1948 (plus a two seat T.3), the first of these flown on 16 February 1950 and the last seven completed as production standard Wyvern S.4s. A TF.2 became the first British turboprop aircraft to operate from a carrier in June 1950.

Testing resulted in changes to the Wyvern's fin and horizontal tail surfaces which gained dihedral and finlets. Serious problems with the engine delayed entry to service, the first production standard S.4 not delivered to a Fleet Air Arm squadron until May 1953 and it was not until April 1954 that full operational clearance was given.

The Wyvern S.4 flew with four FAA front line squadrons until 1958 and some active service was recorded during the 1956 Suez Crisis. One of the Wyvern's features – an ejection seat – created some history in October 1954 when Lt B D Macfarlane successfully ejected from underwater when his aircraft's engined flamed out during a catapult launch and went over the side.

Photo: Wyvern S.4.

Yakovlev Yak-15

Country of origin: Soviet Union.

Type: Single seat fighter.

Powerplant: One 1967lb (8.7kN) Lyulka RD-10 (Junkers Jumo 004B) turbojet.

Dimensions: Wing span 9.20m (30ft 2¼in); length 8.70m (28ft 6½in); height 2.27m (7ft 5½in); wing area 14.9m² (160sq ft).

Weights: Empty equipped 2350kg (5181lb); max takeoff 2735kg (6029lb).

Armament: Two 23mm cannon in nose.

Performance: Max speed 378kt (700km/h) at 8200ft, 424kt (785km/h) at 16,400ft; time to 16,400ft 4.8min; service ceiling 43,800ft; max range 275nm (510km).

Production: 295.

Notes: The first Soviet jet fighter to enter squadron service, the Yak-15 was one of only two production jet fighters to be derived from a piston engined fighter which also saw production and operational service. The other one was the Saab 21R (which see).

Design work by Yevgenii Adler and Leon Shekhter began in May 1945 based on the all metal second generation Yak-3 and retaining its wing, rear fuselage, tail surfaces and tailwheel undercarriage. A new forward fuselage section was incorporated housing an underslung Junkers 004B turbojet. The engine's exhaust exited under the centre section and the main wing spar was arched over the jetpipe. The engine was 'reverse engineered' by I F Koliesov of the Lyulka design bureau and put into production as the RD-10.

Using the Yak-3 as its basis meant the Yak-15 was quickly designed and built, with the first of three prototypes completed in October 1945. A series of taxiing trials and brief 'hops' were carried out but the first proper flight didn't take place until 24 April 1946 (the same day the MiG-9 first flew) while wind tunnel work on the effects of the jet efflux on the aerodynamics of the rear fuselage at high angles of attack was carried out.

The Yak-15 appeared in public for the first time on 18 August 1946 at the Tushino Aviation Day. A batch of 12 pre series aircraft was ordered two days later so they could participate in the October Revolution Parade to be held on 7 November, just 80 days away. The first of these was flown on 5 October and although all 12 were built in time for the parade, it was cancelled due to poor weather. One of the pre series aircraft was then converted to a tandem two seat conversion trainer and redesignated Yak-21.

State acceptance testing was completed in May 1947, and despite its very low limiting Mach number (M0.68 below 10,500ft) and poor range, the Yak-15 was ordered into production as an interim type. The batch of 280 production aircraft had been completed by late 1947 in favour of the tricycle undercarriage Yak-17 (see next entry), the aircraft operated briefly by the *Voenno-Vozdushnye Sily* (VVS – Military Aviation Forces). NATO allocated the aircraft the reporting name 'Feather'.

Apart from the two seat Yak-21, the only variation on the basic Yak-15 theme was the Yak-15U with tricycle rather than tailwheel undercarriage, this concept further developed as the Yak-17.

Photo: Yakovlev Yak-15.

Yakovlev Yak-17

Country of origin: Soviet Union.

Type: Single seat fighter.

Powerplant: One 2205lb (9.8kN) Lyulka RD-10A (Junkers Jumo 004B) turbojet.

Dimensions: Wing span 9.20m (30ft 2¼in); length 8.77m (28ft 9½in); wing area 14.9m² (160sq ft).

Weights: Empty equipped 2430kg (5357lb); max takeoff 3323kg (7326lb).

Armament: Two 23mm cannon in nose.

Performance: Max speed 388kt (719km/h) at 7900ft, 405kt (750km/h) at 19,700ft; time to 16,400ft 5.8min; service ceiling 41,830ft; range 387nm (718km).

Production: 430.

Notes: Even before the first Yak-15 had flown, the Yakovlev design bureau began work on a simple tricycle (rather than tailwheel) under-carriage modification of the aircraft under the designation Yak-15U (for *Uluchshennyi* – modified). The modified aircraft was redesignated Yak-17 and NATO applied the same reporting name as the Yak-15 – 'Feather'.

The new undercarriage configuration necessitated more changes than had at first been thought, other differences between the Yak-17 and its predecessor including some substantial structural modifications resulting from having to relocate the main undercarriage mounting points from the front to the rear wing spar. This in turn resulted in a loss of internal fuel capacity (which was already inadequate), requiring the fitting of jettisonable tanks below each wingtip to compensate.

The position of the engine made it impossible for the new nosewheel to be completely enclosed when retracted, resulting in the incorporation of a fixed fairing under the nose to partially cover it. The engine itself was a more powerful version of the RD-10 (Jumo 004B) unit fitted to the Yak-15 and designated RD-10A.

The structure was also restressed and in production form, the Yak-17 had redesigned and less curvaceous fin and rudder. Armament remained at two 23mm cannon in the nose. A single Yak-17 was supplied to Czechoslovakia for evaluation (as the S.100) and Poland received three. The latter negotiated a manufacturing licence for both the Yak-17 and its RD-10A engine, but the programme was cancelled in late 1950 before any aircraft had been built due to the appearance of more effective types, notably the MiG-15.

The prototype Yak-17 first flew in early 1947 and replaced the Yak-15 on the production line later in the same year. It was built until late 1948, during which time 430 were rolled out of the factory. Of these, about 150 were Yak-17UTI tandem two seat conversion trainers with the second seat located forward of the original, above the engine. The Yak-17UTI was the first jet trainer to enter Soviet service.

Codenamed 'Magnet' by NATO, the first Yak-17UTI flew in April 1948 and about 20 were exported to Poland plus a handful to China. One of Poland's aircraft was operated by the Polish Aero Club to provide local reservist pilots with jet experience. Regular Soviet operational use of the Yak-17 ended in 1951 and Yak-17UTI two years later, while Poland retained some in service until 1955.

Photo: Yakovlev Yak-17.

Yakovlev Yak-23

Country of origin: Soviet Union.

Type: Single seat fighter.

Powerplant: One 3505lb (15.6kN) Klimov RD-500 (Rolls-Royce Derwent) turbojet.

Dimensions: Wing span 8.73m (28ft 8in); length 8.13m (26ft 8in); height 3.30m (10ft 10in); wing area 13.5m² (145sq ft).

Weights: Empty 1980kg (4365lb); max takeoff 3384kg (7460lb).

Armament: Two 23mm cannon in nose.

Performance: Max speed 500kt (925km/h) at sea level, 473kt (875km/h) at 16,400ft; max climb 6693ft (2040m)/min; service ceiling 48,550ft; range with tip tanks 648nm (1200km).

Production: 310.

Notes: Yakovlev temporarily moved away from the 'stepped' fuselage design of the Yak-15 and -17 with their underslung engines with the two Yak-19 fighter prototypes of 1947, these featuring a more conventional 'straight through' configuration with a nose intake, engine mounted behind the cockpit and jet pipe in the tail.

The Yak-19 was not proceeded with, the design bureau instead reverting to the Yak-15/17 layout with the Yak-23 (NATO reporting name 'Flora') to meet a day interceptor requirement. The Yak-23 featured the wings and horizontal tail surfaces of the Yak-19 in combination with larger vertical tail surfaces and a stepped fuselage. Any connection between the aircraft and its ancestor, the piston engined Yak-3, was therefore gone. Slightly smaller than its predecessors, the Yak-23 also had a much more advanced powerplant in the form of the RD-500, a copy of the British Rolls-Royce Derwent.

As has been noted in other early Soviet fighter entries in this book, the British Government of the day supplied Rolls-Royce Derwents and Nenes to the USSR in 1946, these immediately copied and substantially boosting the Soviet industry's lack of knowledge on jet engine technology.

The first of three Yak-23 prototypes (powered by an imported Derwent) flew on 17 June 1947. The manufacturer's trials were completed by the following September and State Acceptance testing by the end of the year. Series production was initiated in May 1948 and initial deliveries to V-VS operational units began early in 1949. All production Yak-23s were powered by the RD-500 engine and manufacture ended in 1950.

The Yak-23 was always regarded as an interim type in Soviet service pending the arrival in numbers of more advanced types such as the MiG-15. It equipped only two V-VS regiments (replacing the Yak-17) but proved to be an agile and reliable fighter.

The Yak-23 began to be supplied to Soviet *Bloc* nations from 1950 including Czechoslovakia (12 as the S.101), Poland (95), Romania (12) and Bulgaria (12). Both Czechoslovakia and Poland had plans to build the aircraft under licence but abandoned them in favour of the MiG-15. The Yak-23 was out of service in these countries by the mid 1950s.

One aircraft was converted to a two seat conversion trainer by Yakovlev as the Yak-23UTI and flown in 1949, while a similar one-off conversion was also performed in Romania.

Photo: Yakovlev Yak-23.

Yakovlev Yak-25

Country of origin: Soviet Union.

Type: Two seat all weather interceptor.

Powerplants: Two 5798lb (25.8kN) dry/7940lb (35.3kN) with after-burner Tumansky RD-9 turbojets.

Dimensions: Wing span 11.00m (36ft 1in); length 15.67m (51ft 5in); height 4.32m (14ft 2in); wing area 31.5m² (339sq ft).

Weights: Empty approx 7484kg (16,500lb); max takeoff 11,350kg (25,022lb).

Armament: Two 37mm cannon in underfuselage pack; two air-to-air missiles under wings (one infrared homing and one radar guided) on some aircraft.

Performance: Max speed 588kt (1090km/h) at 16,400ft, 547kt (1013km/h) at sea level; cruising speed 442kt (818km/h) at 29,500ft; initial climb 9800ft (2987m)/min; service ceiling 45,600ft; max range 1474nm (2730km).

Production: Estimated at 'no more than 1000', probably around 500.

Notes: The Soviet Union's first combat aircraft to carry radar and a radar operator/observer, the Yak-25 (NATO reporting name 'Flashlight') was developed to meet a 1951 requirement for an all weather interceptor capable of carrying sufficient internal fuel to mount 2½ hour standing patrols. It also had to be able to accommodate the large *Sokol* (Falcon) radar with its 80cm (31.5in) diameter dish, three scan modes and weight of about 500kg (1100lb).

Yakovlev and Lavochkin submitted designs, the former's Yak-120 (the design bureau designation) selected. A tandem two seater swept mid wing design with 'bicycle' main undercarriage and wingtip outriggers, the proposed design was powered by two Mikulin AM-5 turbojets mounted in large nacelles under the wings. Basic armament was a pair of 37mm cannon under the fuselage.

The first of three Yak-120 prototypes flew on 19 June 1952 followed by 20 pre series aircraft. Series production as the Yak-25 began in late 1953, the aircraft powered by the more powerful afterburning RD-9 engine. Service entry with the *Istrebitelnya Aviatsiia Protivovozdushnoi Oborony* (IA-PVO or Fighter Armies of the Air Defence Forces) was not until late 1955 due to problems with developing the radar to a satisfactory level of performance and reliability. In service the Yak-25 flew mainly defending sectors to the far north of the Soviet Union. Production was completed in 1958 and retirement from service began in the mid 1960s.

There has been much confusion with Yak-25 designations and variants over the years. The basic production Yak-25 was codenamed 'Flashlight-A', and there was the tactical reconnaissance Yak-25R 'Flashlight-B' with single pilot cockpit and glazed nose behind which the second crew member was accommodated, Yak-25P 'Flashlight-C' enhanced all weather interceptor, and 'Flashlight-D' tactical reconnaissance fighter-bomber with glazed nose.

Some sources have allocated the designation Yak-25F to the RD-9 powered version but more recent information suggests this was the basic all weather interceptor model as described in the data above. Regardless of the details, the NATO name 'Flashlight-A' was applied. The Yak-25L was an ejection seat test bed and the Yak-25RV a high altitude strategic reconnaissance variant.

Photo: Yakovlev Yak-25.

Yakovlev Yak-28

Country of origin: Soviet Union.

Type: Yak-28B/I/L – two seat tactical strike. Yak-28P – two seat all weather interceptor.

Powerplants: Two 10,140lb (45.1kN) dry/13,668lb (60.8kN) with after-burner Tumansky R-11AF-2-300 turbojets.

Dimensions: Yak-28P – wing span 11.64m (38ft 2¼in); length 20.65m (67ft 9in); height 3.96m (13ft 0in); wing area 37.5m² (404sq ft).

Weights: Yak-28P – normal loaded 15,700kg (34,612lb); max takeoff 20,000kg (44,092lb).

Armament: Yak-28B – one 30mm cannon in starboard forward fuselage; internal weapons bay and external hardpoints for max 3000kg (6614lb) ordnance. Yak-28PM – initially two AA-3 'Anab' AAMs under wings (one infrared homing and one radar guided), later four AAMs.

Performance: Yak-28P – max speed 1020kt (Mach 1.78/1890km/h) clean or 848kt (Mach 1.48/1570km/h) with four AAMs at 36,000ft; service ceiling 52,500ft; range with two AAMs and slipper tanks 1420nm (2630km).

Production: 437 Yak-28P plus unknown number of Yak-28B/R models.

Notes: Although having a configurational similarity to the Yak-25 models with swept back shoulder mounted wings, tandem undercarriage with outriggers and two engines in large nacelles under the wings, the Yak-28 family was a completely new design capable of supersonic speeds. Power was provided by two afterburning Tumansky R-11 turbojets.

Intended from the start as a multirole combat aircraft, three basic versions were planned and built: the Yak-28B tactical strike aircraft (NATO reporting name 'Brewer') with weapons bay and single cockpit plus glazed nose for the navigator/bomb aimer; Yak-28P ('Firebar') tandem two seat all weather interceptor with underwing pylons for missiles and a solid nose housing radar; and Yak-28R tactical photo-reconnaissance versions (also 'Brewer').

Development was carried out under the design bureau designation Yak-129 and the Yak-28B 'Brewer-A' tactical strike version was the first to fly on 5 March 1958. Subsequent bomber versions were the improved Yak-28I 'Brewer-B' and Yak-28L 'Brewer-C', most of the original 'A' models upgraded to those standards. The Yak-25R was dubbed 'Brewer-D' and the Yak-28PP 'Brewer-E' was an electronic warfare platform configured mainly for standoff jamming duties. The D and E remained in service well into the 1990s.

The Yak-28P all weather interceptor first flew in 1960 and entered service over the northern hemisphere winter of 1961-62, initial armament comprising two AA-3 'Anab' air-to-air missiles under the wings. Upgraded radar in a longer and sharply pointed low drag radome, lengthened engine nacelles, two additional underwing stores stations and the ability to carry short range AAMs resulted in the revised designation Yak-28PM. A further upgraded fighter, the Yak-28PD, was tested and evaluated in the mid 1960s but not ordered. Production ended in 1967 and a small number remained in service into the 1990s.

A conversion trainer variant of the Yak-28P was also produced with two seats in tandem, but individual single seat cockpits with separate canopies were fitted rather than the single canopy used on the fighter. Designated Yak-28U, the trainer was called 'Maestro' by NATO.

Photo: Yakovlev Yak-28P.

Yakovlev Yak-38

Country of origin: Soviet Union.

Type: Single seat carrier based V/STOL fighter.

Powerplants: One 15,300lb (68.0kN) Tumansky R-27V-300 turbojet and two 7165lb (31.9kN) RKBM RD-36-35FVR lift jets.

Dimensions: Yak-38M – wing span 7.32m (24ft 0in); length 15.49m (50ft 10in); height 4.37m (14ft 4in); wing area 18.5m² (199sq ft).

Weights: Yak-38M – operating empty 7484kg (16,500lb); max takeoff 11,700kg (25,795lb).

Armament: Yak-38M – four underwing hardpoints for 2000kg (4409lb) ordnance including 23mm cannon pods, bombs (up to 500kg/1100lb each), air-to-surface missiles, anti-shipping missiles, air-to-air missiles and fuel tanks.

Performance: Yak-38M – max speed 528kt (978km/h) at sea level, 545kt (1010km/h) at 36,000ft; max initial climb 14,750ft (4495m)/min; service ceiling 39,375ft; combat radius with max warload 130nm (240km) lo-lo-lo or 200nm (370km) hi-lo-hi; radius with four AAMs, external tanks and 75min on station 100nm (185km).

Production: 13 Yak-36M, 2 Yak-36U and 231 Yak-38 of all versions.

Notes: The first Soviet combat aircraft designed specifically for shipboard operations to achieve service, the Yak-38 (NATO reporting name 'Forger') was also the world's second V/STOL combat aircraft to be put into service, after the Harrier.

Yakovlev's first V/STOL design was the experimental Yak-36 'Freehand' of the mid 1960s powered by two vectored thrust turbofans but with only two swivelling nozzles on the centre of gravity. Hover balance was provide by four puffer pipes – one on each wingtip, one under the tail and another on a long boom extending from the nose.

This configuration was abandoned in favour of the completely redesigned Yak-36M, the prototype for the production Yak-38. The Yak-36M was powered by a single Tumansky R-27V thrust vectoring turbojet with two swivelling nozzles behind the wing, their effect balanced in the vertical takeoff, vertical landing, hover and transition modes by two RD-36 lift engines just behind the cockpit. The first Yak-36M flew in 1971 and a pre series of single seaters and Yak-36U tandem two seaters were extensively trialed aboard the carrier-cruiser *Kiev* in 1975-76.

Production of the externally similar operational version, the Yak-38, was initiated in 1976, this featuring a full weapons system, ranging radar and folding wings. Two major versions were built: the single seat 'Forger-A' and tandem two seat Yak-38U 'Forger-B'. Later aircraft with upgrades including a steerable nosewheel, more power and provision to carry underwing fuel tanks were designated Yak-38M (and two seater UM).

The Yak-38 entered Soviet Navy service in 1978 and was evaluated under operational conditions in Afghanistan two years later. Each of the four *Kiev* class carrier-cruisers had a 14 aircraft squadron on board including a pair of two seaters. Production ended in 1987 after 321 Yak-38s of all versions had been completed. Their numbers declined after the disintegration of the Soviet Union and by 1995 only about 30 remained in Russian Navy service with retirement well underway. The remainder had been withdrawn within a year.

Photo: Yakovlev Yak-38M.

Yakovlev Yak-141

Country of origin: Soviet Union/Russia.

Type: Single seat V/STOL multirole fighter.

Powerplants: One 24,205lb (107.7kN) dry/34,170lb (152.0kN) with afterburner Soyuz/Koptchyenko R-79V-300 turbofan and two 9390lb (41.8kN) Rybinsk RD-41 lift engines.

Dimensions: Wing span 10.11m (33ft 2in); length (incl nose probe) 18.29m (60ft 0in); height 5.00m (16ft 5in); wing area 31.7m² (341sq ft).

Weights: Operating empty 11,650kg (25,683lb); max for vertical takeoff 15,800kg (34,832lb); max for rolling takeoff 19,500kg (42,989lb).

Armament: One 30mm cannon under port intake; four underwing hardpoints for max 2600kg (5732lb) ordnance including AAMs, ASMs, TV guided and conventional bombs, cluster bombs and rocket pods.

Performance: Max speed 972kt (Mach 1.69/1800km/h) above 36,000ft, 675kt (Mach 1.02/1250km/h) at sea level; service ceiling 49,215ft; combat radius with 2000kg (4409lb) warload 373nm (690km); range with 1000kg (2205lb) warload 545nm (1010km) at sea level or 1134nm (2100km) at altitude.

Production: 4 built of which 2 flown.

Notes: Designed to meet a 1975 Soviet Navy requirement for an advanced successor to the Yak-38 under the designation Yak-41, what became known as the Yak-141 (NATO reporting name 'Freestyle') fell victim to Russian funding problems and was cancelled in 1993. The Yak-141 was the world's second supersonic V/STOL combat aircraft, after the experimental Dassault Mirage IIIV of 1965.

Two versions were proposed: the basic Yak-41 interceptor and the Yak-41M with added air-to-surface/anti ship missile capability. This was subsequently given the designation Yak-141. A further developed land based variant with a revised and lower radar signature airframe plus greater weapons carrying capability was also discussed in the mid 1990s.

The Yak-141 retained the single main engine/two lift engines configuration of the Yak-38 but differs in having only one thrust vectoring nozzle located at the rear of the fuselage, between the two short tailbooms. The lift engines were mounted immediately behind the cockpit. The Yak-141 incorporated modern design features such as a digital fly-by-wire flight control system (with manual backup) and extensive use of aluminium-lithium alloys in the structure with composites accounting for 26 per cent of the airframe by weight.

The first of two flying prototypes took to the air on 9 March 1987, this representative of the air defence version with secondary attack capability. The second prototype (Yak-41M) flew in April 1989 and supersonic flight was achieved for the first time shortly afterwards.

Flight testing revealed problems with hot gas ingestion while performing vertical takeoffs and the afterburning main powerplant's efflux tended to melt the runway! The first shipboard trials were performed in September 1991 with a landing on the carrier *Admiral Gorshkov*. The programme faltered in November 1991 when the Russian Government stopped financial support and work was terminated in 1993. Plans to revive it have so far come to nought.

Photo: Yakovlev Yak-141.

GLOSSARY OF TERMS AND ACRONYMS

AAA – Anti aircraft artillery.

AAC – Army Air Corps (UK).

AAM – Air-to-air missile.

ABM – Anti ballistic missile. A missile capable of destroying hostile ballistic missiles or their payloads before they impact on their target.

ACC – Air Combat Command (USAF).

ACM – Air combat manoeuvring.

ACMI – Air combat manoeuvring instrumentation.

ACMR – Air combat manoeuvring range.

ADF – Australian Defence Force.

ADIZ – Air defence identification zone.

AEW – Airborne early warning.

AEW&C – Airborne early warning and control.

AF – Air force.

AFB – Air force base (US).

AFMC – Air Force Materiel Command (USAF).

ALBM – Air launched ballistic missile.

ALCM – Air launched cruise missile.

AMC – Air Mobility Command (USAF).

Amraam – Advanced medium range air-to-air missile, the Hughes AIM-120.

ANG – Air National Guard (USA).

APU – Auxiliary power unit.

ARM – Anti radiation missile.

ASM – Air-to-surface missile.

ASPJ – Airborne self protection jammer.

Asraam – Advanced short range air-to-air missile. An advanced IR guided AAM missile developed by Matra BAe.

AST – Air staff target.

ASTOVL – Advanced short takeoff and vertical landing

ASV – Anti surface vessel.

ASW – Anti submarine warfare. All measures designed to reduce or nullify the effectiveness of hostile submarines.

ASuW – Anti surface warfare.

ATBM – Anti tactical ballistic missile.

AUW – All up weight.

AWACS – Airborne Warning and Control System. In particular refers to Boeing E-3 Sentry.

BAe – British Aerospace, now BAE Systems.

BVR – Beyond visual range.

C2 – Command and control.

C3 – Command, control and communications.

C3I – Command, control, communications and intelligence.

CAF – Canadian Armed Forces, now Canadian Forces.

CAP – Combat air patrol.

CAS – Close air support.

CDU – Control display unit.

CEA – Circular error average.

CEP – Circular Error Probable. A measure of the accuracy of missiles or bombs, the CEP is the radius of a circle in which half the shots are statistically likely to fall.

CF – Canadian Forces.

CFE – Conventional Forces Europe.

CIWS – Close-In Weapon System (US).

COIN – Counter insurgency.

CRT – Cathode ray tube.

CV – Attack aircraft carrier, conventionally powered (US).

CVN – Attack aircraft carrier, nuclear powered (US).

DEW – Distant early warning (US).

DFC – Distinguished Flying Cross: air force decoration.

DGPS – Differential GPS.

DoD – Department of Defence.

DVI – Direct Voice Input.

ECCM – Electronic counter countermeasures. A form of electronic warfare designed to overcome enemy use of ECM and thus continue to make effective use of the electromagnetic spectrum.

ECM – Electronic countermeasures. A form of electronic warfare designed totally or partially to prevent effective use by the enemy of part of the electromagnetic spectrum.

ECR – Electronic combat reconnaissance, SEAD Panavia Tornado variant.

EFIS – Electronic flight instrument system.

ELINT – Electronic intelligence. Intelligence derived from enemy electronic transmissions other than telecommunications (ie radar).

Endurance – The length of time an aircraft's fuel load will permit it to remain airborne.

ESM – Electronic support measures.

EW – Electronic warfare • Early warning.

FA – Frontal Aviation, Russian AF command in charge of tactical fighters.

FAA – Fleet Air Arm (UK, Aus) • Fuerza Aerea Argentina, Argentine AF.

FAB – Forca Aerea Brasileira, Brazilian AF.

FAC – Forward air control/forward air controller • Fuerza Aerea de Chile, Chilean AF • Fuerza Aerea Colombiana, Colombian AF.

FAE – Fuel air explosives • Fuerza Aerea Ecuatoriana, Ecuadorian AF.

FBW – Fly-by-wire (electronic signalling of flight controls).

fire and forget missile – AAM or ASM with self guiding capability.

FLIR – Forward looking infrared.

fly-by-wire – Flight-control system with electric signalling.

FMS – Foreign military sale (US).

g – Force of gravity.

GAM – GPS-Aided Munition. Mk 82 bombs with a GPS guidaince tail kit, developed for the B-2.

GCA – Ground controlled approach. An instrument approach procedure provided by a ground controller on the basis of radar displays. The aircraft is 'talked down' to within sight of the runway when weather conditions would otherwise preclude a safe landing. This predates ILS.

GCI – Ground-controlled intercept.

GE – General Electric.

GPS – Global positioning system. A worldwide system by which the user can derive his position by receiving signals from navigation satellites.

HF – High frequency: 3 to 30 MHz.

HOTAS – Hands on throttle and stick.

HOTCC – Hands on throttle, collective and cyclic.

hp – horsepower

hr – Hour/s

HUD – Head-up display.

HUDWAC – HUD weapon aiming computer.

HUDWASS – HUD weapon aiming subsystem.

IADS – Integrated air defence system.

IAS – Indicated airspeed shown on the airspeed indicator, when corrected for instrument error.

ICBM – Intercontinental ballistic missile. Land based missile with range in excess of 5600km (3000nm).

IFF – Identification friend or foe.

IGE – In ground effect.

ILS – Instrument landing system.

Imp – Imperial (UK).

INS – Inertial navigation system. A navigation system in which displacement from the point of departure is determined by measuring the acceleration exerted upon a gyroscopically stabilised platform by vehicle movement.

IOC – Initial operational capability. Date when a weapon system can be considered capable of being used by troops even though not fully developed and troops not fully trained (US).

IR – Infrared.

IRAN – Inspect and Repair As Necessary.

IRBM – Intermediate range ballistic missile. Land based missile with range of 2780km (1500nm) to 5600km (3000nm).

IRCM – Infrared countermeasure.

ISA – International Standard Atmosphere.

IRS – Inertial reference system.

IRST – Infrared search and track.

JASDF – Japan Air Self Defence Force.

JAST – Joint Advanced Strike Technology.

JDAM – Joint Direct Attack Munition. INS and GPS guidance kits for conventional bombs. Mk 84 with JDAM is GBU-31.

JGSDF – Japan Ground Self Defence Force.

JMSDF – Japan Maritime Self Defence Force.

Joint-STAR – Joint Surveillance Target Attack Radar System, as in Northrop Grumman E-8.

JSOW – Joint Stand-Off Weapon. Currently being developed in GPS/INS guided AGM-154 form.

JSF – Joint Strike Fighter (USA), replaced JAST. A current program to find a multirole fighter for the USAF, USN, USMC and RN.

JTIDS – Joint Tactical Information Distribution System.

KCAS – Calibrated airspeed in knots.

kg – Kilogram/s.

KIAS – Knots indicated airspeed.

km – Kilometre.

km/h – Kilometres per hour.

kN – KiloNewton (1000 Newtons, 1 Newton = 0.2248lb of force).

Knot – Aviation and maritime unit of velocity. 1 knot = 1 nautical mile per hour.

KT – Kiloton. Explosive yield equivalent in effect to 1000 tons of TNT.

Kt/kt – Knot/s

KTAS – True airspeed in knots.

kW – KiloWatt. SI measure of power.

LAMPS – Light airborne multi purpose system (US).

LANTIRN – Low altitude targeting infrared for night.

LABS – Low Altitude Bombing System.

LAPES – Low Altitude Parachute Extraction System.

lb – Pounds, either of mass or thrust.

LCD – Liquid crystal display.

LF – Low frequency: 30 to 300 kHz.

LGB – Laser guided bomb.

LO – Low observables, ie stealth.

LRMP – Long range maritime patrol aircraft.

LZ – Landing zone.

Mach number, M – Ratio of true airspeed to speed of sound in surrounding air (which varies as square root of absolute temperature). In standard conditions, the speed of sound (Mach 1) is 1223km/h (661kt) at sea level and 1063km/h (575kt) at 36,000ft.

MAC – Military Airlift Command, now AMC (USAF).

MAD – Magnetic Anomaly Detector. ASW equipment designed to detect disturbances in the Earth's magnetic field.

MAP – Military Assistance Program (USA).

MAW – Marine Air Wing (USMC).

MCM – Mine countermeasures.

MFD – Multi Function Display.

min – Minute/s.

MLU – Mid life update.

MoD – Ministry of Defence.

MPA – Maritime patrol aircraft.

MR – Maritime reconnaissance.

MRBM – Medium range ballistic missile. Land based missile with range of 1100km (600nm) to 2780km (1500nm).

MSIP – Multi Stage Improvement Program (US).

MTOW – Maximum takeoff weight.

NAS – Naval air station.

NASA – National Aeronautics & Space Administration (US).

NATO – North Atlantic Treaty Organisation. Current members are Belgium, Canada, Czech Republic, Denmark, France, Germany, Greece, Hungary, Iceland, Luxembourg, Netherlands, Norway, Poland, Portugal, Spain, Turkey, UK, USA.

Nautical mile – Unit of measurement of distance. 1nm is one minute of great circle of the earth, standardised at 6080ft (1853m) but actually varying with latitude from 6046ft to 6108ft (1842 to 1861m).

nav/attack system – One offering either pilot guidance or direct command of aircraft to ensure accurate navigation and weapon delivery against surface target.

nm – Nautical mile.

OCU – Operational Conversion Unit.

OGE – Out of ground effect; supported by lifting rotor(s) in free air with no land surface in proximity.

OTH-B – Over-the-Horizon Backscatter Radar. This transmits signals that extend beyond the line-of-sight along the ground. Range is of the order of 2900km (1570nm).

OTHR – Over-the-horizon radar.

OTHT – Over the horizon targeting.

PACAF – Pacific Air Force (USAF).

Passive – Not itself emitting. Usually used when describing detection devices which do not use electro-magnetic emissions to operate. They cannot be detected in the way that 'active' devices can.

Payload – Weapon and/or cargo capacity of an aircraft or missile.

PGM – Precision guided munition.

PID – Passive identification device.

PNGDF – Papua New Guinea Defence Force.

R&D – Research and development.

RAAF – Royal Australian Air Force.

RAAWS – Radar altimeter and altitude warning system.

RAF – Royal Air Force (UK).

RAM – Radar absorbing material.

RAN – Royal Australian Navy.

RAST – Recovery assist, secure and (deck) traverse system.

RATO – Rocket assisted takeoff.

RCS – Radar cross section.

Recce – Reconnaissance.

RMAF – Royal Malaysian Air Force.

RN – Royal Navy (UK).

RNeAF – Royal Netherlands Air Force.

RNZAF – Royal New Zealand Air Force.

ROE – Rules of Engagement.

RoKAF – Republic of Korea Air Force (Sth Korea).

RPV – Remotely piloted vehicle.

RR – Rolls-Royce.

RSAF – Republic of Singapore Air Force • Royal Saudi AF.

RWR – Radar warning receiver.

SAAF – South African Air Force.

SAC – Strategic Air Command (USAF, merged into ACC).

SAM – Surface-to-air missile.

SAR – Search and rescue.

SEAD – Suppression of enemy air defences.

SENSO – Sensor operator.

SLAR – Side looking airborne radar.

Sigint – Signals intelligence.

Smart – Device possessing precision guidance. Normally used to describe ASMs and bombs with terminal guidance to differentiate them from iron or gravity bombs.

Sonobuoy – A small sonar device dropped by aircraft into the sea. The device floats for several hours and transmits information to the aircraft above. It then sinks automatically to prevent retrieval by a hostile agency.

SSM – Surface-to-surface missile.

SRAM & SRAM II – Cancelled Short Range Attack Missiles (nuclear) for the B-2 Spirit.

Stealth – Stealth (or low observables) technology is used to render aircraft or satellites invisible or near invisible to visual, radar or infrared detection. The Northrop Grumman B-2 Spirit and the Lockheed F-117 Nighthawk are stealth aircraft.

STO – Short takeoff

STOL – Short takeoff and landing.

STOVL – Short Takeoff Vertical Landing.

TAC – Tactical Air Command (USAF, now merged into ACC).

TACAMO – Take Charge And Move Out.

TACAN – Tactical Aid to Navigation. Military UHF navaid.

TACCO – Tactical coordinator.

TANS – Tactical Air Navigation System.

TBO – Time Between Overhauls.

TFR – Terrain following radar.

TIALD – Target Identification Airborne Laser Designation.

TNI-AU – Tentara Nasional Indonesia-Angkatan Udara, Indonesian AF.

TOW – Tube launched, Optically tracked, Wire guided. Anti armour missile.

TSSAM – Tri Service Stand-Off Attack Missile. Cancelled stealthy stand-off weapon.

UAV – Unmanned aerial vehicle.

UHF – Ultra-high frequency: 300MHz to 3GHz.

UN – United Nations.

USAF – United States Air Force.

USAFE – US Air Forces in Europe.

USMC – United States Marine Corps.

USN – United States Navy.

VHF – Very high frequency: 3 to 300MHz.

V/STOL – Vertical or short takeoff and landing.

VTAS – Voice, throttle and stick.

VTOL – Vertical takeoff and landing.

WSO – Weapon system operator (occasionally weapon systems officer).

zero-zero seat – Ejection seat qualified for operation at zero height, zero airspeed; ie pilot can safely eject from parked aircraft.

INDEX

ALSO IN THIS SERIES

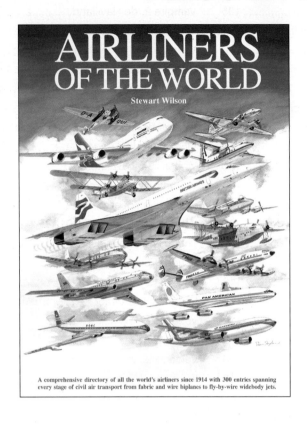

A comprehensive directory of all the world's airliners since 1914 with 300 entries spanning every stage of civil air transport from fabric and wire biplanes to fly-by-wire widebody jets.

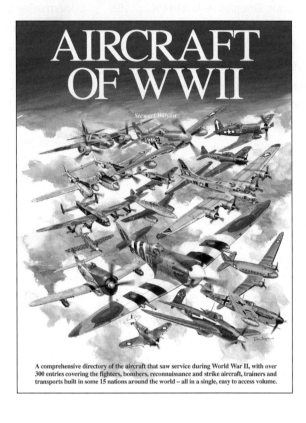

A comprehensive directory of the aircraft that saw service during World War II, with over 300 entries covering the fighters, bombers, reconnaissance and strike aircraft, trainers and transports built in some 15 nations around the world – all in a single, easy to access volume.

Airliners of the World is an indispensable, easy to access reference work which provides an enormous amount of source material within its 160,000 words of text. A comprehensive directory of all the world's airliners since 1914 with 300 entries spanning every stage of civil air transport from fabric and wire biplanes to fly-by-wire widebody jets. From the Benoist XIV to the Concorde, from the Douglas DC-2 to Boeing's 777, they are all described and illustrated in colour where possible in this unique high quality reference directory.

With its 160,000 words of text *Aircraft of WWII* is an indispensable, easy to access reference work which provides an enormous amount of source material. *Aircraft of WWII* includes more than 320 entries covering both the major and minor combat types along with the more important transports and trainers. Many aircraft have multiple entries to cover their variants. Each entry is illustrated and contains details of country of origin, role, powerplant, dimensions, weights, armament, performance, operators, production numbers and a concise history of the aircraft's development and service.

Proudly Printed in Australia by Pirie Printers Pty Ltd, 140 Gladstone St, Fyshwick, ACT 2609.

Distributed throughout Australia by
Network Distribution Company, 54 Park St, Sydney, 2000. Fax (02) 9264 3278

Distributed in North America, Asia and South America by
Motorbooks International,
729 Prospect Ave, Osceola, Wisconsin, 54020, USA. Fax (715) 294 4448.

Distributed throughout Europe and the UK by
Airlife Publishing Ltd,
101 Longden Rd, Shrewsbury SY3 9EB, Shropshire, UK. Fax (743) 232944.

Review and read excerpts of these books on our website: www.ausaviation.com.au